Sport and Nationalism

Sport and Nationalism: Theoretical Perspectives aims to advance the academic study of the interconnections between sport and nationalism by, firstly, reviewing the current 'state of play' in this field of study and, secondly, highlighting the potential for the development of future theoretically informed analysis of the relationship between sport, nationalism, and national identity.

This book offers a critical appraisal of the utility of various theoretical concepts used to explore the nature of contemporary nationalism when applied to the specific topic of sport. Bringing together a range of contemporary academics in this field of study, it offers an opportunity to showcase contrasting theoretical positions on this topic. Furthermore, the central focus of this book regarding extended application of theories of nationalism to the field of sport provides an opportunity for novel and critical contributions to this field of study.

This book will be beneficial to students, researchers, and professionals with an interest in sport and in the relationship between sport, politics, and nationalism. The chapters in this book were originally published as a special issue of *Sport in Society*.

Stuart Whigham is Senior Lecturer in Sport, Coaching and Physical Education at Oxford Brookes University, UK. His research interests revolve around the sociology and politics of sport, with a particular interest in the study of national identity, nationalism, and sport; the politics of sport and sporting events; the politics of the Commonwealth Games; the sociology and politics of Scottish sport; and sport and the Scottish diaspora.

Sport in the Global Society: Contemporary Perspectives
*Series Editor: **Boria Majumdar**, University of Central Lancashire, UK*

The social, cultural (including media) and political study of sport is an expanding area of scholarship and related research. While this area has been well served by the *Sport in the Global Society* series, the surge in quality scholarship over the last few years has necessitated the creation of *Sport in the Global Society: Contemporary Perspectives*. The series will publish the work of leading scholars in fields as diverse as sociology, cultural studies, media studies, gender studies, cultural geography and history, political science and political economy. If the social and cultural study of sport is to receive the scholarly attention and readership it warrants, a cross-disciplinary series dedicated to taking sport beyond the narrow confines of physical education and sport science academic domains is necessary. *Sport in the Global Society: Contemporary Perspectives* will answer this need.

The League of Ireland
An Historical and Contemporary Assessment
Edited by Conor Curran

Forced Migration and Sport
Critical Dialogues across International Contexts and Disciplinary Boundaries
Edited by Ramón Spaaij, Carla Luguetti and Nicola De Martini Ugolotti

The Sport Mega-Events of the 2020s
Governance, Impacts and Controversies
Edited by Jan Andre Lee Ludvigsen, Joel Rookwood, Daniel Parnell

Methodological Advancements in Social Impacts of Tourism Research
Edited by Manuel Alector Ribeiro and Kyle Maurice Woosnam

Cricket in the 21st Century
Edited by Souvik Naha and Dominic Malcolm

Sport and Nationalism
Theoretical Perspectives
Edited by Stuart Whigham

For more information about this series, please visit:
www.routledge.com/Sport-in-the-Global-Society–Contemporary-Perspectives/book-series/SGSC

Sport and Nationalism
Theoretical Perspectives

Edited by
Stuart Whigham

LONDON AND NEW YORK

First published 2024
by Routledge
4 Park Square, Milton Park, Abingdon, Oxon, OX14 4RN

and by Routledge
605 Third Avenue, New York, NY 10158

Routledge is an imprint of the Taylor & Francis Group, an informa business

Introduction, Chapters 1–5 and 7–14 © 2024 Taylor & Francis

Chapter 6 © 2020 Gijs van Campenhouta and Henk van Houtumb. Originally published as Open Access.

With the exception of Chapter 6, no part of this book may be reprinted or reproduced or utilised in any form or by any electronic, mechanical, or other means, now known or hereafter invented, including photocopying and recording, or in any information storage or retrieval system, without permission in writing from the publishers. For details on the rights for Chapter 6, please see the chapter's Open Access footnote.

Trademark notice: Product or corporate names may be trademarks or registered trademarks, and are used only for identification and explanation without intent to infringe.

British Library Cataloguing-in-Publication Data
A catalogue record for this book is available from the British Library

ISBN13: 978-1-032-68013-2 (hbk)
ISBN13: 978-1-032-68014-9 (pbk)
ISBN13: 978-1-032-68016-3 (ebk)

DOI: 10.4324/9781032680163

Typeset in Minion Pro
by codeMantra

Publisher's Note
The publisher accepts responsibility for any inconsistencies that may have arisen during the conversion of this book from journal articles to book chapters, namely the inclusion of journal terminology.

Disclaimer
Every effort has been made to contact copyright holders for their permission to reprint material in this book. The publishers would be grateful to hear from any copyright holder who is not here acknowledged and will undertake to rectify any errors or omissions in future editions of this book.

Contents

Citation Information	vii
Notes on Contributors	x
Introduction: Sport, nationalism, and the importance of theory *Stuart Whigham*	1
1 Sport, British national identities and the land: reflections on primordialism *Alan Bairner and Anthony May*	11
2 Soccer, the Saarland, and statehood: win, loss, and cultural reunification in post-war Europe *Alec S. Hurley*	25
3 Challenges and complexities of imagining nationhood: the case of Hong Kong's naturalized footballers *Andy Chiu*	40
4 Banal Europeanism? Europeanisation of football and the enhabitation of a Europeanised football fandom *Regina Weber*	55
5 Norbert Elias's concept of the 'drag-effect': implications for the study of the relationship between national identity and sport *Tom Gibbons*	72
6 'I am German when we win, but I am an immigrant when we lose'. Theorising on the deservedness of migrants in international football, using the case of Mesut Özil *Gijs van Campenhout and Henk van Houtum*	86
7 Building American Supermen? Bernarr MacFadden, Benito Mussolini and American fascism in the 1930s *Ryan Murtha, Conor Heffernan and Thomas Hunt*	103
8 Sport and the 'national Thing': exploring sport's emotive significance *Jack Black*	118

CONTENTS

9 Everyday bordering. Theoretical perspectives on national 'others' in sport and leisure time physical activity 133
Sine Agergaard and Verena Lenneis

10 Analysing British Asian national sporting affiliations post-London 2012 149
Alison Forbes

11 Hegemony, domination and opposition: fluctuating Korean nationalist politics at the 2018 Winter Olympic Games in PyeongChang 164
Jung Woo Lee

12 They are not 'Team New Zealand' or the 'New Zealand' Warriors! An exploration of pseudo-nationalism in New Zealand sporting franchises 181
Damion Sturm, Tom Kavanagh and Robert E. Rinehart

13 Nation as a product of resistance: introducing post-foundational discourse analysis in research on ultras' nationalism 198
Mateusz Grodecki

14 *Guerrilla patriotism* and mnemonic wars: cursed soldiers as role models for football fans in Poland 212
Przemysław Nosal, Radosław Kossakowski and Wojciech Woźniak

Index 229

Citation Information

The chapters in this book were originally published in the journal *Sport in Society*, volume 24, issue 11 (2021). When citing this material, please use the original page numbering for each article, as follows:

Introduction
Editorial: Sport, nationalism, and the importance of theory
Stuart Whigham
Sport in Society, volume 24, issue 11 (2021), pp. 1839–1848

Chapter 1
Sport, British national identities and the land: reflections on primordialism
Alan Bairner and Anthony May
Sport in Society, volume 24, issue 11 (2021), pp. 1849–1862

Chapter 2
Soccer, the Saarland, and statehood: win, loss, and cultural reunification in post-war Europe
Alec S. Hurley
Sport in Society, volume 24, issue 11 (2021), pp. 1863–1877

Chapter 3
Challenges and complexities of imagining nationhood: the case of Hong Kong's naturalized footballers
Andy Chiu
Sport in Society, volume 24, issue 11 (2021), pp. 1878–1892

Chapter 4
Banal Europeanism? Europeanisation of football and the enhabitation of a Europeanised football fandom
Regina Weber
Sport in Society, volume 24, issue 11 (2021), pp. 1893–1909

Chapter 5
Norbert Elias's concept of the 'drag-effect': implications for the study of the relationship between national identity and sport
Tom Gibbons
Sport in Society, volume 24, issue 11 (2021), pp. 1910–1923

Chapter 6

'I am German when we win, but I am an immigrant when we lose'. Theorising on the deservedness of migrants in international football, using the case of Mesut Özil
Gijs van Campenhout and Henk van Houtum
Sport in Society, volume 24, issue 11 (2021), pp. 1924–1940

Chapter 7

Building American Supermen? Bernarr MacFadden, Benito Mussolini and American fascism in the 1930s
Ryan Murtha, Conor Heffernan and Thomas Hunt
Sport in Society, volume 24, issue 11 (2021), pp. 1941–1955

Chapter 8

Sport and the 'national Thing': exploring sport's emotive significance
Jack Black
Sport in Society, volume 24, issue 11 (2021), pp. 1956–1970

Chapter 9

Everyday bordering. Theoretical perspectives on national 'others' in sport and leisure time physical activity
Sine Agergaard and Verena Lenneis
Sport in Society, volume 24, issue 11 (2021), pp. 1971–1986

Chapter 10

Analysing British Asian national sporting affiliations post-London 2012
Alison Forbes
Sport in Society, volume 24, issue 11 (2021), pp. 1987–2001

Chapter 11

Hegemony, domination and opposition: Fluctuating Korean nationalist politics at the 2018 Winter Olympic Games in PyeongChang
Jung Woo Lee
Sport in Society, volume 24, issue 11 (2021), pp. 2002–2018

Chapter 12

They are not 'Team New Zealand' or the 'New Zealand' Warriors! An exploration of pseudo-nationalism in New Zealand sporting franchises
Damion Sturm, Tom Kavanagh and Robert E. Rinehart
Sport in Society, volume 24, issue 11 (2021), pp. 2019–2035

Chapter 13

Nation as a product of resistance: introducing post-foundational discourse analysis in research on ultras' nationalism
Mateusz Grodecki
Sport in Society, volume 24, issue 11 (2021), pp. 2036–2049

Chapter 14

Guerrilla patriotism *and mnemonic wars: cursed soldiers as role models for football fans in Poland*
Przemysław Nosal, Radosław Kossakowski and Wojciech Woźniak
Sport in Society, volume 24, issue 11 (2021), pp. 2050–2065

For any permission-related enquiries please visit:
http://www.tandfonline.com/page/help/permissions

Notes on Contributors

Sine Agergaard, Department of Health Science and Technology, Aalborg University, Denmark.

Alan Bairner, School of Sport, Exercise and Health Sciences, Loughborough University School of Sport Exercise and Health Sciences, UK.

Jack Black, Academy of Sport and Physical Activity, Collegiate Hall, Collegiate Crescent, Sheffield Hallam University, UK.

Gijs van Campenhout, Department of History, Erasmus School of History, Culture and Communication, Erasmus University Rotterdam, The Netherlands.

Andy Chiu, Department of Sociology, University of Warwick, Coventry, UK.

Alison Forbes, Department of Sport, University of Wolverhampton, UK.

Tom Gibbons, School of Health & Life Sciences, Teesside University, Middlesbrough, United Kingdom of Great Britain and Northern Ireland.

Mateusz Grodecki, Institute of Philosophy and Sociology, The Maria Grzegorzewska University, Warsaw, Poland.

Conor Heffernan, Department of Kinesiology, University of Texas at Austin, USA.

Henk van Houtum, Nijmegen Centre for Border Research, Radboud University, Nijmegen, The Netherlands; University of Eastern Finland, Joensuu, Finland.

Thomas Hunt, Department of Kinesiology, University of Texas at Austin, USA.

Alec S. Hurley, Department of Kinesiology – Physical Culture and Sport Studies, The University of Texas at Austin, USA.

Tom Kavanagh, Department of Sport and Leisure Studies, University of Waikato, Hamilton, New Zealand.

Radosław Kossakowski, Gdansk University, Department of Social Sciences, Gdansk, Poland.

Jung Woo Lee, Moray House School of Education and Sport, University of Edinburgh, UK.

Verena Lenneis, Department of Health Science and Technology, Aalborg University, Denmark.

Anthony May, School of Marketing and Management, Coventry University, UK.

NOTES ON CONTRIBUTORS

Ryan Murtha, Department of Kinesiology, University of Texas at Austin, USA.

Przemysław Nosal, Faculty of Sociology, Adam Mickiewicz University, Poznan, Poland.

Robert E. Rinehart, University of Waikato, Hamilton, New Zealand.

Damion Sturm, School of Management, Massey University, New Zealand.

Regina Weber, Faculty of Society and Economics, Rhine-Waal University, Germany.

Stuart Whigham, Department of Sport, Health Sciences and Social Work, Oxford Brookes University, UK.

Wojciech Woźniak, Faculty of Economics and Sociology, University of Lodz, Poland.

Introduction: Sport, nationalism, and the importance of theory

Stuart Whigham ⓘ

Introduction

This Collection, entitled 'Sport and Nationalism: Theoretical Perspectives', aims to advance the academic study of the interconnections between sport and nationalism by, firstly, reviewing the current 'state of play' in this field of study and, secondly, highlighting the importance of theoretically-informed analysis of the relationship between sport, nationalism and national identity. This collection of articles thus facilitates a critical appraisal of the utility of various theoretical concepts used to explore the nature of contemporary nationalism when applied to the specific topic of sport.

This Collection seeks to build upon the existing literature in the field of sport and nationalism in a number of ways. Firstly, by bringing together a range of contemporary academics in this field of study, it will offer an opportunity to showcase contrasting theoretical positions on this topic within the same issue. Finally, the central focus of the Collection on the application of theories of nationalism to the field of sport provides an opportunity for novel and critical contributions to this field of study.

Each article is dedicated to contrasting theorists, theoretical approaches and/or concepts, and then applied to a specific case study or topic within the field of sport. This structure demonstrates a diverse range of potential approaches for the study of sport and nationalism, thus acting as an innovative resource for academics interested in identifying and utilising influential theoretical concepts in these specific fields. To this end, the central goal of this Collection is to showcase contrasting and competing theoretical approaches to the study of sport and nationalism, with the opportunity to foster critical debate regarding the utility of the contrasting theories presented in the text.

This editorial will commence with a necessarily brief overview of the prevalent theoretical approaches which have influences the academic study of sport and nationalism, signposting influential texts and academics within this domain of study. This introductory discussion will thus provide a foundation against which the original theoretical contributions offered with this Collection can be juxtaposed. The remainder of the editorial is then dedication to introducing the various papers which contribute towards the Collection, signposting the contrasting theoretical approaches and key findings from each article.

Sport, nationalism, and the importance of theory

The relationship between sport, nationalism and national identity has remained an important issue in sociological and political studies of sport, and this has resulted in a vast number of contrasting theoretical approaches and concepts applied in case studies from various geographic locations. Although it is outwith the scope and constraints of this brief editorial to provide a thorough examination of such literature, it is important to acknowledge that the various theoretical contributions offered in this Collection is situated in this wider field of literature.

Nonetheless, it is important to signpost the contrasting theoretical explanations which have been offered in eminent studies on nationalism and national identity in sport in order to appreciate why this issue retains significant academic interest.

In the academic study of sport, Anderson's (1991) concept of the 'imagined community' has acted as one of the most frequently deployed theoretical tools, with Bairner (2009: 225) arguing that "Anderson is regularly invoked in discussions on the relationship between sport and national identity formation". Indeed, in his comprehensive study of sport and national identity in various locations in Europe and North America (Bairner 2001), he argues that the centrality of sport in contemporary expressions of nationalism results from its ability to bring the 'imagined community' of the nation to life:

> Benign or aggressive, the relationship between sport and nationalism is, nevertheless, inescapable… Except in times of war, seldom is the communion between members of the nation, who might otherwise be classed as total strangers, as strongly felt as during major international [sport] events. There is nothing great or glorious about writing one's nationality in a hotel register. (Bairner 2001: 17)

However, in his more recent work which has drawn upon primordialist theory to examine the role of landscape in relation to 'national sports' (Bairner 2009), he equally cautions against the over-dependence on the notion of the 'imagined community' in the study of sport and nationalism, arguing that its use can result in an over-simplification of the nuanced relationship between sport and national identity which results in arguments that "represent nothing other than the claim that national identity is all in the mind with no material basis" (Bairner 2009: 225).

Although Maguire's (1999) adoption of an Eliasian, figurational sociological perspective contrasts with the position of Bairner, his arguments regarding the relationship between sport and nationalism share certain elements of common ground. Maguire similarly argues for the importance of the 'imagined community' for sporting national identities, but instead claims that that the community of the nation is brought to life through the medium of national 'habitus codes' which shape and reinforce nationalist behaviours. Maguire's theorisation of the relationship between sport and national identity therefore initially appears to sit within the modernist paradigm, having been significantly influenced by the work of these theorists from the 'constructionist' approach to nationalism. However, Maguire also draws upon the 'personal pronoun model' espoused in the process/figurational sociological approach advocated by Norbert Elias, arguing that discourse relating to sport and the nation has a tendency to semantically frame its content through the use of phrases such as 'I' and 'we' as a means of delineating between the 'established' self-group of the nation and othering of the 'outsiders' of competitor nations.

These arguments find similar support in Billig's (1995) work on 'banal nationalism' which makes specific reference to the role of sports media coverage in terms of personal pronoun usage as a means of nationalist flagging, as well as highlighting the emphasis given to British teams and individuals in newspaper coverage of sport in the mainstream British press. Billig argues that the nature of media discourses relating to sport and the nation therefore provides the opportunity to foster a sense of a shared expressing within the nation through sports media consumption.

In contrast, the position outlined by Silk, Andrews, and Cole (2005) is somewhat less circumspect regarding an adherence to a modernist approach to nationalism in their explication of their concept of 'corporate nationalisms' in sport. Their stance draws upon modernist principles in their discussion of the nation in sport, arguing that:

> Despite appearances of antiquity, the genesis of the modern nation-state can in fact be traced to the relatively recent past in history [sic] of human civilization … the Peace of Westphalia in

> 1648 brought the Thirty Years War to an end ... [m]ore importantly, this covenant instantiated the very idea of the sovereign state—and indeed that of an international community of states—through a mutual agreement as to the common independence of state formations. (Silk, Andrews, and Cole 2005: 5)

Silk, Andrews and Cole expand on this stance by outlining the frequent use of sport by Western nations as a means of nation-building in the twentieth century, arguing that the appeal of sport acts as a tool for encouraging popular identification with the nation-state and developing sporting traditions, invoking the modernist arguments of Hobsbawm and Ranger (1983; Hobsbawm 1983). With their emphasis on the development of a 'corporate-cultural nation', the position of Silk, Andrews and Cole arguable aligns with the 'socioeconomic' strand of modernist thought identified by Smith (2010).

Cronin's (1999) extensive analysis of the interrelationship between sport and nationalism in Ireland also aligns with a modernist theorisation of the origins of nationalism. Although he acknowledges the merits of arguments of perennialists such as Hastings who identify pre-modern examples of nationalism in various contexts, Cronin explicitly outlines his agreement with the "majority verdict" (Cronin 1999: 25) of a modernist stance in his definition of nationalism. Although this articulation of the origins of nationalism clearly echoes the arguments of 'modernist' theorists, it is equally important to note that Cronin's caveat regarding the pre-modern existence of nationalist movements avoids a rigid alignment with a modernist perspective for all national contexts. Indeed, Cronin's thesis provides a detailed acknowledgement of the contrasting perspectives within the wider study of nationalism, categorising theorists into 'primordialists', 'modernists', 'statists' and 'political mythologists'. These categories demonstrate some obvious similarities to those of Anthony Smith's (2010) oft-cited typology of nationalism theories, although Cronin's categorisation appears to exclude 'perennialist' and 'ethnosymbolist' perspectives.

Whilst the positions outlined above have placed emphasis on the potential analytical utility of 'modernist' theoretical concepts in the study of nationalism in sport, other academics have highlighted the necessity to consider the importance of pre-modern ethnic and cultural factors as suggested within 'perennialist', 'primordialist' and 'ethnosymbolist' approaches to the study of nationalism. Bairner's (2009) analysis of the relationship between national landscapes and 'national sports' is a prime example of such an argument, highlighting that a "claim that a discussion of modern sports can generate support for a qualified primordial perspective is far less absurd or irrational than initial reactions might suppose" (Bairner 2009: 224). He contends that the debate between 'primordialist' and 'modernist' approaches in contemporary reflections on nationalism has often led to 'primordialist' and 'ethno-symbolist' approaches to nationalism being "mocked by those who prefer the modernist interpretation" (Bairner 2009: 224). Disputing such a stance, Bairner's explication of the links between the national sports and the national anthems involved in international sports events to notions of landscape demonstrates that a purely 'modernist' understanding of nationalism in sport is limiting, and that the imagery and symbolism associated with 'primordialist' approaches is equally evident in contemporary examples of nationalism in sport.

Edensor's (2002) theorisation of 'everyday nationalism' draws upon postmodern conceptualisations on the nature of national identity, as underlined in its inclusion within this category of Smith's (2010) typology of nationalism theories. For Edensor, sport allows the opportunity to "explore occasions where bodily expression and emotional participation manifest highly charged expressions of national identity" (Smith 2010: 78). In particular, he highlights the existence of 'national sporting styles' in various team sports which act as a medium for explicit performances of national identity, thus invoking specific stereotypes regarding the nature of a given nation on a global stage. Although Edensor is careful not to valorise such 'styles' and their associated stereotypes in a simplistic and uncritical manner, he argues that the lack of questioning of such sporting stereotypes by fans and the media demonstrates that these styles can be viewed as part of a 'habitus' for a given nation.

In summary, whilst the above account by no stretch of the imagination does justice to the abundance of contrasting theoretical approaches adopted within the study of sport, nationalism and national identity, it does at least begin to illustrate the diversity evident within past influential analyses of this phenomena. Furthermore, the centrality of nationalism theory within these accounts further underlines the importance of academics endeavouring to explicitly identify their theoretical stances. It is in this light the forthcoming Collection aims to contribute to this effort to promote theoretically-informed analyses of sport and nationalism, thus placing nationalism theory front and centre within such analyses.

The 'sport and nationalism: theoretical perspectives' collection: an overview

Without doubt, the toughest task in writing this editorial introduction to the Collection is attempting to do justice to the outstanding scholarship and theoretical breadth evident within the various articles incorporated within this issue. Nonetheless, below follows a brief introduction to each article which signposts the contrasting theoretical approaches adopted by the authors of each article, as well as an explanation of their order of presentation within the issue.

The opening articles of the Collection focus their attention upon theoretical perspectives which have been frequently used within the study of nationalism and sport, and thus provide an opportunity to reflect upon the analytical merits of such theoretical approaches for the study of sport and nationalism in the contemporary.

To this end, the Collection commences with an excellent reflection from Alan Bairner and Anthony May (2021) on the merits of 'primordialism' for understanding the complex relationship between sport, nationalism, and nationhood. Bairner and May open their piece with a concise explanation of the fundamental principles of the primordialist approach to the study of nationalism, drawing upon the seminal work of Clifford Geertz and Walker Connor which has critically examined the nature of the primordial roots of nationalist public sentiment. As Bairner and May argue, primordialism "is widely regarded with suspicion, evoking as it does the Nazi ideal of blood and soil" (p. 1) but "it nevertheless represents a valuable analytical tool for understanding the emotional attachment which many nationalists have to their natural landscape, whether real and imagined" (pp. 1–2). The authors illustrate these sentiments with an engaging comparative case study of the relationship between sport and regional identities in the Scottish and English context, specifically focusing upon the Scottish Borders region and the 'Black Country' region of England. Drawing upon an analysis of contrasting narrative forms in both autobiographical and fictional literature on these two contexts, Bairner and May illustrate the ways in which the nature of sporting identities formed in each locale are intrinsically linked to their respective surrounding landscapes. To this end, the authors insightfully illustrate the ways in which "landscapes work in terms of forging both regional and national identities" (p. 12), thus concluding that the "contrasting stories … tell us something but not everything about how different landscapes in the United Kingdom reflect and contribute to different ideas about being and belonging" (p. 12).

In the second and third articles from Alec Hurley (2021) and Andy Chiu (2021), respectively, attention turns towards two contrasting applications of Benedict Anderson's oft-cited notion of the 'imagined community' in relation to the importance football in two different national contexts. In Hurley's article, discussion centres on the unique case of Saarland, now a regional state within Germany, but during the inter-war and post-war era, a nation which fluctuated between French and German control for a number of decades, prior to its reunification with West Germany in 1957. Hurley's work therefore examines Saarland's brief existence within international football through the application of Anderson's notion of the imagined community, offering an exploration of the intersection of imagined communities and the unique nationalising role of football. As Hurley argues, Saarland represents an interesting illustration of the allure of the imagined community of the nation, contending that "Saarland employed football in the post-war period to reject both French occupation and independent governance to reunite with West Germany, the imagined community from which it had been torn" (p. 5). Hurley therefore concludes that Saarland's eventual reunification with West Germany was in many ways symbolised in the actions of the Saarland football team, endeavouring to reject any attempts to align the nation with the influence of the French government in the post-war era and instead perpetuating an affinity with a German cultural and sporting identity.

Chiu's contribution to the Collection offers an equally insightful analysis of the relevance of Anderson's 'imagined community' thesis, again focusing on a contested nation and national identity in his focus on football in contemporary Hong Kong. Specifically, Chiu's article focuses on "the case of Hong Kong's naturalized football representatives to recon-textualize Anderson's work considering the naturalization of athletes in international sports and its impact to the understanding of 'Hong Kongness' and 'Chineseness'" (p. 2). Chiu outlines the benefits of Anderson's 'modernist' and 'constructionist' theoretical position in relation to the study of nationalism for understanding both the mediatised representation and lived experience of national identity through sport, providing a concise overview of an array of studies which have explored this theoretical argument. His attention then turns to an analysis of an array of original empirical data on the role of football in contemporary Hong Kong, including such representations by fans and sporting organisation in posters, chants, slogans and promotional material, combined with interviews with professional footballers and fans in Hong Kong. Chiu skillfully illustrates the contested nature of national identity in Hong Kong given the intersection between 'Hong Kongness' and 'Chineseness', concluding that the context of football demonstrates that "the consumption and repetition of chants, slogans, tifos and posters act as constant reminders of the 'Hong Kongness' of the naturalized players that differentiate a civic and cultural 'Hong Kongness' from a racial and political 'Chineseness'" (p. 12).

Changing theoretical tack, the fourth article in the Issues from Regina Weber (2021) draws upon Michael Billig's work on 'banal nationalism' as the theoretical underpinning of her analysis of identity in European football. In her contribution, Weber argues that the 'Europeanisation' of football structures and competitions in the late twentieth and early twenty-first century has in turn led to the growth of 'banal Europeanism' for football fans, contending that "football can provide its fans with an everyday, banal practice of Europe … and contribute to subconscious identification through symbols of the European leagues and due to the increased presence of actors from across Europe" (p. 2). Weber charts the impact of various factors in the perpetuation of banal Europeanism over recent decades, such as the growth of pan-European league competitions such as the UEFA Champions League and UEFA Europa League, the establishment of Europe-wide freedom of movement in the football transfer market, the centralisation of football broadcasting rights, and growing transnational club coordination between football clubs. For Weber, these developments resonate with the arguments of Billig in relation to the mundane, everyday practices which slowly shape the nature of contemporary national identities in relation to Europeanism, whilst equally reiterating the ongoing primacy and power of pre-existing regional and national identities for fans of European football clubs.

The next two articles in the Collection mark an end to the opening section of the Issue which has focused on common and well-established theoretical approaches within the sociology of sport, with Gibbons (2021) and van Campenhout and van Houtum (2021) both drawing upon Eliasian, 'figurational' sociology to underpin their analyses. Tom Gibbons' contribution provides an extensive account of past literature which have deployed Elias' theoretical concepts to study the relationship between sport and nationalism, illustrating the relatively frequent deployment of Eliasian approaches in sport, in contrast to the 'mainstream' study of nationalism where figurational sociology has been comparatively marginalised. Gibbons then plays particular attention to Elias' concept of the 'drag-effect', arguing that "the drag-effect can be applied to understanding the complexities of the relationship between sport and contemporary English national identity, using examples from the popular sport of football" (p. 3). He illustrates this argument through a case study of the complexities of national identity in British context, emphasising the nuanced nature of contemporary English national identity in relation to competing notions of Britishness, Scottishness, Welshness, and Northern Irishness within the UK's constitutional arrangements. To this end, Gibbons argues that Elias' work offers unique insights which overcome the potential limitations of other theoretical approaches to nationalism in this regard. van Campenhout and van Houtum focus their attention on Elias' work (alongside John Scotson) on the 'established-outsider model' as their central theoretical concept, applying this model in their analysis of the case of Mesut Özil, a German-born international football of Turkish descent. Their analysis of Özil's experiences and treatment by the German media and fans therefore aims to "understand who, under what conditions, are accepted as representatives of the football nation and are recognised as (conditionally and temporally) belonging to the nation" (p. 2) in the German context. The article deconstructs the resignation statements released by Özil in 2018 when he declared that he no longer wished to be selected by the German national team, drawing upon analysis of the statements themselves as well as the reactions to this event. To this end, van Campenhout and van Houtum argue that Özil's treatment emphasises his position as an 'outsider' in relation to German identity due to his migrant descent, whilst illustrating the resonance of the 'established-outsider' model to other footballers of similar descents in both the German context and beyond. They thus regretfully conclude that what "should be kept in mind is that Özil, like many other, especially non-Western, immigrants, will never be able to fully meet the current, prevailing conditions of Germany's national belonging, which seem to be biased towards Western, Christian and White characteristics" (p. 13).

Following on from the above analyses which draw upon more established theoretical approaches to the study of nationalism and sport, the second half of the Collection provides an eclectic range of theoretical approaches and concepts which have been deployed less frequently in past analyses of the sport-nationalism nexus.

For example, the contribution from Ryan Murtha, Conor Heffernan and Thomas Hunt (2020) focuses its attention on the notion of 'embodied nationalism', using this concept in their historical case study of American health entrepreneur Bernarr Macfadden. Their paper contends that "Macfadden attempted to create a form of American nationalism which began with the physique and came to represent patriotic traits such as fighting and dying for one's country", with "a distinctly embodied form of nationalism … promoted during these years" (p. 3). The authors illustrate the theoretical influences which shape the notion of 'embodied nationalism', again illustrating the relevance of constructionist and modernist theoretical perspectives such as the work of Benedict Anderson and Ernest Gellner in this regard. The article charts the role of Macfadden's *Physical Culture* magazine in perpetuating narratives in relation to embodied nationalism in the early 1900s, whilst highlighting controversies with regards to Macfadden's alignment with eugenicist thought and Mussolini's fascist regime in Italy. Murtha, Heffernan and Hunt conclude that the "kind of nationalism promoted by Macfadden was in many ways a palimpsest, one which built on prevailing trends linked to fitness, eugenics, nationalism, and American identity" (p. 13), whilst illustrating that such visions of American patriotism still linger to this day.

Jack Black's (2020) article adopts a starkly contrasting theoretical position, offering an engaging account of the potential analytical utility of the work of Slavoj Žižek for the study of nationalism in sport, given the lack of attention afforded to Žižek in this regard to date. Specifically, Black emphasises how Žižek's arguments on "fantasy, ideology and the Real. can prove useful for examining the extent to which examples of nationalism are underscored by forms of enjoyment (jouissance)" (p. 1) within the context of sport. Black commences his contribution with a concise review of the commonly-deployed theoretical approaches within the study of sport and nationalism, before situating the work of Žižek in juxtaposition to these analyses to articulate the unique contribution of Žižekian theory to shed new light on these issues. Black then further develops his arguments through the application of a number of Žižek's central concepts to the study of sport and nationalism, such as Žižek's arguments on the 'national Thing', his position on ideology and 'fantasy', the 'Other/other' dynamic, and his contentions on 'the Real'. Black interweaves discussion of the nature of the relationship between sport and nationalism, with specific reference to the English and British context to illustrate Žižek's theoretical position in this regard.

The article by Sine Agergaard and Verena Lenneis (2021) again offers a contrasting theoretical approach to the study of nationalism and sport through their use of postcolonial and transnational feminist theory, with specific reference to work of Nira Yuval-Davis. Agergaard and Lenneis thus draw upon the work of Yuval-Davis in their analysis of the "current political and public discourses about Muslim women's sports and leisure practices that demarcate this group from belonging to the nation" (p. 1) in the Danish context. The article firstly maps the development of postcolonial and transnational feminist thought in relation to the study of the nation, with a concise overview of the findings of past literature which have adopted such theoretical approaches in the broader study of nationalism, as well as the specific context of sport. Attention then turns to the specific focus on Muslim women's experiences of sport and physical activity in the Danish context, drawing upon recent empirical work which focused on political discourses, mediatised narratives, and personal experiences in relation to this issue. Concluding their analysis, Agergaard and Lenneis contend that "Yuval-Davis' conceptual framework contributes to analysing how groups and individuals that are marked as 'others' may be excluded from belonging to the nation in connection with their sports and leisure practices", thus illustrating the marginalisation of the other similarly found in other articles within this Collection.

Ally Forbes (2021) article on the nature of British Asian national affiliations in sport in the period following the London 2012 Olympic Games similarly sheds light on the complexity of national identity for ethnic minorities in the British context. In contrast to Agergaard and Lenneis' use of Yuval-Davis, Forbes instead draws upon notions of 'hybridity' to understand the identities for diasporic groups in relation to sport and nationhood. To this end, Forbes draws upon Homi Bhabha's work on 'hybrid identities' in relation to diasporic groups to explore the challenges for British Asians in relation to negotiation their Britishness and diasporic identities in a hybridised manner. Forbes firstly outlines the contested nature of Britishness in contemporary sport, emphasising that expressing a coherent notion of Britishness in sport is nigh-impossible for all members of the British public, regardless of race, ethnicity, or gender. She then develops upon this further by identifying the additional layers of complexity faced by British Asians in this regard, drawing upon discussions of such manifestations in sports such as cricket, football, before exploring the hybridised nature of identities for her British Asian interviewees. In conclusion Forbes argues that exploring "national identity formation through a diasporic lens enables us to appreciate the fragmented nature of British Asian identities, thus moving away from essentialist conceptualisations and associated accusations that differential supporter preferences must be evidence of 'divided loyalties'" (p. 13).

Jung Woo Lee (2021) focuses upon constructions of national identity in relation to a more recent international sporting event, namely the 2018 PyeongChang Winter Olympics. In his article, Lee outlines four different manifestations of Korean identity which fluctuated throughout the period of PyeongChang 2018: (1) unified Korean ethnic nationalism; (2) South Korean state patriotic nationalism; (3) postcolonial anti-imperialist nationalism; and (4) cosmopolitan Korean identity. Lee underlines the heightened politicisation of PyeongChang 2018 given the increasing diplomatic and military tensions between North Korea and South Korea, leading to contrasting political discourse from political actors with divergent ideological stances on the nature of Korean nationhood and identity. For Lee, these tensions are best conceptualised as an indicator of the importance of the concept of 'hegemony' in relation to discourses of the nation, drawing upon the work of Seiler and Anderson in this regard to argue that "the hierarchy of national identity politics is by no mean fixed but there is a constant struggle between different nationalist groups for the hegemonic position" (p. 3). To this end, Lee concludes that the four variants of nationalism "he identifies have been vying for a dominant position in the hierarchy of South Korean politics ... and in the midst of intensifying national identity wars, the Winter Olympics presented a unique platform on which each nationalist group asserts the legitimacy of their sense of nationhood" (p. 12).

Turning attention to a contrasting Pacific geographic context, Damion Sturm, Tom Kavanagh and Robert Rinehart (2021) offer an exploration of 'pseudo-nationalism' within the promotional strategies of sporting franchises in New Zealand. The authors commence their article by outlining their conceptualisation of 'pseudo-nationalism', describing this phenomenon where "sports, syndicates and franchises masquerade as a national team and rely upon tapestries of national identity, affiliation and symbolism" (p. 1), often for commercial ends through the harnessing of public support and interest. Sturm, Kavanagh and Rinehart juxtapose the notion of 'pseudo-nationalism' with the arguments of Anderson on 'imagined communities', Hobsbawm on 'invented traditions' and Silk, Andrews and Cole on 'corporate nationalism', articulating the ways in which these constructionist conceptualisations of nationalism and national identity resonate with the practices of sporting franchises in New Zealand. To this end, the authors interrogate evidence from the activities of 'Team New Zealand' in sailing's America's Cup and the 'New Zealand Warriors' in the Australia-based National Rugby League competition, illustrating the manufactured nature of the imagery and identities associated with each team to project forms of 'pseudo-nationalism'. The authors highlight their scepticism regarding the potential success of this strategy, concluding that the "claimed links between sport, nation and corporation are tenuous, dubious to non-existent, with expressions of pseudo-nationalistic sentiment predominantly having commercial, global and mediated interests at heart" (p. 12), thus leading to their likely failure.

The Collection is subsequently brought to a close by two complementary contributions from Mateusz Grodecki (2021) and Przemysław Nosal, Radosław Kossakowski and Wojciech Woźniak (2021) which both focus on the topic of football fandom in Poland, whilst adopting contrasting theoretical approaches which help to illuminate contrasting elements of the relationship between sport and nationalism in this context. Firstly, Grodecki's article uses a post-foundational discourse analysis approach to examine the nationalistic discourses of Polish football supporters. He commences his article with a concise introduction to the principles of post-foundational discourse analysis, outlining its alignment with both structuralist, post-structuralist and constructivist approaches to discourse, and emphasising the analytical utility of this approach which has been absent from the study of sport and nationalism. Grodecki's attention then turns to the application of his post-foundational discourse analysis approach in his case study of nationalist discourses espoused by Polish 'ultras', highlighting the existence of specific discourses concerning such constructs as the traditional Polish family, anti-communism, 'national heroes', and anti-refugee sentiment. For Grodecki, this analysis illustrates that "ultras groups have been proven to create distinctive meanings of nation ... analysing the process of how these meanings are produced in this environment can bring new insights into our understanding of the process of (re)production of nation in general" (p. 12).

In contrast, the final article from Nosal, Kossakowski and Woźniak centres its analysis on the concept of 'guerilla patriotism' to examine the nature of the nationalistic symbolism which is often associated with football fans in Poland. For Nosal, Kossakowski and Woźniak, 'guerilla patriotism' should be understood as "an example of anti-establishment, victimised, ready-to-fight pro-national attitude" (p. 2), contending that this form of national identity is the result of the gradual withdrawal of fans of a number of Polish football clubs from supporting the Polish national football team. The article specifically focuses upon the status of the 'Cursed Soldiers', a term used to describe "a large spectrum of heterogeneous underground movements which continued the guerrilla war against the Soviet Army operating on the Polish territory and against the institutions of the emerging Polish communist state in the aftermath of World War II" (p. 5). They argue that the Cursed Soldiers maintain an important symbolic role for football fans who align with the concept of 'guerilla patriotism' identified by Nosal, Kossakowsi and Woźniak, thus symbolising the marginalised hero status which Polish football fans aim to align with in their own notions of national identity. Whilst the authors conclude by posing a number of future questions with regards to the notion of 'guerilla patriotism', the article exemplifies the potential for theoretical innovations for the study of sport and nationalism found across the collection contained with this Collection, thus successfully concluding an excellent and diverse set of articles.

Conclusion

Drawing upon an eclectic range of theoretical approaches to the study of nationalism, this Collection showcases the theoretical diversity of contemporary scholarship on sport and nationalism. This theoretical diversity is evidenced in the deliberate selection of articles which offer contrasting theoretical approaches, applied to a range of contrasting national contexts as outlined above. Given this international emphasis, coupled with the ongoing academic interest in the nature of contemporary nationalist movements in the European and global context, this Collection acts as a timely reminder of the ongoing importance of theoretically-informed analysis of the nexus between sport and nationalism. We therefore hope that this collection of articles can act as a catalyst and inspiration for future analyses of sport, nationalism and national identity, encouraging similar high-quality, theoretically-informed accounts of this complex issue.

Disclosure statement

No potential conflict of interest was reported by the author.

References

Agergaard, S., and V. Lenneis. 2021. "Everyday Bordering. Theoretical Perspectives on National 'Others' in Sport and Leisure Time Physical Activity." *Sport in Society*. doi:10.1080/17430437.2021.1904904.

Anderson, B. 1991. *Imagined Communities: Reflections on the Origins and Spread of Nationalism*. 2nd ed. London: Verso.

Bairner, A. 2001. *Sport, Nationalism and Globalization: European and North American Perspectives*. Albany, NY: State University of New York Press.

Bairner, A. 2009. "National Sports and National Landscapes: In Defence of Primordialism." *National Identities* 11 (3): 223–239. doi:10.1080/14608940903081101.

Bairner, A., and A. May. 2021. "Sport, British National Identities and the Land: Reflections on Primordialism." *Sport in Society*. doi:10.1080/17430437.2021.1887142.

Billig, M. 1995. *Banal Nationalism*. London: Sage.

Black, J. 2020. "Sport and the 'National Thing': Exploring Sport's Emotive Significance." *Sport in Society*. doi:10.1080/17430437.2020.1865928.

Chiu, A. 2021. "Challenges and Complexities of Imagining Nationhood: The Case of Hong Kong's Naturalized Footballers." *Sport in Society*. doi:10.1080/17430437.2021.1944116.

Cronin, M. 1999. *Sport and Nationalism in Ireland: Gaelic Games, Soccer and Irish Identity since 1884*. Dublin: Four Courts Press.

Edensor, T. 2002. *National Identity, Popular Culture and Everyday Life*. Oxford: Berg.

Forbes, A. 2021. "Using Diaspora and Hybridity as Conceptual Tools to Analyse British Asian National Sporting Affiliations post-London 2012." *Sport in Society*.

Gibbons, T. 2021. "Norbert Elias's Concept of the 'Drag-Effect': Implications for the Study of the Relationship between National Identity and Sport." *Sport in Society*. doi:10.1080/17430437.2021.1900119.

Grodecki, M. 2021. "Nation as a Product of Resistance: Introducing Post-Foundational Discourse Analysis in Research on Ultras' Nationalism." *Sport in Society*. doi:10.1080/17430437.2020.1865927.

Hobsbawm, E. 1983. "Introduction: Inventing Tradition." In *The Invention of Tradition*, edited by E. Hobsbawm and T. Ranger, 1–14. Cambridge: Cambridge University Press.

Hobsbawm, E., and T. Ranger. eds. 1983. *The Invention of Tradition*. Cambridge: Cambridge University Press.

Hurley, A. S. 2021. "Soccer, the Saarland, and Statehood: Win, Loss, and Cultural Reunification in Post-War Europe." *Sport in Society*. doi:10.1080/17430437.2021.1902992.

Lee, J. W. 2021. "Hegemony, Domination and Opposition: Fluctuating Korean Nationalist Politics at the 2018 Winter Olympic Games in PyeongChang." *Sport in Society*. doi:10.1080/17430437.2021.1883588.

Maguire, J. 1999. *Global Sport*. Cambridge: Polity Press.

Murtha, R., C. Heffernan, and T. Hunt. 2020. "Building American Supermen? Bernarr Macfadden, Benito Mussolini and American Fascism in the 1930s." *Sport in Society*. doi:10.1080/17430437.2020.1865313.

Nosal, P., R. Kossakowski, and W. Woźniak. 2021. "Guerrilla Patriotism and Mnemonic Wars: Cursed Soldiers as Role Models for Football Fans in Poland." *Sport in Society*. doi:10.1080/17430437.2021.1892644.

Silk, M., D. Andrews, and C. Cole. 2005. "Corporate Nationalism(s): The Spatial Dimensions of Sporting Capital." In *Sport and Corporate Nationalisms*, edited by M. Silk, D. Andrews, and C. Cole, 1–13. Oxford: Berg.

Smith, A. D. 2010. *Nationalism*. 2nd ed. Cambridge: Polity Press.

Sturm, D., T. Kavanagh, and R. E. Rinehart. 2021. "They Are Not 'Team New Zealand' or the 'New Zealand' Warriors! An Exploration of Pseudo-Nationalism in New Zealand Sporting Franchises." *Sport in Society*. doi:10.1080/17430437.2021.1957835.

van Campenhout, G., and H. van Houtum. 2021. "'I Am German When We Win, But I Am an Immigrant When We Lose'. Theorising on the Deservedness of Migrants in International Football, Using the Case of Mesut Özil." *Sport in Society*. doi:10.1080/17430437.2020.1865314.

Weber, R. 2021. "Banal Europeanism? Europeanisation of Football and the Enhabitation of a Europeanised Football Fandom." *Sport in Society*. doi:10.1080/17430437.2021.1893697.

Sport, British national identities and the land: reflections on primordialism

Alan Bairner and Anthony May (iD)

ABSTRACT
The paper begins by outlining the key elements of the primordial approach to nations and nationalism central to which is the belief that national attachments and relations can be attributed to criteria that are perceived to be objective – language, ethnicity, geography – and which are likely to predate the emergence of the modern nation state and of nationalism as a modern political ideology. Although the approach is widely regarded with suspicion, evoking as it does the Nazi ideals of blood and soil, it nevertheless represents a valuable analytical tool for understanding the emotional attachment which many nationalists have to their natural landscape, whether real and imagined. Following a preliminary discussion of primordial theories of the nation, the paper then explains the two slightly different methodological approaches that have been used to examine two case studies which we argue demonstrate the value of a certain type of primordial perspective. Drawing upon autobiographies and biographies of former rugby union players from the Scottish border region, the first of these case studies examines the relationship between landscape, rugby union and culture in a unique part of the nation, not only in relation to its landscape, its most popular sport and the relationship between the two but also in terms of what it means to be Scottish. The second case study examines the relationship between sport, place and national identity in the industrial towns and cities of the English Midlands, drawing upon contemporary literature which discusses these concepts as defined by primordial ties to the land. Novels examined include Anthony Cartwright's *Heartland* and *Iron Towns*.

Introduction

The paper begins by outlining the key elements of the primordial approach to nations and nationalism central to which is the belief that national attachments and relations can be attributed to criteria that are perceived to be objective – language, ethnicity, geography – and which are likely to predate the emergence of the modern nation state and of nationalism as a modern political ideology. Although the approach is widely regarded with suspicion, evoking as it does the Nazi ideal of blood and soil, it nevertheless represents a valuable analytical tool for understanding the emotional attachment which many nationalists have to their natural landscape, whether real and imagined. The paper then focuses on two case studies which we argue further demonstrate the value of a primordial perspective. Drawing upon autobiographies and biographies of former rugby union players from the Scottish border region, the first of these case studies examines the relationship between landscape, rugby union and culture in a unique part of the country, not only in relation to its landscape, its most popular sport and the relationship between the two but also in terms of what it means to be Scottish. The second case study examines the relationship between sport, place and national identity in the industrial towns and cities of the English Midlands, drawing upon contemporary literature which discusses these concepts as defined by primordial ties to the land. Novels examined include Anthony Cartwright's *Heartland* (2009) and *Iron Towns* (2016).

On primordialism

Whatever its origins, the nation has long been associated with a rarely consistent combination and complex of language, law, economy, race, custom, geography and collective will (Pecora 2001). In relation to understanding nations and nationalism, primordialism nowadays almost certainly offers the least popular and most frequently criticised explanation except perhaps in the eyes of a certain type of xenophobic nationalist. Shils (1957, 131) claimed that modern society is held together, in part, by *primordial affinities*. For Geertz (1973, 259) such affinities or attachments stem mainly from 'immediate contiguity and kin connection'. Kellas (1991, 35), however, referred to 'the controversial "primordial" type of theory', controversial because many of its adherents have traced nationalism back to instinctive human behaviour, involving an ethnic or, in some instances, a racial (and potentially racist) form of biological determinism. Eller and Coughlan (1993, 183) went so far as to call for primordialism to be dropped from 'the sociological lexicon'. They argue that 'there are logically no circumstances in which ethnicity can be described as primordial' (1993, 183). Yet, as Bayar (2009, 164) points out, 'there is a fundamental difference between *explaining* and *justifying* a phenomenon'. The primordial theorist is not necessarily a primordial or ethnic nationalist.

There are more nuanced and complex arguments which fall under the umbrella of primordialism and describe nationalism as neither ethnically defined nor a naturally occurring phenomena; it is instead discussed as a constantly changing artefact produced by the culture of any given territory. Geertz's work examines the cultural factors behind the formation of ethnic groups and argues that 'blood, language, religion, and certain social practices' play a key role (Özkirimli 2010, discussing the work of Geertz 1993, 55). However, this is not an argument that such factors are biologically determined; rather, the strength of the ties that are produced by these factors comes from the fact that people assume that they are a 'given' within their society. Nations and national groups are maintained by the perception of similarity between individuals, but this similarity is not solely ethnic or racial.

In Geertz's (1993) conception of the growth and maintenance of group ties, what matters is the importance that is attributed to cultural factors. Attachments 'seem to flow' from a 'sense of natural affinity' and this is not a biological process; rather, its strength is derived from people believing it to be one (Geertz, 1993, cited in Özkirimli 2010, 57). Geertz is not necessarily arguing that nationalism is the result of primordial attachments, but it is partly the result of people believing in the strength of such an explanation. A similar argument is made by Connor: 'To those who would object that national and ethnic groups are not closely related kin [...] it is not the fact, but the perception that matters' (Connor, cited in Hearn 2006, 28)

Connor (1994, 93) further argues that when analysing nationalism, 'what ultimately matters is not what is but what people believe is. A subconscious belief in the group's separate origin and evolution is an important ingredient of national psychology'. The explanation offered in the arguments of both Geertz and Connor is not that nationalism is natural to humans, but that many people believe nationalism to be a natural part of the human condition. The theorists themselves are not primordialists, but they do believe that a majority of people are, and that nations appear natural as a result of this.

It can be argued that the roots and persistence of nationalism owe much to something that can be described as primordial, has material substance, changes little over time and does not assign primacy to ethnicity. National and regional landscapes, unlike built environments, have generally evolved relatively slowly even though the climate change emergency is speeding up this process in many parts of the world (Bairner 2009). The interrelationship between identity, memory and place has been increasingly recognised (Stewart and Strathearn 2003). Often idealised, these landscapes become important influences on how people relate to and identify with the places from which they come and that relationship need not discriminate in the slightest in terms of ethnic differences.

Methodological considerations

The data used in this study consist of two very different forms of narrative. The primordial approach to the Scottish borders involves a reading of autobiographies and biographies of former rugby union players who grew up in that region of Scotland. The second study is based on works of fiction. Neither of these data sources has been commonly used in social scientific studies of sport although the personal stories of research participants have become increasingly prominent, especially in psychology and health sciences. Indeed, as early as 1993, it was noted that 'a burgeoning interest in sociological research perspectives which offer access to 'the subjective' in social life has led to a consideration of autobiography as a particular methodological strategy and/or form of data for this purpose' (Harrison and Lyon 1993, 101). In 1988, Robert Merton reflected on the concept of sociological autobiography (Merton 1988) and Liz Stanley sought to develop Merton's work, emphasising that 'it is a very rare autobiography that does not contain within its pages, many, shorter or longer, biographies of other people who figure, in different times and places, in the subject's life' (Stanley 1993, 47). This a reflection of the fact that 'lives are composed by a variety of social networks of others that the subject of 'a life' moves between; and how these overlapping but not coterminous collectivities of people understand a life, character, relationships, achievement, death, may differ or even clash, but the differences will be associated with particular social groupings' (Stanley 1993, 50). While in-depth interviews have been used to learn about the lives of relatively ordinary people including lower league footballers (Gearing 1999), the autobiographies and biographies of better known athletes offer an alternative data source (Woolridge 2008). With a focus on class as a constituent of social groupings and, with direct reference to sport research, Woolridge (2008, 638) argued that 'instead of dismissing the football autobiography as a formulaic source whose poor quality and uncertain provenance renders it peripheral, it should be recognized as providing one of the main types of evidence for the study of representations of the professional footballer's image, and for forms of acceptable and oppositional working-class masculinity'. What is missing from each of these arguments is the relationships that individuals have with places as well as with people.

The rugby players whose stories are told in the books that have been analysed are Jim Telfer (born in Melrose, 22 caps for Scotland), Jim Renwick (Hawick, 52 caps), John Rutherford (Selkirk, 42 caps), Roy Laidlaw (Jedburgh, 47 caps), Doddie Weir (Edinburgh but brought up in the Borders, twelve miles from Galashiels, 61 caps) and Gregor Townsend (Galashiels, 62 caps) as well as Bill McLaren (Hawick) who was a good enough player to take part in a trial match for the Scottish national team but went on to make his name as a BBC radio and television commentator.

As for novels, it has been argued that, although novelists are not usually trained social scientists, they could be and, although the stories which they tell are not true, they too could be. It is these qualities that make works of fiction potentially valuable sources of data (Bairner 2017). Generally, historians of sport have recognised this with greater alacrity and enthusiasm than exponents of other cognate disciplines (Hill 2007). However, in light of the central aim of this paper, it is worth noting that poets and novelists have long been in the forefront of representing people's relationships with the natural environment, relationships which have been argued to be associated with the concept of national sports (Bairner 2009).

One issue with examining works of fiction in order to gain some insight into a society (or societies) or cultural form is the totally reasonable contention that they are works of the imagination, and not 'real life'. However, as Anderson (2006, 30) argues, the novel is an ideal vehicle for the development and maintenance of a sense of community, with the action often taking place 'through a sociological landscape of a fixity that fuses the world inside the novel with the world outside'. Novels are ideal vehicles for examining societies, depicting their characteristics and inequities, and for exploring ideas about how societies might be understood. The contention made here is that as well as studying how a society is 'lived', researchers interested in social practices should also consider how communities are imagined. This is a well-established theory, particularly in the study of nationalism, but it has not permeated the study of sport's role (s) in society as much as might be expected.

Sport, borders and the South of Scotland

It has been argued that, in the case of Ireland, 'sport has allowed some border nationalists to generate a regional identity that assumes pre-eminence over association with either of the two states on the island ...' (Hassan 2006, 26; see also Donnan and Wilson 1999). For different reasons, there is an equally complex relationship between nation and region in the Scottish Border region, specifically those areas in the south east which adjoin neighbouring north-east England. It differs markedly from the other region adjoining the border with England to the south-west which has a less embedded culture and identity and has been aptly referred to as 'the debatable land' (Robb 2018). The Border region discussed in the paper possess a distinct, and distinctive landscape, as well as a sports culture that differs markedly from that of the rest of Scotland. Yet both the landscape and the sporting culture, like those of the highlands and islands and the coastline, contribute to a sense of Scottishness that is felt throughout the entire country.

The Border landscape is one of rolling hills, sheep farms and rivers highly prized by anglers, punctuated by small historic towns with their own traditions usually harking back to cross-border skirmishes in the past. Rugby union is played elsewhere in Scotland but nowhere with the same passion derived from local community engagement as it is in the Borders. This goes a long way to explaining the significant contribution of the region to the national rugby team and, by extension to the nation, because of the Six Nations tournament and guaranteed annual games against England, whereby rugby has arguably assumed a more important place in Scottish sporting nationalism than football in recent years, even in those parts of the country where it is very much a minority activity.

The Borders landscape, while distinctive and not one with which most Scots are even very familiar, has come to represent a widely imagined Scottish landscape both by Scots and by foreigners. This process owes much to Scotland's literary giants and, in the case of the Borers, particularly to Sir Walter Scott. According to Obert (2019), Scott wrote about the Borders to promote cultural nationalism but also to critique the demand for Scottish independence. Herein may lie a partial explanation for an apparent anomaly in Scotland's recent political history. On 18th September, the nation took part in a referendum on Scotland's constitutional status with 44.7% of those who voted opting for independence and 56.3% voting against. In the Scottish Border region, the gap was considerably wider with 66.6% voting no and only 33.4% in favour of independence from the United Kingdom. Only Orkney recorded a higher no vote than the Borders.

Walter Scott was long gone. However, his legacy to Scotland lives on and may well have resonated even more in the Borders than elsewhere. Scott is often credited with having resurrected, or as has been argued simply invented, Scottish traditions such as the wearing of the kilt, to instil pride in being Scottish while simultaneously consolidating the Union (Trevor-Roper 1983). In so doing, he may also have contributed to what was once dismissed by a leading Scottish National Party member as '90- minute patriotism' which, given the popularity of rugby union in the Borders, should perhaps be renamed for present purposes as '80 minute patriotism', with both terms describing passionate support for Scotland's sporting representatives without any concomitant support for Scottish independence (Jarvie and Walker 1994). The autobiographies and biographies of prominent members of the Borders rugby fraternity offer illuminating insights into what makes the region distinct but also what makes it Scottish, including cross-border skirmishes now remembered in the Border towns with annual so-called Common Riding festivals. These are captured under the headings of The Border Towns, Rugby in the Borders, and The Border Landscape.

The Border towns

Neville (1994, 3) observes that 'in the vast moorland known as the borders of Scotland, the ancient towns, or *burghs*, are sentinels of civic order amid an otherwise sparsely populated expanse of heath and meadow dominated by hills and Cheviot sheep'. The extent to which the reference to 'civic order' has survived into the twenty-first century is a moot point. There is no doubt, however, that strong civic identities persist.

It is likely that, at least, until the advent of professionalism, the names of the larger Border towns would have been known to many, in Scotland itself and beyond, because of their rugby teams – Langholm, Kelso, Selkirk, Jedburgh (Jed-Forest) and, to an even greater extent, Melrose, Galashiels (Gala) and Hawick. Rugby and the past have conspired to create a sense of civic pride that is increasingly rare in the modern world. This pride, and an idealised version of reality, are widely present in the rugby autobiographies.

According to McLaren (2004, 166), 'Every Scottish Border town is proud of its own identity, and nothing can be allowed to tarnish it' and, for him, 'Hawick is a small community and if you are in any sort of trouble, people will help' (McLaren 2004, 128). He continues, 'Borders folk who have moved away never lose their love for their native town, and the Common Riding weekend regularly attracts two or three hundred exiles from Hawick' (McLaren 2004, 168). Finally, he declares, 'I have always been and always will be a man of Hawick – indeed, I am extremely proud to have been granted the Freedom of the Town some years ago – and that description certainly goes for me' (McLaren 2004, 291). Another Hawick man is Jim Renwick who, according to his co-author, 'has seen a fair bit of the world on rugby tours and family holidays, but, apart from an enforced sabbatical in Galashiels soon after he was married, he has never had any inclination to move away from Hawick's West End...' (Renwick and Barnes 2006, 3).

With reference to Galashiels, the current Scottish national coach, Gregor Townsend writes, 'Gala folk much prefer to be known as "Braw Lads or Lasses"' (Townsend 2007, 2) The reference is to The Braw Lad Gathering which celebrates annually an event in 1337 when a group of locals defeated a party of English soldiers. Comparable events, the Common Riding for example, take place in all the Border towns. In the winter months, however, it has long been rugby that has served to keep the sense of civic pride alive.

Rugby in the Borders

The Border League was established in 1903 and went on to become 'one of the best things in Scottish Rugby, for it fostered a competitive spirit of a sort rarely found at club level (though there were of course those to say that rivalries between the Border towns were already sufficiently intense to render any artificial form of competition superfluous)' (Massie 1984, 15). Even earlier, in 1883, Melrose had been the birthplace of seven-a-side rugby, invented by Ned Haig, a local butcher, and now an integral part of the Summer Olympic Games (Massie 1984).

Commenting on the Borders in relation to the development of rugby talent, a book that focuses on the half back pairing of John Rutherford and Roy Laidlaw, describes the region as 'The Border Cradle' (Rutherford and Laidlaw 1988, 19). As McLaren (2004, 293) observed, 'there is a football club in Hawick, Hawick Royal Albert, and football does function here, but it has always been a rugby town'. The importance of rugby is also noted when he compares New Zealand with home. New Zealand, he writes is 'a marvellous place from the rugby point of view, because everybody there talks about the game. So even though it is on the other side of the world, it feels very much like a home from home; very like Hawick, where rugby is the main topic of conversation among many folk' (McLaren 2004, 51–52).

Jim Telfer, a former Scotland and British and Irish Lions player and national coach, comments, 'there is no doubt that the opportunities available to me at Melrose and in the Borders generally were instrumental in shaping my future as a player, coach and administrator' (Telfer 2005, 36). According to Townsend (2007, 13), 'for a Borders youngster with a talent for sport, rugby was seen as the only true way to express your natural abilities' (Townsend 2007, 13). He goes on, 'the abundance of rugby knowledge in the area was plain to see and I was lucky that I had been able to come under the influence of some very astute teachers' (Townsend 2007, 9). These included Jim Telfer and Jim Renwick, another Borderer and 'one of the best ever Scottish players' (Townsend 2007, 10).

As a primary school pupil, Renwick's first coach was actually Bill McLaren who 'had a crucial role in the number of players produced in Hawick during the sixties, seventies and eighties who were capable of playing at the highest level' (Renwick and Barnes 2006, 23).

Reference is also made to the way that rugby had been organised in the town which was 'instrumental in ensuring that Hawick was able to maintain a strength in depth which no other club in Scotland could match' (Renwick and Barnes 2006, 34). Reflecting on the period in which he first took up the game, Weir (2018, 3) writes that 'the Borders and the clubs that made up the Border League at that time – Melrose, Gala, Hawick, Selkirk, Jed-Forest, Kelso and Langholm – were a real hotbed of talent and competition'. In recent years, however, many of the smaller feeder clubs have been disbanded and the autobiographies regularly reflect on the fact that Borders rugby has been left behind in the professional era.

According to Telfer (2005, 270), 'it's a poor reflection on Scottish rugby that an area like that, which produces so many good players, does not enjoy the advantages of having a professional team and I hope that ceases soon'. He recognises, however, that

> the pendulum of strength in club rugby has swung towards the central Lowlands, especially the cities of Edinburgh and Glasgow' and 'even though the sport is uniquely a way of life here, I don't think Borders teams will ever dominate Scottish rugby again… (Telfer 2005, 271).

Townsend is more sanguine: 'As a Borderer, not having a professional team is a bitter pill to swallow and I know this will have dire effects for the region. But, as a supporter of Scottish rugby, I would have been less upset if the team had been allocated elsewhere in the country' (Townsend 2007, 369). Aside from the impact, whether good or bad, on Scottish rugby, one wonders how civic pride in the Border towns and the sense of what it means to be a Borderer will survive intact with the steady decline of one of its main building blocks. Yet comfort is to be found in words written as recently as 2011 about the achievements of the sport, 'much of which is down to the vision and the dedication of so many people in the Borders, for whom rugby continues to be an activity of beautiful noise and passionate intensity, and who have passed that message on from one generation to another' (Drysdale 2011, 260). All of this takes place against the backdrop of the slowly evolving Border landscape - the Greenyards, for example, home to Melrose Rugby Football Club and birthplace of rugby sevens, 'completely surrounded by hills' and 'a beautiful setting' (McLaren 2004, 299).

The Borders landscape

A theme that runs through the auto/biographies and brings us closer to the essence of one aspect of the primordial is an appreciation of the Borders landscape. Gray (2000, 32) points out, 'landscapes are a particular form of "scaping," a concept that highlights an idea prevalent in Western society about a mode of seeing and representing nature'. McLaren (2004, 325) refers directly to '…this wonderful Border and to '…the lovely countryside in the Borders and all the beautiful walks so close to our home' (McLaren 2004, 144). He continues, 'it is a wild part of the country, yet for all its remoteness and ruggedness, it has a raw beauty which, as I grew up, I came to appreciate more and more' (McLaren 2004, 149) and again New Zealand is invoked as a point of comparison: 'Parts of New Zealand, with its rivers, streams, hills and trees, remind so much of Scotland' (McLaren 2004, 52).

Both Telfer and Weir refer to the remoteness of the Border farms. Telfer recalls, 'our family lived in a very remote place in the borders, up the Bowmont Valley, which disappears south of Kelso into the Cheviot Hills. My father was a shepherd on a farm called Calroust Hopehead, near the village of Yetholm, where the burn runs right up to the border with England' (Telfer 2005, 25). Weir remembers the days before he was an enrolled as a day pupil at an Edinburgh school: 'We were remote, on the farm, in the middle of nowhere, and...I was at school with a couple of dozen kids, who I knew everything about' (Weir 2018, 15).

In his anthropological account of living and working on hill sheep farms in the Border region of Scotland, Gray (2000, 29) uses the idea of frontier to conceptualise the drawing of a boundary between what, prior to 1707, were two states, with the Borders region being 'distant from the seats of both governments geographically and politically in different ways'.

As with most sporting autobiographies, however, direct references to politics in the life stories of the Borders rugby greats are limited. McLaren had clearly been in favour of the restoration of a Scottish parliament. He writes, 'in my view it is a good thing that we have our own people looking after our affairs. When policy was dictated from London, you could hardly say it was decided by those who knew Scotland best' (McLaren 2004, 369). There is no clue, however, as to whether such sentiments might have inclined him towards support for full independence. We can only assume that commitment to their sport combined with the satisfaction derived with representing the nation have largely superseded any temptation to make more overt political statements on the part of the former international players.

Littlejohn (1963, 1) described the Scottish Borders as 'a not clearly defined area of Scotland whose inhabitants regard themselves as a slightly different group within the nation, different for example in dialect and in the Common Riding ceremonies of border towns', It is different too because of the attachment to rugby as a cross-class sport unlike in Edinburgh and Glasgow where the former pupils of a select group of schools dominate the local rugby scene. Of course, not a everyone who lives in the Borderers is a Borderer by birth and/or upbringing and we should keep in mind the distinction made by Frankenberg in his social study of religion, politics and football in a North Wales community between 'Outsiders' and those whom he refers to as 'Pentre people' (Frankenberg 1957, 149). Gill (2005, 83) writes, for example, about the problem that is caused in her 'Bordertown' by 'the close relationship between national identity and territory, and the integration of this geographic reality with social structures'. This can manifest itself in hostility to the Scottish other as well as to England (Smith 1993). Furthermore, not every native Borderer likes rugby or likes living in the region because s/he likes the landscape. The fact remains, however, that these are material aspects of the Borders which offer support to a primordial explanation not only of a regional identity but also of a Scottishness that to date has not needed independence in order to feel adequately Scottish. But what about the regions of England and the emotions which they arouse?

Anthony Cartwright's Black Country

As Ignatieff (1994) discusses, primordial attachments to the land can form an element of 'blood and soil' nationalism. This exclusionary, ethnically defined nationalism has tended to be the preserve of right-wing extremists but is becoming more visible in modern politics, both in Europe and in North America. Primordial attachments to landscapes and regions are not necessarily the preserve of 'hot' nationalism. However Stewart and Strathearn (2003) stress the significance of memory and place to identity, and it does not always follow that interest in the landscape of a place leads to exclusionary ethnic nationalism. It does need to be acknowledged however that an interest in the primordial can be problematic.

This is important to note because in the particular case study examined here, the novelist Anthony Cartwright arguably attempts to develop what might be termed a positive case for primordialism. This particularly relates to the Black Country, a region of the English west Midlands which is multi-cultural, multi-ethnic, and multi-racial. It is also a region that, as Cartwright discusses in his fiction and also in essays on the topic, has suffered due to neo-liberal government policy adopted since the late 1970s and early 1980s. There have been numerous examinations of the region's historical identity, many emanating from the prolific West Midlands cultural and social historian Carl Chinn, but relatively few analyses of the region's contemporary identity. Lawrence's (2016) exploration of fan identities at Walsall FC, one of three professional football clubs based in the Black Country, is perhaps the most useful of these. Lawrence (2016) finds that this centres on largely white, working-class cultural tropes, such as drinking beer, the local dialect, and a particular camaraderie built in part on identification as 'other' to the West Midlands' largest city, Birmingham. However, the identity is not monolithic.

While Lawrence's (2016) findings are of value in a number of ways, two particular elements inform the analysis undertaken here. The first is his contention that analyses of the Black Country must not be reliant on historical reductionism – certainly this is a concern of Cartwright's. The second is that anyone wishing to gain some understanding of the area's social and cultural identity should certainly concern themselves with how this is expressed through football. Cartwright uses football as a tool for exploring wider issues of social, cultural and political importance, and the argument made here is that, as in the work of Irvine Welsh (May 2018), football serves a useful shorthand that allows informed readers to understand the wider issues discussed without extensive exposition.

Given that the region was, in large part, given its current identity through its significance to the UK's manufacturing and mining industries – the name 'Black Country' itself is thought to derive from the smog which hung over the area in its industrial prime – it can reasonably be said that the region's identity is under question in the post-industrial age. In the Borders of Scotland, it appears that the landscape itself plays a part in shaping people's identities. The same is true of the Black Country, although it is a largely man-made environment that is seen as having played a key role. Cartwright, particularly in *Iron Towns* (2016) tries to develop a sense of identity which looks further back into history. The relatively brief industrial era, although significant, is not all that shapes the region's identity in Cartwright's work.

As Bairner (2009) discusses, national and regional landscapes, unlike built environments, have generally evolved relatively slowly. In the case of the Black Country, the region's identity has come to be defined through its modern history as a key element of the United Kingdom's industrial heyday. However, that role is over, and in its place there is uncertainty about the present and the future. Cartwright's work addresses the fact that the Black Country has a far longer history than the relatively brief industrial era and stresses the importance of the primordial to a region's identity in order to present a wider, more nuanced view of the region.

With regard to Connor's (1994) assertion that it is belief and perception that fuels primordialist views, rather than fact, the novel can play a key role in developing the perception of a 'through line' from the distant past into the present day. The sense of a 'core' identity which is always present, even if it is lying dormant, is one of the key elements of the narrative in *Iron Towns* (2016). This is less immediate and visceral than the performed Black Country identity discussed by Lawrence (2016), but also in some ways more tangible. Fiction gives Cartwright the freedom to discuss ideas with social and cultural relevance, and to present these ideas in a unified whole.

One of the key characters in *Iron Towns* (2016) is a one-time England international footballer, now seeing out his playing days at his home town club. Not the player he was in his prime, Liam Corwen's decline mirrors that of the town he grew up in. The player's struggle to maintain his former standard in the twilight of his career is representative of a wider regional decline. The Iron Towns are somewhat similar to Dudley – in a piece written for *Granta*, Cartwright discusses his upbringing in this Black Country town, a place where the municipal cricket ground collapsed into the earth due to subsidence caused by mining but of which Cartwright (2016) says 'Thatcher's malice [did] more to undermine us all than cutting coal and limestone ever did'.

The decline of the football club that Corwen plays for also reflects the fortunes of the town – the stands in the stadium are crumbling, and the club is struggling to stay in the professional system. The numbers of fans making their way to the club's Anvil Yards stadium have greatly reduced since its halcyon days. The stadium is a signifier for parts of the wider region – crumbling, in disrepair, and surviving on a greatly reduced level of income. As in Welsh's fiction, Cartwright's work is not specifically 'about' football in the sense of being an examination of the sport as it is played. Rather, football's social role in the communities that sustain it (and that it can sometimes help to sustain) is the focus.

Professional football in the UK is a product of modernity, having grown out of developments in the work and leisure patterns of working class people. The decline of the football club in *Iron Towns* (2016) mirrors the decline of the society and patterns of living that initially supported the club and hundreds like it. There are dozens of clubs in the English and Scottish league systems whose situation is not dissimilar to that of the Irontown club.[1] In *Iron Towns*, the decline of the football club despite the dramatic growth of revenue levels in the upper echelons of the game reflects not just the situation in English football below the top two levels, but is also symbolic of the differences between the lives led by those who have experienced the type of post-industrial decline depicted by Cartwright and the lives of metropolitan elites. Even nearby Birmingham is presented as a distant metropolis, mirroring ways that Lawrence (2016) suggests fans of Walsall FC 'other' this famous industrial city.

As a novelist who grew up in Dudley but now lives in London, Cartwright may appear to be one of the 'liberal elite', as he has acknowledged in articles about his home region. However, he has sided with the 'left behind', arguing that to understand the way that (in particular) the Brexit vote played out, we also need to understand that the UK is a state where:

a section of society might impoverish people, *a people* (and this is where we might choose to go down a long, dark tunnel), and then blame them for their impoverishment, mock them for any attempt to either change or ease that impoverishment (Cartwright 2016).

Of particular relevance to our examination of primordialism is the phrase that Cartwright chooses to italicise: *a people*. While he acknowledges that the term itself is problematic, Cartwright's novels frequently depict the Black Country as a region which has primordial roots. He presents the region as having a distinct character, shaped not just by its recent industrial past or its experience of decline, but by earlier history and mythology. The people of that region have a distinct character also, defined by their recent history, but also by the distant past. Primordialism and concepts related to ethnicity are often linked, and as Ignatieff (1994) documents, the idea that people might 'belong' to a particular geographical area is a significant element of 'blood and soil' types of exclusionary ethnic nationalism. This might be considered the 'long, dark tunnel' that Cartwright refers to and wants to avoid.

The sense in which the author employs a type of primordialism in his fiction is the implicit, rather than explicit suggestion that the ancient history of the region somehow still affects its character. This is not exclusionary in terms of race or ethnicity. In Cartwright's work, the characters are from a number of different ethnic backgrounds, reflecting the modern character of the Black Country. There is no sense in which these characters are presented as being in any way not 'of' the region. However, he does acknowledge that racial tensions are an element of the Black Country, particularly in *Heartland* (2009) in which a football match between a largely white pub team and a largely Asian team is used as a vehicle for exploring wider tensions between modern communities. Cartwright's work is a mixture of the primordial and the modern; it would be inaccurate to suggest that an entirely primordial, pre-industrial identity is promoted. However, the importance of the primordial to the present is addressed, alongside its possible role in a future regional identity.

As in novels by other contemporary British authors which concern life in the post-industrial UK (notably Irvine Welsh and Niall Griffiths), Margaret Thatcher is a bête noire in Cartwright's work. The decision taken by the Conservative governments of the 1980s and 1990s to greatly reduce the UK's supposedly unprofitable industrial output defines the opportunities, or lack thereof, that Cartwright's characters have. Where independence is not an option, and there appears no way out of the neoliberal style of government that Cartwright is clearly opposed to and that has lasted more than 40 years, the region takes on a higher level of significance as a place with which to identify. Cartwright's discussion of the primordial appears to be specifically targeted towards developing an alternative identity for the Black Country, one that is not defined by its recent industrial past. What Cartwright presents might be seen as a kind of 'progressive primordialism', where the multi-ethnic, multi-racial community of the modern Black Country are aware of the history of the region that they live in without seeing that history as exclusive. The format of the novel allows this difficult, contested enterprise to be explored in a way that would be far more difficult in other forms of text.

Conclusion

In his fiction, and also in essays and interviews on the topic, Cartwright presents England and the wider UK as a divided nation with no single clear sense of identity. This is somewhat similar to how Welsh (1999, 2003, 2012) presents the UK; Scotland is a place with an increasingly different collective conscience than England, as May (2018) discusses in his analysis of Welsh's increasingly positive presentations of Scottish nationalism. The schism that Cartwright discusses takes place within England itself, and there are significant differences in outlook and experience between those who have benefitted from what we might term neoliberal politics in the United Kingdom, and those who feel they have been left behind. Although Kelly (2018) argues, in one of the relatively few published discussions of Cartwright's work, it is in communities far removed from London that the highest concentration of Leave voters can be found, and amongst those whose skills in manufacturing industries are no longer marketable or indeed valued, the highest national concentration of Remainers was in Scotland. Nevertheless, the independence referendum should not be forgotten with its resultant tension between no doubt proud Scottish borderers and their compatriots in the populous Central Belt which revealed that there are many who believe that being Scottish does not mean forsaking Britishness.

According to Mitchell (1994, 1), we should approach landscape as a verb rather than a noun, 'a process by which social and subjective identities are formed'. Our approach 'involves a recognition of the mutually constitutive relationship between bodies and spaces' (Martin 1997, 108). Thus, we have sought to understand how landscapes work in terms of forging both regional and national identities since, although the Scottish Borders and the English West Midlands are regions, they also feed into place-based representations of the Scottishness and English national respectively. The contrasting stories that are told by the Borders rugby men and by Cartwright tell us something but not everything about how different landscapes in the united Kingdom reflect and contribute to different ideas about being and belonging.

The position of sport within our analysis varies, reflecting differences in place. In the Scottish Borders, sport is connected to a celebrated primordial landscape, while in the West Midlands of England it is more connected with heavy industry (and its decline). In Cartwright's work, sport is linked with modernity and industrialisation, but in the case of rugby in the Scottish borders, there appear to be links at the primordial level. Sport itself does not play one unchanging role in the construction of identity and in analysing the influence of place and landscape on identity, it is not possible to take one monolithic approach but the significance of place, whether rural or industrial, is apparent in both parts of an increasingly disunited kingdom.

It is appropriate that the regions of Scotland and England have been discussed in the paper for, as Matless (2016, 13) has it, 'Scotland and Europe put England in question in the late twentieth century, and continue to do so'. The attitudes that the people of these regions hold were not forged in some dim and distant past. However, they are reflective of the evolution of their surroundings and, to that extent, they can be regarded as primordial. To repeat, however, we do not write this as primordialists but we are secure in the knowledge that many people are and believe regions and nations to be natural as a result.

Note

1. However, unlike (for example) Irvine Welsh's frequent references to Hibernian (May 2018), Cartwright has had to invent the Irontown club because the two clubs nearest to Dudley do not fit his narrative. West Bromwich Albion are a global business, owned by Chinese business interests, just as Wolverhampton Wanderers are. The latter club were close to going out of

business in the 1980s but were saved by heavy investment by a wealthy local businessman, Sir Jack Hayward, and are now owned by the Fosun conglomerate.

Disclosure statement

No potential conflict of interest was reported by the authors.

ORCID

Anthony May ⓘD http://orcid.org/0000-0001-7288-4990

References

Anderson, Benedict. 2006. *Imagined Communities Revised Edition*. London: Verso.
Bairner, Alan. 2009. "National Sports and National Landscapes: In Defence of Primordialism." *National Identities* 11 (3): 223–239. doi:10.1080/14608940903081101.
Bairner, Alan. 2017. "Sport, Fiction and Sociology: Novels as Data Sources." *International Review for the Sociology of Sport* 52 (5): 521–535. doi:10.1177/1012690215617758.
Bayar, Murat. 2009. "Reconsidering Primordialism: An Alternative Approach to the Study of Ethnicity." *Ethnic and Racial Studies* 32 (9): 1639–1657. doi:10.1080/01419870902763878.
Cartwright, Anthony. 2009. *Heartland*. Birmingham: Tindal Street.
Cartwright, Anthony. 2013. *How I Killed Margaret Thatcher* Birmingham: Tindal Street.
Cartwright, Anthony. 2016. *Iron Towns* London: Serpent's Tail.
Connor, Walker. 1994. "A Nation Is a Nation, Is a State, is an Ethnic Group, Is a…." In *Nationalism*, edited by J. Hutchinson and A. Smith, 36–46. Oxford: Oxford University Press.
Donnan, Hastings, and Thomas Wilson. 1999. *Borders: Frontiers of Identity, Nation and State*. Oxford: Berg.
Drysdale, Neil. 2011. *Southern Comfort. The Story of Borders Rugby*. Edinburgh: Birlinn.
Eller, Jack David, and Reed M. Coughlan. 1993. "The Poverty of Primordialism: The Demystification of Ethnic Attachments." *Ethnic and Racial Studies* 16 (2): 183–202. doi:10.1080/01419870.1993.9993779.
Frankenberg, Ronald. 1957. *Village on the Border. A Social Study of Religion, Politics and Football in a North Wales Community*. London: Cohen and West.
Gearing, Brian. 1999. "Narratives of Identity among Former Professional Footballers in the United Kingdom." *Journal of Aging Studies* 13 (1): 43–58. doi:10.1016/S0890-4065(99)80005-X.
Geertz, Clifford. 1973. *The Interpretation of Cultures*. New York: Basic Books.
Gill, Fiona. 2005. "Public and Private: National Identities in a Sottish Borders Community." *Nations and Nationalism* 11 (1): 83–102. doi:10.1111/j.1354-5078.2005.00193.x.
Gray, John N. 2000. *At Home in the Hills. Sense of Place in the Scottish Borders*. New York: Berghahn Books.
Harrison, Barbara, and E. Stina Lyon. 1993. "A Note on Ethical Issues in the Use of Autobiography in Sociological Research." *Sociology* 27 (1): 101–109. doi:10.1177/003803859302700110.
Hassan, David. 2006. "Sport, Identity, and the People of the Irish Border Lands." *New Hibernia Review* 10 (2): 26–43. doi:10.1353/nhr.2006.0039.
Hearn, Jonathan. 2006. *Rethinking Nationalism*. Basingstoke: Palgrave MacMillan.
Hill, Jeffrey. 2007. *Sport and the Literary Imagination. Essays in History, Literature and Sport*. New York: Peter Lang.
Ignatieff, Michael. 1994. *Blood and Belonging*. London: Vintage.
Jarvie, Grant, and Graham Walker. 1994. "Ninety Minute Patriots? Scottish Sport in the Making of the Nation." In *Scottish Sport in the Making of the Nation: Ninety Minute Patriots?*, edited by G. Jarvie and G. Walker, 9–26. Leicester: Leicester University Press.
Kellas, James G. 1991. *The Politics of Nationalism and Ethnicity*. London: Macmillan.

Kelly, Richard T. 2018. "Brexit in Fact and Fiction: A Few First Drafts of History." *Critical Quarterly* 60 (2): 74–85. doi:10.1111/criq.12416.

Lawrence, Stefan. 2016. "'We Are the Boys from the Black Country!' (Re) Imagining Local, Regional, and Spectator Identities through Fandom at Walsall Football Club." *Social & Cultural Geography* 17 (2): 282–299. doi:10.1080/14649365.2015.1059481.

Littlejohn, James. 1963. *Westrigg. The Sociology of a Cheviot Parish*. London: Routledge and Kegan Paul.

Martin, Angela K. 1997. "The Practice of Identity and an Irish Sense of Place." *Gender, Place and Culture: A Journal of Feminist Geography* 4 (1): 89–114. doi:10.1080/09663699725512.

Massie, Allan. 1984. *A Portrait of Scottish Rugby*. Edinburgh: Polygon Books.

Matless, David. 2016. *Landscape and Englishness*. 2nd expanded ed. London: Reaktion Books.

May, Anthony. 2018. "The Relationship between Football and Literature in the Novels of Irvine Welsh." *Soccer and Society* 19 (7): 924–943.

McLaren, Bill. 2004. *The Voice of Rugby. My Autobiography (with Peter Bills)*. London: Bantam.

Merton, Robert. 1988. "Some Thoughts on the Concept of Sociological Autobiography." In *Sociological Lives*, edited by M. W. Riley, 17–21. Newbury Park: Sage.

Mitchell, William J. T. 1994. *Landscape and Power*. Chicago: University of Chicago Press.

Neville, Gwen Kennedy. 1994. *The Mother Town. Civic Ritual, Symbol and Experience in the Borders of Scotland*. New York: Oxford University Press.

Obert, Julia C. 2019. "The Political Ecologies of the Borders in Walter Scott's *Minstrelsy of the Scottish Borders and the Lay of the Last Minstrel* and in Contemporary Scottish Poetry." *Scottish Literary Review* 11 (2): 81–96.

Özkirimli, Umut. 2010. *Theories of Nationalism: A Critical Introduction Second Edition*, Basingstoke: Palgrave MacMillan.

Pecora, Vincent P. 2001. *Nations and Identities: Classic Readings*. Oxford: Blackwell.

Renwick, Jim, and David Barnes. 2006. *Centre of Excellence: The Jim Renwick Story*. Edinburgh: Birlinn.

Robb, Graham. 2018. *The Debatable Land. The Lost World between Scotland and England*. London: Picador.

Rutherford, John, and Roy Laidlaw. 1988. *Rugby Partnership (with Norman Mair)*. London: Stanley Paul.

Shils, Edward. 1957. "Primordial, Personal, Sacred and Civil Ties: Some Particular Observations on the Relationships of Sociological Research and Theory." *The British Journal of Sociology* 8 (2): 130–145. doi:10.2307/587365.

Smith, Susan J. 1993. "Bounding the Borders: Claiming Space and Making Place in Rural Scotland." *Transactions of the Institute of British Geographers* 18 (3): 291–308. doi:10.2307/622461.

Stanley, Liz. 1993. "On Auto/Biography in Sociology." *Sociology* 27 (1): 41–52. doi:10.1177/003803859302700105.

Stewart, Pamela J., and Andrew Strathearn. 2003. "Introduction." In *Landscape, Memory and History. Anthropological Perspectives*, edited by P. J. Stewart and A. Strathearn, 1–15. London: Pluto Press.

Telfer, Jim. 2005. *Jim Telfer. Looking Back…for Once*. Edinburgh: Mainstream.

Townsend, Gregor. 2007. *Talk of the Toony*. London: HarperSport.

Trevor-Roper, Hugh. 1983. "The Invention of Tradition: The Highland Tradition of Scotland." In *The Invention of Tradition*, edited by E. Hobsbawm, 15–42. Cambridge: Cambridge University Press.

Weir, Doddie. 2018. *My Name's Doddie. The Autobiography*. Edinburgh: Black and White Publishing.

Welsh, Irvine. 1999. *Trainspotting* London: Vintage.

Welsh, Irvine. 2003. *Porno* London: Vintage.

Welsh, Irvine. 2012. *Skagboys* London: Jonathan Cape.

Woolridge, Joyce. 2008. "These Sporting Lives: Football Autobiographies 1945-1980." *Sport in History* 28 (4): 620–640. doi:10.1080/17460260802580669.

Soccer, the Saarland, and statehood: win, loss, and cultural reunification in post-war Europe

Alec S. Hurley (iD)

ABSTRACT
Football proved to be one of the few areas that fueled West Germany's ambition to reintegrate Saarland into the fractured post-war republic. Denied participation with the German football federation in the wake of the Second World War, yet unwilling to don French colors, Saarland's national football team (*Saarländische Fußballnationalmannschaft*) epitomised the uneasy space embodied by its citizens. Unable to compete in the 1950 World Cup – despite FIFA recognition – Saarland focused instead on dominating the lower French leagues and creating their own tournament. Despite two losses to eventual champions West Germany in the qualifying round of the 1954 World Cup, Saarland's footballers and their supporters left no doubt as to their cultural and political desire to reunite with the nation that had been denied to them. Studying Saarland and its football team this way, this paper juxtaposes sport, politics, and nationalism within the context of post-WWII German history.

Introduction

Saarland's inspired performance in the 1954 World Cup qualifying round – where they fell to eventual champions West Germany – spilled into the political sphere. The small nation's unrelenting style of play inspired impassioned rallies culminating in the 1955 Saar Statute. On January 1, 1957, with enthusiasm rivaled only by the echoes of the football pitch, Saarland rejoined West Germany. In the aftermath of reunification, Saarland continued to provide a meaningful aspect of Germany's success in international football. In conjunction with their region's bounty of natural resources, the *Saarländische Fußballnationalmannschaft* secured itself a position as a vital part of West German cultural identity in the late twentieth century. Several former Saarland footballers dedicated their lives to the development and formalization of German football and by extension the nation's post-war identity, both nationally and internationally. Helmut Schön, the manager of Saarland's squad between 1952 and 1956, continued his role with the merged West German team through the 1960s and 70s. At the time of his retirement in 1978 he held records for the most wins and most match appearances in World Cup history with sixteen and twenty-five, respectively. After impressive performances in the 1954 and 1958 World Cup, Schön and the West German side emerged victorious at the 1974 World Cup. His impeccable run that year resulted in one of just three teams from the post-war era to win the tournament as the host nation. He was not Saarland's lone representative in the annals of West German football. In 1962, Herman Neuberger, the former president of the Independent Saarland Football Association, played a leading role in the foundation of the Bundesliga, the top league for German association football. These deeply rooted connections necessitate the present examination of the importance of sport, public spectacle, and German nationalism through Saarland's brief but brilliant appearance on the international football stage.

Soccer, imagined communities, and Saarland

Nations are nothing more than imagined political communities. This lasting sentiment authored by Benedict Anderson in the early 1980s continues to dominate academic literature on social and national formations of sport. The 'image of communion' was critical to Anderson's thesis because as members of a nation, whether small or expansive, individuals involved would likely never all meet (Anderson 2006, 7). Though Anderson himself wrote rarely on the impact of sport, his contemporary Eric Hobsbawm, aptly reconciled the two when he wrote, 'the imagined community of millions seems more real as a team of eleven named people' (Hobsbawm 1992, 142).

Before examining Saarland's brief existence within international football, a discussion on the intersection of imagined communities and nationalism will precede an analysis of the unique nationalising role of football. Nationalism, according to Anderson, is an ideology based on paradox. In brief, nations are both modern and timeless, universal but unique, and influential yet undefinable (Anderson 2006, 5). The proposed duality eventually defined the shift in sport scholarship during the social turn. At a crossroads, football and nationalism became 'contested terrain' (Falcous and Booth 2017, 1826).

Writing in the run-up to the 2006 World Cup, one sport sociologist asserted that 'nowhere are imagined communities better manifested... than in football, the world's most popular sport' (Burdsey 2006, 12). Studies tracing the historical intersection between football and national identity are nearly all focused through the narrow framework of the nation state (Adam 2017, 1371). Football, more than any other sport, lends itself to examining the construction of national cultures, the reinforcement of national sentiment, and the flourishing presence of Anderson's 'imagined community.'

Anderson's nationalism paradox will serve as the crux of this paper as football is often understood through the same self-contradiction. Recognizing the potential of sport as an arena of nationalism in the interwar period, an English sport journalist wrote, 'whatever his nationality, every sensible man knows the thud of the football is sweeter than the rattle of the sabre' (*The Leeds Mercury*, December 7, 1934). Sensibility, however, is a characteristic often absent under nationalism. Harnessing the power of myth and popular sentiment, nationalism hinges on the element of irrationality as a defining trait (Emmerich 2009, 244). Anderson was among the first to argue that national self-consciousness belongs in the realm of the mythic. In his seminal work, he presented nations as 'imagined political communities' necessitated upon 'a deep, horizontal comradeship' that itself is a fiction that seeps 'quietly and continuously into reality' (Anderson 2006, 7). The irrationality inherent within nationalism is what allows for the presence of the paradoxes

Anderson highlighted, as its purpose is to generate and feed off popular emotion (Gibernau 1996, 1003).

Irrationality provides another link between nationalism and sport as both rely on popular emotion as opposed to logical sobriety. The emotion and paradox which pervades the myopic focus of nationalism distinguishes it from the nation-state itself. Nationalism, as an identifying philosophy, is distinct from the geopolitical reality of a nation-state (Rowe 2017, 1471). As evidenced in the post-war Saar, the logical option was to embrace the economic and political recovery instituted by the French occupation. However, the emotional attachments of the quasi-autonomous region remained with the economically battered, but culturally aligned West Germany (*The Guardian*, August 30, 1954). In an analysis of World Cup fandom, Kersting determined that nationalism and national pride are often conflated. The latter is a personal connection whereas the former constitutes an ideological sense of communal superiority. Both, ultimately, differ from the far-less emotionally charged category of 'national identity' (Kersting 2007, 1302). His distinctions support the previously theorized shift from patriotism to nationalism. The two '-isms' are perhaps best understood as an evolution of cultural processes and acceptance within a state, both having significant overlap and influence on the other (Gems 2013, 101).

Malleable identities often coalesce around a singular moment, one which is brimming with 'passionate intensity' (Cassels 1996, 31). It should therefore come as little surprise that sport, a physical expression of such a phenomenon, served as an imagined community's spatial anchor. Existing on the extreme end of mythic and romantic interpretations of nationalism, sport is attractive to a given community through the *power of fascination* (Bonde 2009, 1309). If, therefore, the identity of individuals is best understood as a fluid process, then national identities – Anderson's 'imagined communities' – would be best viewed in like fashion. This outpouring of political and eventual social rights within post-war Europe coincided with desire for acceptance and participation in the 'full social heritage' of a given community (Guschwan 2014, 859–860). Part of the reason football aligns well with the constructs Anderson set down in the early 1980s is due to the need for unifying narratives within imagined communities. The inherent passion of nationalism as an ideology is neatly packaged and presented through football. In its dual capacity as a political tool and romantic ideal sport became a medium through which fascination with past heroes and a reengagement with a common folk history, culminated in a specific and highly visible form of cultural nationalism (Rowe 2017, 1471).

It is worthwhile to remember that national football teams do not always represent a nation in the traditional sense (Hesse 2014, 2–3). More accurately, they are teams which define an idea, a shared, communal identity – in short, an imagined community.

In the interwar period, as nations were reimagined and reconstructed through mandates from the League of Nations, continental European identity experienced a new reckoning. Faced with the daunting task of addressing competing post-war identities that did not fit neatly into prescribed camps, German scholars welcomed the return of the nation as a cultural entity despite its partitioned geopolitical status (Berger 1995, 201). Historically, though, wrestling with a national cultural identity in the face of political partition was nothing new for the German people. Since the formation of the modern German state in 1871, there have been 'at least six different states, each with its own rationale, borders, economy, population, society, and political order' (Dann 1992, 285–290). Among German historians, there continues to be a sense of *disequilibriam* in the recording of the immediate post-war histories. That makes reducing the fractured German identity to that of an easier to grasp asymmetric relationship insufficient (Kleßmann 2001, 142). An inability to reconcile or comprehend one's national existence was not only a question for scholars, as most Germans in the immediate post-war era initially questioned whether they still existed – either as a nation or a people (Hermand 2012, 284). The deeply personal and communal existential question was such a powerful and constant point of reflection that it was granted its own word, *Vergangenheitsbewältigung* (Henke and Woller 1991, 32). Translated as 'coming to terms with one's own and one's nation's past,' the process articulated the struggle of acknowledging an unconscionable legacy with a desire to embrace a renewed communal identity (Huth 1994, 489).

In 1966, the then-West German newspaper *Die Zeit* claimed an irrefutable reality, that 'sport is the continuation of politics by other means' (Balbier 2009, 548). Their claim was centered immediately on the rising tensions between the German Democratic Republic and the Federal Republic of Germany as contested through medals tables and Olympic glory. That quote could also apply to an earlier intersection of West German cultural identity and sport. Two decades prior, nestled in the dense woods southwest of Germany's Rhineland and bordering France's Alsace-Lorraine, a collection of local footballers – players and managers – embarked on one of international football's finest forgotten five-year stretch.

Due to the absence of a traditional nationalized space, Saarland's sport history has been overlooked in sport literature. Studies on post-war Germany focus either on Germany's relationship with the Allied powers or on the struggle between the 'two Germanies' (Planert 2002, 25–30). Saarland's role in unifying West Germany is a crucial and understudied aspect of the re-emergence of sport and the reconstruction of identity in post-war Europe (Harres 1997, 12). The process of reformulating German cultural memory in the immediate post-war period provides an appropriate vehicle to examine Anderson's paradox. Through the dynamic – often unconscious – creation of social memory, remembering is always pitted against forgetting (Figlio 2017, 121). New social memory requires a stimulus. Setting the stage for football, Saarland's lone appearance at the Olympic games in Helsinki in 1952 became a 'place' of glorious memory for the Saarland's collective culture of recollection (Großmann 2005, 510–515). Internal stimuli can be found through religion or prayer, whereas external stimuli can be centered around momentous cultural events such as a ritual or experience (Assmann 1992, 36–43). A football match perfectly satisfies the criteria for an external stimulus. Also, the western border of Germany was where football first gained national appeal, so its return in some ways satisfied the internal stimulus of a spiritual like reflection (Assmann 2000, 106). Football's return in Germany accelerated and strengthened its post-war identity (Assmann 1988, 11–14). Along Germany's lush, industrial western border burned a passion for football. Under alternating French and German control, the region increasingly rewrote the English roots of the imported game and replaced them with the national narratives of each continental power (Adam 2017, 1372). However, cultural memories derived from and entrenched by football's passionate allure fostered a sense of national belonging that superseded the constant redrawing of national borders. The 1954 World Cup qualifying match in Stuttgart between West Germany and Saarland, overshadowed by the *Miracle at Bern* several months later, bound together the culturally unified but politically separated entities in a 'symbolic order' that heightened calls for national reunification.

It is worth examining a recent critique of Anderson's thesis. Renowned transnational historian Thomas Adam, in an essay on the intercultural contexts of football in longtime rival nations Argentina and Germany, argued that 'the game created its own space [and] is not determined by the imagined and constructed spaces ascribed to particular nations' (Adam 2017, 1372). The transnational critique is one which requires acknowledgement because it shares two crucial elements with Anderson's nationalism. First, the transnational critique exists without a specific methodology. Like Anderson's thesis, the focus is on the importance of communal connections and generalized rather than personal developments. Secondly, the transnational critique highlights those individuals who forged such connections through which scholars can refashion social history. As Anderson's thesis rapidly approaches its fiftieth anniversary it is important to remember that his imagined communities served a similar purpose; to return the agency of nations to the sovereign people who founded them. This paper adds a unique wrinkle to Adam's transnational critique, as Saarland actively voted against self-governance and independence in deference to a desire to rejoin their culturally cohesive German family. The unusual decision to forgo the isolating but passionate allure of nationalism for the comfort of a familiar cultural community aligns itself well with the framework provided by Anderson. Shedding light on the previously unexplored history of Saarland's football team, this paper examines the role football played in Saarland's eventual reunification with West Germany. Anderson's thesis, critiques and all, will now be examined through the delicately intertwined history of football, sovereignty, and collective cultural identity in the small, overlooked, mineral-rich German State. Caught in the midst of the struggle – waged militaristically, ideologically, and eventually athletically – Saarland employed football in the post-war period to reject both French occupation and independent governance to reunite with West Germany, the imagined community from which it had been torn.

Soccer and Saarland

In Anderson's seminal work, he presents nations as 'imagined political communities' necessitated upon 'a deep, horizontal comradeship' that itself is a fiction that seeps 'quietly and continuously into reality' (Anderson 2006, 7). Studies of sport and nationalism have prioritized discussions vis à vis nation states and assertions of international recognition. There exists, however, another use for sport within the framework of the nation-state: a use that rejects national autonomy in favor of reconciliation. While admittedly a less common approach, the implications for favoring a cultural community beyond geopolitical borders, lends weight to the validity of Anderson's imagined community. Saarland, a small German state nestled to the southwest of Germany's Rhineland and just to the east of France's Alsace-Lorraine, presents an intriguing case study for sport and nationalism. This is a region that voluntarily rejected independent nationhood and relinquished all emblems of nationalism (*Belfast News-Letter*, October 24, 1955).

Over the first half of the twentieth century, Saarland had been torn apart by contentious Franco-German relations and the broader global conflicts of two world wars. The region swung between French and German control throughout the late nineteenth and early twentieth centuries. As early as 1870 the Prussian leadership in Germany established nationalized mining and manufacturing complexes throughout Saarland (*The Guardian*, August 30, 1954). Following the First World War, the region was granted quasi-independence under the League of Nations after the First World War. In 1935, Saarlanders voted to rejoin the German Third Reich. The outcome of the vote was as consequential as it was surprising.

Over ninety percent of the votes cast were in favor of full reunification, vastly outperforming the other two options on the ballot which included an adherence to France or a continuation of governance by an international committee (*The Los Angeles Times*, February 7, 1954). The overwhelming vote was most surprising to the French. After World War I, France attempted to override the provisions of the 1920 Peace Treaty to establish Saarland as a French province. As such, leaders of the occupation were frustrated by the preference of Saarlanders for reabsorption into Germany (*The Guardian*, August 30, 1954). A return to Germany led to renewed control of the national mines and manufacturing apparatus founded more than half a century earlier. Despite economic relationships and cultural traditions linking Saarland with Germany, a reunion with Hitler's Reich was uncomfortable. Home to a strong tradition of socialist movements and connection with the Catholic Church most international observers were stunned that Saarland chose to align with a Nazi regime who had ruthlessly interfered with those two institutions (*The Age*, December 3, 1952). Ignoring pleas from their own local leadership to embrace autonomy, Saarlanders once more chose to reunite with its cultural home over independence.

After the Second World War, Saarland once more fell under French control during the Allied partition of Germany. In the war's immediate aftermath, West German leaders feared that any possible reconciliation with Saarland was lost. The temporary measures taken by the Allied powers in 1948–1950 seemed more than likely permanent to German leadership in Bonn who believed the drafters of post-war peace treaties would not be inclined to disturb French control (*The Guardian*, January 17, 1950). Envisioning their new territory as an economic goldmine over which they could exert full control, French occupational leaders officially maintained a desire for an autonomous Saar state (Heinen 1996, 175). The post-war occupation by France placed the German-aligned population in a difficult environment. Economically the region prospered via increased commercial traffic driven by French coal interests, but culturally suffered from an uncertain future (Sander 1990, 110–111). One diplomatic correspondent presciently noted in the early 1950s that a territory could not be tied economically to one sovereign state and politically to another (*The Guardian*, January 17, 1950). The majority consensus during the initial post-war decade was that Saarland would resume its status as an international protectorate, as it had been during the interwar era. The whole of Europe – often argued under the case for unity – believed to have as much of a say in Saarland's affairs as its 950,000 residents. An American foreign affairs correspondent best articulated the thoughts of the European elite when he wrote, 'it is obvious that the Saar is the last place on earth where the future of the Saar will be determined' (*The Los Angeles Times*, February 7, 1954).

Instead, the fate of Saarland hinged, at least partially, on the football pitch. It was the return of football in 1948–1949 that catalyzed national passions and roused national sentiment, which once embraced could not be rescinded (Cassels 1996, 64). One way the divisions of the nineteenth century remained a present reality for Saarlanders in the immediate post-war era was linguistic. In romance languages, such as French, the word 'nation' can mean either a state or a people. In German, however, each concept has its own word. *Staat* is the geopolitical entity while *Nation* is cultural. From 1947 to 1957, Saarland was a French *Staat* that identified with the German *Nation*. The fight between cultural identity and political authority found a symbolic battleground within soccer stadiums.

Saarland football, both provincial and national, during the late 1940s and 1950s became a principal driver of nationalism (Hüger 2009, 429). As Danish historian Hans Bonde argued, the 'dramatic bodily acts' inherent to sport builds identification through 'the excitement of results and hope of release' (Bonde 2009, 1309). International matches, beginning with a dominant run through the French second league, offered Saarland an avenue for direct international confrontation. The region effectively confronted – and triumphed over – their French occupiers on the pitch.

Channeling Anderson's thesis, Gleaves and Llewelyn argued that national sports offer imagined communities a cultural text (Gleaves and Llewellyn 2014, 6). Saarland's national football team, through international competition, rewrote their own cultural texts to the astonishment and embarrassment of their French occupiers. Germany, which longed to reclaim Saarland, used the region's football success – and French inadequacy – as the rationale for cultural unity. FC Saarbrücken, the club team within Saarland's capital, provided the catalyst.

A dominant squad within the German league as recently as 1943, FC Saarbrücken laid waste to the second tier of the French Football Association to which they had been invited as a non-point-scoring member. Their inclusion into the league came reluctantly, as the French league did not believe Saarland capable of playing at the demanding pace customary of the French style of play. Such claims were rudely doused by the Saarlanders themselves as they defeated a first-tier team, AS St. Etiene by four goals in Saarbrücken. The following year, with a team of just fourteen players, FC Saarbrücken returned to play in the French second league (Haas and Freyer 2020). The pride of Saarland decimated their French opponents, including blowout victories facilitated by a dynamic, high-scoring offense. Operating as a 'guest' participant in the league they won it by six points. Saarland's 59-53 final point margin over the 'official' champions from Bordeaux is even more impressive considering Bordeaux's refusal to play the Saarlanders. The undermanned team won 26 of their 37 games, out-scored their opponents by over three goals per game and landed half of their squad in the top ten rankings for total goals scored (Haas and Freyer 2020). It was a thorough domination and an abject humiliation for the French who witnessed control of Saarland slipping further away with each victory. For the Saarlanders, the victories were defiant triumphs over an unwelcome occupied presence. The inclusion of Saarland's most dominant club team portended the demise of French plans for regional cultural supremacy. Even coverage of the matches refused to acknowledge the embarrassing French defeats, because praise of an ex-German club would have been blasphemous (Laurent 1984, 26–28). Saarland's success in France lasted only one year, which coincided with resumption of the German football association.

Territorial rights along the Ruhr, Rhineland, and Alsace-Lorraine have long been the driver of nationalized sporting movements among old rivals. German *Turnen* gymnastics was born in response to the Prussian defeat at the hands of Napoleon. Likewise, French Olympism was spurred on in part by France's territorial losses at the hands of a revitalized Prussia. Ill-will continued to define Franco-German relations in the interwar period as France banned international football competitions with Germany in 1938. France's crackdown on expressions of Germanic culture in Saarland was vehemently opposed. Most Saarlanders, outraged at their continental occupiers, believed they had to accept the French terms of occupation under duress and that the Allies had manipulated their way into power (*The Guardian*, April 21, 1952). French resistance to German international sport participation continued in the post-war era, stalling attempts for German inclusion into the global football community until the mid-1950s. This resistance did not apply to Saarland. All too readily, the French initiated physical education schools as well as national club-level football to instill their own cultural values. Both efforts, endorsed by the French high commissioner Gilbert Grandval, failed spectacularly within a few short years (Joyce 2008). While the schooling efforts were plagued by poor weather and inadequate facilities, it was Saarland's proficiency in professional and national football that proved the ultimate humiliation for the French (Dichter 2008, 91).

Reviewing the remaking of the national landscape in the post-war era, German scholar Dietmar Hüger argued that political battles over Saarland were waged in legislative houses, but the 'symbolic battlefield' was the football field where 'politicians negotiated autonomy and internal contradictions melted away' (Hüger 2009, 438). National teams embody this impassioned coalescence by 'invoking *our* [sic] team… into our daily routines, reminding us with whom we stand' (Meier and Leinwather 2013, 1202). Even at the club level, representing a localized intimate community, professional football provided an outlet for an increasingly urbanized Europe over the long nineteenth century (Hobsbawm 2003, 298). In Germany, Hobsbawm's observation manifested itself. As the English Game made inroads on the continent in the late 1800s, the sport quickly became the preference of the German working class. The Ruhr area, a similarly heavily industrialized region just north of Saarland, became – and remains – the geographic stronghold of national football (Merkel 2007, 223–224). This is a somewhat unsurprising development as Anderson contended that nationalist movements in general were typically 'populist in outlook and sought to induct lower classes into political life,' often channeling popular class energies – such as football (Anderson 2006, 48).

Despite slipping in recent years, Saarland's footballing success allowed it to maintain a connection to the German state even when disconnected politically and economically. It is the personal connection vis-à-vis the passion aroused through the on-field action which makes football such a potent driver of communal identity. This is especially true for rural communities where football has long enjoyed pride of place for both the athletes and the community. Football's ability to occupy spaces in memory by way of heroic figures or mythic narratives increases the likelihood of remembrance by a population (Briegleb 1997, 31–35).

The Allies allowed the Germans to resume limited football activity as early as 1947. However, the geographic regions of the revitalized national league excluded the French controlled Saarland. The four regional leagues of the Oberliga – Berlin, North, West, and South – were joined by a fifth region in 1950. Having thoroughly whipped and embarrassed the French football establishment in the 1948–1949 season, the occupation government of Saarland relented and allowed FC Saarbrücken to rejoin the German league as the South-West region (Hesse-Litchtenberger 2003, 108–112). By 1951, supported by the rebirth of its national football league, Germany began to re-establish itself in the international community. For their part, the German leadership attempted to depoliticize sport. Under the guidance of Willi Daume, the inaugural years of the *Deutsche Sportbund (DSB)* were focused as much on national unification as in opposition to the communist East German state (Missiroli 2002, 9–10). The message of nominal apoliticism resonated with Saarland's weary population. Worn down by attempts at external fights for control of imposed sovereignty, Saarland's footballers expressed an antipathy for politics, preferring to identify solely as sportsmen. The region's continued presence and success through international athletics during the early 1950s forced an uneasy reconciling of national politics between French control and German cultural adherence. Before being fully accepted into the German

Football Association, West Germany watched as Saarland – then operating as an independent sporting community – entered the 1952 Olympic stadium in Helsinki in front of them. The opening ceremony combined with an inspired performance by Saarland's athletes shifted the attitudes of both the German and the French when it came to vying for the supremacy of internalized cultural allegiance (Großmann 2009, 515–520).

One prominent historian built on Anderson's thesis by proposing the concept of 'banal nationalism.' Distinct from the brow-beating, shortsighted characteristics typical of nationalism, his argument centered on sport operating as an 'unnoticed flag of nationhood, embedded within everyday media' where it can draw 'readers, viewers, and listeners together as a part of a community' (Billig 1995, 174–175). These 'symbol-laden conflicts' and 'ritualized gestalt' of sport provided the breeding ground for the cultivation of national sentiment (Bonde 2009, 1309). As such, the roots of sport within a given community – tangible and imagined – run deep and have become an integral part of those identities.

After thoroughly dominating the French league, Saarland football was granted an exceptional recognition. The international football federation, FIFA, granted the small protectorate independent competitive status in the summer of 1950, mere months before West Germany (Vonnard 2020, 23). Perceptions of Saarland as a separate, though slightly weaker, German side was a harbinger of the community's future. One thing Saarlanders did well was play football. In a belated assessment of Saar's ability to utterly dominate the pitch, the coach of the heavily favored Hungarian side in 1954 remarked that Saarland could outplay the best Europe had to offer (Haas and Freyer 2020). After success in the French league, Saarland opted to create their own tournament. In the uncertain years between their expulsion from the French league and their acceptance into the German sport federation, Saarland hosted, then won, the inaugural Internationaler Saarlandpokal – a forerunner of today's European Cup. Fifteen European clubs and one from Chile (although notably none from Germany) all bowed out to the hosts who claimed the trophy and the two-million-franc prize (Joyce 2008). The prizes, however, were a small consolation for a nation facing a crisis of identity. In the face of stiff opposition from the French occupiers and international community, football had rekindled hope of reconciliation with West Germany. In 1951, that ember of hope burst into a fully formed flame when Saarland was granted re-entry into the German league. Their national hopes again rested primarily on the footballers from FC Saarbrücken. Wasting no time, the men from Saar's capital swiftly advanced to the championship where they faced neighboring Stuttgart in a closely contested final (Potter and Chaplin 2015). The location of the match foreshadowed the pinnacle moment in Saarland's crash-course of unification with West Germany. Stuttgart's home stadium provided the venue for one of the most nationally charged football matches since the end of World War II.

Unity through sport

Fall 1953 saw national football galvanize a rare movement of cultural reintegration. Among German historians, 1953 is often described as the best year since the war. One reason for the unusual optimism came courtesy of the first World Cup since 1938 (Wolfgang 1972, 26). The draw for the 1954 World Cup placed West Germany in the same qualifying group as Saarland. Only one team, though, could advance to the knockout stage. Concurrent with the football drama came increased calls for Saarland's return to West Germany. Led by the head of the German SPD political party Kurt Schumacher, sport reinforced the similarities between the two nations. Global media coverage, driven by Schumacher, heightened the political importance of the first match between the two sides. (*The Tampa Tribune*, February 4, 1952) On October 11, 1953, fifty thousand culturally homogenous fans packed Stuttgart's national stadium for the first qualifying match between Saarland and West Germany. Adding to the tension was Saarland's early lead in the group standings. From the beginning, any notion that the match was strictly about football was laughable. Navigating a diplomatic minefield, the West German hosts opted not to fly the national flags of either side (Joyce 2008). Far from being a festive embellishment, the flags of West Germany and Saarland stirred up questions of national imagination, including autonomy and power (Hill 1999, 5). At the time, the questions of 'who represented Germany' and, more broadly, 'who were Germans' were at the forefront of both populations, including those in the stadium and those listening on the radio (Hughes and Owen 2009, 447). The game itself was less dramatic, with West Germany coasting to a three-goal shutout.

Five months later, with West Germany's bid to the World Cup on the line, the two teams met again in Saarbrücken. Notes from a private collection reveal that the game being played had far more riding on it than just a chance to gain entry to the World Cup. Several months prior to the game, the French Commissar of Saarland – Andre François-Poncet – sent a telegraph back to the administration in Paris warning his superiors that the match would offer declarations in favor of a return to Germany by the Saar, which would result in an unpleasant turn for France. Fulfilling the commissar's fears, tensions and excitement descended on the full-capacity stadium of fifty-three thousand Germans. A state of emergency was implemented for the contest in and around Saarbrücken. In a report from the day, four minutes prior to kickoff, the powder keg went off. A group of pro-German sympathizers took to the field with an illegally obtained loudspeaker and proclaimed, rightly, that 'the separatist government wanted to prevent this game against our German brothers!' Over the loudspeaker the rebels then led the crowd in chants of 'We are Germans! The Saar is German! The Saar remains Germany!' before playing the first stanza of the German national anthem 'Deutschlandied' (Hüger 2009, 442). The sold-out crowd was treated to a game that lived up to its pre-match hype. Although the West Germans ultimately prevailed by a score of three to one, Jules Rimet the French president of FIFA remarked that Saarland had played better that day and was perhaps 'the most interesting team in Europe' (*11Freunde*, December 3, 2013). Herbert Brinker, the legendary scorer for the Saarland side, recalled in a 2009 interview that game was – despite the loss – the greatest game he had ever played in (Haas and Freyer, 2020).

Saarland's defeat at the hands of West Germany did little to drive a wedge between the two nations. If anything, passion for reconciliation and national reunification soared higher than ever. One Saarland winger recalled his emotions after the game, remembering that he was not unhappy. He saw himself as a German and as such, did not want to prevent the team he had cheered on as a boy from making it into the World Cup (Haas and Freyer 2020). As an olive branch to their soon-to-be countrymen, the West German team invited the Saarland national side to Wankdorf Stadium in Switzerland to watch the World Cup final. Following a match now known as 'The Miracle at Bern,' Saarland's footballers were extended another invitation, this time to celebrate with the recently crowned West German world champions at their hotel (Haas and Freyer 2020). Celebration seems too small a word for the overflowing of emotions that poured out of Saarland as Herbert Zimmerman's exasperated voice called out the go-ahead goal '*Tor für Deutschland! Drei zu zwei führt*

Deutschland. Halten Sie mich für verrückt, halten Sie mich für übergeschnappt!' ('Finale 1954 – Rahn Schießt' 2010). The author of the digital collection of Saarland football materials recalled his face pressed against the glass of a television shop in Saarbrücken as a child watching the final moments in sheer joy as his neighbors crowded into pubs and radio shops to listen to their long-separated countrymen fulfil the miracle victory (Haas and Freyer 2020). Fifteen months later, with public euphoria still at peak levels from the German victory, Saarlanders overwhelmingly voted against a referendum on independent statehood in October of 1955 (Wiskemann 1956, 287). This rejection was widely perceived as a vote for reunification with Germany. The passionate intensity present in Saarland ever since the first football match with West Germany two years prior, guided a fiercely nationalistic course. Saarlander's nationalist ambitions rejected offers for self-governance as well as status as an independent protectorate. A pro-German Saarland vote in 1955 concluded with the reintegration into West Germany on January 1, 1957. As a result, Saarland's national football team, after nearly a decade of hard-earned respect and international recognition, left FIFA and resumed play as a regional member of the top German football league (Hesse 2014, 3). The region and its people, embodied by their football team, basked in the reunification with their imagined community.

Despite the West German desire for sport to remain divorced from politics, they could not halt the injection of nationalism and increasing calls for unification highlighted by Saarland's football prowess. By 1955, the French owned up to their cultural losses in the region. Exacerbated by the brilliance of Saarland's footballers, the French occupational government agreed to return control of the region to Germany. Economically, the transfer of power would take nearly a decade (E.W 1957, 27). Culturally, the battle for Saarland's soul had already been won in the soccer stadiums in Stuttgart and Bern in 1953–1954.

Celebrating the official re-entry of the Saarland into West Germany, German Chancellor Konrad Adenauer remarked that Saarland's journey invited European powers to rethink reconciliatory capabilities in building a united Europe. The congratulatory mood masked the occasionally turbulent road both nations traversed to arrive at their unification. While sport had been a catalytic factor in accelerating the reunion, for many Saarlanders cheering on their nation against a nation they hoped they would again call their own, constituted a bizarre spectacle (Heffernan 2015, 4–5). Also, despite early claims to the contrary, the German Sport Federation came to represent the whole of the German people, an overtly political position (Hughes and Owen 2009, 448). Far from a contradictory stance, the *Deutsche Sportbund* and the *Saarländische Fußballnationalmannschaft* embraced a word often used along the Franco-German border. The word is 'Verechtungen,' which refers to the interwoven nature of things (Gardner and Kries 2017, 1). Just as the communities of Saarland and West Germany remained interwoven despite external partitions, so too were football and politics.

Saarland's tale offers sport historians a glimpse into the unifying power that can be achieved even in the absence of on-field victory. The legacy of Saarland's team lingered in the German consciousness for years to come. When West Germany repeated as World Cup champions in 1974 their coach was Helmut Schön, the same man who managed Saarland's unifying World Cup run twenty years prior. Schön's time at the helm resulted in one of the finest eras of German football, in many ways an extension of the resilient performances of his Saarland squad. The following year, in 1975, Hermann Neuberger president of Saarland's national football association during its magical era in the 1950s, was elected the seventh president of the German Football Federation, an organization credited as one of the most public symbols of modern German nationalism.

Conclusion

It is hardly coincidence that the rise of sport emerged concomitant with nationalist ideology. The intertwined nature of sport and nationalism rests on the inherent competitiveness associated with both phenomena. It is therefore little surprise that the image of Saarland's football team defying French influence and proving itself loyal to Germany still evokes strong emotions in the collective memory of the region's inhabitants (Großmann 2005, 525–530). Perhaps Anderson channeled the likes of 'sub'-nationalisms like Saarland when he argued that the era of nationalism was still going strong because of its legitimizing value in our collective political life (Anderson 2006, 3).

The hierarchical valuation of worth and intense competitive pride binds people to created dominant traditions – observable in both the rise of the nation-state and organized sport (Maguire 2011, 978). The lengthy tenure of sport's presence as an intimate thread in the cloak of national identity was recognized by Hobsbawm, who wrote that sport was 'one of the most significant practices [during the late nineteenth century]' and the institutionalization of sports on a national and even international stage marked a decisive transformation from recreational pursuits and ad hoc nature of sports from the early nineteenth century. In perhaps the most direct connection between sport and nationalism made outside the confines of sport studies, was Hobsbawm's own assertion that 'the very act of cheering for one's side is an expression of nationalism' (Hobsbawm 2003, 31).

From the start, wrote Anderson, 'the nation was conceived in language… and that one could always be "invited into" the imagined community' (Anderson 2006, 145). As the West German players, managers, and fans erupted in celebration at the Miracle of Bern, so too joined their brothers and sisters from Saarland. There could have been no more apt invitation than one delivered from a strong left foot just inside the box. Saarland's brief and remarkable appearance on the international football stage is a strong reminder to historians to reflect on the unifying aspects of nationalism, even in defeat. Within established nation-states, imagined communities have their place, and they can often be found gathered around the nearest pitch.

Disclosure statement

No potential conflict was reported by the author.

ORCID

Alec S. Hurley ⓘ http://orcid.org/0000-0003-4969-9492

References

Adam, Thomas. 2017. "The Intercultural Transfer of Football: The Contexts of Germany and Argentina." *Sport in Society* 20 (10): 1371–1389. doi:10.1080/17430437.2016.1221059.

Anderson, Benedict. 2006. *Imagined Communities: Reflections on the Origin and Spread of Nationalism, Revised Edition*. London: Verso.

Assmann, Jan. 1992. *Das kulturelle Gedächtis: Schrift, Erinnerung un dpolitische Identität in Frühen Hochkulturen*. Munich: Beck.

Assmann, Jan. 1988. "Kollectives Gedächtis und kulturelle Identität." In *Kultur und Gedächtnis*, edited by Jan Assmann and Tonio Hölscher, 9–19. Frankfurt.

Assmann, Jan. 2000. *Religion und kulturelle Gedächtis: Zehn Studien*. Munich: Beck.

Balbier, Uta Andrea. 2009. ""A Game, a Competition, an Instrument?": High Performance, Cultural Diplomacy and German Sport from 1950 to 1972." *The International Journal of the History of Sport* 26 (4): 539–555. See footnote 39, for the full German source ('Sport auf Kinderbeinen.' *Die Zeit*. December 27, 1966).

Berger, Stefan. 1995. "Historians and Nation-Building in Germany after Reunification." *Past and Present* 148 (1): 187–222. doi:10.1093/past/148.1.187.

Billig, Michael. 1995. *Banal Nationalism*. London: Sage Publication.

Bonde, Hans. 2009. "Prologue: Globalization, Regionalism, Nationalism: Danish Idiosyncrasy." *The International Journal of the History of Sport* 26 (10): 1307–1314. doi:10.1080/09523360903057401.

Briegleb, Klaus. 1997. "Ingeborg Bachmann, Paul Celan. Ihr (Nicht-)Ort in der Gruppe 47 (1952-1964/65): Eine Skizze." In *Ingeborg Bachmann und Paul Celan: Poetische Korrezpondenzen*, edited by Bernhard Böschenstein and Sigrid Weigel. Frankfut: a.M. Suhrkamp.

Burdsey, Daniel. 2006. "'If I Ever Play Football Dad, Can I Play for England or India?' British Asians, Sports, and Diasporic National Identities." *Sociology* 40 (1): 11–28. doi:10.1177/0038038506058435.

Cassels, Alan. 1996. *Ideology and International Relations in the Modern World*. London: Routledge.

Dann, Otto. 1992. *Nation und Nationalismus in Deutschland, 1770–1990*. München: Beck.

Dichter, Heather. 2008. "Sporting Democracy: The Western Allies Reconstruction of Germany Through Sport, 1944-1952." PhD diss., University of Toronto.

Diplomatic Correspondent. 1950. "Saar Lost to Germany?" *The Guardian*. January 17.

Emmerich, Wolfgang. 2009. "Cultural Memory East v West: Is What Belongs Together Really Growing Together?" *Oxford German Studies* 38 (3): 242–253. doi:10.1179/007871909x475553.

E.W. 1957. "The Return of the Saar to Germany." *The World Today* 13 (1): 27–36.

Falcous, Mark, and Douglas Booth. 2017. "Contested Epistemology: Theory and Method of International Sport Studies." *Sport in Society* 20 (12): 1821–1837. doi:10.1080/17430437.2017.12 32350.

Figlio, Karl. 2017. "Conflict of Remembering: The *Historikerstreit*." In *Remembering as Reparation: Psychoanalysis and Historical Memory*, edited by Karl Figlio, 119–143. London: Palmgrave Macmillan.

"Finale 1954 – Rahn schießt, Rahn schießt! TOOR!" 2010. YouTube.com. October 22. https://www.youtube.com/watch?v=G3I684BzNRM

Gardner, Nicky, and Susanne Kreis. 2017. "Saarland, January 1957." *Hidden Europe*, January 15. https://www.hiddeneurope.co.uk/saarland-january-1957

Gems, Gerald R. 2013. *Sport and the Shaping of Italian American Identity*. New York: Syracuse University Press.

Gibernau, Montserrat. 1996. "Nationalism and Intellectuals in Nations without States: The Catalan Case." *Political Studies* 48 (5): 989–1005.

Gleaves, John, and Matthew Llewellyn. 2014. "Ethics, Nationalism, and the Imagined Community: The Case against Inter-National Sport." *Journal of the Philosophy of Sport* 41 (1): 1–19. doi:10.108 0/00948705.2013.785427.

Guschwan, Matthew. 2014. "Sport and Citizenship: Introduction." *Sport in Society* 17 (7): 859–866. doi:10.1080/17430437.2013.806038.

Großmann, Johannes. 2005. Sportpolitik im Saarland 1945-1954, in Jahrbuch für westdeutsche Landesgeschichte 31.

Haas, Steffan, and Rainer Freyer. 2020. "Der 1 FC Saarbrücken." http://www.saar-nostalgie.de/FCS.htm

Harres, Wolfgang. 1997. *Sportpolitik an der Saar, 1945–1957*. Saarbrücken: Saarbrücker Dr. und Verlag.

Heinen, Amin. 1996. *Saarjahre: Politik und Wirtschaft im Saarland, 1945–1955.* Stuttgart: F. Steiner.

Heffernan, Conor. 2015. "War, Politics and Football: Saarland Versus West Germany." February 14. https://punditarena.com/football/cheffernan/war-politics-football-saarland-versus-west-germany

Henke, Klaus-Dietmar and H. Woller. Eds. 1991. *Politische Suduberungin Europa. Die Abrechnung mit Fachismus und Kollaboration nach dem Zweiten Weitkrieg* Munich: Deutscher Taschenbuch Verlag.

Hermand, Jost. 2012. *Verlorne Illusionen Eine Geschichte des deutschen Nationalismus.* Köln: Böhlau Verlag.

Hesse, Uli. 2014. "Saarland – The Forgotten International Team within Germany." September 23 www.espen.com/soccer/name/10/blog/post/2050535/headline

Hesse-Lichtenberger, Ulrich. 2003. *Tor! The Story of German Football.* London: WSC Books.

Hill, Jeffrey. 1999. "Cocks, Cats, Caps, and, Cups: A Semiotic Approach to Sport and National Identity." *Culture, Sport, Society* 2 (2): 1–21. doi:10.1080/14610989908721836.

Hobsbawm, Eric. 1992. *Nations and Nationalism since 1780: programme, Myth, Reality.* 2nd ed. Cambridge: UK: Cambridge University Press.

Hobsbawm, Eric. 2003. "Mass-Producing Traditions: Europe, 1870-1914." In *The Invention of Tradition,* edited by Eric Hobsbawm and Terrance Ranger. Cambridge, UK: Cambridge University Press.

Hüger, Dietmar. 2009. "Fußball, Politik, und Identität an der Saar nach dem Zweiten Weltkreig – was heißt und zu welchem Ende studiert man Sportgeschichte?" In *Kultur, Politik und Öffentlichkeit: Festschrift für Jens Flemming,* edited by Dagmar Bussiek and Simona Göbel, 428–445. Kassel: Kassel University Press.

Hughes, R. Gerald, and Rachel Owen. 2009. ""The Continuation of Politics by Other Means": Britain, the Two Germanys and the Olympic Games, 1949-1972." *Contemporary European History* 18 (4): 443–474. doi:10.1017/S0960777309990099.

Huth, Sabine. 1994. "Einigkeit und Recht un Freiheit: Selected Themes in Contemporary German Post- War History." *The Historical Journal* 37 (2): 487–503. doi:10.1017/S0018246X00016629.

Joyce, Paul. 2008. "Saarland, 1950-55." *When Sunday Comes.* https://www.wsc.co.uk/the-archive/923-Europe/4367-saarland-1950-1955

Kersting, N. 2007. "Sport and National Identity: A Comparison of the 2006 and 2010 FIFA World Cups." *Politikon* 34 (3): 277–293. doi:10.1080/02589340801962551.

Kleßmann, Christoph, ed. 2001. *The Divided past: Rewriting Post-War German History.* Oxford: Berg.

Laurent, Michel, 1984. *Histoire du football en Lorraine..* Metz: Lorraine University Press.

Maguire, Joseph A. 2011. "Globalization, Sport and National Identities." *Sport in Society* 14 (7-8): 978–993. doi:10.1080/17430437.2011.603553.

Meier, Henk Erik, and Marcel Leinwather. 2013. ""Finally a Taste for Diversity"? National Identity, Consumer Discrimination, and the Multi-Ethnic German National Football Team." *European Sociological Review* 29 (6): 1201–1213. doi:10.1093/esr/jct011.

Merkel, Udo. 2007. "Milestones in the Development of Football Fandom in Germany: Global Impacts on Local Contests." *Soccer & Society* 8 (2-3): 221–239. doi:10.1080/14660970701224426.

Missiroli, Antonio. 2002. "European Football Cultures and Their Integration: The "Short" Twentieth Century." *Sport in Society* 5 (1): 1–20.

Planert, Ute. 2002. "Wann beginnt der "moderne" deutsche Nationalismus? Plädoyer für eine nationale Sattelzeit." In *Die Politik der Nation: Deutscher Nationalismus in Krieg und Krisen, 1760-1960,* edited by Jörg Echternkamp and Sven Oliver Müller, 25–60. München: R. Oldenbourg Verlag.

Potter, Steffen, and Mark Chaplin. 2015. "The Remarkable Story of Saarbrücken." November 3. https://www.uefa.com/uefachampionsleague/news/newsid=2300972.html

Rowe, David. 2017. "We're All Transnational Now: Sport in Dynamic Sociocultural Environments." *Sport in Society* 20 (10): 1470–1484. doi:10.1080/17430437.2016.1221075.

Sander, Michael. 1990. "Politiker an der Saa zwischen Frankreich und Deutschland." In *Von der 'Stunde 0'zum Tag X: Das Saarland 1945-1959*. Merzig: Merzig Druckeri und Verlang GmbH.

Vonnard, Phillippe. 2020. *Creating a United Europe of Football: The Formation of UEFA (1949-1961)*. London: Palmgrave.

Wiskemann, Elizabeth. 1956. "The Saar Moves toward Germany." *Foreign Affairs* 34 (2): 287–296. doi:10.2307/20031161.

Wolfgang, Michalski. 1972. *Export und Wirtschaftswachstum: Schlussfolgerungen aus der Nachskriegsentwicklung in der Bundesrepublik Deutschland*. Tranlated by Henry Hellmann and Udo Hammar. Hamburg: Welt Archiv GmbH.

Challenges and complexities of imagining nationhood: the case of Hong Kong's naturalized footballers

Andy Chiu

ABSTRACT
In the field of sports and nationalism, little has been done to explore the process of how a member from another nation become representatives of another imagined community. In view of the growing significance of naturalization of foreign sporting talents in international sports, this paper highlights the complexities of the imagining a '*deep, horizontal comradeship*' through the case of Hong Kong's naturalized football representatives, with a focus on the negotiation of 'Hong Kongness' and 'Chineseness' among fans and naturalized representatives regarding selected contents in the stadium. It is argued that fans and naturalized players are constantly reminded of an inclusive Hong Kongness and an exclusive Chineseness that facilitated the acceptance of naturalized footballers as representatives of Hong Kong's imagined community. But at the same time, paradoxes are identified in the imagination of a 'deep, horizontal comradeship' between Hong Kong citizens and the naturalized footballers.

Introduction

Anderson's *Imagined Communities* thesis provided an alternative explanation to the theoretical debate on the origin of nations and nationalism with a macro, historical approach. Instead of positioning nationalism ideologically, Anderson (2006) proposed to regard nationalism as a specific way to make sense of belonging through the imagination of a '*deep, horizontal comradeship*'. He argued that our social world is consisted of imagined communities, ranging from sizes and ways that are being imagined.

> (a nation) is imagined because the members of even the smallest nation will never know most of their fellow-members, meet them, or even hear of them, yet in the minds of each lives the image of their communion (Anderson 2006, 6).

For Anderson, the concept of nation is imagined, as it requires one's imagination to consider the sharing of a common membership with people that he or she had not met before; limited, as the sovereign land of a nation is always finite but subjecting to changes; sovereign, as the legitimacy of a nation is embedded in its nature for the making of its citizens. He proposed the idea of printed capitalism as a crucial element in the making of nations in modernity, which emphasized the significance of language and media in the construction of nationhood that is possible for the imagination among different individuals. From a modernist and constructionist position, Anderson's work contributed to the primordialist-modernist debate in nationalism studies, as his work emphasized the important role of vernacular language, modes of communication (print-capitalism), and the concept of time as homogeneous and empty, as essential elements that contribute to the imagining of nationhood.

This article uses the case of Hong Kong's naturalized football representatives to recontextualize Anderson's work considering the naturalization of athletes in international sports and its impact to the understanding of 'Hong Kongness' and 'Chineseness'. Although Anderson had not further elaborated the process of imagining the nation at a personal, self-identified level in his work, this article supplements the complexities in the negotiation and making of a '*deep horizontal comradeship*' as suggested in Anderson's work when racial and ethnic others become representatives of another imagined community. This could lead to different imaginaries regarding the identities of naturalized national representatives as members of the same imagined community, which is a consequence of the inter-connectedness of various forms of imagined communities (national or subnational) that people are feeling attached to (Anderson 2006). By exploring the understanding of 'Hong Kongness' and 'Chineseness' among Hong Kong's naturalized footballers and fan groups members through their perceptions of contents (chants, slogans and posters) in the stadium, this article highlights the complexities in the process of imagining and accepting 'others' as 'we', and the challenges arise in the imagination of a 'deep, horizontal comradeship' under the trend of naturalization of foreign sporting talents. Through the Cantonese and English contents, Hong Kong fans are constantly reminded of the authenticity of the naturalized football representatives' distinctive 'Hong Kongness'. And the latter sections of this article discuss the paradoxes identified in the process of imagining racial and ethnic others as members and representatives of Hong Kong's imagined community.

Researching sports, imagined communities and naturalization

A modernist and constructivist perspective, as found in Anderson and many others' work, has successfully staged the discursive power of media discourses, especially those in traditional printed media, at the centre of the discussion, but the medium and the process of imagining and negotiating nationhood has gone beyond novels and newspapers. For instance, the use of social media and other online platforms might have taken over the position of printed media and the simultaneous reading of newspapers as a ritual of creating national consciousness (Sofer 2013), and the significance of competitive sports as the medium for the demonstration of national performance (Edensor 2002) and inculcation of nationalistic sentiments among members of the nation are being acknowledged in nationalism studies. As Hobsbawm (1996) pointed out,

> The imagined community of millions seems more real as a team of eleven named people. The individual, even the one who only cheers, becomes a symbol of the nation himself (Hobsbawm 1996, 147).

There are adequate researches of the negotiation of national identity and nationhood through the lens of sports with various theoretical and methodological approaches, ranging from the study of national press (Vincent and Hill 2011; Jiang 2013; Vincent and Harris 2014; Falcous 2015; Skey 2015), television (Erik Meier and Leinwather 2013), online discussion platforms (Gibbons 2015; Ho and Chiu 2016), perspectives of the elite athletes (Back, Crabbe, and Solomos 2001; Holmes and Storey 2011; Bowes and Bairner 2019; Kyeremeh 2020), other members of the nation (Bradley 2011; Ho and Bairner 2013; Whigham 2014), and particular cases or sporting events (Lechner 2007; Bocketti 2008: Goig 2008; Harris 2008; Ewen 2012; Choi 2020; Lee 2018; Penfold 2019; Storey 2020). However, there is also the need to address the call from Bairner (2015) to revisit Anderson's framework instead of casually referring to the concept of imagined community in a taken-for-granted fashion. As Choi (2020) argued, the imagination of racial others becoming national representatives could be limited by historical, economic, and political conditions in different societies – the increasing presence of naturalized athletes has made the formation of a 'deep, horizontal comradeship' problematic.

Furthermore, the active role of fans and athletes as members and embodiments of the nation, and their agencies regarding the changing socio-political circumstances in the era of globalization and migration should not be overlooked, especially when naturalization of sporting talents has become a common practice across the globe. National identity has not yet deterritorialized as Poli (2007) proposed, as cases have suggested that the introduction of naturalized athletes remains contested, while the case of Taiwan supported the idea and naturalized athletes become the 'significant others' (Chen and Chiang 2019), the case of South Korea has highlighted the difficulties of such practice in a perceived racially and ethnically homogenous society (Choi 2020), and it was under heated debate in England (Gibbons 2015). If the existence of a 'deep, horizontal comradeship', as Anderson proposed, has the power to create meanings and willingness for one to make sacrifices for the community regardless of the existence of inequality and exploitation, would the presence of naturalized representatives as racial others in Hong Kong's case, challenge or reaffirm people's understanding of nationhood? This issue of naturalized athletes is becoming more relevant among the rising tides of nationalism, populism, migration, and outcry for racial justice in our societies.

Contextualizing football and (sub)national identity in Hong Kong

Hong Kong had a vital role in the development of football in Asia: it launched the first professional football league in Asia in 1968, and Hong Kong was one of the founding members of Asian Football Confederation (AFC) in 1954 (Bridges 2016). Football was introduced by the British as an elite sport among expatriates at the beginning of the colonial era, but the local Chinese community in Hong Kong soon gained access to football and took over their colonizers in the early 20th Century. Nurtured outstanding Chinese footballers, the advancement of football development in Hong Kong had earned the fame to be known as the 'Football Kingdom of the Far East' – Team Republic of China (ROC), which mainly consisted of ethnic Chinese players from Hong Kong, won nine gold medals in the Far East Games between 1915 and 1934 (Lee 2018). Yet, the recruitment of Hong Kong Chinese footballers soon became a political tug of war between the two Chinese regimes, given that Hong Kong's elite footballers preferred to play as Chinese representatives (Lee 2018), despite of Hong Kong's separate membership in International Federation of Association Football (FIFA) and International Olympic Committee (IOC).

ROC lost the membership in AFC in the 1970s and most local elite Chinese players in Hong Kong decided to represent British Hong Kong when Hong Kong was drawn against North Korea in the Asian Cup Qualifying. Although Hong Kong lost to North Korea by penalties, Lui (2012) argued that this match is one of the key moments that lead to the emergence and acceptance of a Hong Kong identity, but it should also be noted that this formation of Hong Kong identity was first emerged from cultural space without nationalistic imperatives and the focus was on the cultural difference between Hong Kong and mainland China, through the interplay between media and non-media processes (Ma 1999).

Because of Hong Kong's specific socio-political context, there was a lack of top-down construction of national identity in Hong Kong during the colonial era, which makes Hong Kong an exception when having a national identity is being perceived as natural and taken-for-granted (Mathews, Ma, and Lui 2008),

> China has been their cultural home, but also a dictatorship from which many in Hong Kong once fled; and Great Britain was felt as no home for most, but only a distant colonizer. Today this detachment from national belonging is beginning to fade, as more in Hong Kong come to accept that they indeed emotionally belong to the Chinese nation, if not necessarily to the Chinese state; but this issue of identity continues to be a matter of intense debate. (Mathews, Ma, and Lui 2008, Prologue)

A sign of this process of identity negotiation and ambivalence among Hong Kong citizens could be shown by the variations in identification as the handover of Hong Kong's sovereignty was approaching (Ma 1999; Law 2018). Hong Kong citizens have developed different understandings of their self-identified national identity, namely, 'Hong Konger', 'Chinese living in Hong Kong', 'Hong Konger living in China' and 'others' (Fung 2004; Ma and Fung 2007; Steinhardt, Li, and Jiang 2018). The variations in this categorization also shown the cultural, racial and political dimensions in perceiving Chinese identity (Ortmann 2018).

Unlike other former colonies of Britain, decolonization and self-determination did not happen in Hong Kong, the return of Hong Kong to China is portrayed as '*a child's sentimental return from his 'foster father' back to his 'biological mother'*' (Law 2018, 14). The consequence of this delay of decolonization, in the forms of cultural and socio-political conflicts, soon led to the intensification of nativist and separationist ideologies, distrust of Chinese authorities resulted as waves of major social movements such as the Umbrella Movement in 2014 (Lam and Cooper 2018) and the Anti-extradition Bill movement in 2019 (Lee 2020). In Hong Kong football's context, a significant event would be the Chinese Football Association poster incident (CFA poster incident) which took place shortly after the Umbrella Movement in 2015: Hong Kong and China were in the same group in the World Cup Qualifying Stage, together with Bhutan, Maldives, and Qatar. For publicity purpose, CFA issued a series of promotional posters about each of its opponent, and this had led to controversies regarding the description of the naturalized players of Team Hong Kong, as the CFA poster said,

> HK's team has black skin, yellow skin and white skin people, playing a team with such diverse background, you'd better be prepared (translated to English)

The emphasis on the skin colour of the naturalized representatives of Hong Kong resulted in an outrage in Hong Kong, many found the poster's message racist, and Hong Kong

Football Association (HKFA) responded by a poster that highlighted the diverse but equal nature of every player in the squad (Ho and Chiu 2016).

> Don't let other people look down on you, our team has black skin, yellow skin and white skin, but the goal is the same to fight for Hong Kong, you are Hong Kongers so you must support us! (translated in English)

Although some, including footballers of Team Hong Kong, regarded the CFA poster as 'a poor sense of humour', the controversies of the CFA poster have drawn huge attention to the qualifying stage matches and Hong Kong's naturalized footballers.[1] For many Hong Kong citizens, matches of Team Hong Kong had become a channel to expressing their anger and sentiments in defending the pride and values of Hong Kong as a multi-ethnic society, fans expressed their discontent by booing the national anthem[2] *The March of Volunteers* in 2015 (Bridges 2016), a similar phenomenon could also be observed in 2019 during the Anti-extradition Bill movement as some fans jeered the national anthem and sang the protest anthem *Glory to Hong Kong* in the stadium before and after the match against Iran, which highlighted the significant role of football in Hong Kong as the field of identity negotiation as these actions have yet been found in other sporting encounters between Hong Kong and China.

Challenges to the imagining of a unified Chineseness in football

The performance of Hong Kong's footballers in the two draws against China have attracted interests from clubs in Chinese Super League (CSL) and China League One, as several Hong Kong footballers took the chance to play in Chinese leagues. However, the CFA adjusted their player registration regulations in the professional leagues in China during the 2016 season, which no longer regard players (passport holders) from Hong Kong, Macau, and Taiwan region as local players. Interestingly, this change in player registration is then reversed in early 2018, allowing each club in CSL and China League One to register one player from Hong Kong, Macau, and Taiwan region as local player. Naturalized players are being recognized as 'foreign players' and only those who previously held a contract in China or who only been registered in HKFA throughout their whole career are eligible to register as local players.

Although there are no actual proofs towards CFA's intention, the controversies of the poster incident and the changes in CFA's regulation of player registration have raised questions on the different understanding of citizenship and nationality between Hong Kong and mainland China. As Hong Kong citizens are constantly reminded of their identity as Chinese nationals and the articulation of Hong Kong being an inseparable part of China, what happened in the football world seem to be challenging the imagining of 'Hong Kongness' into a homogenic, unified 'Chineseness' as promoted by the PRC regime.

Methodology

This paper aims to re-contextualized Anderson's framework using the case of Hong Kong's naturalized players, with a focus on both naturalized footballers and fans' perspectives towards posters, chants and slogans in the stadium to explore how the presence of naturalized footballers, as racial others, are being imagined, perceived and justified. This approach articulates the agencies of fans and footballers as their interactions in and outside the football stadium are contributing to the production of meanings of these contents, which facilitate the imagining of nationhood via football. A particular focus would be the understandings and interpretations of 'Hong Kongness' and 'Chineseness' of the naturalized players by both naturalized players and fans. By outlining the imagination and negotiation process of a distinctive Hong Kong identity that is argued to be increasingly incompatible to a homogenous Chinese identity, this article could enrich the understanding on the dynamics and complexities of Hong Kong people's imagination of the 'deep, horizontal comradeship' as stated in Anderson's work, particularly on how the imagination of Hong Kong's naturalized footballers may succeed or fail to transcend the presence of a strong, common cultural root through contents created in Cantonese and English.

To explore the different understanding of 'Hong Kongness' and 'Chineseness' in Hong Kong's football world, certain contents in the stadium are being selected, reviewed and analysed, as shown in the following:

1. The 'We are Hong Kong' chant from fans (in English)
2. The 'Hong Kong Kickass' (香港勁揪) chant and slogan from fans and HKFA (in Cantonese and Traditional Chinese script)
3. The 'We Stand Together' diversity tifo from fans
4. The 'Support you own people' (撐自己人) slogan from HKFA (in Cantonese and Traditional Chinese script)
5. Poster issued by HKFA in CFA incident (in Traditional Chinese script)

These materials were used by fans and HKFA in official matches of Team Hong Kong from 2015 to 2019, this particular period of time is identified because it is right after the CFA poster incident which led to a heated discussion of the identity of Hong Kong's naturalized footballers. In-depth interviews of ten Hong Kong's naturalized footballers (call-ups from 2014 to 2019) and twenty fans from two major fan groups were conducted from January to September 2019 to explore the perspectives from both parties.

Imagining through the repetitive contents in the stadium

Anderson highlighted the role of media and the practice of simultaneous reading of newspapers in the imagination of nation as an imagined community. In the context of competitive sports, a similar ritual would be the consumption, creation and repetitions of chants, slogans, and other contents or national symbols in and out of the stadium. As reflected by both fans and naturalized footballers in the interviews, the chants 'We are Hong Kong' and 'Hong Kong Kickass' have contributed to the consolidation of imagining of a distinctive Hong Kongness through a selected remembering and forgetting process. Although the contents being imagined by the fans and naturalized footballers may not be as significant as the narratives of official history as highlighted in Anderson's thesis, it is argued that the elements of remembering and forgetting, and the bottom-up approach of the creation and use of the contents for the 'ritual in the stadium', have similarities to Anderson's argument about the construction of a nation's past.

The slogan 'Hong Kong Kickass' was invented by fans and first appeared in Kai Tak International airport in 1985, as hundreds of Hong Kong citizens welcomed the return of

Team Hong Kong after defeating China by 2:1 at Beijing Workers Stadium, which shattered Team China's dream to proceed to the next round of the 1986 FIFA World Cup Qualifying. This victory, also known as the '519 incident', marked the beginning of the rivalry between China and Hong Kong in football, some Chinese fans in Beijing started a riot because of the devastation caused by the humiliating defeat to a weaker British Hong Kong team (Xu 2008). But it is argued that this rivalry had appeared in a lukewarm manner as the celebration of the '519 incident' in Hong Kong did not come across the humiliation of Team China and the focus was on Hong Kong's success into the group stage of the competition (Lee 2018). Also, the verbal use of 'Hong Kong Kickass' has a distinctive cultural meaning as the phase 'Kickass' (勁揪) is a vernacular Cantonese expression. The use of the chant and slogan 'Hong Kong Kickass' serves as a symbolized reminder of the '519 incident' and Hong Kong's Cantonese culture, and was reintroduced in Hong Kong's football circle by fans and HKFA in 2011. When Hong Kong played against China in 2015, 'Hong Kong Kickass' was the official slogan and could be found in HKFA's official merchandise, promotional posters, and repeated in banners and chants among fans.

As Anderson tried to illustrate how nations construct their own narratives of identity through remembering and forgetting certain historical events, a similar approach could be observed in the selection and creation of 'official' contents as representations of Hong Kong football's history among fans and HKFA. Through the re-emergence of the Cantonese 'Hong Kong Kickass' chant and slogan that was exclusively used in football, although many younger fans have not witnessed the historical victory or knowing the names of the footballers in Hong Kong's squad at that time, the remembering of the '519 incident' through the chant became a shared experience of Hong Kong people and naturalized footballers while many other victories and defeats of Hong Kong seem to be forgotten.

> The 519 incident is a good example of how football works......If Team Hong Kong had done that before, we can do that again against stronger teams. (Naturalized footballer A)

> I was not born yet when it happened (519 incident), but this is a huge encouragement to us and our players. This reminds me of the spirit of Hong Kong as we always work our best and do not give up. (Fan group representatives A)

For both fans and naturalized footballers, the articulation of a sense of 'we' as found in the 'We are Hong Kong' chant and the remembering the '519 incident' are crucial to their imagination and understanding of Hong Kongness in football.

> This reminds me of Hong Kong's unique role. Hong Kong is not a country, but we have our own team to compete internationally......Having a representative team means a lot to me as a Hong Konger and a local football fan. It means we have something to fight for. (Fan Group Representative B)

As this fan had articulated, Hong Kong's independent membership in international sporting bodies is significant to the imagining of Hong Kong as unique compare to other regions of China. As promised in the principle of 'One Country, Two Systems', the uniqueness of Hong Kong, namely a capitalist style of living, common law system, westernized understanding of freedom and civil rights, and a hybridized culture, all contribute to the formation of a distinctive subnational Hong Kong identity and values, as legacies of a former British colony and advantages of being a Special Administrative Region of China. By articulating a sense of 'we' as Hong Kong people in the chants, the consumption and repetition of this sense of 'we' contribute to the boundary setting process that separate Hong Kongers from others.

As the CFA poster incident stirred up a heated debate regarding the different understanding of citizenship and sense of belonging in Hong Kong and China (Ho and Chiu 2016), the message of HKFA's poster as a response to the CFA poster had highlighted the civic inclusiveness that is being embedded in 'Hong Kongness'. Both fan group representatives and naturalized footballers have mentioned the idea of a relatively civic understanding of Hong Kongness and emphasized the practice of naturalization as a lawful, common phenomenon, as they recalled their experiences during the CFA poster incident in 2015.

> I couldn't agree more with FA's poster (HKFA) because we (naturalized footballers) are also Hong Kongers. It's ironic, isn't it? They (CFA) were picking on us few years ago, but now they have their naturalized players. It (naturalization of foreign talents) is so common now in modern football. I don't understand why they did that at that time. (Naturalized footballer D)

This naturalized footballer's view is being shared by most interviewees as both footballers and fans named examples of naturalizing footballers in France, Germany and recent opponents of Team Hong Kong, such as Qatar, Guam and Taiwan. Fans and naturalized footballers have also highlighted the 'irony' mentioned by naturalized footballer D as they are aware of CFA's introduction of naturalized footballers in 2019.[3] Some naturalized footballers admitted that there are certain cultural similarities between 'Hong Kongness' and 'Chineseness', but there are also many differences as Hong Kong society appeared to be more 'westernized and progressive', a fan group representative's response to the HKFA poster made a good supplement to this view.

> FA did the right thing to defend the diversity of Team Hong Kong. All Hong Kongers are Chinese nationals but not all Chinese are Hong Kongers, if you know what I mean. Maybe they could tell who a Chinese is by skin colour in mainland, but it is not how it works here in Hong Kong......There are locally born and raised South Asians who are browner than us, there are African Hong Kongers, there are European Hong Kongers, there are even mainland Chinese who became Hong Kongers...... (Fan group representative E)

The response from this fan has implied a mixed civic and cultural understanding of Hong Kongness, as a person's 'Hong Kongness' could be acquired and should not bounded by race or place of birth. Contrastingly, his understanding of 'Chineseness' is closely related to racial and political identity, which is argued to be influenced by a state-driven, Han-Chinese racial discourse in China (Ortmann 2018) and the political reality of Hong Kong being a Special Administrative Region of China. For many locally born and raised fans in Hong Kong, this understanding of Chinese as a racial identity is prevalent, as many have abided to a socially constructed definition of Chinese as a race of '*yellow skin, black hair, and black eyes*' and the mythical description of '*heirs of dragon*', which placed the understanding of Hong Kongness and Chineseness into the two ends of the civic-ethnic dichotomy as Kohn (1944) proposed.

Imagining Hong Kong as a diverse, international city

> I know some people still question our identity and passion to fight for Hong Kong, I am not born and raised here but I am a Hong Konger and this is my home now. Yes, we are Hong Kong...... (Naturalized Footballer B)

Naturalized footballer B's response served as a typical answer for the naturalized footballers being interviewed, all naturalized footballers have shown similar understanding of Hong Kong as home and expressed their eagerness to represent Hong Kong, yet, an apolitical attitude also stood out among some naturalized footballers, which is different from most fans' responses.

> To be honest I don't know much about politics, I am just a footballer. Some fans are very upset with China and booed the anthem…I understand their feelings, but that's not appropriate as this is putting the FA and us to risk (being punished by FIFA). I know we (Hong Kong and China) are very different after living here for ten years. I could tell who a Hong Konger is and who is not on the streets……Hong Kong is very international; it is convenient to live here. People are polite and could speak very good English. And you could succeed if you work hard…… (Naturalized Player C)

Although Naturalized footballer C did not go further to elaborate the differences between 'Hong Kongness' and 'Chineseness', his response had again articulated the significance of Hong Kong's 'internationalness', as an element that is being valued highly in Hong Kong. In fact, this narrative of Hong Kong being an international city is being used repeatedly by the interviewees to justify Hong Kong's ethnic and racial diversity, as a contrast to the imagining of China's Han-ethnocentric nationhood, which becomes an ambiguous boundary setting criteria to be drawn between the imagination of 'Hong Kongness' and 'Chineseness'. An example of the promotion of racial diversity and solidarity in Team Hong Kong's squad would be the use of the 'We Stand Together' tifo that is created by fans against the criticisms of increasing reliance on naturalized footballers in Hong Kong's squad. The tifo depicts an image of footballers with different skin colour supporting each other, as a celebration of Hong Kong's 'multi-racial' squad. Most interviewees have stressed the importance of ethnic and racial diversity in Hong Kong as an international city.

> Hong Kong is an international city and embraces values of freedom and respect of each other. Our naturalized footballers have fulfilled the requirements of naturalization and therefore they should be accepted as members of Hong Kong, not to mention the sacrifices they have made on and off the pitch fighting for us. I agree that total reliance on naturalized talents is not a sustainable approach for the advancement of Hong Kong football, but it does not mean that foreign born players should be rejected and excluded. (Fan groups representative B)

> They (naturalized players) have stayed in Hong Kong for more than seven years; they are holders of HKSAR passport and therefore they could represent us internationally. It has nothing to do with their colour of skin or place of origin. They are Hong Kongers and a part of our society. (Fan groups representatives C)

To most of the fan groups representatives, this understanding of a strong civic 'Hong Kongness' is key to justify their acceptance of non-ethnic Chinese footballers as representatives of Hong Kong. In fact, the same narrative of Hong Kong's internationalness is being celebrated by both the government and the Hong Kong society to justify the positive presence of non-ethnic Chinese population in Hong Kong, allowing ethnic and racial others to become members of the same imagined community through citizenship and the adoption of a Hong Kong style of living. However, it should be noted that the acceptance of naturalized talents in Hong Kong football may not guarantee a general acceptance of racial others in the city, as some naturalized footballers who are originally from Africa have experiences of being racially discriminated in Hong Kong.

Yes, it is the reason why FIFA is working so hard to deal with racism in football. I am happy to see the fans doing it (showing the tifo on the stand). I could remember when I first arrived Hong Kong, there were people who refused to sit with me and my friends on the train just because we are black. People used to call me names from the stands, but it has improved a lot now as I am doing better. More people recognize me on the street and welcome me. I think everyone has a chance here (in Hong Kong) because we all speak the same language (football) on the pitch and we train hard. I have friends and teammates from all over the world here, I met my wife here, my child is born here......Hong Kong gave me everything. This is my home and I want to give back to Hong Kong and fight for Hong Kong. (Naturalized footballer A)

The personal story of this naturalized footballer had shown a different side of the politically correct narrative of the embracement of internationalness and diversity in Hong Kong. As he said, despite his strong emotional attachment to Hong Kong, he is welcomed because he was recognized by other people on the street as a representative of Hong Kong. This echoes with Yung, Chan and Phillips's work (2020) on Hong Kong's naturalized footballers, which suggested that the acceptance of the 'racial other' as Hong Kongers is influenced by a mix of meritocratic and civic values. While Anderson tried to put aside the existing inequalities as preconditions of the imagining of nationhood, the case of Hong Kong's naturalized footballers shows that racial 'others' have to prove his or her worth to the society to be recognized as members or even representatives of the same imagined community. The 'deep, horizontal comradeship' being imagined by the fans appeared to be de-ethnicized and inclusive, but at the same time conditional, exclusive and grounded on values of pragmaticism, as long as the introduction of naturalized footballers could strengthen the squad and is allowed by the rules of FIFA.

Paradoxes of imagining your 'own people'

In order to publicize the matches of Team Hong Kong, HKFA created the 'Support your own people' slogan as a reminder of the Hong Kongness that is being shared by fans and Team Hong Kong. Yet, the slogan's message is paradoxical as fans need to be reminded of the naturalized footballers' 'Hong Kongness'. This is even more ironic as most fans tried to describe their support of Team Hong Kong as 'natural' and obligated, regardless of its rankings or fame.

I used to be a big fan of English Premier League and had never watched local league before. But after the CFA poster incident, I realize that if we do not support our league or our players, then no one would...we have to support our people. (Fan group representative C)

I see myself as a Hong Konger, so it is natural to support my people (Team Hong Kong). Yes, some of our players are not born and raised in Hong Kong, but they chose to become Hong Kongers and fight for us, if they are eligible to wear the red jersey, they are Hong Kongers...... Different colour of skin or birthplace would not disqualify their Hong Konger identity. If you embrace the values and culture of Hong Kong, and regard here as home, you are a Hong Konger. (Fan group representative D)

The naturalized footballers' intentions behind the naturalization process, ranging from 'careerist' to 'nationalist' position (Holmes and Storey 2011), are being questioned by fans. Different intentions behind naturalization were also mentioned by a naturalized footballer as he voiced out his doubts over a pragmatic, careerist consideration in contrast to his love of Hong Kong.

I know some treat Hong Kong as a working place, some may leave after retiring, but I love Hong Kong and I want to stay here with my family for the rest of my life. After retirement, I want to help as a coach to develop players for Hong Kong. (Naturalized footballer E)

Fan group representative D stressed the importance of embracing Hong Kong's core values, alongside with the adaptation of Hong Kong's culture and its style of living, which is a typical response from the fans regarding their imagination of the Hong Kongness of the naturalized footballers. Apart from the uniqueness of Hong Kong as mentioned in previous sections of this article, around half of the fans mentioned the 'Lion Rock Spirit'. Similar to the storyline of the 'American dream', the 'Lion Rock Spirit' symbolizes Hong Kong people's collective experience of perseverance, diligence and solidarity (Ortmann 2018), and is often emphasized in the story of Hong Kong's success from a village being transformed into a prosperous international financial centre.

I support the team because I am a Hong Konger. The question is 'who is your people?', the reality is, apart from the white communities, many ethnic minorities are being neglected in Hong Kong. South Asians and Africans are being labelled as troublemakers or fake asylum seekers......it is not fair to exclude the remaining 8% of the population as 'our people'. The hardships they are experiencing as immigrants are the same when my grandparents came to settle in Hong Kong after the civil war. People often forget the difficulties the naturalized footballers have experienced in Hong Kong. I am not sure if the players know much about the Lion Rock Spirit but what they have experienced is close enough to it. (Fan group representative E)

While a few naturalized footballers talked about the experience of being racially discriminated, most naturalized footballers tended to mention the experience of hardships, ranging from adopting a fast-paced style of living, learning a new language, to the competitiveness and expectations they experienced as foreign players. A naturalized footballer highlighted the challenge to pick up Cantonese and the efforts he had made as a justification of his 'Hong Kongness'.

Yes, I am a Hong Konger too (repeated 'I am a Hong Konger' in Cantonese)......I could not speak good English and Cantonese when I came, I am lucky that my teammates helped me to learn the basics of Cantonese. You know, many foreign players can speak English, so they are not learning Cantonese because it is difficult...... Personally, it is important to speak good Cantonese in Hong Kong because it helps me to connect with local people, it is why I am learning and practicing it every day. (Naturalized footballer E)

Some naturalized footballers are very good at Cantonese, but many are not. Of course, they are all Hong Kongers because of more than seven years of residency, but I feel closer to those who could speak Cantonese. It stands out when you approach them after a match outside the stadium......I mean, most naturalized footballers look like foreign tourists if you don't know them, so their Cantonese ability is a proof of their eagerness to be Hong Kongers and fit in. (Fan group representative F)

The articulation of one's Cantonese proficiency as a determinant of 'Hong Kongness' seems contradictory to the ability to speak English as a sign of the internationalness being celebrated as an element of 'Hong Kongness', but one's Cantonese proficiency is commonly accepted as a proof of one's 'Hong Kongness' among the bilingual local fans whose mother tongue is Cantonese. This sense of cultural sameness could not be substituted by one's English proficiency in Hong Kong, but at the same time it seems difficult for a local citizen to expect a non-ethnic Chinese person to be able to communicate in Cantonese until he or she speaks. The perspectives from fans and naturalized footballers of Hong Kong show two sides of the influence of vernacular language as Anderson had articulated in his thesis: on one hand the vernacular language enables an imagined community being imagined as inherently limited by becoming a criterion in the boundary setting process between the in-group and out-group; on the other hand it may limit the imagination of ethnic others as members of the same imagined community just because their outlook may not fit to the existing understanding of members within the in-group. These resulted in the paradoxes being identified in the contents in the stadium, Hong Kong citizens (including non-football fans) may find difficult to imagine the naturalized footballers as representatives and members of Hong Kong's imagined community even if they are well-accepted by the fans who have prior knowledge of the Hong Kongness of the naturalized footballers.

Conclusion

This paper has illustrated the complexities of imagining nationhood through the case of Hong Kong's naturalized football representatives. It is argued that the imagining of a 'deep, horizontal comradeship' as proposed by Anderson is being challenged by the practice of naturalization of foreign sporting talents. The selected contents that are created and repeated in English and Cantonese in Hong Kong football circle have shown certain difficulties of imagining 'Hong Kongness' and 'Chineseness' as compatible identities. The different perceptions of the two identities as reflected by fans and naturalized footballers on one hand facilitated the imagining of racial others to become representatives of Hong Kong in football, and on the other hand challenged a homogenous Chinese identity, as shown in contestations surrounding the CFA poster and China's recent introduction of non-ethnic Chinese naturalized footballers. The case of Hong Kong suggested that the consumption and repetition of chants, slogans, tifos and posters act as constant reminders of the 'Hong Kongness' of the naturalized players that differentiate a civic and cultural 'Hong Kongness' from a racial and political 'Chineseness'.

Furthermore, the imagining and negotiation of 'Hong Kongness' among fans have shown a 'layered and conditional' imagining of comradeship rather than a horizontal one as proposed by Anderson. On one hand Hong Kong's internationalness is articulated by respondents to justify the presence of ethnic others and a multi-ethnic football squad in Hong Kong, and on the other hand the fans' acceptance of naturalized footballers in Hong Kong's squad may be grounded by meritocracy. And the paradoxes being identified in the chants have shown the difficulties and challenges of imagining naturalized footballers as representatives and members of Hong Kong's imagined community. As the naturalization of sporting talents remains a common practice for sporting nations across the globe, the acceptance and imagination of racial and ethnic others as embodiment of nationhood may continue to challenge the construction of a homogenized imagined community.

Notes

1. All home games of Team Hong Kong in the Group Stage were sold out as fans were motivated to support Hong Kong. In view of the political tension after the Umbrella Movement, extra police officers were deployed to separate home fans and away fans from mainland China in Hong Kong's home game against China.

2. The booing of the March of Volunteers occurred the world cup qualifying match against Qatar in 2015 soon led to disciplinary actions from FIFA, but this has not stopped the fans from booing the national anthem, as the same deviant behaviour has been continued since then until the outbreak of COVID-19 in early 2020. But it is expected that the booing will be stopped by the recent introduction of the National Anthem Law in Hong Kong.
3. In August 2019, the CFA made a historical announcement of the naturalization of Brazil-born striker Elkeson as the first player of non-Chinese heritage to represent PRC for the World Cup qualifying. Elkeson's naturalization is crucial as he fulfilled the five-year residency requirement by FIFA as he first joined the CSL club Guangzhou Evergrande in 2013. It is reported that all naturalized players (including those with Chinese heritage) are monitored and educated by their correspondent clubs in CSL regarding the knowledge of Chinese history, culture and knowledge of the Communist regime, so that they could develop patriotic feelings towards China.

Disclosure statement

No potential conflict of interest was reported by the author.

References

Anderson, B. 2006. *Imagined Communities: Reflections on the Origin and Spread of Nationalism.* London: Verso.
Back, L., T. Crabbe, and J. Solomos. 2001. *The Changing Face of Football.* Oxford, UK: Berg.
Bairner, A. 2015. "Assessing the Sociology of Sport: On National Identity and Nationalism." *International Review for the Sociology of Sport* 50 (4-5): 375–379. doi:10.1177/1012690214538863.
Bocketti, G. P. 2008. "Italian Immigrants, Brazilian Football, and the Dilemma of National Identity." *Journal of Latin American Studies* 40 (2): 275–302. doi:10.1017/S0022216X08003994.
Bowes, A., and A. Bairner. 2019. "Three Lions on Her Shirt: Hot and Banal Nationalism for England's Sportswomen." *Journal of Sport and Social Issues* 43 (6): 531–550. doi:10.1177/0193723519850878.
Bradley, J. M. 2011. "In-Groups, out-Groups and Contested Identities in Scottish International Football." *Sport in Society* 14 (6): 818–832. doi:10.1080/17430437.2011.587298.
Bridges, B. 2016. "Booing the National Anthem: Hong Kong's Identities through the Mirror of Sport." *Contemporary Chinese Political Economy and Strategic Relations: An International Journal* 2 (2): 819–843.
Chen, T. H., and Y. Chiang. 2019. "The Absent Savior? Nationalism, Migration, and Football in Taiwan." *The International Journal of the History of Sport* 36 (7-8): 698–713. doi:10.1080/09523367.2019.1675642.
Choi, Y. 2020. "Running for Korea: Rethinking of Sport Migration and in/Flexible Citizenship." *International Review for the Sociology of Sport* 55 (3): 361–379. doi:10.1177/1012690218807364.
Erik Meier, M., and M. Leinwather. 2013. "Finally a 'Taste for Diversity'? National Identity, Consumer Discrimination, and the Multi-Ethnic German National Football Team." *European Sociological Review* 29 (6): 1201–1213. https://www.jstor.org/stable/24480016.
Falcous, M. 2015. "White Is the New Black? Football, Media and the New Zealand Imagination." *Soccer & Society* 16 (4): 555–572. doi:10.1080/14660970.2014.891987.
Fung, A. 2004. "Postcolonial Hong Kong Identity: hybridising the Local and the National." *Social Identities* 10 (3): 399–414. doi:10.1080/1350463042000230854.
Gibbons, T. 2015. "Fan Debates on English National Identity Surrounding the Almunia Case." *Soccer & Society* 16 (2-3): 344–359. doi:10.1080/14660970.2014.961386.
Goig, R. L. 2008. "Identity, Nation-State and Football in Spain. the Evolution of Nationalist Feelings in Spanish Football." *Soccer & Society* 9 (1): 56–63. doi:10.1080/14660970701616738.
Harris, J. 2008. "Match Day in Cardiff: (Re)Imaging and (Re)Imagining the Nation." *Journal of Sport & Tourism* 13 (4): 297–313. doi:10.1080/14775080802577219.

Ho, G., and A. Bairner. 2013. "One Country, Two Systems, Three Flags: Imagining Olympic Nationalism in Hong Kong and Macao." *International Review for the Sociology of Sport* 48 (3): 349–365. doi:10.1177/1012690212441160.

Ho, L., and A. Chiu. 2016. "'Indigenous' or 'All Stars': Discourses on 'Team Hong Kong' in a FIFA World Cup Tournament." *The International Journal of the History of Sport* 33 (11): 1226–1241. doi:10.1080/09523367.2016.1267150.

Hobsbawn, E. J. 1992. *Nations and Nationalism Since 1780: Programme, Myth, Reality*. Cambridge UK: Cambridge University Press.

Holmes, M., and D. Storey. 2011. "Transferring National Allegiance: Cultural Affinity or Flag of Convenience?" *Sport in Society* 14 (2): 253–271. doi:10.1080/17430437.2011.546550.

Jiang, Q. 2013. "Celebrity Athletes, Soft Power and National Identity: Hong Kong Newspaper Coverage of the Olympic Champions of Beijing 2008 and London 2012." *Mass Communication and Society* 16 (6): 888–909. doi:10.1080/15205436.2013.789528.

Kohn, H. 1944. *The Idea of Nationalism: A Study in Its Origins and Background*. New York: Macmillian.

Kyeremeh, S. A. 2020. "Whitening Italian Sport: The Construction of 'Italianness' in National Sporting Fields." *International Review for the Sociology of Sport* 55 (8): 1136–1151. doi:10.1177/1012690219878117.

Lam, W. M., and L. Cooper, eds. 2018. *Citizenship, Identity and Social Movements in the New Hong Kong*. London: Routledge.

Law, W. S. 2018. "Decolonisation Deferred Hong Kong Identity in Historical Perspective." In *Citizenship, Identity and Social Movements in the New Hong Kong*, edited by W. M. Lam and L. Cooper, 13–33. London: Routledge.

Lechner, F. J. 2007. "Imagined Communities in the Global Game: Soccer and the Development of Dutch National Identity." *Global Networks* 7 (2): 215–229. doi:10.1111/j.1471-0374.2007.00166.x.

Lee, C. W. 2018. "PRC v. Hong Kong: Politics and Identity from the Cold War Years to the Twenty-First Century." *Soccer & Society* 19 (5-6): 858–874. doi:10.1080/14660970.2017.1399606.

Lee, F. 2020. "Solidarity in the Anti-Extradition Bill Movement in Hong Kong." *Critical Asian Studies* 52 (1): 18–32. doi:10.1080/14672715.2020.1700629.

Lui, T. L. 2012. 那似曾相識的七十年代 *[That Familiar 1970s]*. Hong Kong: Chung Hwa.

Ma, E. 1999. *Culture, Politics, and Television in Hong Kong*. London; New York: Routledge.

Ma, E., and A. Fung. 2007. "Negotiating Local and National Identifications: Hong Kong sIdentity Surveys 1996-2006." *Asian Journal of Communication* 17 (2): 172–185. doi:10.1080/01292980701306555.

Mathews, G., E. Ma, and T. Lui. 2008. *Hong Kong, China: Learning to Belong to a Nation*. Florence: Routledge.

Ortmann, S. 2018. "The Development of Hong Kong Identity from Local to National Identity." in *Citizenship, Identity and Social Movements in the New Hong Kong*, edited by W. M. Lam and L. Cooper, 114–131. London: Routledge.

Penfold, T. 2019. "National Identity and Sporting Mega-Events in Brazil." *Sport in Society* 22 (3): 384–398. doi:10.1080/17430437.2018.1490266.

Poli, R. 2007. "The Denationalization of Sport: De-Ethnicization of the Nation and Identity Deterritorialization." *Sport in Society* 10 (4): 646–661. doi:10.1080/17430430701388798.

Skey, M. 2015. "'What Nationality He Is Doesn't Matter a Damn!' International Football, Mediated Identities and Conditional Cosmopolitanism." *National Identities* 17 (3): 271–287. doi:10.1080/14608944.2014.934214.

Sofer, O. 2013. "The Internet and National Solidarity: A Theoretical Analysis." *Communication Theory* 23 (1): 48–66. doi:10.1111/comt.12001.

Steinhardt, H. C., L. Li, and Y. Jiang. 2018. "The Identity Shift in Hong Kong since 1997: Measurement and Explanation." *Journal of Contemporary China* 27 (110): 261–276. doi:10.1080/10670564.2018.1389030.

Storey, D. 2020. "National Allegiance and Sporting Citizenship: identity Choices of 'African' Footballers." *Sport in Society* 23 (1): 129–141. doi:10.1080/17430437.2018.1555228.

Vincent, J., and H. Hill. 2011. "Flying the Flag for the En-Ger-Land: The Sun's (Re)Construction of English Identity during the 2010 World Cup." *Journal of Sport & Tourism* 16 (3): 187–209. doi:10.1080/14775085.2011.635006.

Vincent, J., and J. Harris. 2014. "'They Think It's All Dover!' Popular Newspaper Narratives and Images about the English Football Team and (Re)Presentations of National Identity during Euro 2012." *Soccer & Society* 15 (2): 222–240. doi:10.1080/14660970.2013.849188.

Whigham, S. 2014. "'Anyone but England'? Exploring Anti-English Sentiment as Part of Scottish National Identity in Sport." *International Review for the Sociology of Sport* 49 (2): 152–174. doi:10.1177/1012690212454359.

Xu, G. 2008. *Olympic Dreams: China and Sports, 1895–2008.* Cambridge, MA: Harvard University Press.

Yung, S. C., A. H. N. Chan, and D. R. Phillips. 2020. "Athletic Naturalisation, Nationality and Nationalism – Naturalised Players in Hong Kong's Representative (National) Football Team." *International Review for the Sociology of Sport.* doi:10.1177/1012690220964770.

Banal Europeanism? Europeanisation of football and the enhabitation of a Europeanised football fandom

Regina Weber ⓘD

ABSTRACT

Michael Billig's seminal work 'Banal nationalism' described how everyday practice and habits reinforce national identity. Football fans provide a fertile ground for an application of this concept. The community among supporters of the same team is constitutional for football. 20 years after his book, the Europeanisation of football structures could have caused banal national identifications to expand to the European level, contributing to a 'banal Europeanism'. In contrast to the crises of political Europe, football could provide fans with an everyday practice of Europe. This might change the understanding of in- and out-groups among supporters and beyond. The article discusses 'banal nationalism' in the arena of European club football. It elaborates in how far 'banal' football fandom related practice is related to the European level. The leading question of the article is How does football create an arena for 'banal Europeanism' among football fans?

Introduction

Michal Billig's 'Banal nationalism' (Billig 1995) has provided a thorough understanding of how unconscious national symbols are incorporated in self-understandings of groups and how they shape group identification. His distinction between explicit, 'hot' nationalism and unconscious, 'banal' nationalism, which remains underneath the surface of attention in everyday life has become an important approach in nationalism studies, particularly those focusing on the well-established nations of the Western world (Koch and Paasi 2016; Skey and Antonsich 2017). His approach also served to understand how sport spectatorship corroborates national identification (Bora and Senyuva 2011; Fox 2006; Juncà Pujol and Inglés Yuba 2014).

More than two decades after his seminal book, this influence might still hold true for national sport teams. Contrary to that, the example of top-level club football in Europe provides a valuable case to discuss how the focus of attention has shifted from the national to the European level, influencing the subtle self-identification of the spectators. Following 25 years of Europeanisation of football structures, fans are regularly exposed to a pan-European quasi-league system (Champions League and Europa League) and face squads with an increasingly high number of non-native players, mostly from other European countries (FIFA 2019b; Velema 2020). While the European competitions are exceptionally relevant for supporters of the top teams in a few top leagues, the cross-national transfer activities and the Europeanisation of teams are prevalent across the continent (FIFA 2019a).

Given the current state of Europe – the European Union (EU) being confronted with severe crises – this Europeanised football might subliminally influence the consciousness of Europeans against all odds. A 'hot' and conscious *Europeanism* understood here as the shift of citizens' identities towards Europe, faces serious setbacks in rising anti-European sentiments and respective parties across European countries. In contrast, football can provide its fans with an everyday, banal practice of Europe – so-called *banal Europeanism* by Cram (2001) – and contribute to subconscious identification through symbols of the European leagues and due to the increased presence of actors from across Europe. This might change the understanding of in-group and out-group belongings among supporters and – as football remains an arena of mass attention – across wider parts of society.

The aim of the article is to evaluate whether football can contribute to *banal Europeanism* and how this could look like given what we know about European identity formation. It connects with European identity studies by taking nationalism studies to better understand identity formation vis-à-vis Europe (Cram 2001). At the same time, this work goes further as it does not limit its understanding of 'Europe' to the EU. A wider focus on Europe seems necessary, as the EU has become a focus of strong anti-sentiments. For a thorough understanding of such anti-EU sentiments, it is relevant to study whether this attitude formation is restricted towards the institutions and symbols of the political project or in general towards the idea of a common Europe, the latter with much severe implications for the future of the project of European unification.

The developments of European club football indicate that football fandom is increasingly a Europeanised everyday practice, as 'Europe' became the 'gold standard' for fans across the continent and potentially beyond (Niemann, García, and Grant 2011b; Pyta and Havemann 2015; Vonnard, Quinn, and Bancel 2016). Europe is reiterated through everyday practise, symbols, and cultural praxis of following football as a spectator. Billig calls such routine exposure *enhabitation*, referring to Bourdieu's idea of *habitus*, the practice that is internalised as a 'second nature', to be able to pass through everyday life (Billig 1995, 42; Bourdieu 1990).

The arena of football provides a valuable research field for studies on 'banal' identity formation. In many European countries, it is a mass project in which relevant parts of society invest resources and emotions. At the same time, while several developments in the field have been influenced by European Union institutions, this influence remains mostly hidden to the followers. From the fans' perspective, the football associations, especially the European Football Association (UEFA) and International Football Association (FIFA) are the relevant actors. Football provides an arena to study subliminal identity formations outside of the 'hot' areas of politics, while it is indeed deeply connected to the European integration project.

This work theoretically discusses the potential of *banal Europeanism* in football using the knowledge on European identity formation and the main strands of Europeanisation of football structures. European identity is a complex and intertwined construct, it is no zero-sum game between national and European identity (Checkel and Katzenstein 2009; Herrmann, Risse, and Brewer 2004). Consequently, 'banal Europeanism' should be conceptualised maybe not as the only normal, but as increasingly normalised through practice side-by-side with an ongoing normal of the nation.

Banal nationalism and European identity

The seminal work of Michael Billig (Billig 1995), introducing the term *banal nationalism*, contributed to the understanding of nationalism in two ways. His first argument was that 'we', in 'the West's nation states' (5) conceive of nationalism something that happens elsewhere, in less developed areas of the world or in the political extreme in 'our' societies. He illustrates this argument with cases on the public perception of the Gulf war in the USA, the Falkland war, and the 'Troubles' in Northern Ireland. The examples show how public discourses close the ranks of the nation and – especially in the case of Northern Ireland – clearly locates nationalism only on one side:

> British media typically use the term 'nationalist' to describe those who seek to abolish the border between the United Kingdom and Eire, especially if they advocate violence in the pursuit of these aims. The government of the British nation-state, by contrast, is not called 'nationalist', although it, too, can use force to maintain present national boundaries. (48)

Following this, nationalism is a constitutional aspect of our societies which gets often overlooked. He elaborates this with his second argument, which is about the core difference between 'hot' and 'banal' nationalism. *Hot nationalism* marks outbreaks that 'arise in times of social disruption and which are reflected in extreme social movements' (44). *Banal nationalism* is the 'form of life which is daily lived in a world of nation states' (68). It causes the news reporting about foreign events, such as thunderstorms or earthquakes with the added information about how many of 'us' have been affected. It is what Billig calls the 'unwaved flags' (10) that silently establish the nation as the norm. This banal nationalism remembers citizens in an unconscious way about 'their' nation.

Everyday practice of *banal nationalism* comes in flags displaced in front of public buildings, in illustrations or in private business communication, i.e. on a loaf of baguette indicating French baking tradition (40). It relates to symbols, such as coins and their imprints that convey a notion of the nation that is overlooked because it is so regular. Billig relates this everyday experience of the nation to Bourdieu's notion of 'habitus' (Bourdieu 1990): the nation is internalised through the banal routines of everyday life, it is practiced, 'enhabited' (42) in practice and behaviour.

This is where identity steps in. For Billig, the puzzle is 'why people in the contemporary world do not forget their nationality' (7). His answer is that the banality of reminders underneath the level of explicit attention re-informs the subtle identification with the nation (8). Such approach can help in understanding how European identity may be formed through a seemingly unpolitical, maybe even irrelevant leisure activity such as watching football.

Billig's concept has been used in very different national contexts (for an overview see Skey and Antonsich 2017, 3–4) and for local, trans-national and global contexts (Aksoy and Robins 2002; Cram 2001). These works made use of the theoretical concept of *banal nationalism*, developed it further and clarified it. Billig work has been praised for paving the way to understand nationalism from 'below', the everyday life of citizens (Duchesne 2018; Edensor 2002). At the same time, criticism target its lack of complexity and its failure to relate to the nation in a globalised world. Some critical points are relevant for this study. The *banal nationalism* approach is rather stable and does not consider changing circumstances (Skey 2009). Its unified understanding of the 'banal' falls short the everyday (re-) production of a national 'we' in ethno-culturally diverse contexts (Antonsich 2016). Paasi (2016) emphasised the need for an integrated understanding of hot and banal forms of nationalism by tracing how the remembrance of independence struggles in Finland merge hot and banal nationalism.

The few works on banal nationalism in football highlight the role of football for identity formation. Bora and Senyuva (2011) applied banal nationalism to Turkish football. They emphasised that despite football being used as nationalistic tool in official propaganda, especially with the national team, football fans have become more Europeanised recently, both due to the European orientation of the top team and because of a changed fandom towards modern consumer-oriented citizens. Fox (2006) elaborated how the European championship fostered and corroborated differences between Romanian students of different backgrounds. While ethnic Romanians used the matches to celebrate the Romanian team, those with Hungarian background enthusiastically supported its respective opponents. Both examples show how football serves as banal tool for national identification not only with a certain nation, but also with larger and trans-national in-groups.

Cram (2001) departed from *banal nationalism* and invented the term *banal Europeanism*. The lack of a widespread 'hot' Europeanism invites to study whether subtle, yet 'banal' Europeanism is at place given the decades of European integration. She elaborated this as 'implicit identification with the European Union' (Cram 2012, 77) and stressed how banality matters in the 'normalisation' of the EU for its citizens: carrying passports and the omnipresence of EU flags in its member states constitute banal experiences of the EU (Cram 2012, 79).

The political integration project in Europe triggered questions about the impact on identity formation from its very beginning. Pioneers in European integration research have been considering the potential impact of the integration project on identity formation (Deutsch 1957; Haas 2004 (1958)). Back in the beginning days of the European Communities, the main concern was to understand why people – foremost political elites – shift their loyalties from the national to the European level (Haas 2004 (1958)). Three reasons have been deemed relevant: 1. because the new centre is valued as an end in itself; 2. because the new centre of power pressures into conformity, or 3. as a haphazard side-product of instrumental behaviour towards another end (Haas 2004 (1958), 14). While the first factor is related to a more ideological conviction as cause for loyalty shift, the latter two factors relate directly to the *enhabitation* of a new normal, as a result of either conformity pressure or rational action. This loyalty shift does not result from a conscious identification with the European level but a side-product of strategic behaviour (Cram 2009; Risse 2005).

A different explanation argues that increased communication, political and economic cooperation across borders in Europe causes more transaction across citizens and fosters their sense of a common European community (Deutsch 1957). This *transactionalist theory* has triggered many works on the impact of increased communication, traffic, and transfer across European boarders (Gustafson 2009a, 2009b; Kuhn 2011, 2012, 2015). So far, the results are mixed. While more cross-border transaction indeed relates to a stronger sense of cross-border community and identification with Europe, the direction is not always straightforward. Kuhn (2011, 2012) argues that those more prone to have transnational identities tend to establish more cross-border experiences, as the highly selective cases of

Erasmus students illustrates. Also, financial resources and opportunities for cross-border work relations are heavily stratified across societies towards well-educated white-collar workers (Favell 2011). This raises the question if sport as an area of mass attention can serve as a channel to circumvent conventional social stratifications, given that in this arena, the Europeanisation of the structures allows for a continuous exposure to cross-border experiences.

Both understandings of European identity formation offer approaches to study how Europeanised football creates banal experiences of Europe and has the power to influence identification with a European collective. The banality of everyday experience of Europe has been attempted with promising results, i.e. in the case of the effect of a common European currency and the usage of its coins and bills (Hanquinet and Savage 2013; Risse 2003). This work is limited to the EU or even smaller areas, e.g. the Eurozone. Given the growing discontent with the political project of the EU with Brexit at its apex (Kuhn et al. 2016), it might make sense to access citizens attitudes towards Europe beyond the official political project of the EU.

If there is one consensus about European identity, it is that it is complex and intertwined with some form of national identity. Different forms of intertwined identities have been discussed, e.g. nested (Medrano and Gutiérrez 2001) or marble cake-like layered forms (Herrmann, Risse, and Brewer 2004; Risse 2003). They conceptualise the interplay between national and European identifications not as a zero-sum-game: Both national and Europeanised identities are possible at the same time within the same person. Time and circumstances might influence which identity is stronger at a particular moment (Bruter 2005, 15–17).

Against that background, Europeanised football fan identities can be understood as *identifications, self-understandings*, and *feelings of groupness and belonging* (Brubaker and Cooper 2000) in the context of football and fandom that relate to the European level or across national borders within Europe. Billig's approach has been summarised as focusing not 'on the emergence of the nation' but on 'what happened once the nation was established' (Skey and Antonsich 2017, 1). This is exactly the approach that is needed to understand how 'Europe' might matter for the minds of football fans. Europe is there, in whatever contingent form, institutionalisation and function. How does this influence fans in their everyday, how do they *enhabit* it? What makes 'Europe' persistent and pervasive?

Europeanisation of football and banal Europeanism among fans

A cautious perspective on the role of football in the global world concludes that football follows politics and globalisation but does not shape it (Waalkes 2017). This approach will lead the following section on Europeanisation in football. While football has prominently been called a 'global game' (Giulianotti 1999) – its epicentre is in Europe. Here, the game has developed common structures, institutions, and policies. These developments reach back more than 70 years, but they have enormously accelerated since the mid-1990s (Niemann, García, and Grant 2011b).

The Europeanisation of football can be understood in four constituting mechanisms: most prominently, the *establishment of a pan-European league system* with the Champions League (CL) and the Europa League (EL). Then, two direct interventions of European institutions: the *acceleration of a European transfer market after the Bosman rulings* by the

European Court of Justice (ECJ) and the intervention of the European Commission (EC) in the *central marketing of broadcasting rights*. And both resulting from and corroborating the above: an increased *transnational coordination and cooperation between clubs* in addition to national associations and UEFA (Mittag 2018). The ambiguous relationship between football and the European structures is officially constituted in the EC's 'White Paper on Sport' (2007) which enshrined exemptions of *football as a sport* from competition regulations, thus defines football as not just a business. As a result, EU pressure spurred adjustment in football governance (e.g. in the transfer market), while other core policies remain intact despite their potential friction with European legislation, as it was the case for central marketing of broadcasting rights (Niemann and Brand 2008, 100–1).

Initial research of how these developments of Europeanisation in football might influence fan identifications has indicated that fans tend to show more Europeanised self-understandings when following their team in European competitions (King 2000, 2003; Millward 2006, 2009). The internationalisation (and Europeanisation) of the squads seems not to compromise the fans' ability to identify with their team (Ranc 2012). This part discusses how the four mechanisms of Europeanisation of football induce banal experiences of Europe among fans.

The pan-European league system

The evolution of cup competitions between national champions into a *pan-European league system* is the most approachable sign of Europeanisation in football. The Champions League (CL) was introduced in 1992 to replace the European Champion Clubs' Cup to allow multiple clubs from certain national leagues to participate. 1999, the remaining two European cups were merged and finally, in 2009 called Europa League (EL). Over time, a relatively stable pattern of the ever-same clubs in this continent-wide competitions has resulted in a pan-European 'league mode', dividing between frequent participants and a few occasional guest clubs (Niemann and Brand 2020; Pawlowski, Breuer, and Hovemann 2010).

This new system favours large teams from the most affluent leagues. With a handful of exceptions since 1992, all matches from the semi-final stages onwards were played between teams from the 'big five' leagues: Spain, England, Italy, Germany and France (Bullough 2018; Renz 2020). At the same time, expanded stages increased the number of matches and expanded the competition to cover clubs also from leagues with a low UEFA 5 year-coefficient – if only for the qualification round. This has created a continuous prevalence of matches between clubs across national borders throughout the season.

Although the participation of clubs is very selective, the increased opportunities to regularly watch European level club football have two possible implications for fans: first, matches, especially semi-finals and the final create a European 'fireplace' where fans meet across the continent watching the same match at the same time on TV, also in countries where clubs have low chances of participation (Niemann and Brand 2020). Additionally, fans are exposed to matches regularly through broadcasting and media coverage of teams, players and matches. Second, travel opportunities have increased for fans of clubs that regularly play in European competitions. In connection with the increase in cheap travel options (esp. cheap flights) and the lack of travel restrictions within the EU, travelling became more attractive and accessible. It could even be combined with visits to the cities or regions of away matches. Such development applied to the pre-Covid-19 era. The ongoing pandemic has brought tremendous change for football related travel. It is currently not foreseeable when the situation will change again and whether it will at all return to the old state, but so far, travel should still be understood as a strong and potentially influential cross-border experience of football fandom.

Potential banal experiences through the pan-European league system stem from several sources. First, clubs from the own national league, or even the own club, regularly play a rival from another European country. The media coverage before and after the match provides information about the rival, including information about its 'foreign' national league. Then, matches are organised around a certain ceremony, including an anthem and a logo, the star ball (King 2004). The anthem is played before each match. The logo – a football made up of eight stars under which the words 'UEFA Champions League' are written – has a decisive football connection, but it is also reminiscent of the EU flag in using a round shape and stars. Billig emphasises flags and hymns as banal experience of the nation (Billig 1995, 39ff.). Others underlined the explicit role of performances for the symbolic formation of nationhood (Fox and Miller-Idriss 2008). In that sense, the regularity of CL matches (and to a lesser extent EL matches) can provide a well-equipped stage for experiences of banal Europeanism.

The European competitions also contributed to an increasing hierarchy among clubs and leagues. Mostly rich clubs from West European leagues dominate the European competitions. Also, within the national leagues the system causes inequalities, as mostly the same clubs reach the competitions every year and receive important revenues from playing in the different rounds (Bullough 2018; Niemann and Brand 2020). Fans from less successful clubs might, as a result, feel excluded from what is seen as gold standard in football. Their club has no chance to reach the European stages.

Resulting from such differences, Europe can become a negative antidote as being capitalist and commercialised. Fans have conceptualised such protest in the slogan 'against modern football' (Hill, Robin, and Millward 2018). A very different reaction to the importance of the European football is the perspective of following a second club, which competes in European competitions (Bora and Senyuva 2011, 46–47). Given rivalries in the national league, this will probably be a club from another country that competes on the European level (as some European top clubs have several fan clubs outside of their country but within Europe, this is much likely). Both reactions have in common the potential *enhabitation* of Europe as main reference frame. While in the first case, fans demarcate themselves from European football, their reference point remains Europe. In the second case, Europe as reference frame is normal in a way that Europe is the normal level for competition, and it is worth following a team that competes there.

While these aspects contribute to an *enhabitation* of Europe by football fans through the ubiquity of European football competitions, the concomitant remaining relevance of national football may not be downplayed. The aspects above deliver arguments why it will still play a role:

1. Travel and match attention are easier if distances are smaller and travel is cheap. Match calendars still foresee most national matches taking place on the weekends while European competitions play during weekdays. This influences how prevalent and accessible travel will be among fans.

2. Media consumption is still focussed on national media (language barriers, reporting costs and assumed interest), information about other leagues is mostly related to players or managers from the own country or highlights matches such as Champions League finals, but not the day-by-day competitions in a foreign country (Mutz 2018).
3. While the idea of European competitions as commercialised evil still relates to Europe, it bears the chance of self-retraction to the national framework. Some fans might just abandon European football, especially if their team is not competing on that level (Koenigstorfer, Groeppel-Klein, and Kunkel 2010).

The accelerated European transfer market following the Bosman case

The *Bosman case* is the most prominent cases of official EU interference in football. It refers to the rulings of the ECJ in 1995 abrogating a system of transfer fees to be paid for out-of-contract players as it infringed upon the freedom of movement under Article 48 of the Treaty of Rome and abolishing 'nationality restrictions' that limited the number of foreign players in a team. Both practices of clubs were ruled illegal as they discriminated against EU-nationals. Consecutively, national Football Associations (FAs) reformed their transfer rules. Player restrictions range now from very liberal (e.g. in Germany) to restrictive but supposedly within the legally accepted frame (e.g. Austria) (Niemann, Brand, and Spitaler 2011a). The ruling was essential as it clarified that sport governing bodies have to follow EU free movement rights, but restrictions can be justified to keep up higher aims such as competitive balance in sports (Duval and van Rompuy 2016, 2). The implications for player markets of European leagues were enormous. Even though the role of the rulings as only cause for the deregulation of player markets has been challenged (see e.g. García 2016), they accelerated the Europeanisation of player markets enormously (Duval and van Rompuy 2016; Niemann, García, and Grant 2011b).

The transfer market acceleration bore tremendous changes in how current squads of top-level football teams look like (Velema 2018; Velema, Wen, and Zhou 2020). For most teams in Europe, a significant share of players has a foreign passport and stays with the club only for a short time. While the transfer market is international, its focus for European clubs remains Europe: most players (also non-Europeans) play in several European countries, increasing the interest of fans to get information about players and teams from other European countries when in/out rumours appear regarding their club (FIFA 2019a; Herm, Callsen-Bracker, and Kreis 2014; Velema 2018). As national FAs reacted to the Bosman case, some applied restrictions that differentiate between European and non-European players and few even introduced incentives to employ national players (Binder and Findlay 2012; Duval and van Rompuy 2016; Niemann, Brand, and Spitaler 2011a). As a result, players from European countries or those who have played across Europe are the majority in most teams.

Given this Europeanised transfer market, *enhabitation* of Europe among fans emerges in two different ways: first, information gathering about players from other countries becomes normal when these players are discussed as incoming for the own or a rival team. Websites such as *transfermarkt* contain information about players from most European leagues (and beyond) and serve as important information tool for fans (Velema 2020). The fact that the website is available in several European languages and with specific domains (i.e. fr, co.uk, es, pt) indicates that this resource is used across the continent. Such availability of information helps fans to acquire knowledge about clubs and players in other European countries. Second, fans are exposed to predominantly European squads, both with their own club and the rivals of their club. It becomes normal that players speak English or another language in press conferences and are translated to the national language. They address their fans in English, the club's language, or another language relevant to their expected audience on social media. This normalises the experience of being exposed to someone from a different country and in a different language even if not travelling or going abroad.

Despite such normalisation of Europeanism, aspects of banal nationalism are not vanished completely. The nationality of players is still relevant, not only because in some leagues, e.g. in the Austrian Bundesliga, financial revenues of the clubs depend on the playing time of domestic players, but also because the need of national teams often serves as an argument to favour domestic players in the country's top league (Binder and Findlay 2012). Generally, national team players enjoy attention, even when they play outside their home country. They are often the only reason why media covers foreign clubs and their matches. The example of Mesut Özil showed how this attention mirrors conflicts of the domestic societies: When the German team player posed on a photo together with the Turkish president the following public discussion finally led to his resignation from the national team (Sonntag and García 2020).

Another factor corroborating the remaining importance of the national is the degree of 'foreigness' of the Europeanised teams and the role of nationality for player judgement. It has been analysed that player markets often play out biased: i.e. English Premier League clubs draw foremost on non-domestic players from areas 'that most resemble local sources in terms of climate, culture, language and style of football' (McGovern 2002). Even though this was concluded based on an analysis before Bosman, the migration of football players still follows generic migration and trade patterns, as well as proximity. A very recent analysis of top teams' recruiting patterns concludes that only top-team in Europe scout on a Europeanised transfer market, while lower level teams scout mainly in neighbouring countries, and to a lesser extent in Latin America, mostly in the case of Portugal and Spain (Velema 2020). The transfer market and player migration are deeply embedded in social, economic and cultural inequalities and historical trajectories (Darby 2007; Poli 2010). This indicates that there are many different transfer markets with a heterogeneous diversity of players and thus a very different exposure to Europeanised squads among football fans.

Central marketing of broadcasting rights

The issue of *broadcasting rights of football matches* caused trouble during the mid-2000s between the FAs and the EU. Match broadcasting is one of the most profitable aspects in sports (Izquierdo and Troncoso Ferrer 2014). The EC considered the central marketing of broadcasting rights for football events (i.e. Bundesliga, Champions League matches) as a potential restriction of competition and violating EU law. On the other side, FAs argued for a central marketing as tool to preserve equal competition within a league (Hill 2009). Through a mere strategy of lobbying on the European level, especially through UEFA, the agreement saw a compromise with the EC that partly exempted football broadcasting from common market rules (Niemann and Brand 2008, 100–01). Broadcasting rights (and subsequently copy right issues) have kept the EC and the ECJ busy ever since. The EC has reviewed copy right and sport broadcasting issues and the ECJ has interfered in cases where broadcasting within the common market has been restricted to certain national boundaries. While most of these interferences targeted satellite TV, the ever-increasing infrastructural availability of content through live streaming over the internet will rather fortify cross border availability of match streams and coverage (Boyle 2015).

The interest in football across borders is volatile and follows certain trends: matches during the final stages of the CL are almost pan-European events that are covered across the continent. But media coverage of teams and matches in 'foreign' leagues follows mainly domestic players or managers who have been transferred abroad (Mutz 2018). Against the background of the Europeanisation of the transfer markets and the increasing prevalence of European club competitions, this broadcasting is most likely to expand accordingly.

The central marketing of broadcasting rights seems to be an issue of market regulations with little impact on the direct experience of the match for fans. But the long-term implications of central marketing arrangements shape both the financial conditions for clubs and the prevalence of football on TV or through live streaming. While the top clubs challenged the central marketing system to increase their revenue by marketing their bestselling matches to a larger audience, they aimed at having a better market position compared to other clubs and compared to a centralised system through the leagues (Izquierdo and Troncoso Ferrer 2014; Kruse and Quitzau 2003). The final agreement to keep the centralised marketing rights and sell them in 'packages' thus contributes to a more balanced competition and at least indirectly decreases inner-league disparities to a certain extent. To a certain extent, this equalises the chances for clubs to reach top positions in the league and thus qualify for European competitions. Broadcasting also has a secondary effect on the prevalence of football on TV: a not-centralised broadcasting right would have provided incentives for broadcasters to only buy the rights for matches between top clubs or clubs where teams from the own country are involved. As the broadcasters buy rights in packages, they also must buy the rights for matches between the less interesting clubs.

The banalisation of Europe can derive from the greater availability of matches through the central marketing of broadcasting rights in two ways. First, broadcasters stream/show matches, both top selling matches between the European elite clubs, and further matches between less interesting teams. They anyway must pay for them and might still get advertising income from less valuable matches. Consequently, the prevalence of matches in general increases, as not only top matches are broadcasted, but also the lower ones. This is especially relevant for the European competitions, e.g. matches of the Europa League and the qualification stages of the competitions. Then, streaming became increasingly easier and new competitors developed formats that were online only (DAZN, Amazon Prime). This has led to an increased market with several competitors, thus offering the fans more options to see matches. The business models led to the situation that suppliers needed to find new business models, e.g. the German streaming service DAZN screens English Premier League matches in addition to the CL and EL matches it mainly advertises.

Similarly, this has led to new differences that have the power to re-establish nationalism. The new broadcasters will probably target a certain population that pays for additional TV streams, while others are exempted from watching, e.g. elderly people that are not so acquainted with the internet or others who cannot afford pay TV (Johnsen and Solvoll 2007). A case study in Germany indicates that broadcasting of the English Premier League is rather a supplement to the national Bundesliga, not as important for broadcasting (Schreyer, Schmidt, and Torgler 2018). This reiterates national perspectives, as those sticking to the public TV channels are more dependent on what the public media in the county provides them with: Football restricted to the national leagues (e.g. sportschau (Germany), Match of the day (England/UK), sport sections in regular news).

Transnational club coordination

Resulting from the developments described above, the *transnational coordination among football clubs* has increased. The history of international and regional football associations reaches back to the first half of the 20th century, but these football associations, FIFA on the world level and UEFA in the European context, are built as umbrella organisations of national FAs. This implies only indirect influence of individual clubs. The national associations usually outbalance diverging interests of their heterogeneous members, let alone their own organisational interests. This resulted in a formation of 'top' clubs from several European countries into what became known as the G14. Their main aim was to influence UEFA and FIFA by using their power position as 'best-selling' clubs in European football. Issues of conflict were i.e. the compensation for players playing for national teams, but above all stood the aim to reform the European club competition system, mainly the Champions League, to the benefit of the top clubs (Mittag 2018). G14 dissolved in 2008, but the transnational club coordination remained intact – in the now bigger and more encompassing European Club Association (ECA), which, despite its about 200 member clubs, still merely represents top clubs and their particular interests (Keller 2018). This coordination led to orchestrated decision making and increased influence of the big clubs on the European level.

The increased coordination among top level clubs has rather indirect effects on the fans' experience of the game. The organisation of top clubs improved the articulation of interests by the strong players in the arena. They form the debate and influence the official decision making in the associations. The founding of the G14 during crucial times of a Champions League reform is the perfect example how this influences fans experiences. The top clubs have the interest to play in as many matches as possible against other top clubs for increased visibility and attractive competitions. They nurture pan-European debates and thus corroborate the European level as standard level in football. The discussion about the introduction of a European Super League, revealed through the football leaks papers saw the chairman of the European club association (ECA) as important actor, UEFA and the association of European leagues as strong opposition (der Spiegel 2018; The Guardian 2018).

Such developments changes fans' experiences of how the competitions take place. Much of what applies here has been elaborated above in the section on the development of the European club competitions. Additionally, European club coordination contributes to a normalisation of Europe in the discourse on football. As ECA influences public debates about how football should change, the media coverage of these debates gets Europeanised, thinking Europe as a whole and normalising interviews with actors from other countries in the context of a larger debate (by not interviewing e.g. ECA president as an Italian or Milan president, but as an European actor). These aspects are definitively rather a 'second layer' effect on how fans perceive Europeanisation, as they do not necessarily see the increased coordination, but they probably experience the results of such coordination.

Also, the European club coordination reiterates the national level as relevant. The mentioned debates about the future of football still have a national focus. Public discourse focuses on the question of how the national football will be influenced. In the example of the super league proposal, the German participants, e.g. officials from Bayern München, were dominantly present in German media debates and similarly across countries. Additionally, as European top club coordination is experienced openly as a closed shop (as the super league debates indicated), those fans that perceived their clubs to be excluded from this top clubs could identify the European level as potentially endangering 'their' football. Thus, the national football has the potential to become an antidote to the European super football.

Conclusions

The work explored how the concept of *banal nationalism* can be transferred to the European level. It discussed *banal Europeanism* as approach to understand the potential impact on football fans given the Europeanisation of the sport. In other words: How, if at all can *banal Europeanism* be identified among football fans? The aim was to use the added value of nationalism studies to understand Europeanism, meaning a shift of identification towards the European level, in the field of sports.

The work departed from four main strands of material Europeanisation in football: the development of a pan-European league system, ECJ interventions in the player market and their aftermath, EC interventions in broadcasting rights regulations and the cross-national organisation of top-club interests. These strands of Europeanisation in football have been discussed in their potential impact on the *enhabitation* of Europe as the new normal for football fans. Such *banal Europeanism* is a very much likely impact of the material changes that could be witnessed throughout the past decades. These four strands likely have different impact on fans: The development of a pan-European league system and the accelerated European transfer market directly affect match experiences and changed the face of clubs. The EC intervention in broadcasting rights and the establishment of cross-border top club interest organisations had a sustaining and perpetuating effect on how football is organised. The two latter developments influence the experiences of fans rather indirectly, but nonetheless.

The discussions of the potential *banal Europeanism* highlight that subtle and subliminal identification opportunities for fans are ubiquitous. The gold standard in football is the European level with its best-selling product, the CL as 'mega-event' (Alpan, Schwell, and Sonntag 2015) and 'myth' (Niemann and Brand 2020). Even though fans are exposed to this football differently, depending on the club they are following, it is unlikely that they can avoid the Europeanisation of the game in general. Not least through the transfer market and the *potential* impact that this market has on every professional club's team building strategies, Europe as reference frame is relevant.

Enhabitation, understood in the sense of Billig (1995, 42) as 'process of routine formation', is visible in everyday football related activities, such as (football related) media consumption, match attention or watching on TV. The dynamics of Europeanisation of football have increased the opportunities for fans in that regard. Additionally, the accessibility of information through the internet at low costs can accelerate the experience of a Europeanised sport. Such change is not exclusive to football or sports but reflects larger trends of globalisation and global information flow. In that regard, football does not create, it follows more generalised economic trends (Waalkes 2017). Unlike other factors that have been identified as driving force for European identities, such as educational or professional cross-border activities (Favell 2011; Kuhn 2012), football is not an exclusive arena for a happy few and might transport Europeanisation into a larger group of average citizens. *Banal Europeanism* in football could provide a gateway to Europe for those that are traditionally not much prone to hold pro-European views. Any empirical evidence of such assumptions is still weak (van Tuyckhom 2006), but the potential effect of 'sport as a vehicle' (van Tuyckhom) cannot be neglected.

Despite such arguments underlining the potential power of football in building and fostering Europeanised identities, this power has its limitations: Earlier criticism of Billig's work has emphasised his Western-European point of view and challenged the *banality* of national symbols, e.g. from a Serbian perspective (Spasic 2017). This general criticism on the Western dominance might hold true for banal Europeanism in football as well. Most clubs participating in the final stages of the CL come from the same few leagues (Bullough 2018). Against the backdrop of economic power, it is no coincidence that these 'big five', England, Germany, Spain, France, and Italy, are exclusively Western European countries. Adding to that, the travel opportunities for matches are also much easier for Schengen citizens than for Europeans who need a visa to enter the Schengen area. It might be valid to ask whether the *banal Europeanism* is prevalent with very specific inner-European boundaries.

At the same time, national and regional reference points remain relevant in the context of football. The Europeanisation of football potentially creates new divides between clubs that participate on the European level and those that will probably never do so. Already as early as 2000, in the very beginning of the accelerated Europeanisation of football, King (2000) identified the tendency among football fans of Manchester United F.C. to relate both to the locale of Manchester and to the European level but leaving out the national level. He has called this shift of reference frames 'post-national identity' among football fans. The discussion of the *enhabitation* of Europe as reference frame leaves open the opportunity for relevance of national and local reference frames. We may not forget that the nation has not lost its position as 'the most universally legitimate value in the political life of our time' (Anderson 1991, 3). This potentially holds true also for the arena of football, given that language barriers remain and the developments of European football towards a commercialised experience is met by many fans with disaffirmation.

It is unlikely that the reference point of the nation easily disappears. The results connect well to what we know about European identity formation: Such an identification is usually intertwined, complex and no zero-sum game with national identifications (Herrmann, Risse, and Brewer 2004; Medrano and Gutiérrez 2001). A conceptionalisation of banal Europeanism will always have to incorporate other reference points. The mix is of a new normal that covers local, regional, national, and European understandings of groupness. Such a mix seems to be habitualised in football, when 'Europe' becomes the new norm, while other aspects of the arena are still organised in national terms.

Disclosure statement

No potential conflict of interest was reported by the author.

ORCID

Regina Weber http://orcid.org/0000-0001-9892-214X

References

Aksoy, Asu, and Kevin Robins. 2002. "Banal Transnationalism: The Difference that Television Makes." WPTC-02-08.

Alpan, Basak, Alexandra Schwell, and Albrecht Sonntag, eds. 2015. *The European Football Championship: Mega-Event and Vanity Fair*. London: Palgrave.

Anderson, Benedict. 1991. *Imagined Communities*. London: Verso.

Antonsich, Marco. 2016. "The 'Everyday' of Banal Nationalism – Ordinary People's Views on Italy and Italian." *Political Geography* 54: 32–42. doi:10.1016/j.polgeo.2015.07.006.

Billig, Michael. 1995. *Banal Nationalism*. London: SAGE.

Binder, John J., and Murray Findlay. 2012. "The Effects of the Bosman Ruling on National and Club Teams in Europe." *Journal of Sports Economics* 13 (2): 107–129. doi:10.1177/1527002511400278.

Bora, Tanil, and Özgehan Senyuva. 2011. "Nationalism, Europeanization and Football: Turkish Fandom Transformed?" In *Football, Europe et Régulations*, edited by G. Robin, 35–51. Villeneuve: PUS.

Bourdieu, Pierre. 1990. *The Logic of Practice*. Stanford: Stanford University Press.

Boyle, Raymond. 2015. "Battle for Control? Copyright, Football and European Media Rights." *Media, Culture & Society* 37 (3): 359–375. doi:10.1177/0163443714567020.

Brubaker, Rogers, and Frederick Cooper. 2000. "Beyond 'Identity'." *Theory and Society* 29 (1): 1–47. doi:10.1023/A:1007068714468.

Bruter, Michael. 2005. *Citizens of Europe?: The Emergence of a Mass European Identity*. Basingstoke: Palgrave.

Bullough, Steve. 2018. "UEFA Champions League Revenues, Performance and Participation 2003–2004 to 2016–2017." *Managing Sport and Leisure* 23 (1-2): 139–156. doi:10.1080/23750472.2018.1513341.

Checkel, Jeffrey T., and Peter J. Katzenstein, eds. 2009. *European Identity*. New York: Cambridge University Press.

Cram, Laura. 2001. "Imagining the Union: A Case of Banal Europeanism?" In *Interlocking Dimensions of European Integration*, edited by H. Wallace, 233–236. London: Palgrave.

Cram, Laura. 2009. "Identity and European Integration: Diversity as a Source of Integration." *Nations and Nationalism* 15 (1): 109–128. doi:10.1111/j.1469-8129.2009.00367.x.

Cram, Laura. 2012. "Does the EU Need a Navel? Implicit and Explicit Identification with the European Union*." *JCMS: Journal of Common Market Studies* 50 (1): 71–86. doi:10.1111/j.1468-5965.2011.02207.x.

Darby, Paul. 2007. "African Football Labour Migration to Portugal." *Soccer & Society* 8 (4): 495–509. doi:10.1080/14660970701440774.

der Spiegel. 2018. "Documents Show Secret Plans for Elite League of Top Clubs." https://www.spiegel.de/international/world/football-documents-show-secret-plans-for-elite-league-of-top-clubs-a-1236447.html.

Deutsch, Karl W. 1957. *Political Community and the North Atlantic Area*. Princeton: Princeton University Press.

Duchesne, Sophie. 2018. "Who's Afraid of Banal Nationalism?" *Nations and Nationalism* 24 (4): 841–856. doi:10.1111/nana.12457.

Duval, Antoine, and Ben van Rompuy, eds. 2016. *The Legacy of Bosman*. The Hague: Asser.

Edensor, Tim. 2002. *National Identity, Popular Culture and Everyday Life*. Oxford: Berg.

Favell, Adrian. 2011. *Eurostars and Eurocities: Free Movement and Mobility in an Integrating Europe.* Malden: Wiley.

FIFA. 2019a. *Global Transfer Market Report* 2019: *Men Professional Football.* https://resources.fifa.com/image/upload/global-transfer-market-report-2019-men.pdf?cloudid=x2wrqjstwjoailnncnod.

FIFA. 2019b. *Professional Football Report 2019.* https://resources.fifa.com/image/upload/fifa-professional-football-report-2019.pdf?cloudid=jlr5corccbsef4n4brde.

Fox, Jon E. 2006. "Consuming the Nation: Holidays, Sports, and the Production of Collective Belonging." *Ethnic and Racial Studies* 29 (2): 217–236. doi:10.1080/01419870500465207.

Fox, Jon E., and Cynthia Miller-Idriss. 2008. "Everyday Nationhood." *Ethnicities* 8 (4): 536–563. doi:10.1177/1468796808088925.

García, Borja. 2016. "He Was Not Alone: Bosman in Context." In *The Legacy of Bosman*, edited by A. Duval and B. van Rompuy, 13–30. The Hague: Asser.

Giulianotti, Richard. 1999. *Football: A Sociology of the Global Game.* Malden, MA: Blackwell.

Gustafson, Per. 2009a. "Mobility and Territorial Belonging." *Environment and Behavior* 41 (4): 490–508. doi:10.1177/0013916508314478.

Gustafson, Per. 2009b. "More Cosmopolitan, No Less Local: The Orientations of International Travellers." *European Societies* 11 (1): 25–47. doi:10.1080/14616690802209689.

Haas, Ernst B. 2004 (1958). *The Uniting of Europe: Political, Social, and Economic Forces, 1950-1957.* Notre Dame: University of Notre Dame Press.

Hanquinet, Laurie, and Mike Savage. 2013. *The Europeanisation of Everyday Life: Cross-Border Practices and Transnational Identifications among EU and Third-Country Citizens: Europeanisation and Globalisation.* EUCROSS Working Paper. No. 6.

Herm, Steffen, Hans-Markus Callsen-Bracker, and Henning Kreis. 2014. "When the Crowd Evaluates Soccer Players' Market Values: Accuracy and Evaluation Attributes of an Online Community." *Sport Management Review* 17 (4): 484–492. doi:10.1016/j.smr.2013.12.006.

Herrmann, Richard, Thomas Risse, and Marilynn Brewer, eds. 2004. *Transnational Identities: Becoming European in the EU.* Lanham: Rowman & Littlefield.

Hill, Jonathan. 2009. "The European Commission's White Paper on Sport: A Step Backwards for Specificity?" *International Journal of Sport Policy and Politics* 1 (3): 253–266. doi:10.1080/19406940903265533.

Hill, Tim, Canniford Robin, and Peter Millward. 2018. "Against Modern Football." *Sociology* 52 (4): 688–708. doi:10.1177/0038038516660040.

Izquierdo, S. M., and M. Troncoso Ferrer. 2014. "Football Broadcasting Business in the EU." *Journal of European Competition Law & Practice* 5 (6): 353–363. doi:10.1093/jeclap/lpu042.

Johnsen, Hallvard, and Mona Solvoll. 2007. "The Demand for Televised Football." *European Sport Management Quarterly* 7 (4): 311–335. doi:10.1080/16184740701717048.

Juncà Pujol, Albert, and Eduard Inglés Yuba. 2014. "Constructing the National through Sports News in Catalonia (2007–2009)." *Catalan Journal of Communication & Cultural Studies* 6 (2): 239–256. doi:10.1386/cjcs.6.2.239_1.

Keller, Berndt K. 2018. *Sectoral Social Dialogue in Professional Football: Social Partners, Outcomes and Problems of Implementation.* etui Working Paper. No. 2018.04. Brussels. Accessed October 7, 2020. https://www.etui.org/publications/working-papers/sectoral-social-dialogue-in-professional-football-social-partners-outcomes-and-problems-of-implementation.

King, Anthony. 2000. "Football Fandom and Post-National Identity in the New Europe." *British Journal of Sociology* 51 (3): 419–442. doi:10.1080/00071310050131602.

King, Anthony. 2003. *The European Ritual: Football in the New Europe.* London: Routledge.

King, Anthony. 2004. "The New Symbols of European Football." *International Review for the Sociology of Sport* 39 (3): 323–336. doi:10.1177/1012690204045599.

Koch, Natalie, and Anssi Paasi. 2016. "Banal Nationalism 20 Years on: Re-Thinking, Re-Formulating and Re-Contextualizing the Concept." *Political Geography* 54: 1–6. doi:10.1016/j.polgeo.2016.06.002.

Koenigstorfer, Joerg, Andrea Groeppel-Klein, and Thilo Kunkel. 2010. "The Attractiveness of National and International Football Leagues." *European Sport Management Quarterly* 10 (2): 127–163. doi:10.1080/16184740903563406.

Kruse, Jörn, and Jörn Quitzau. 2003. *Fußball-Fernsehrechte: Aspekte der Zentralvermarktung.* Diskussionspapier. Helmut-Schmidt-Universität Hamburg. Fächergruppe Volkswirtschaftslehre. No. 18.

Kuhn, Theresa. 2011. "Individual Transnationalism, Globalisation and Euroscepticism: An Empirical Test of Deutsch's Transactionalist Theory." *European Journal of Political Research* 50 (6): 811–837. doi:10.1111/j.1475-6765.2011.01987.x.

Kuhn, Theresa. 2012. "Why Educational Exchange Programmes Miss Their Mark: Cross-Border Mobility." *JCMS: Journal of Common Market Studies* 50 (6): 994–1010. doi:10.1111/j. 1468-5965.2012.02286.x.

Kuhn, Theresa. 2015. *Experiencing European Integration: Transnational Lives and European Identity.* Oxford: Oxford University Press.

Kuhn, Theresa, Erika J. van Elsas, Armen Hakhverdian, and Wouter van der Brug. 2016. "An Ever Wider Gap in an Ever Closer Union: Rising Inequalities and Euroscepticism in 12 West European Democracies." *Socio-Economic Review* 14 (1): 27–45. doi:10.1093/ser/mwu034.

McGovern, Patrick. 2002. "Globalization or Internationalization? Foreign Footballers in the English League, 1946-95." *Sociology* 36 (1): 23–42. doi:10.1177/0038038502036001002.

Medrano, Juan D., and Paula Gutiérrez. 2001. "Nested Identities: National and European Identity in Spain." *Ethnic and Racial Studies* 24 (5): 753–778. doi:10.1080/01419870120063963.

Millward, Peter. 2006. "'We've All Got the Bug for Euro-Aways': What Fans Say about European Football Club Competition." *International Review for the Sociology of Sport* 41 (3-4): 375–393. doi:10.1177/1012690207077706.

Millward, Peter. 2009. *Getting into Europe: Identification, Prejudice and Politics in English Football Culture.* Saarbrücken: VDM.

Mittag, Jürgen. 2018. "Aufstieg und Auflösung der G14: Episode oder Paradebeispiel der Konfliktregulierung europäischer Sportpolitik?" In *Europäische Sportpolitik*, edited by J. Mittag, 193–216. Baden-Baden: Nomos.

Mutz, Michael. 2018. "Die Europäisierung im Fußball und seines Publikums: Zur Messung und Analyse von transnationalem öffentlichen Interesse im Fußball." In *Europäische Sportpolitik*, edited by J. Mittag, 315–328. Baden-Baden: Nomos.

Niemann, Arne, and Alexander Brand. 2008. "The Impact of European Integration on Domestic Sport: The Case of German Football." *Sport in Society* 11 (1): 90–106. doi:10.1080/17430430701717822.

Niemann, Arne, Alexander Brand, and Georg Spitaler. 2011a. "The Europeanisation of Football: Germany and Austria Compared." In *The Making and Mediatization of Modern Sport in Europe*, edited by C. Young, D. Holt, and A. Tomlinson, 187–204. London: Routledge.

Niemann, Arne, Borja García, and Wyn Grant, eds. 2011b. *Transformation of European Football.* Manchester: Manchester University Press.

Niemann, Arne, and Alexander Brand. 2020. "The UEFA Champions League: A Political Myth?" *Soccer & Society* 21 (3): 329–343. doi:10.1080/14660970.2019.1653859.

Paasi, Anssi. 2016. "Dancing on the Graves: Independence, Hot/Banal Nationalism and the Mobilization of Memory." *Political Geography* 54: 21–31. doi:10.1016/j.polgeo.2015.07.005.

Pawlowski, Tim, Christoph Breuer, and Arnd Hovemann. 2010. "Top Clubs' Performance and the Competitive Situation in European Domestic Football Competitions." *Journal of Sports Economics* 11 (2): 186–202. doi:10.1177/1527002510363100.

Poli, Raffaele. 2010. "Understanding Globalization through Football." *International Review for the Sociology of Sport* 45 (4): 491–506. doi:10.1177/1012690210370640.

Pyta, Wolfram, and Nils Havemann, eds. 2015. *Football Research in an Enlarged Europe, European Football and Collective Memory.* London: Palgrave.

Ranc, David. 2012. *Foreign Players and Football Supporters: The Old Firm, Arsenal, Paris Saint-Germain.* Manchester: Manchester University Press.

Renz, Michael. 2020. "Ausgeglichenheit des Wettbewerbs europäischer Fußballligen." In *Internationaler Wettbewerb europäischer Profiligen*, edited by M. Renz, 133–220. Wiesbaden: Springer.

Risse, Thomas. 2003. "The Euro between National and European Identity." *Journal of European Public Policy* 10 (4): 487–505. doi:10.1080/1350176032000101235.

Risse, Thomas. 2005. "Neofunctionalism, European Identity, and the Puzzles of European Integration." *Journal of European Public Policy* 12 (2): 291–309. doi:10.1080/13501760500044033.

Schreyer, Dominik, Sascha L. Schmidt, and Benno Torgler. 2018. "Game Outcome Uncertainty in the English Premier League." *Journal of Sports Economics* 19 (5): 625–644. doi:10.1177/1527002516673406.

Skey, Michael. 2009. "The National in Everyday Life: A Critical Engagement with Michael Billig's Thesis of Banal Nationalism." *The Sociological Review* 57 (2): 331–346. doi:10.1111/j.1467-954X.2009.01832.x.

Skey, Michael, and Marco Antonsich, eds. 2017. *Everyday Nationhood*. London: Palgrave.

Sonntag, Albrecht, and Borja García. 2020. "National Teams, Multiple Loyalties. A Discussion of Three Football Case Studies." *Papeles Del CEIC* 2020 (1): 224. doi:10.1387/pceic.20832.

Spasic, Ivana. 2017. "The Universality of Banal Nationalism, or Can the Flag Hang Unobtrusively outside a Serbian Post Office?" In *Everyday Nationhood*, edited by M. Skey and M. Antonsich, 31–52. London: Palgrave Macmillan.

The Guardian. 2018. "European Super League Would Threaten Football's Future, Says Group of 900 Clubs." https://www.theguardian.com/football/2018/nov/06/european-super-league-threaten-football-future-warns-association-european-leagues.

van Tuyckhom, C. 2006. "Sport as a Vehicle for Postnational Identity?" Paper presented at the 2006 Sport&EU-Workshop, Loughborough.

Velema, Thijs A. 2018. "A Game of Snakes and Ladders: Player Migratory Trajectories in the Global Football Labor Market." *International Review for the Sociology of Sport* 53 (6): 706–725. doi:10.1177/1012690216679967.

Velema, Thijs A. 2020. "Globalization and Player Recruitment: How Teams from European Top Leagues Broker Migration Flows of Footballers in the Global Transfer Network." *International Review for the Sociology of Sport*: Online First.

Velema, Thijs A., Han-Yu Wen, and Yu-Kai Zhou. 2020. "Global Value Added Chains and the Recruitment Activities of European Professional Football Teams." *International Review for the Sociology of Sport* 55 (2): 127–146. doi:10.1177/1012690218796771.

Vonnard, Philippe, Grégory Quinn, and Nicolas Bancel. 2016. *Building Europe with the Ball*. Frankfurt am Main: Peter Lang.

Waalkes, Scott. 2017. "Does Soccer Explain the World or Does the World Explain Soccer? Soccer and Globalization." *Soccer & Society* 18 (2-3): 166–180. doi:10.1080/14660970.2016.1166782.

Norbert Elias's concept of the 'drag-effect': implications for the study of the relationship between national identity and sport

Tom Gibbons

ABSTRACT

In this paper Norbert Elias's concept of the 'drag-effect' is argued to be important for exploring the complexities of the relationship between national identity and sport. Elias's distinct sociological perspective is briefly outlined before the importance of Elias's drag-effect is considered alongside other much more popular concepts commonly used in the study of nationalism and sport. The concept of the drag-effect is then applied to help make sense of the relationship between contemporary English national identity and sport, using specific examples from the sport of association football. Future researchers are encouraged to make greater use of Elias's drag-effect for studying the complex relationships between other national identities and sports.

Introduction: the sociological perspective of Norbert Elias

Elias's figurational or process sociological approach focused specifically on "how human beings and societies interconnect and develop" (Smith 2001, 1). Elias (1978, 15) contended that, "people make up webs of interdependence or figurations of many kinds, characterized by power balances of many sorts." These figurations are fluid and ever changing depending on the dynamics of the relationships people form and the situational context within which they exist. Elias (1978, 74) created what he termed 'game models' to help explain how power pervades in all human relationships. Through regarding power relations as analogous to invasion games (team sports) - like association football (referred to hereafter as football), rugby or hockey - Elias was able to show that all relationships are processes subject to change. In such sports, the relationship between teams and the individuals which make them up on the field of play is constantly changing depending on a number of related factors, including: who has possession of the ball; where players are positioned on the field; and, so on. Here Elias conceives of the way power operates as: processual; fluid; multi-dimensional; relational; and, situational, instead of being static; fixed; one-sided; and, uni-directional, as for example a classic Marxist conception of class relations maintains where members of the proletariat are always subordinate to the dominance of the bourgeoisie (cf.

Marx and Engels 1967). For Elias (1978, 93), in any given figuration all individuals have a degree of power in the interdependent relationships they form:

> We depend on others; others depend on us. In so far as we are more dependent on others than they are on us, more directed by others than they are by us, they have power over us, whether we have become dependent on them by their use of naked force or by our need to be loved, our need for money, healing, status, a career, or simply for excitement ... all relationships—like human games—are processes.

Since the European Middle Ages, if not before, webs of interdependency (figurations) have gradually increased in size to such an extent that in the modern world, "millions of people may have some relationship to each other and be dependent on each other" (Elias 1978, 100). The task for sociologists, according to Elias, is to study these figurations in order to make them more transparent. This requires a necessarily developmental sociological approach because "people's interdependencies change as societies become increasingly differentiated and stratified" (Elias 1978, 134). Thus, it is important to conceive of figurations as if they are in a constant state of flux because people form interpersonal bonds with one another as well as with larger units of which they have become part (such as nation-states) because of the ways in which societies have developed. Elias (1978, 137) states that people's "attachments to such large social units is often as intense as their attachment to a person they love." Elias argues that throughout history units or alliances of people have always held the function of survival units or attack and defence units. Whereas they have previously been in the form of smaller groups such as tribes or clans, at the present stage of human development nation-states act as the main units into which people are bound. Elias's (2000) seminal work, *The Civilizing Process*, is essentially concerned with making strong links between large-scale social processes that have occurred in Western Europe over the last millennium and visible alterations in the psychological make-up or 'habitus' of individuals.

Habitus refers to a specific set of acquired dispositions of thought, behaviour and actions that are embedded in individuals through long-term socialisation into particular cultures as part of everyday life so that they become second nature (Bourdieu 1977; Mennell 1994). Elias uses the phrase 'social habitus' which he contends exists within the personality structure of any individual human being and the idea of the 'national habitus' figures prominently in a number of Elias's works (Elias 1978; 1991; 1996; Elias and John 1994). Despite Elias's (1991; 1996; 2000) clear focus on the link between long-term processes of state-formation, the development of national habitus amongst Europeans and the persistence of nationalism within an increasingly global and European age, his work still remains somewhat under-utilised in the diverse academic study of nationalism. Although Elias (cf. 1991; 2000) specifically theorised about the development of globalisation and its impact on European nation-states as a long-term process, even recent texts focused on globalisation and Europeanisation often pay scant attention to his contributions to understanding in this area. Delanty and O'Mahony (2002, 72) argue that Elias may simply be placed "before his time". Nevertheless, through focusing on both structure (in terms of European state formation processes) and agency (in terms of the affective impacts of national culture building on citizens within states) Elias

> is the theorist par excellence of the national habitus, a position that insofar as nationalism is increasingly seen as intrinsic to modernity, places his work at the core of the theorisation of modernity itself (Delanty and O'Mahony 2002, 71).

The aims of this paper are two-fold. First, to provide an argument to suggest Elias's (1991) concept of the 'drag-effect' should not be overlooked alongside other much more popular concepts commonly used in the study of nationalism and sport. Second, that the drag-effect can be applied to understanding the complexities of the relationship between sport and contemporary English national identity, using examples from the popular sport of football. In the remainder of this paper each of these two arguments are discussed in turn before a conclusion is provided.

The importance of Elias's drag-effect in relation to theories of nationalism

Smith (2010) suggests that there are many theories to explain how nations and their national identities have developed. In order to begin to appreciate why Elias's drag-effect can be considered important alongside more commonly used concepts within the study of nationalism and sport, it is important to briefly consider the latter.

Commonly used concepts within the study of nationalism and sport

In sociological terms, a 'nation' is a community of history and culture, possessing a compact territory, whilst a 'state' has a unified economy and common legal rights and duties for its members (Smith 2010). 'Ethnic' nationalism refers to ideas of the 'nation', and the 'civic' nationalism refers to ideas about the 'state'. Essentially, 'nationalists' operating within modern nation-states have aimed to put the 'roof' of statehood over the nation or multiple nations—as is the case in the United Kingdom of Great Britain and Northern Ireland (UK), whereas others have pointed to the 're-invention' of traditions that are symbolic of the cultural and often ethnic history of the nation—for example, 'Celtic' ethnicity is used to underpin the nationalism of the Republic of Ireland.

The 'modernist' paradigm of nationalism contends that nation-states; nationalisms; and, the national identities evident in contemporary Europeans, need to be viewed as completely 'modern' in that they have been developed since the 'Enlightenment' of the mid-seventeenth century, which led to the modernising revolutions of the eighteenth and nineteenth centuries signalling the onset of modernity (Smith 1998). Modernists contend that nation-states and nationalism emerged through the modernisation of western society and state politics of the elite classes and are therefore *not* deeply rooted in history. This is recognised as the most dominant paradigm of nationalism to date and has largely stemmed from influential scholars like Gellner (1964; 1983) and Kedourie (1960).

Smith (1996) describes how most (but not all) modern nation-states are simultaneously and necessarily 'civic' and 'ethnic'. He observes that it is often assumed, by liberal theorists in particular, that ethnic sentiments of collective belonging that enter into the life of a state inevitably breed exclusiveness and intolerance leading to conflict. Marxist theorists often tend to claim that states are modern capitalist inventions that seek to divide workers of different nations and disguise their common interests. Hobsbawm's (1983, 1) is an example of a Marxist interpretation of the production of nationalism as a political ideology because he regards the practices that are associated with modern nation-states as 'invented traditions', which he describes as a term taken to mean a set of practices, normally governed by overtly or tacitly accepted rules and of a ritual or symbolic nature, which seek to inculcate certain values and norms of behaviour by repetition, which automatically implies continuity with the past. In fact, where possible, they normally attempt to establish continuity with a suitable historic past.

In later work, Hobsbawm (1990) proposed that the ruling political elites who had power throughout the industrial and modernising periods created or 'invented' certain 'national' symbols such as flags and anthems to symbolise particular nation-states. Though, as Smith (1998) clarifies, Hobsbawm does not adequately explain that traditions are not only invented by elites and neither are they always successful in binding society as if it were a homogenous community. Traditions also need to appeal to the majority of people within a nation in order to be successful. It is important not to divorce romantic symbols from historically lived experience and, therefore, because national traditions necessarily need a connection to the past, it is perhaps more accurate to conceive of them as 'selected' rather than completely 'invented'.

Stemming from a similar Marxist position, Anderson (1991) sought to emphasise the cultural and subjective aspects in producing modern feelings of national belonging or sentiment, which Hobsbawm leaves aside to some extent. Instead of nations and their nationalisms being 'invented', they are actually 'imagined' according to Anderson. Therefore, nations are modern cultural artefacts and not ideological for Anderson (1991, 5), who states that it "would, I think, make things easier if one treated it [nationalism] as if it belonged with 'kinship' and 'religion', rather than with 'liberalism' or 'fascism.'" Anderson (1991, 6) defines the modern nation-state as being "an imagined political community—and imagined as both inherently limited and sovereign." According to Anderson, the reason the nation is 'imagined' is because citizens will rarely meet or hear about the majority of other people existing within their nation. Still they will imagine similarities between themselves and the wider community of people existing within the limited boundaries of their country.

Billig (1995) helps one understand how what Hobsbawm termed 'invented traditions' are used to maintain the 'imagined national community' Anderson theorised. Billig conceives of national 'identity' as constructed through the nation being 'flagged up' in many areas of everyday life, including sport. Billig recognises that representations in the national media and other areas of everyday life, although not overt, still act to 'flag the nation' on a subtle but routine basis. He argues that it is by continual reference to national symbols, such as flags or anthems, and aspects of a nation's history, such as successes in wars, that what he terms 'banal nationalism' occurs. In this regard, Billig (1995, 93) contends that small "words, rather than grand memorable phrases, offer constant, but barely conscious, reminders of the homeland, making 'our' national identity unforgettable."

The opposing paradigm to modernism is that of traditionalism. Taking this perspective, primordialists have the view that ethnic ties, often from the ancient past, explain that 'nationalism' has been apparent for as long as people have been in existence. Clifford Geertz (1994) notes how post-colonial societies have created a shared sense of collective belonging through six essentially ethnic elements, including: assumed blood ties; race; language; region; religion; and custom. These are what he calls 'primordial' ties. Perennialists, being similar to primordialists, derive modern nations from fundamental ethnic ties rather than from the processes of modernisation (Smith 2010). Perennialists locate myths that relate to the ethnic majority in society and may often be formalised through civic commemoration in order to make certain citizens feel more like a community.

Finally, there are post-modernist approaches which focus upon how the modernist paradigm needs to be adapted or extended to include more recent themes, including: postcolonial perspectives; feminist critiques; and, the impact of globalisation processes on national cultures (Smith 1998; 2010).

Elias's the drag-effect

Now that some of the most popular theoretical concepts commonly used to study nationalism and sport have been briefly outlined, the goal of this section is to provide an explanation of Elias's concept of the drag-effect. A more thorough examination of Elias's ideas relating to nationalism can be found elsewhere (see Delanty and O'Mahony 2002; Smith 2001).

Elias is neither a modernist nor a traditionalist. Nor is he even a postmodernist. Elias (2000) posits that nation-states are not entirely modern, and in fact, state-formation processes extend to a far earlier time than the onset of modernity. According to Elias's (2000) empirical research, modernisation is part of the overall process of state-formation, but it is reductionist to see it as *the only* process within state-formation, often the argument of the Modernist paradigm of nationalism (James 2006).

In the second volume of *The Civilizing Process* Elias (2000) investigated how personality structure and standards of behaviour are linked to the broader structure of society in his enquiry into the 'Sociogenesis of the State'. This is where Elias differs significantly from Marx himself, as well as the Modernist theorists of nationalism alluded to above. Marx saw the rise of nation-states as a particular outgrowth of the modern period and especially of the rise of industrial capitalism, thus viewing it in purely economic terms. Unlike Marx, Elias's (2000) discussion of processes of European state-formation neither reduces this process to economics alone, nor does he see the rise of the nation-state idea purely as a consequence of capitalism. Instead Elias posits that such a process is not only more complex than a mere reflection of capitalism, but also that it occurred much earlier than the onset of modernity. Elias (2000) contends that it is more accurate to accept that state-formation, the social division of functions and lengthening of interdependency chains, the growth of towns, trade and money, all intertwine and reinforce one another. Any attempt to separate out one strand as the prime cause, or to represent history as a sequence of static stages, distorts the essentially processual character of social reality.

The monopoly mechanism is one of three principal elements in Elias's (2000) discussion of state-formation and refers to two intimately related processes: the gradual concentration of the means of violence and taxation in the hands of a single ruler and administration in each territory; and, the enlargement of the territory through competition with and elimination of neighbouring rulers. Another is what Elias terms the royal mechanism, which refers to the internal balance of social forces within the developing state. The third of these elements is the transformation from private to public monopolies. These are not successive stages, all intertwine and other strands including the growth of towns, of money economy and trade, of intermediate bourgeois strata, are also tied together within this overall process of development. This relatively blind or unplanned complex set of processes can be traced back as far as the beginning of the European Middle

Ages, the end of the Roman Empire, where there were great migrations of people across Europe (Roche 2010).

For Elias, individuals and their figurations (collectives of individuals or groups such as: families; clans; tribes; ethnic groups; or, nations/states) complement one another in that they are part and parcel of the same phenomenon, what Elias (1991) called the 'society of individuals'. In short, Elias (1991) contended that the involvement or commitment expressed by the use of the pronoun 'we' is probably usually strongest in relation to family, domicile or native region, but it has also grown to be just as strong in relation to an individual's affiliation to a nation or state.

According to Elias (1978, 128), long-term and largely unplanned processes shape the figurations which link people, groups and institutions interdependently to one another and this means that the habitus of individuals is also impacted. Elias (1991; 2000) considered the fate of European nation-states in the expanding European project (European Union) in this way. He argued that a central aspect of the development of Europe over the last millennium has been a tendency towards increasingly dense and complex figurations. Elias (1991, 222) terms the conflict between newer and older planes of habitus the 'drag-effect' but expects that incorporation into larger and more complex integration planes will gradually increase over time.

In a case study on the Germans, Elias (1996) referred to the national habitus as a particular form of we-group identification noting that the fortunes of a nation become internalised and deeply embodied as part of the second nature (or habitus) of its citizens. As such, he contended that one of the most potent 'I-We' identities belonging to individual citizens in modern European nation-states like Germany, France and Britain, is that associated with their nation. Elias also recognised that people in contemporary European nation-states have come to develop multi-layered identifications that are simultaneously: local; regional; national; European; and, even global. It is these overlapping affiliations that form the flexible and complex network of the habitus of a person (Elias 1991). Thus, instead of viewing a person's habitus as fixed and immovable, it is perhaps more appropriate to view habitus as a process that may be subject to change.

Anderson (1991) and Hobsbawm (1983) have been used by many scholars to suggest that national communities are continually re-imagined or re-invented in the face of more recent political developments such as European integration. Although this may be true, few have realised the potential of Elias's contribution to this area. Elias (1991, 202) observed as a general trend that "in the earlier stages [of human existence], the we-I balance first tilted strongly towards the we. In more recent times it has strongly swung towards the I." Furthermore, in a study on a small community in England, referred to as Winston Parva, Elias and Scotson (1994) came up with the theory of established–outsider relations, which can help explain what Elias refers to as the we-I balance. Elias and Scotson (1994, xliii) noted how a

> person's we-image and we-ideal form as much a part of a person's self-image and self-ideal as the image and ideal of him- or herself as the unique person to which he or she refers as "I".

Thus, wider group identities (such as a nation, class or religion) cannot often be separated from an individual's personal habitus, meaning that in the same moment any individual is both an 'I' and a 'we'.

Elias (1991, 209) also contends that powerful as the advance of individualization has been in recent times due to globalisation processes, "in relation to the nation-state plane we-habitus has actually strengthened." This is because people regard themselves as individual representatives of a we-group (an Englishman or Welshwoman for example). In fact, the traits of national group habitus—what we call the national character—are a layer of the social habitus built very deeply and firmly into the personality structure of an individual (Elias 1991; Fletcher 1997, 99).

Elias (1991; 2000) urges that the state's role as nation-state, is of relatively recent date and he posits that the emergence of European states happened gradually and in complex stages, not all of which were linear. It is of importance to note that absolutist states such as France at the time of Louis XIV (1643-1715) were ruled autocratically by kings and nobles. England, although never absolutist, was still ruled largely by the monarch with the aid of the upper classes at this time. They alone, as the established group, formed the state and the mass populace were perceived only as a they group and as outsiders (Elias and Scotson 1994). Even in the late nineteenth and early twentieth centuries, parts of the populace in France—first peasants, then the industrial proletariat—were excluded from the citizens' we habitus by the ruling classes—the nobility and the rising bourgeoisie (Elias 2000).

Thus, these outsiders perceived the state as a 'they' rather than a 'we' group. The more complete integration, or what Elias (2000) terms 'functional democratisation', of all citizens into the state within European multi-party states really only happened during the course of the twentieth century—only with parliamentary representation of all classes and both genders did all members of the state begin to perceive it more as a we-unit and less as a they-group. Democratisation can be defined as "the gradual historical tendency towards more equal—though not wholly equal—power balances between different groups and sub-groups in society" (Murphy, Sheard, and Waddington 2000, 94). For Elias (2000), this is part of the process of movement from private to public monopolies.

Furthermore, Elias observed that it was only during the course of the two great wars of the twentieth century that the populations of the more developed industrial European states—Britain, Germany and France—took on the character of nation-states in the modern sense of the word. This leads him to suggest that nation-states, "one might say, are born in and for wars" (Elias 1991, 208). For Elias this is the reason why, among the various layers of habitus, the nation-state level of integration today carries such an emotional charge. The integration plane of the nation-state, more than any other layer of habitus, has in the consciousness of most members, the function of a survival unit, a protection unit on which depends their physical and social security in conflict between human groups.

In this section, I have argued that Elias's concept of the drag-effect should not be over-looked alongside other much more popular concepts commonly used in the study of nationalism and sport. In the following section this argument is substantiated through the application of the drag-effect to help make sense of the relationship between contemporary English national identity and sport, using examples from the popular sport of football.

Using Elias's drag-effect to understand the relationship between contemporary English national identity and sport

The place of sport in regard to the rise or resurgence in national consciousness amongst contemporary Europeans is significant since this extremely popular social practice has the power to both unite and divide large numbers of citizens. Recent figurational studies have demonstrated this to be the case (see for example Liston and Deighan 2019; Liston and Kitching 2020; Liston and Maguire 2020). Throughout the history of British sport one can observe division between the nations of the UK (England, Scotland, Wales and Northern Ireland) in terms of the organisation of international sporting contests, including for instance, football, cricket and rugby World Cups as well as the Commonwealth Games. Yet, at the same time, the nations of the UK have also united as Great Britain and Northern Ireland, perhaps most significantly as 'Team GB' in the Olympic and Paralympic Games as well as in many other sports, such as the British Lions rugby union tour.

Sport has often been used in attempts to integrate Europeans, yet due to the drag-effect of national identity within the habitus of European citizens, such attempts have been unsuccessful. British identity politics in media coverage of football were discussed by Maguire and Poulton (1999) in their seminal figurational study of the UEFA (Union of European Football Associations) European Football Championship tournament hosted by England in 1996 (known as EURO 96). Here Maguire and Poulton demonstrated how the British (England-based) national press sought to reinforce national stereotypes and xenophobia in relation to their reports of other European nations, reinforcing division rather than integration between the nations of Europe.

Fast-forward a quarter of a century and one can observe that attempts to integrate Europeans through the EUROs have become even more pronounced. EURO 2020 was moved from the summer of 2020 to the summer of 2021 following the COVID-19 pandemic. For the first time in its 60-year history, the tournament matches would be held in 12 cities in 12 countries across Europe rather than in just one or two host countries. As such, UEFA dubbed the tournament a 'EURO for Europe' (FA 2019). Two of the host cities include Glasgow (Hampden Park) and London (Wembley). Wembley Stadium is host to three Group D matches (the other three being staged at Hampden Park), as well as a round of 16 match, two semi-finals and even the tournament final.

The irony of this situation is that by that point the UK will have been out of the European Union for over a year (since 31 January 2020), a result of the Brexit negotiations which began following the UK EU (European Union) membership referendum on 23 June 2016 in which 51.9% Brits voted to leave the EU (see O'Rourke 2019 for more on the historical processes underpinning Brexit). Added to this, the reality of Brexit has recently re-ignited the possibility of a second referendum on Scottish independence (following the first one on 18 September 2014 in which 55.3% voted for Scotland to remain part of the UK), considering a majority in Scotland (62%) voted to remain in the EU (Wishart 2019).

A key question asked by many a sports fan, athlete and pundit at the time of writing is: 'How will the British compete in sport following Brexit?' It is doubtful whether the long-standing divisions within the UK regarding international sporting competition will be altered unless absolutely necessary and demanded by international governing bodies. Such a case became a huge issue in the lead up to the 2012 London Olympics. Bringing the UK nations together under the Team GB banner for the men's football competition at the London 2012 competition was extremely controversial (see Gibbons, Dixon, and Braye 2015). The British Olympic Committee and the four separate UK Football Associations each formally recognised in world football – the (English) Football Association (FA), the Scottish FA (SFA), the Football Association of Wales (FAW) and the governing body for the Northern Irish football team, the Irish FA (IFA) - were forced to comply because it was demanded by the International Olympic Committee (IOC) that the host nation must field a team in every event. Yet, the actual Team GB football squad was not representative of the UK *at all* as it contained 13 English and five Welsh, but no Scottish or Northern Irish players (Ziegler 2012). A British football team for a FIFA World Cup or UEFA EUROs is inconceivable in the minds of football fans in the UK given the history of competition as separate national teams since 1950 (see Gibbons 2014).

The Brexit situation and how it relates to the relationship between sport and competing national identities within the UK (English, Scottish, Welsh and Northern Irish) highlights the complexities underpinning the relationship between sport and national identity politics within Europe, and within the UK specifically. Here we have four 'national' identities within one nation-state. Whilst sport has the potential to overcome national divisions between European nations, those political divisions are continually reinforced through sporting competition, as has often been the case between England and Scotland national football teams for example (Whigham and Gibbons 2018). Whilst EURO 2020 represents an attempt to unite the nations of Europe, ironically it could be regarded as reinforcing their division both within Europe and the UK. The supranational layer of identity has not (yet) engendered the emotional habitus of citizens within European nations meaning that competitions like the EUROS act to highlight and even reinforce the kind of drag-effect that Elias (1991: 222-223) contended is symptomatic of the persistence among citizens of contemporary European nation-states;

> the feeling that the fading or disappearance of a … state as an autonomous entity would render meaningless everything which past generations had achieved and suffered in the framework and in the name of this survival unit.

What Elias explains here in relation to the drag-effect has similarities to Anderson's (1991) conception of nations as imagined communities that survive in the minds of the people partly due to having continuity with a nation's past achievements. Sport, like war, as George Orwell famously alluded, helps to maintain this continuity (Maguire, Poulton, and Possamai 1999).

For the English, the fate of the national team or individual athletes who represent Britain or England in international competitions in a variety of sports has been regarded as a major source of national pride. Examples include: cricket (Malcolm 2009; Malcolm and Velija 2017); tennis (Lake 2017); cycling (Griggs et al. 2014; Groves and Griggs 2016; Rees, Kevin, and Gibbons 2017); both rugby codes (Falcous 2017); and of course, football (Bowes 2017; Gibbons and Lusted 2007; Gibbons 2010; 2011; 2014; Gibbons, Dixon, and Braye 2015; 2017; Gibbons, Dixon, and Braye 2015; Griggs and Gibbons 2014; Whigham and Gibbons 2018). Nowadays the St George Cross becomes ubiquitous whenever the English are involved in international sporting competitions. However, if ones looks more closely, this is not the only flag on display when an England team/English athlete competes. Nor is it the only layer of the English national habitus on display.

Research on media representations of English national identity during World Cup coverage (Gibbons 2010; Griggs and Gibbons 2014); observations of fans at subsequent international football tournaments (Gibbons and Lusted 2007; Gibbons 2014); surveys of fans' views (Gibbons 2011) and analysis of discussions between fans (Gibbons 2014; Gibbons, Dixon, and Braye 2015; Gibbons, Dixon, and Braye 2015; Griggs and Gibbons 2014; Whigham and Gibbons 2018), has revealed that multiple layers of English place-based identity have been manifest surrounding the men's England national football team. These layers are: the *specifically English*, the *British*, and the *local/regional* (see Gibbons 2014 for a detailed explanation of each layer). Whilst the complexity of the identities that exist within the UK was not a topic Elias himself wrote about in any detail (Fletcher 1997), his concept the drag-effect is useful to explain how identities of many different ages and sizes – i.e. for the English: city/town/village, region (e.g. north vs. south), nation (England), state (Britain) and supra-nation (Europe) - conflict with one another and how national identity is challenged by global integrative forces.

Perhaps the clearest example of the conflict between different layers of identity and the drag-effect for the English can be found in the (con)fusion of British with specifically English layers of identity. This has endured for centuries yet it is something the English have only recently been forced to think about. The English character depicted in media coverage of World Cup competitions has often been defined by references to British achievements rather than specifically English ones (Gibbons 2010; Griggs and Gibbons 2014). Whilst the distinctively English national symbol of St George continues to be ubiquitous when the national team play, English fans have always been reminded of aspects of British history, including: the singing of the British national anthem 'God, Save the Queen' prior to each England match; the strong presence of the British union flag (Union Jack), particularly prior to the 1990s; the winning of the two world wars; and, the once globally dominant (now former) British Empire. Press reports regarding the presence of British figureheads such as members of the British Royal family at England matches has also been used by certain sections of the media to remind English readers of their strong attachment to all things British.

Similarly, the behaviour of English fans surrounding the national team has also been based on British attachments rather specifically English ones. For example, the song *Ten German Bombers* has often been sung when the England team have played Germany. Its lyrics, according to the version in Locken's (2009, 14-15, emphasis added) *The Best England Football Chants Ever*, specifically state: "There were ten German bombers in the sky…" ending with "The RAF from *England* had shot them all down!" Parsons (2005), writing in the British daily national newspaper *The Mirror*, argued that a "residual resentment of Germany remains in our national consciousness" and that the *British* cannot forget the war because "it is just too soon". This evidence echoes Elias's (1991; 1996; 2000) argument that the identities of individuals living in European nation states is rooted in their national pasts, despite political attempts to integrate all Europeans (Chryssochoou 2001; Guibernau 2011; Roche 2010).

Conclusions

Elias (1991) argued that there has been a very-long unplanned trend-line in the development of human society towards integration into larger and more diverse networks of interdependent people organised into more and more interlocking layers. This is clearly observable in the long-term unplanned movements in the size and complexity of figurations into which human beings have been socialised throughout history. Whilst Elias (2000) has previously been criticised for showing a preference for civilizing processes (van Krieken 1998), in seeking to highlight the importance of Elias's simultaneous recognition of decivilising processes, Mennell (1990) gave a number of examples of de-civilised spurts throughout history. Among other aspects, decivilising processes are "marked by … shorter chains of social interdependence" according to Mennell (1990, 205). Elias's (1991) concept of the drag-effect is a particularly good example of the possibilities for reversals in the direction of the civilising process—a process that is still widely misunderstood by many sociologists both within and outside the study of national identity and sport, who suggest it simply follows a linear incremental trajectory. On initial inspection, the persistence of the national we-image in the face of a more European we-image (the drag-effect) appears to be moving in the opposite direction to the civilizing process Elias (2000) theorised. However, essentially the civilizing process entails a necessary transitional phase involving conflict between three interrelated layers of identity distinguished by their different vintages – *the nation, the state and the supranational.*

At the time Elias (1991) was writing in the mid-late twentieth-century, the European community consisted of only twelve member states (Chryssochoou 2001). The European Union (EU) currently consists of twenty-seven member states and this is clear evidence that centripetal forces are still advancing, and 'Europe' is expanding, at least on the 'political' level, but importantly, perhaps not so much at the 'emotional' level (Guibernau 2011; Roche 2010), and this helps explain why the majority of citizens within the UK voted to leave the EU in 2016. Elias (1991) succinctly explained how individuals living in nation-states within Western Europe at the latter end of the twentieth century were in a 'double-bind'. Whilst they were being moved towards increasing assimilation into a 'united' Europe politically via virtue of various agreements between the ruling elites of leading Western European nations, at the same time the personality habitus or 'we-image' of individual European citizens was still firmly rooted in their national contexts. Hobsbawm's (1983) idea of how 'invented traditions' such as flags and anthems were created by ruling elites to instil emotional attachments to nations; Anderson's (1991) understanding of how nations became 'imagined communities' in the minds of individuals; and, Billig's (1995) notion of how the national ideology is maintained on an 'everyday' basis via 'banal nationalism', all highlighted the significance of the nation to citizens living in many nation-states in late twentieth-century Europe. In the twenty-first century sport still holds the emotional attachment of European citizens to their nation rather than to the larger supranational unit of Europe.

Despite the strength of the national layer of habitus, Elias (1991) suggested that the European political unit had already taken over from the nation-state as the principal survival unit for Western Europeans in the late twentieth century and that this was evidence that Western European society as a whole was undergoing a civilizing spurt. Yet, as always with the civilizing process, Elias was careful to note that it is *not* simply a uni-linear process. Elias recognised that Western European nations were in a transitional phase as the habitus of the vast majority of European citizens, aside from some elites, was still clearly dragging along the baggage of 'nationalism'. This drag-effect was therefore emotionally holding European citizens back from further integration into a united Europe which has thus far failed to instil anything like as deep a 'we' feeling as has 'nationalism' (Elias 1991; 1996).

Although he fails to mention the work of Elias (1991), Guibernau (2011, 303), argued that the EU had still, at the beginning of the second decade of the twenty-first century, only succeeded in generating a 'non-emotional identity' amongst the vast majority of European citizens largely because it has thus far been "a top-down project designed and carried out by selected intellectuals and political leaders after 1945." Guibernau (2011, 311) states that "Europe shares a history of internal confrontation and war that is more conducive to enmity and distrust than to collaboration", a point which Elias (1991; 1996; 2000) often made when explaining how the European civilizing process did not always follow a linear trajectory and necessarily involved various de-civilizing spurts. Even though he was writing towards the end of the twentieth century, Elias's (1991) drag-effect can be used to help explain the late twentieth/early twenty-first century rise or resurgence in a national consciousness amongst citizens within European nations. The latter is something which a number of scholars have recently highlighted (see for example Crescenzi, Fratesi, and Monastiriotis 2020; Dijkstra, Poelman, and Rodriguez-Pose 2020), though none have made use of Elias's theoretical contributions to explain why this may be happening.

Elias (1986, 19) recognised the value of studying sport to help understand wider social processes in detail, stating that "knowledge about sport was knowledge about society." Elias (1986, 26) noticed that there are "specialists in the study of sport, specialists in the study of society ... each group working as it were in its own ivory tower", and he sought to stimulate further sociological studies using sport as a lens through which to make particular aspects of societies more transparent. For these reasons, future researchers are encouraged to make greater use of Elias's drag effect for studying the complex relationships between other national identities and sports.

Disclosure statement

No potential conflict of interest was provided by the author(s).

References

Anderson, Benedict. 1991. *Imagined Communities: Reflections on the Origins and Spread of Nationalism*. London: Verso.

Billig, Michael. 1995. *Banal Nationalism*. London: Sage.

Bourdieu, Pierre. 1977. *Outline of a Theory of Practice (Originally Published in French 1972, Trans. Richard Nice)*. Cambridge: Cambridge University Press.

Bowes, Ali. 2017. "England's Lionesses: English Women and Sport." In *Sport and English National Identity in a 'Disunited Kingdom*, edited by Tom Gibbons and Dominic Malcolm, 110–124. London: Routledge.

Chryssochoou, D. N. 2001. *Theorizing European Integration*. London: Sage.

Crescenzi, Riccardo, Ugo Fratesi, and Vassilis Monastiriotis. 2020. "Back to the Member States? Cohesion Policy and the National Challenges to the European Union."*Regional Studies* 54 (1): 5–9. doi:10.1080/00343404.2019.1662895.

Delanty, Gerard, and Patrick, O'Mahony. 2002. *Nationalism and Social Theory*. London: Sage.

Dijkstra, Lewis, Hugo Poelman, and Andrés Rodriguez-Pose. 2020. "The Geography of EU Discontent." *Regional Studies.*" *Regional Studies* 54 (6): 737–753. doi:10.1080/00343404.2019.1654603.

Elias, Norbert. 1986. "Introduction." In *Quest for Excitement: Sport and Leisure in the Civilising Process*, edited by Norbert Elias and Eric Dunning, 19–62. Oxford: Basil Blackwell.

Elias, Norbert. 1978. *What is Sociology?* London: Hutchinson.

Elias, Norbert. 1991. *The Society of Individuals*. Oxford: Basil Blackwell.

Elias, Norbert. 1996. *The Germans*. Cambridge: Polity Press.

Elias, Norbert. 2000. *The Civilizing Process* (Revised Edition). Oxford: Basil Blackwell.

Elias, Norbert, and L. Scotson John. 1994. *The Established and the Outsiders: A Sociological Inquiry into Community Problems*. London: Frank Cass.

Falcous, Mark. 2017. "Rugby League and the Negotiation of Englishness." In *Sport and English National Identity in a 'Disunited Kingdom*, edited by Tom Gibbons and Dominic Malcolm, 79–92. London: Routledge.

Fletcher, Jonathan. 1997. *Violence & Civilization: An Introduction to the Work of Norbert Elias*. Cambridge: Polity Press.

Geertz, Clifford. 1994. "Primordial and Civic Ties." In *Nationalism*, edited by John Hutchinson and Anthony D. Smith, 29–34. Oxford: Oxford University Press.

Gellner, Ernest. 1964. *Thought and Change*. London: Weidenfeld and Nicholson.

Gellner, Ernest. 1983. *Nations and Nationalism*. Oxford: Blackwell.

Gibbons, Tom. 2017. "Is St George Enough? The Relationship between English National Identity and Football." In *Sport and English National Identity in a 'Disunited Kingdom*, edited by Tom Gibbons and Dominic Malcolm, 34–48. London: Routledge.

Gibbons, Tom, Kevin, Dixon, and Stuart, Braye. 2015. "The GB Football Team for London 2012: What's All the Fuss about?." In *The Impact of the London 2012 Olympic & Paralympic Games: Diminishing Contrasts, Increasing Varieties*, edited by Kevin Dixon and Tom Gibbons, 35–55. Hampshire: Palgrave Macmillan.

Gibbons, Tom. 2010. "Contrasting Representations of Englishness during FIFA World Cup Finals." *Sport in History* 30 (3): 422–446. doi:10.1080/17460263.2010.505408.

Gibbons, Tom. 2011. "English National Identity and the National Football Team: The View of Contemporary English Fans." *Soccer & Society* 12 (6): 865–879. doi:10.1080/14660970.2011.609685.

Gibbons, Tom. 2014. *English National Identity and Football Fan Culture: Who Are ya?* London: Routledge.

Gibbons, Tom. 2015. "Fan Debates on English National Identity Surrounding the Almunia Case." *Soccer & Society (Society)* 16 (2-3): 344–359. doi:10.1080/14660970.2014.961386.

Gibbons, Tom, and Jim Lusted. 2007. "Is St George Enough? Considering the Importance of Displaying Local Identity While Supporting the England National Soccer Team." *Annals of Leisure Research* 10 (3-4): 291–309. doi:10.1080/11745398.2007.9686768.

Griggs, Gerald, and Tom Gibbons. 2014. "Harry Walks, Fabio Runs': A Case Study on the Current Relationship between English National Identity, Soccer and the English Press." *International Review for the Sociology of Sport* 49 (5): 536–549. doi:10.1177/1012690212463917.

Griggs, Gerald, Tom Gibbons, Anthony Rees, and Mark Groves. 2014. "Allez Wiggo': A Case Study on the Reactions of the British Print Media to Bradley Wiggins's Victory in the Tour de France." *International Journal of Sport Communication* 7 (1): 113–125. doi:10.1123/IJSC.2013-0040.

Groves, Mark, and Gerald Griggs. 2016. "Riding in the Shadows: The Reaction of the British Print Media to Chris Froome's Victory in the 2013 Tour de France." *International Review for the Sociology of Sport* 51 (4): 428–445. doi:10.1177/1012690214534848.

Guibernau, Montserrat. 2011. "The Birth of a United Europe: On Why the EU Has Generated a 'Non-Emotional' Identity." *Nations and Nationalism* 17 (2): 302–315. doi:10.1111/j.1469-8129.2010.00477.x.

Hobsbawm, Eric. 1983. "Introduction: Inventing Traditions." In *The Invention of Tradition*, edited by Eric Hobsbawm and Terrence Ranger. Cambridge: Cambridge University Press.

Hobsbawm, Eric. 1990. *Nations and Nationalism since 1780*. Cambridge: Cambridge University Press.

James, Paul. 2006. "Theorizing Nation Formation in the Context of Imperialism and Globalism." In *The SAGE Handbook of Nations and Nationalism*, edited by Gerard Delanty and Krishan Kumar, 369–381. London: Sage.

Kedourie, Ellie. 1960. *Nationalism*. London: Hutchinson.

Krieken, Robert van. 1998. *Norbert Elias*. London: Routledge.

Lake, Robert J. 2017. "Tennis in an English Garden Party': Wimbledon, Englishness and British Sporting Culture." In *Sport and English National Identity in a 'Disunited Kingdom*, edited by Tom Gibbons and Dominic Malcolm, 49–64. London: Routledge.

Liston, Katie, and Matthew Deighan. 2019. "Whose 'Wee Country'?: Identity Politics and Sport in Northern Ireland." *Identities* 26 (2): 203–221. doi:10.1080/1070289X.2017.1392103.

Liston, Katie, and Niamh Kitching. 2020. "Our Wee Country': national Identity, Golf and 'Ireland." *Sport in Society* 23 (5): 864–879. doi:10.1080/17430437.2019.1584186.

Liston, Katie, and Joseph Maguire. 2020. "Making Sense of 'Ireland', Sport and Identity: The Craft of Doing Sociology." *Sport in Society* 23 (10): 1587–1605. doi:10.1080/17430437.2020.1814572.

Locken, Eric. 2009. *The Best England Football Chants Ever*. Interviewbooks.com.

Maguire, Joseph, and Emma Poulton. 1999. "European Identity Politics in Euro 96: Invented Traditions and National Habitus Codes." *International Review for the Sociology of Sport* 34 (1): 17–29. doi:10.1177/101269099034001002.

Maguire, Joseph, Emma Poulton, and Catherine Possamai. 1999. "Weltkrieg III?: Media Coverage of England versus Germany in Euro 96." *Journal of Sport and Social Issues* 23 (4): 439–454. doi:10.1177/0193723599234006.

Malcolm, Dominic. 2009. "Malign or Benign? English National Identities and Cricket." *Sport in Society* 12 (4-5): 613–628. doi:10.1080/17430430802702897.

Malcolm, Dominic, and Philippa Velija. 2017. "Cricket: The Quintessential English Game?." In *Sport and English National Identity in a 'Disunited Kingdom*, edited by Tom Gibbons and Dominic Malcolm, 19–33. London: Routledge.

Marx, Karl, and Frederick Engels. 1967. *The Communist Manifesto* (with an introduction and notes by A.J.P Taylor). London: Penguin.

Mennell, Stephen. 1990. "Decivilising Processes: Theoretical Significance and Some Lines of Research." *International Sociology* 5 (2): 205–223. doi:10.1177/026858090005002006.

Mennell, Stephen. 1994. "The Formation of We-Images: A Process Theory." In *Social Theory and the Politics of Identity*, edited by Craig Calhoun, 175–197. Oxford: Blackwell.

Murphy, Patrick, Ken Sheard, and Ivan Waddington. 2000. "Figurational Sociology and Its Application to Sport." In *Handbook of Sports Studies*, edited by Jay Coakley and Eric Dunning, 92–105. London: Sage.

O'Rourke, K. 2019. *A Short History of Brexit: From Brentry to Backstop*. London: Penguin

Parsons, Tony. 2005. "Forget the war? It's far too soon." *The Mirror*, December 12. http://www.mirror.co.uk/news/columnists/parsons/2005/12/12/forget-the-war-it-s-far-too-soon-115875-16474483/

Rees, Anthony, Dixon Kevin, and Tom Gibbons. 2017. "We Are Just Going to Draw the Raffle Numbers': The English History of the Cycling Time-Trial." In *Sport and English National Identity in a 'Disunited Kingdom*, edited by Tom Gibbons and Dominic Malcolm, 65–78. London: Routledge.

Roche, Maurice. 2010. *Exploring the Sociology of Europe*. London: Sage.

Smith, A. D. 1998. *Nationalism and Modernism: A Critical Survey of Recent Theories of Nations and Nationalism*. London: Routledge.

Smith, Anthony D. 1996. *Nations and Nationalism in a Global Era*. Cambridge: Polity Press.

Smith, Anthony D. 2010. *Nationalism: Theory, Ideology, History* (Second Edition). Cambridge: Polity Press.

Smith, Dennis. 2001. *Norbert Elias and Modern Social Theory*. London: Sage.

Whigham, Stuart, and Tom Gibbons. 2018. "The Auld Enemy'? Exploring the England vs. Scotland Rivalry from the Perspective of Soccer Fans." *Soccer & Society* (Special Issue 'Face to Face." *Soccer & Society* 19 (5-6): 673–686. doi:10.1080/14660970.2017.1399617.

Wishart, Ruth. 2019. "A second referendum on Scottish independence is suddenly very likely." *The Guardian*, October 18. https://www.theguardian.com/commentisfree/2019/oct/18/second-referendum-scottish-independence-brexit-scots

Ziegler, Martyn. 2012. "No Scottish or Northern Ireland players as Team GB football squad is announced for the Olympics." *The Independent*, July 2. https://www.independent.co.uk/sport/olympics/no-scottish-or-northern-ireland-players-as-team-gb-football-squad-is-announced-for-the-olympics-7904093.html 𝗱 OPEN ACCESS

'I am German when we win, but I am an immigrant when we lose'. Theorising on the deservedness of migrants in international football, using the case of Mesut Özil

Gijs van Campenhout (iD) and Henk van Houtum (iD)

ABSTRACT

'I am German when we win, but I am an immigrant when we lose'. With this powerful statement Mesut Özil resigned from Germany's national football team. His resignation act not only highlights growing controversies and uneasiness around the representation of the football nation by players with migration backgrounds, but also marks the fragility of national belonging. In this article, we deconstruct in detail Özil's powerful resignation elaborating upon Norbert Elias and John Scotson's (1994 (1965)) 'established–outsider model'. With this, we will analyse the power dynamics underlying the processes of national belonging. Moreover, we extend the established-outsider approach by using the fluid and contextual borders between *formal* and *moral* deservedness of citizenship. In our conclusion, we revisit Özil's statement and recapitulate our theoretical explanations on the sensitivities of this case as well on how to navigate a way out of the contested competition between nationalities in the context of international football.

'I have two hearts, one German and one Turkish'

For years, the talented Arsenal-midfielder Mesut Özil was one of the key players in the German national football team. Özil, born, raised, and schooled in the German city of Gelsenkirchen as a third-generation Turkish immigrant,[1] is a practicing Muslim who recites from the Quran when he enters the field (Merkel 2014) and who considers himself to be a blend of both of his cultures; 'Whilst I grew up in Germany, my family background has its roots firmly based in Turkey. I have two hearts, one German and one Turkish' (Özil 2018). Because Özil is a German-born of Turkish descent, he was eligible to play for both national football teams. After long considerations with his family, being torn back and forth between the two countries, he finally decided to play for Germany (Özil 2017). What is more, to make this possible, he had to legally renounce his Turkish passport, which, arguably, can be considered as an ultimate act of formally distancing himself from Turkey and, simultaneously, expressing his formal - and arguably moral - belonging to the state of Germany.

This is an Open Access article distributed under the terms of the Creative Commons Attribution-NonCommercial-NoDerivatives License (http://creativecommons.org/licenses/by-nc-nd/4.0/), which permits non-commercial re-use, distribution, and reproduction in any medium, provided the original work is properly cited, and is not altered, transformed, or built upon in any way.

Soon after, probably also because of the high societal status of the German national football team, Özil was regarded as one of Germany's 'model minorities' (Kalman-Lamb 2013). To illustrate, he won a so-called Bambi Award[2] in the category 'Integration' in 2010 (Martin 2010; Özil 2017; 2018), and was publicly voted *German* footballer of the year five times between 2011 and 2016 (Freemantle 2018).

Yet, the take on Mesut Özil radically changed from a 'German Bambi' to an imagined 'Turkish grey wolf' when he, together with his German-Turkish teammate Ilkay Gündogan, posed with Turkey's president Recep Tayyip Erdoğan in front of the media a month before the start of the 2018 football World Cup (Freemantle 2018; Hirsch 2018). Suddenly, Özil's 'Germanness' became topic of big national dispute. Where many Germans saw in Özil's action 'support for an increasingly autocratic ruler' (Freemantle 2018), for Özil it was a matter of paying respect to highest office of his family's country (Özil 2018). Things, however, really came to a head after Germany's early knock-out in the group stage of the 2018 football World Cup when, especially, Özil, one of the stars of the team, became the convenient scapegoat for the disappointing results of the entire 'Mannschaft' (Hirsch 2018; Özil 2018). While football connoisseurs seemed to comment on Özil's football performances only, the criticisms in the public debate went beyond this and were also directed at his cultural allegiance with Turkey and the Turkish nation. As a consequence of all the controversies around him, Özil resigned from the German national football team on July 22, 2018 by placing a three-parted statement, in English, on his Instagram and Twitter profiles (figure 1). In this statement, Özil marked out the precariousness of national belonging by claiming 'I am German when we win, but I am an immigrant when we lose' (Özil 2018).[3]

Özil's statement for us is a most interesting case to question not only who belongs to which (football) nation, but also who deserves to represent the football nation. 'With deserve we not necessarily point to football qualities per se. For in many ways, this deserving question seems a no-brainer for the average football fan, as we are, as the answer would be the best players of the nation, obviously. To answer that question, it is of importance to verify which players are considered the best in terms of football capabilities, which is and will obviously be a big topic of debate, and it requires verifying which football players are (*formally*) eligible to play for which national football team. But, as Özil's example clarifies, this is not where it stops. The question of deserving also seems to be a *moral* issue. Players with dual citizenship or footballers with migration backgrounds, seem to carry the extra burden of having to prove to unquestionably belong to the nation, to be the model-citizen, at the risk of being seen as untrustworthy or even a traitor if not.

Using Özil's case as an example throughout this paper, we aim to understand who, under what conditions, are accepted as representatives of the football nation and are recognised as (*conditionally* and *temporally*) belonging to the nation. To this end, in the first part of the paper, we sketch the regulations and its implications of national representation in international football, and how this complicates the debates on national belonging of players with migration backgrounds. In the second part, as a prelude to discussing *moral* belonging to the (football) nation, we will introduce and critically engage with Elias and Scotson's (1994 (1965)) established–outsider model, to shed light on the power dynamics between the established and outsiders in the representation of the football nation. In the third part of the paper, we will extend this establish-outsider framework to discuss the dynamic *moral* negotiations around the acceptance and recognition of players with migration backgrounds. We will end by going back to the main character of our plot, Mesut Özil, and reflect upon, with the theoretical insights gained, how this painful rupture, in which there seem to be no winners, only losers, could have happened, and maybe could be prevented in the future.

'Who did I want to play for if the possibility ever came about?'

It has been argued in the literature that one of the reasons why the issue of national belonging in international football 'is so sensitive is because international sporting competitions, such as the Olympic Games and the football World Cup, have become a 'magnifying lens through which critical elaborations of the idea of the nation come to the fore' (Mauro 2020, 5). The competition between nations, including the coinciding performativity of cheering for 'your' nation, with all its theatrical elements of a stadium, flag-waving, winners and losers, (*temporally*) provides 'a uniquely effective medium for inculcating national feelings' (Hobsbawm 1992, 143) and for one's patriotic place attachment, one's topophilia (Van Houtum and Van

I / III MEETING PRESIDENT ERDOGAN

The past couple of weeks have given me time to reflect, and time to think over the events of the last few months. Consequently, I want to share my thoughts and feelings about what has happened.

Like many people, my ancestry traces back to more than one country. Whilst I grew up in Germany, my family background has its roots firmly based in Turkey. I have two hearts, one German and one Turkish. During my childhood, my mother taught me to always be respectful and to never forget where I came from, and these are still values that I think about to this day.

In May, I met President Erdogan in London, during a charitable and educational event. We first met in 2010 after he and Angela Merkel watched the Germany vs. Turkey match together in Berlin. Since then, our paths have crossed a lot of times around the globe. I'm aware that the picture of us caused a huge response in the German media, and whilst some people may accuse me of lying or being deceitful, the picture we took had no political intentions. As I said, my mother has never let me lose sight of my ancestry, heritage and family traditions. For me, having a picture with President Erdogan wasn't about politics or elections, it was about me respecting the highest office of my family's country. My job is a football player and not a politician, and our meeting was not an endorsement of any policies. In fact, we spoke about the same topic that we do every time we have met - football - as he too was a player in his youth.

Although the German media have portrayed something different, the truth is that not meeting with the President would have been disrespecting the roots of my ancestors, who I know would be proud of where I am today. For me, it didn't matter who was President, it mattered that it was the President. Having respect for political office is a view that I'm sure both the Queen and Prime Minister Theresa May share when they too hosted Erdogan in London. Whether it had been the Turkish or the German President, my actions would've been no different.

I get that this may be hard to understand, as in most cultures the political leader cannot be thought of as being separate from the person. But in this case, it is different. Whatever the outcome would've been in this previous election, or the election before that, I would have still taken the picture.

Figure 1. Mesut Özil's statement on his resignation from Germany's national football team (Özil 2018).

II / III MEDIA & SPONSORS

I know that I am a footballer who has played in arguably the three toughest leagues in the world. I've been fortunate to receive great support from my teammates and coaching staff whilst playing in the Bundesliga, La Liga and the Premier League. And in addition, throughout my career, I've learnt to deal with the media.

A lot of people talk about my performances - many applaud and many criticise. If a newspaper or pundit finds fault in a game I play in, then I can accept this - I'm not a perfect footballer and this often motivates me to work and train harder. But what I can't accept, are German media outlets repeatedly blaming my dual-heritage and a simple picture for a bad World Cup on behalf of an entire squad.

Certain German newspapers are using my background and photo with President Erdogan as right-wing propaganda to further their political cause. Why else did they use pictures and headlines with my name as a direct explanation for defeat in Russia? They didn't criticise my performances, they didn't criticise the team's performances, they just criticised my Turkish ancestry and respect for my upbringing. This crosses a personal line that should never be crossed, as newspapers try to turn the nation of Germany against me.

What I also find disappointing are the double standards that the media has. Lothar Matthaus (an honorary German national team captain) met with another world leader a few days back, and received almost no media criticism. Despite his role with the DFB (German national team), they have not asked him to publicly explain his actions and he continues to represent the players of Germany without any reprimand. If the media felt that I should have been left of the World Cup squad, then surely he should be stripped of his honorary captaincy? Does my Turkish heritage make me a more worthy target?

I've always thought that a 'partnership' infers support, both in the good times and also during tougher situations. Recently, I planned to visit my former school Berger-Feld in Gelsenkirchen, Germany, along with two of my charitable partners. I funded a project for one year where immigrant children, children from poor families and any other children can play football together and learn social rules for life. However, days before we were scheduled to go, I was abandoned by my so-called 'partners', who no longer wanted to work with me at this time. To add to this, the school told my management that they no longer wanted me to be there at this time, as they "feared the media" due to my picture with President Erdogan, especially with the "right-wing party in Gelsenkirchen on the rise". In all honesty, this really hurt. Despite being a student of theirs back when I was younger, I was made to feel unwanted and unworthy of their time.

In addition to this, I was renounced by another partner. As they are also a sponsor of the DFB, I was asked to take part in promotional videos for the World Cup. Yet after my picture with President Erdogan, they took me out of the campaigns and cancelled all promotional activities that were scheduled. For them, it was no longer good to be seen with me and called the situation 'crisis management'. This is all ironic because a German Ministry declared their products have illegal and unauthorized software devices in them, which puts customers at risk. Hundreds of thousands of their products are getting recalled. Whilst I was being criticised and asked to justify my actions by the DFB, there was no such official and public explanation demanded of the DFB sponsor. Why? Am I right in thinking this is worse than a picture with the President of my family's country? What does the DFB have to say about all this?

As I said before, 'partners' should stick with you in all situations. Adidas, Beats and BigShoe have been extremely loyal and amazing to work with in this time. They rise above the nonsense created by the German press and media, and we carry out our projects in a professional manner that I really enjoy being part of. During the World Cup, I worked with BigShoe and helped get 23 young children life-changing surgeries in Russia, which I have also done previously in Brazil and Africa. This for me is the most important thing that I do as a football player, yet the newspapers find no space to raise awareness about this sort of thing. For them, me being booed or taking a picture with a President is more significant then helping children get surgeries worldwide. They too have a platform to raise awareness and funds, but choose not to do so.

Figure 1. Continued

III / III DFB

Arguably the issue that has frustrated me the most over the past couple of months has been the mistreatment from the DFB, and in particular the DFB President Reinhard Grindel. After my picture with President Erdogan I was asked by Joachim Low to cut short my holiday and go to Berlin and give a joint statement to end all the talk and set the record straight. Whilst I attempted to explain to Grindel my heritage, ancestry and therefore reasoning behind the photo, he was far more interested in speaking about his own political views and belittling my opinion. Whilst his actions were patronising, we came to agree that the best thing to do was to concentrate on football and the upcoming World Cup. This is why I did not attend the DFB media day during the World Cup preparations. I knew journalists discussing politics and not football would just attack me, even though the whole issue was deemed to be over by Oliver Bierhoff in a TV interview he did before the Saudi Arabia game in Leverkusen.

During this time, I also met with the President of Germany, Frank-Walter Steinmeier. Unlike Grindel, President Steinmeier was professional and actually was interested in what I had to say about my family, my heritage and my decisions. I remember that the meeting was only between myself, Ilkay and President Steinmeier, with Grindel being upset that he wasn't allowed inside to boost his own political agenda. I agreed with President Steinmeier that we would release a joint statement about the matter, in another attempt to move forward and focus on football. But Grindel was upset that it wasn't his team releasing the first statement, annoyed that Steinmeier's press office had to take lead on this matter.

Since the end of the World Cup, Grindel has come under much pressure regarding his decisions before the tournament started, and rightly so. Recently, he has publicly said I should once again explain my actions and puts me at fault for the poor team results in Russia, despite telling me it was over in Berlin. **I am speaking now not for Grindel, but because I want to.** I will no longer stand for being a scapegoat for his incompetence and inability to do his job properly. I know that he wanted me out the team after the picture, and publicised his view on Twitter without any thinking or consultation, but Joachim Low and Oliver Bierhoff stood up for me and backed me. In the eyes of Grindel and his supporters, I am German when we win, but I am an immigrant when we lose. This is because despite paying taxes in Germany, donating facilities to German schools and winning the World Cup with Germany in 2014, I am still not accepted into society. I am treated as being 'different'. I received the 'Bambi Award' in 2010 as an example of successful integration to German society, I received a 'Silver Laurel Leaf' in 2014 from the Federal Republic of Germany, and I was a 'German Football Ambassador' in 2015. But clearly, I am not German…? Are there criteria for being fully German that I do not fit? My friend Lukas Podolski and Miroslav Klose are never referred to as German-Polish, so why am I German-Turkish? Is it because it is Turkey? Is it because I'm a Muslim? I think here lays an important issue. By being referred to as German-Turkish, it is already distinguishing people who have family from more than one country. I was born and educated in Germany, so why don't people accept that I am German?

page 1

Figure 1. Continued

Page 2

Grindel's opinions can be found elsewhere too. I was called by **Bernd Holzhauer (a German politician)** a "goat-f*ker" because of my picture with President Erdogan and my Turkish background. Furthermore, Werner Steer (Chief of German Theatre) told me to "piss off to Anatolia", a place in Turkey where many immigrants are based. As I have said before, criticising and abusing me because of family ancestry is a disgraceful line to cross, and using discrimination as a tool for political propaganda is something that should immediately result in the resignation of those disrespectful individuals. These people have used my picture with President Erdogan as an opportunity to express their previously hidden racist tendencies, and this is dangerous for society. They are no better than the German fan who told me after the game against Sweden "Ozil, verpiss Dich Du scheiss Türkensau. Türkenschwein hau ab", or in English "Ozil, fk off you Turkish s*t, piss of you Turkish pig". I don't want to even discuss the hate mail, threatening phone calls and comments on social media that my family and I have received. They all represent a Germany of the past, a Germany not open to new cultures, and a Germany that I am not proud of. I am confident that many proud Germans who embrace an open society would agree with me.

To you, Reinhard Grindel, I am disappointed but not surprised by your actions. In 2004 whilst you were a German member of Parliament, you claimed that "multiculturalism is in reality a myth [and] a lifelong lie" whilst you voted against legislation for dual-nationalities and punishments for bribery, as well as saying that Islamic culture has become too ingrained in many German cities. This is unforgivable and unforgettable.

The treatment I have received from the DFB and many others makes me no longer want to wear the German national team shirt. I feel unwanted and think that what I have achieved since my international debut in 2009 has been forgotten. People with racially discriminative backgrounds should not be allowed to work in the largest football federation in the world that has many players from dual-heritage families. Attitudes like theirs simply do not reflect the players they supposedly represent.

It is with a heavy heart and after much consideration that because of recent events, I will no longer be playing for Germany at international level whilst I have this feeling of racism and disrespect. I used to wear the German shirt with such pride and excitement, but now I don't. This decision has been extremely difficult to make because I have always given everything for my teammates, the coaching staff and the good people of Germany. But when high-ranking DFB officials treat me as they did, disrespect my Turkish roots and selfishly turn me into political propaganda, then enough is enough. That is not why I play football, and I will not sit back and do nothing about it. Racism should never, ever be accepted.

Mesut Özil

Figure 1. Continued

Dam 2002). As Alan Bairner (2001, 17) argues: 'It [international sports] provides a form of symbolic action which states the case for the nation itself'. Moreover, it emphasises the enduring relevance of Eric Hobsbawm's (1992, 143) observations that 'sportsmen [sic] representing their nation or state' in international sporting competitions are 'primary expressions of their imagined communities', and that 'the imagined community of millions seems more real as a team of eleven named people'. The national make-believe show that a football competition between nations allows for, is a seductive phantasy-reality that comfortably borders and orders the at times chaotic world, even if it is only temporal, and creates an amusing and carnavelesque feeling of seemingly innocent togetherness (Van Houtum 2010; Van Houtum and Van Naerssen 2002). It makes the imagined community (Anderson 1983), the 'we' of the nation feel 'real' (Hobsbawm 1992), at least for some time, provided of course that the national football team performs well, as the ecstasy of national togetherness works best on success (Van Houtum 2010).

But who is included in this 'we'? Who or what defines the *formal* borders of the football nation? It seems that within the nationalistic context of international football these borders are of an inflexible, dichotomic nature. Fluidity in terms of multiple nationality does not seem to exist. It really is either-or: 'one can either be Dutch or Surinamese, or French or Moroccan, but not both' (Lanfranchi and Taylor 2001, 10). The regulations of the, the regulations of the Fédération Internationale de Football Association (FIFA) around the eligibility of players to play for representative teams forces footballers with dual nationality to *choose* a national football team (Iorwerth, Hardman, and Jones 2014; Seiberth, Thiel, and Spaaij 2019). Having dual nationality, also Özil (2017, 42) had to address this issue and struggled with making his decision: 'Who did I want to play for if the possibility ever came about? For the German national side or the Turkish one? It wasn't a decision I made in a couple of minutes, just in passing'. Deciding on one's sporting nationality is often hard for players with dual nationality as it feels like choosing between 'your' two countries. Moreover, being permanent, it is a decision that fundamentally shapes their whole career in football (Özil 2017, 42), and one that will, regardless of the outcome, upset people. Özil experienced the impact of this *forced* decision first-hand after he chose in favour of Germany and, against his will, 'publicly became a bone of contention between Germany and Turkey' (Özil 2017, 46).

It could be argued that to organise international sports competitions, like the football World Cup, solely around the principles of (legal) nationality, is principally sustaining a rigid 'inter-state world view' (Mauro 2020, 2); something that Wimmer and Schiller (2003, 576) refer to as 'methodological nationalism' and John Agnew (1994) has referred to as' the territorial trap'. FIFA's eligibility regulations are, arguably, not only insensitive to the growth of internationalisation overall but also seem to camouflage that, on average per edition of the football World Cup since 1930, nearly 10% of the players can be counted as 'foreign-born' (Van Campenhout et al. 2018, 1079); meaning that these players compete for another national football team than the one of their country of birth. The 23-headed selection of Morocco's 2018 national football team, for example, existed of 17 foreign-born players (74%), with the majority of these players born in European countries like France and the Netherlands (Van Campenhout and Van Sterkenburg 2019). Further, a review of the 2018 victorious 'French national football team's roster reveals its multiculturality, as 19 out of the 23 players had a 'genuine connection' with a country other than France' (Van Campenhout and Van Sterkenburg 2019, 2); most of them with roots in one of France its former African colonies. In a similar vein, England's prospect players such as Declan Rice (Republic of Ireland), Callum Hudson-Odoi (Ghana), Dele Alli (Nigeria), and James Tarkowski (Poland) all have genuine migration backgrounds and, therefore, could have opted to pledge their sporting allegiance to another country (Ronay 2019). The strategic implication of the increasing numbers of (young) football players with dual nationality is, as can be expected, that national football federations increasingly attempt to select these talented prospects as young as possible and to secure their sporting nationality by letting them play in an A-status match of their national football team (Iorwerth, Hardman, and Jones 2014; Seiberth, Thiel, and Spaaij 2019).

The consequence of this nationalised perspective on international football is that the decision on national deservedness then is not only a sportive one but by and large also a political one. And is made to depend on formal regulations as well as on a range of arbitrary and invisible moral norms and (cultural) markers, which are socially constructed by the established 'insiders', that 'outsiders' have to accumulate (Hage 1998; Jansen 2020, 101; Loyal 2011; Pratsinakis 2018, 6; Monforte, Bassel, and Khan 2019; Skey 2011). To this power struggle in defining insiders from outsiders, we turn now.

'I am still not accepted into society. I am treated as being 'different''

In their canonical work *The Established and the Outsiders*, Elias and Scotson (1994 (1965)) studied the uneven balance of power between dominant ('established') and subordinate ('outsider') group(s) within a community near the English city of Leicester in the 1960s. They found that the power ratio between the established and outsider groups was based on the notable distinction in 'length of residence' in the area; whereby the former were (long-term) residents while the latter were relatively new to the area (Black 2016; Dunning and Hughes 2014; Hughes and Goodwin 2016; Pratsinakis 2018). In addition, Elias and Scotson pointed to the importance of understanding the mutual entanglement processes between natives and newcomers, and argued, drawing on Elias' earlier figurational approach, that human relationships should be seen as interdependent and in a constant state of flux and transformation (Dunning and Hughes 2014; Hughes and Goodwin 2016; Loyal 2011). Borders between people, in other words, as also recent literature in border studies has made clear, are not to be seen as fixed and permanent lines, but as discursive power struggles, with room for interpretation, negotiation and hence also as a window of opportunity (Van Houtum and Van Naerssen 2002; Yuval-Davis, Wemyss, and Cassidy 2019). Borders, Orders and Others should therefore be seen as processes, rather than ends, and hence as verbs rather than nouns: b/order*ing* and other*ing* (Van Houtum and Van Naerssen 2002).

Despite, or maybe even because, of its rather straightforward established-outsiders dichotomy (Bloyce and Murphy 2007), the established-outsider model has proven to be a conductive framework to analyse these processes of 'b/ordering' and 'othering' (Black 2016; Pratsinakis 2018; Van Houtum and Van Naerssen 2002). The established-outsider framework has been used to study a wide range of social phenomena, also within sport studies, to illustrate unequal power balances related to processes of globalisation (Maguire and Falcous 2011), race relations (Black 2016; Van Sterkenburg, Peeters, and Van Amsterdam 2019), gender inequalities (Liston 2005; Black and Fielding-Lloyd 2019), and (national) identities (Engh, Agergaard, and Maguire 2013; Jansen 2020).

A key element in the model is the explanation of processes of domination and discrimination, that together continuously (re)construct the differential in the power ratio between groups (Loyal 2011, 188). The most powerful groups are able to (re)construct 'understandings of self that posit them as having superior human value' and in doing so (implicitly) define the characteristics to those of the outsider groups (Engh, Agergaard, and Maguire 2013, 783). The dominant position is mainly upheld by the established group's social cohesion and is displayed through subtle or not so subtle acts of exclusion – in example setting (invisible) norms of standard behaviour (Duemmler 2015) – and forms of shame and stigma – like daily gossip and (public) humiliation – directed at various outsider groups. Often, such acts of 'othering' can be seen as a response by people belonging to the dominant group to subjective feelings of threat from (national) outsiders (Pratsinakis 2018; Skey 2010, 2011). It is through these everyday 'b/ordering and ordering' practices that the dominant group (re)constructs the (cultural) boundaries of belonging.

Still, in today's world, the determination of who is 'we' and who are 'they' and who are 'in' and 'out' is dominantly bordered along national lines (Yuval-Davis 2011; Yuval-Davis, Wemyss, and Cassidy 2019). It is not that (national) identities can (still, if it ever could) only or foremost be grounded on a supposedly naturally existing world of mutually exclusive nation-states (Skey 2010, 2011; Wimmer and Schiller 2003), but what matters here is that these national identities are still imagined to dominantly define the conditions of belonging (Skey 2010): they are imagined and therefore real communities (Anderson 1983). As Benedict Anderson (1983, 6) famously has put it, a nation 'is imagined because the members of even the smallest nation will never know most of their fellow-members, meet them, or even hear of them, yet in the minds of each lives the image of their communion'. The thus socially constructed cultural boundary-makers are prescribed as the national normality, as real and existing model norms and tested among the newcomers (in example through citizenship exams) (Duemmler 2015; Skey 2010). The newcomers, such as foreign-born footballers, in their turn, precisely because the conditions of national belonging are 'continuously negotiated, since social actors engage in struggles over social categories and distinctions' (Duemmler 2015, 4), may 'negotiate their position by presenting and adapting their behaviour in particular ways in order to gain access to established domains' (Black 2016, 984). Interestingly, as Elias earlier had made clear in his writings (Elias 1978 (1970)), an everyday indication of power struggles on belonging and representation is self-identification. How and when personal pronouns – such as 'I', 'you', 'he', she', 'we' and 'they' – are used, could be giveaways of figurative acts of b/ordering and othering (Van Houtum and Van Naerssen 2002).

In his resignation letter, Özil (2018) implicitly refers to his experiences of the power struggles between (ethnic) groups of people within German society arguing – and also explicitly using personal pronouns to illustrate the power figurations – that 'I am still not accepted into society' and it feels that 'I am treated as being 'different''. Özil wonders whether his family's country (Turkey) or the fact that he is a practising Muslim might be reasons to 'other' him from the German nation. Moreover, Özil (2018) seems to be amazed that his position in German society has changed over time and that he recently has become positioned as an outsider to the German nation by proclaiming: 'I was born and educated in Germany, so why don't people accept that I am German?'

What these statements on national belonging illustrate is the inability of (individual) outsiders – even those who previously had the power to negotiate their position into established domains like Özil – to become or remain accepted and recognised as 'fully' belonging to the nation. Some outsiders might, depending on the *situational conditions*, be accepted as 'established-outsiders', yet in other contexts or for other people, some of their personal characteristics will still mark them as outsiders to the imagined (comm)unity of the nation (Black 2016; Dunning and Hughes 2014; Van Sterkenburg, Peeters, and Van Amsterdam 2019). Or as Michael Skey (2010, 718) has argued, we 'must attend to the different ways in which membership categories are contextually negotiated and transformed over time, [and] we must also acknowledge the degree to which distinctions continue to be drawn between different groups, with some seen to be more national than others'. So, what Özil's case alludes to, is that there seems to be a crucial difference between *formal* and *moral* citizenship that can vary over time as well over different kinds of outsider groups that needs to be studied further (Schinkel 2017), an insight that could further enrich the established-outsider approach. To this, we turn next.

'I had to ask myself what I was, or what I wanted to be, on paper at least'

In a *formal* sense, legal nationality or citizenship can be regarded as a political relationship between an individual and a state in which a 'citizen' has certain duties and obligations to a state and in return enjoys certain rights within the legal borders of that state. In terms of power figurations, it is a state's government that decides on a country's citizenship regimes and therefore holds the power to grant citizenship to individuals (Iorwerth, Hardman, and Jones 2014). '*Formal* citizenship', according to Ghassan Hage (1998, 50), 'can reflect a practical mode of national belonging'. This, however, only occurs 'in the ideal situation where the formal decision to include a person as a citizen reflects a general communal will' (Hage 1998, 50). Besides its *formal* dimension, citizenship suggests that citizens of the same state are members of the aforementioned (imagined), socially constructed, political community: the nation. This idea of an imagined-and-therefore-real nation reflects the *moral* dimension of citizenship which can be considered as a personal and collective form of identification with people who perceive themselves as part of the same group. And imagined communities will often be, then, communities of value in which some members are considered to be of higher value, more deserving its membership than others (Anderson 1983; Schinkel 2017).

In a similar vein, Hage (1998, 51) analytically distinguishes between *institutional-political* national acceptance of belonging, referring to legal membership of a state, and *practical-cultural* national acceptance of belonging relating to derivatives of the nation like (practical) nationality. Where the former refers to the power of the state to legally accept and recognise outsiders as belonging to the state [related to *formal* citizenship], the latter can be understood as – in line with Pierre Bourdieu's notion of 'social and cultural capital'– 'the sum of accumulated nationally sanctified and valued social and physical cultural styles and dispositions (national culture) adopted by individuals and groups, as well as valued characteristics (national types and national character) within a national field: looks, accent, demeanour, taste, nationally valued social and cultural preferences and behaviour, etc.' [related to *moral* citizenship] (Hage 1998, 53).

The idea of *moral* citizenship, that what we bring forward here, is helpful in making clear that '*formal* citizenship alone', to use the words of Joost Jansen (2020, 102), 'is often not a sufficient prerequisite for immigrants, or even the children of immigrants, to be recognised as fully 'integrated' members of the (national) society'. Being born on the nation's territorial soil seems to be an insufficient criterium then for second, third, or even fourth generation immigrants to be accepted as fully belonging to the nation (Jansen 2020). So, while *formal* 'recognition and acknowledgment of one's rights and one's belonging become pivotal for the final grounding of one's belonging' (Kryżanowski and Wodak 2008, 104), '"citizenship" in a highly *moralized* sense has become a marker to identify membership of society' (Schinkel 2017, 197). It also implies, that using the notion of citizenship simply as a synonym or in association with national belonging would thus not do justice to capture this *moral* dimension and the inherent 'subtleties of the *differential modalities of national belonging* as they are experienced within society' (Hage 1998, 51). Both dimensions of national acceptance of belonging, the *formal* and the *moral*, are thus important in understanding power figurations between the established and outsider.

As *formal* German citizenship law did not (yet) allow dual nationality, and Özil stood on the brink of an international football career, 'I [Özil] had to ask myself what I was, or what I wanted to be, on paper at least' (Özil 2017, 42). By giving up his Turkish passport in order to acquire a German one, Özil (2017, 44) *formally* expressed his (national) belonging to the German state and nation and, as a consequence, decided in favour of Germany's national football team. Özil's decision on his *formal* and sporting nationality was, according to himself, 'not an explicit rejection of Turkey. Just because I'd chosen to play for Germany didn't mean that Turkey wasn't close to my heart. I wasn't shutting myself off from Turkey and its people' (Özil 2017, 47). Özil 'changed' his nationality mainly because FIFA's eligibility regulations forced him to make a decision between his two countries (Seiberth, Thiel, and Spaaij 2019): 'I had to make the decision about whether I wanted to play for Germany or Turkey. Logically I had to opt for one or the other; there was no way around it' (Özil 2017, 50). This in itself, should not necessarily be a problem. However, as we have seen, it is precisely the *moral* dimension of national belonging that has become pivotal in the whole discussion on Özil's 'Germanness', and which in the end has caused the rupture between him, as a native German, and his performances for the German national football team.

Özil's case is by no means an exception, but rather the rule. Many football players with migration backgrounds are, or have been, subject to public value judgments regarding their eligibility and loyalty to the (football) nation (Van Sterkenburg, Peeters, and Van Amsterdam 2019). In the eyes of Özil (2018), several German newspapers crossed a personal line ('one that should never be crossed') when 'they didn't critique my performances, they didn't criticise the team's performances, they just criticised my Turkish ancestry and respect for my upbringing'. Further, by repeatedly asking questions directed at specific *practical-cultural* markers of belonging, such as loyalty, pride, and affection, the media – as both part and representatives of the established – try to tacitly 'other' players with migration backgrounds thereby simultaneously 'b/order*ing*' an imaginary of the 'true' nation (Pratsinakis 2018; Skey 2010). As a consequence of these mutual processes of b/ordering and othering, players with migration backgrounds need to constantly prove their allegiance to the nation – something native players never have to – and show that they deserve to become or remain accepted and recognised as part of the nation (Hage 1998; Pratsinakis 2018).

'Are there criteria for being fully German that I do not fit?'

The (increasing) discrepancy between *formal* and *moral* citizenship can be indicative of 'the crucial link between recognition and belonging and the unequal relations of power that exist in the attribution and acceptance of identity claims' (Skey 2010, 718–719). In recent debates, in the processes of marking out 'insiders' from 'outsiders', particular attention is paid 'to the continuing power of gendered, racist and classist categories to define who counts as truly national' (Jansen 2020, 100), resulting in 'powerful distinctions between different social groups within the nation' (Skey 2011, 2). Whether outsiders are seen as 'proper' nationals thereby 'remains largely dependent on the judgements and (re) actions of others' (Skey 2010, 719). Interestingly, certain outsiders are 'able to position themselves (and are recognised) as unconditionally belonging to the nation' (Hage 1998; Skey 2010, 718), which largely seems to depend 'on the positions a person is assigned on various markers of difference and sameness, most notably those of race, ethnicity, culture, nation and religion' (Van Sterkenburg, Peeters, and Van Amsterdam 2019, 208). As these markers of difference and sameness differ per country, differences in hierarchies of national belonging exist between countries. Whereas, for example, in Germany, the

(German) Turks are, arguably, at the bottom of this hierarchy (Seiberth, Thiel, and Spaaij 2019), this dubious honour seems to fall to (British) Asians in Great Britain (Clarke 2020). Further, as not all outsider groups have the power to accumulate enough (but when is enough?) national cultural capital, rankings of national belonging can also change over time. The result is that we are witnessing continuously shifting hierarchies of national belonging ranking different immigrant groups in relation to the dominant one (Clarke 2020; Skey 2011). And how this, consequentially, has led to a competition for national acceptance and recognition between individuals and these groups (Pratsinakis 2018, 13–14). For example, whereas the (Dutch) Surinamese were placed low bottom in terms of belonging to Dutch society in the 1970s/1980s, they have arguably moved up this hierarchy due to an increased recognition of the colonial linkages between the two countries (Van Amersfoort and Van Niekerk 2006). In terms of ethnicity and nationality, although this is not uncontested, the (Dutch) Surinamese, are now dominantly seen as more 'properly' Dutch than the (Dutch) Moroccans and the (Dutch) Turks, indicating an overtime re-ordering within this hierarchy of national belonging in the Netherlands (Van Amersfoort and Van Niekerk 2006; Van Sterkenburg, Peeters, and Van Amsterdam 2019). Moreover, in most (West) European countries, non-western immigrants are quite often 'less accepted and their categorization as culturally different burdens their interaction with the dominant society on many occasions' (Pratsinakis 2018, 15). 'Even in German elite football', according to Klaus Seiberth, Ansgar Thiel and Ramón Spaaij (2019, 788), 'the treatment of German national players with a Turkish background also appears to still be different compared to members of other immigrant groups'.

Özil (2018) also explicitly addresses the issue of hierarchy among outsiders when he complains about the fact that 'he is still labelled as a 'German Turk' even though he has been playing for Germany since the age of 17' (Seiberth, Thiel, and Spaaij 2019, 788), whereas his foreign-born former-national teammates Miroslav Klose and Lukas Podolski were never referred to as 'German Poles' (Özil 2018; Seiberth, Thiel, and Spaaij 2019). Apparently, indeed, not all markers of national belonging are practically acquirable for every outsider or outsider group(s) at every moment or in any situation.

In today's (international) football, in Western Europe but also elsewhere, obvious acts of stigmatisation mainly seem to happen to players whose 'race/ethnicity' – being easily identifiable markers – differs from the one of the dominant group. Besides German-Turkish players like Özil, similar forms of othering have been directed at black German football players, most of them having roots that can be traced back to different African countries, such as Gerald Asamoah (Ghana), David Odonkor (Ghana), and Patrick Owomoyela (Nigeria). It was, in particular, Hamburg-born Owomoyela who in 2006 became subject of 'right-wing backlash' as a calendar was produced showing 'the national shirt with Owomoyela's squad number on it and the slogan: "White: not just the colour of the shirt! For a real National team!"' (Merkel 2014, 246). Although biologically informed racism is 'officially' accepted to be not accepted, and other hidden forms of in/exclusion such as references to nationhood or religion have become more 'accepted' (Van Sterkenburg, Peeters, and Van Amsterdam 2019, 198), Owomoyela's case does imply that race/ethnicity still remains one of the distinctive markers in determining who is 'in' or 'out'; arguably, even overtaking someone's place of birth in Western countries.

'You can definitely belong to two cultures. And you can certainly be proud of two cultures'

We come to a conclusion, after our close theoretical reading of Özil's powerful resignment, by going back to his painful rupture with his 'Germanness' once more and then try to look ahead. Born in Germany as a child of second-generation Turkish immigrants, and since the age of seventeen only in the possession of *formal* German citizenship, Mesut Özil felt that he was *morally* excluded from the German national football team after its dramatic 2018 football World Cup. Özil's resignation was a good example of the widespread tendency to portray the complex issues of citizenship and national identity in dichotomies; an 'us versus them', and a 'here versus there'. Özil's exemplary painful rupture has made clear that the arena of international football should come to terms in recognizing that feelings and experiences of national belonging of players with migration backgrounds are – at the very least – dual in the sense that they, in most cases, identify themselves with both their country of birth and the country of their family: 'You can definitely belong to two cultures. And you can certainly be proud of two cultures' (Özil 2017, 51). In addition, Özil's recent public performances outside of football, especially the photo-posing with the Turkish leader Erdoğan which in itself may indeed be seen as politically clumsy given Erdoğan's spiteful anti-western and autocratic leadership, did not necessarily have to backlash on his football affiliation. That it did, and to this extent, is telling for the power of *moral* deservedness for outsiders in the social construction of imagined communities.

Deservedness to represent the (football) nation seems to depend on the accumulated national cultural capital by players with migration backgrounds and the relentless demonstrations of their loyalty, pride, and affection that would mark them as being 'in', as 'one of us'. Further, as the established have the power to (re)construct and maintain the borders of national belonging, they are also powerful in deciding who *morally* deserves to belong to the (football) nation. Obviously, as both the established and outsiders are a constitutive part of the power balance determining national belonging (Pratsinakis 2018), then, arguably, both have the ability to, at least to a certain degree, and also the potential to change the borders of national belonging. What, however, then should be kept in mind is that Özil, like many other, especially non-Western, immigrants, will never be able to fully meet the current, prevailing conditions of Germany's national belonging, which seem to be biased towards Western, Christian and White characteristics (Van Sterkenburg, Peeters, and Van Amsterdam 2019). This highlights the conditional and temporal character of national belonging. It is therefore that many individuals belonging to the second, or even third or fourth generation of non-western immigrants within their country of birth experience that 'their presence and acceptance as legitimate members of the nation remains contested' (Kyeremeh 2020, 1137). The result is, that the acceptance and recognition of players with migration backgrounds will crucially be a matter of *moral* deservedness then, in the sense that their (national) belonging lasts as long as their performances on the field and in public are on (or above) the expected (invisible) norms set by the established: Only 'if "we" win…'.

What Özil's intriguing as well as most smarting case, above all, thus marks out is the fragility of national belonging for multiple generations and naturalised migrants, even for players who have been selected, accepted and recognised as key persons to represent 'the' nation in international football. We would, therefore, argue that more research is needed towards the power (re)figurations of the (invisible) norms of national belonging, and how these norms are experienced in practice by (various) outsiders and between different outsider groups. Further, we would be in favour of loosening the bounds of football nationality and to allow for more flexibility and interchangeability of football players in the context of international football. The current rather fixed eligibility regulations for players to play for representative teams (FIFA 2019) are out of touch with the growth in international migration, the diversification of societies, and the increasing acceptance of dual citizenship (Castels, de Haas, and Miller 2014; Iorwerth, Hardman, and Jones 2014). In this respect, we provocatively postulate here, it would be worthwhile to investigate to what extent international football could become (more) like club football, where footballers of different origins are, in most instances, accepted and (morally) recognised as 'one of us', as long they play – and perform well – for 'our' team.

Mesut Özil played for various teams in his life, also clubs who are competitors of each other in either domestic and international leagues, like FC Schalke 04, Werder Bremen, Real Madrid CF, and Arsenal FC. Barely ever did he have to show his undivided *formal* and *moral* belonging to the clubs he played for to the extent that he had to do for his selection to the German national football team.[4] Never were there discussions on Özil's assumed 'Schalkeness', or whether he would be an Arsenal' Wolf, or anything like it. Whether the team Özil played for won or lost, they would be in it together. As a team. Maybe, it is time, to rethink if we are winning really as a national football team, when the battle is not only or no longer an 'us *versus* them', 'our national football team *versus* the other national football team', but also an 'us *versus* us' within our national football teams.

Notes

1. While Özil's father grew up in Germany, his ancestors are from Devrek, located in the province of Zonguldak in Turkey (Özil 2017).
2. The Bambi Awards are Germany's most important media prizes and have been awarded to 'people with vision and creativity, whose outstanding successes and achievements have been reported in the media' (Martin 2010).
3. Although this statement received a lot of media coverage, Özil's remark is certainly not unique. There have been other players in international football and athletes in other international sports who said similar things, like the French striker Karim Benzema, who has Algerian roots, in 2011: 'Basically, if I score, I'm French. And if I don't score or there are problems, I'm Arab' (Rosenthal and Conrad 2014).
4. Just recently, on October 21st 2020, Mesut Özil placed a statement on his Twitter account expressing his disappointment of not being registered as an Arsenal player for the Premier League season in which he literally pledges his loyalty and allegiance to the club he loves, Arsenal (Özil 2020).

Disclosure statement

No potential conflict of interest was reported by the authors.

ORCID

Gijs van Campenhout ⓘ http://orcid.org/0000-0001-5150-061X
Henk van Houtum ⓘ http://orcid.org/0000-0003-3719-143X

References

Agnew, John. 1994. "The Territorial Trap: The Geographical Assumptions of International Relations Theory." *Review of International Political Economy* 1 (1): 53–80. http://www.jstor.com/stable/4177090. doi:10.1080/09692299408434268.

Anderson, Benedict. 1983. *Imagined Communities: Reflections on the Origin and Spread of Nationalism*. 1st ed. London: Verso.

Bairner, Alan. 2001. *Sport, Nationalism, and Globalization. European and North American Perspectives*. 1st ed.Albany: State University of New York Press.

Black, Jack. 2016. ""As British as Fish and Chips": British Newspaper Representations of Mo Farah during the 2012 London Olympic Games." *Media, Culture & Society* 38 (7): 979–996. doi:10.1177/0163443716635863.

Black, Jack, and Beth Fielding-Lloyd. 2019. "Re-Establishing the "Outsiders": English Press Coverage of the 2015 FIFA Women's World Cup." *International Review for the Sociology of Sport* 54 (3): 282–301. doi:10.1177/1012690217706192.

Bloyce, Daniel, and Patrick Murphy. 2007. "Involvement and Detachment, from Principles to Practice: A Critical Reassessment of the Established and the Outsiders." *Irish Journal of Sociology* 16 (1): 3 21. doi:10.1177/079160350701600101.

Castels, Stephen, Hein de Haas, and Mark J. Miller. 2014. *The Age of Migration: International Population Movements in the Modern World*. 5th ed. Houndmills: Palgrave Macmillan Higher Education.

Clarke, Amy. 2020. "Hierarchies, Scale, and Privilege in the Reproduction of National Belonging." *Transactions of the Institute of British Geographers* 45 (1): 95–108. doi:10.1111/tran.12338.

Duemmler, Kerstin. 2015. "The Exclusionary Side Effects of the Civic Integration Paradigm: Boundary Processes among Youth in Swiss Schools." *Identities* 22 (4): 378–396. doi:10.1080/1070 289X.2014.992435.

Dunning, Eric, and Jason Hughes. 2014. *Norbert Elias and Modern Sociology Knowledge, Interdependence, Power, Process*. 1st ed. London: Bloomsbury Academic. http://dx.doi.org.eur.idm.oclc.org/10.5040/9781780933405.

Elias, Norbert. 1978. *What Is Sociology?* 1st ed. New York: Columbia University Press.

Elias, Norbert, and John L. Scotson. 1994/1995. *The Established and the Outsiders. A Sociological Enquiry into Community Problems*. 2nd ed. London: Sage Publications.

Engh, Mari Haugaa, Sine Agergaard, and Joseph Maguire. 2013. "Established – Outsider Relations in Youth Football Tournaments: An Exploration of Transnational Power Figurations between Scandinavian Organizers and African Teams." *Soccer & Society* 14 (6): 781–798. doi:10.1080/146 60970.2013.843907.

FIFA. 2019. "FIFA Statutes (June 2019 Edition)." Statutes. Zurich: Fédération Internationale de Football Association. https://resources.fifa.com/image/upload/fifa-statutes-5-august-2019-en.pdf?cloudid=ggyamhxxv8jrdfbekrrm

Freemantle, Iriann. 2018. "When Özil Doesn't Win: The Dangers of Celebrating Migrant "Contributions"." *Daily Maverick*, 30 July 2018. https://www.dailymaverick.co.za/article/2018-07-30-when-ozil-doesnt-win-the-dangers-of-celebrating-migrant-contributions/amp/?__twitter_impression=true

Hage, Ghassan. 1998. *White Nation. Fantasies of White Supremacy in a Multicultural Society*. 1st ed. New York: Routledge.

Hirsch, Afua. 2018. "Mesut Özil Reminds Us Why Minorities Have More than One Identity." *The Guardian*, 25 July 2018, sec. Opinion. https://amp.theguardian.com/commentisfree/2018/jul/25/mesut-ozil-minorities-identity-germany-football-turkish-heritage?__twitter_impression=true

Hobsbawm, Eric J. 1992. *Nations and Nationalism since 1780: Programme, Myth, Reality*. Cambridge: Cambridge University Press.

Hughes, Jason, and John Goodwin. 2016. "Introduction: Established-Outsider Relations and "Figurational" Analysis." *Historical Social Research/Historische Sozialforschung* 41 (3): 7–17. https://www.jstor.org/stable/43997036.

Iorwerth, Hywel, Alun Hardman, and Carwyn Rhys Jones. 2014. "Nation, State and Identity in International Sport." *National Identities* 16 (4): 327–347. doi:10.1080/14608944.2014.897316.

Jansen, Joost. 2020. "Who Can Represent the Nation? Migration, Citizenship, and Nationhood in the Olympic Games." Rotterdam: Erasmus University. hdl.handle.net/1765/127634.

Kalman-Lamb, Nathan. 2013. "The Athlete as Model Minority Subject: Jose Bautista and Canadian Multiculturalism." *Social Identities* 19 (2): 238–253. doi:10.1080/13504630.2013.789219.

Kryżanowski, Michal, and Ruth Wodak. 2008. "Multiple Identities, Migration and Belonging: "Voices of Migrants"." In *Identity Trouble Critical Discourse and Contested Identities*, edited by Carmen Rosa Caldas-Coulthard and Rick Iedema, 1st ed., 95–119. Houndmills: Palgrave Macmillan Ltd.

Kyeremeh, Sandra Agyei. 2020. "Whitening Italian Sport: The Construction of "Italianness" in National Sporting Fields." *International Review for the Sociology of Sport* 55 (8): 1136–1151. doi:10.1177/1012690219878117.

Lanfranchi, Pierre, and Matthew Taylor. 2001. *Moving with the Ball. The Migration of Professional Football Players.* 1st ed. Oxford: Berg.

Liston, Katie. 2005. "Established-Outsider Relations between Males and Females in the Field of Sports in Ireland." *Irish Journal of Sociology* 14 (1): 66–85. doi:10.1177/079160350501400105.

Loyal, Steven. 2011. "A Land of a Hundred Thousand Welcomes? Understanding Established and Outsiders Relations in Ireland." *The Sociological Review* 59 (1_suppl): 181–201. doi:10.1111/j.1467-954X.2011.01984.x.

Maguire, Joseph, and Mark Falcous. 2011. *Sport and Migration. Borders, Boundaries and Crossings.* 1st ed. London: Routledge.

Martin, Michelle. 2010. 'Soccer Stars Steal Show at Germany's Bambi Awards'. *Reuters*, 12 November 2010, sec. Sport. https://in.reuters.com/article/idINIndia-52875620101112

Mauro, Max. 2020. "Media Discourse, Sport and the Nation: Narratives and Counter-Narratives in the Digital Age." *Media, Culture & Society* 42 (6): 932–951. doi:10.1177/0163443720902910.

Merkel, Udo. 2014. "German Football Culture in the New Millennium: Ethnic Diversity, Flair and Youth on and off the Pitch." *Soccer & Society* 15 (2): 241–255. doi:10.1080/14660970.2013.849189.

Monforte, Pierre, Leah Bassel, and Kamran Khan. 2019. "Deserving Citizenship? Exploring migrants' experiences of the 'citizenship test' process in the United Kingdom." *The British Journal of Sociology* 70 (1): 24–43. doi:10.1111/1468-4446.12351.

Özil, Mesut. 2017. *Gunning for Greatness. My Life.* 1st ed. London: Hodder & Stoughton Ltd.

Özil, Mesut. 2018. "Özil's Resignation Letter for the German National Football Team." Twitter. *Twitter @MesutOzil1088* (blog). 22 July 2018. https://twitter.com/MesutOzil1088/status/1020984884431638528; https://twitter.com/MesutOzil1088/status/1021017944745226242; https://twitter.com/MesutOzil1088/status/1021093637411700741

Özil, Mesut. 2020. "Arsenal Statement." Twitter. *Twitter @MesutOzil1088* (blog). 21 October 2020. https://twitter.com/MesutOzil1088/status/1318874490646953984/photo/1

Pratsinakis, Manolis. 2018. "Established and Outsider Nationals: Immigrant–Native Relations and the Everyday Politics of National Belonging." *Ethnicities* 18 (1): 3–22. doi:10.1177/1468796817692838.

Ronay, Barney. 2019. "Why Societal Change Makes Mockery of England's Dual Nationality Debate." *The Guardian*, 20 March 2019, sec. Sport. https://www.theguardian.com/football/2019/mar/20/societal-change-mockery-england-dual-nationality-debate

Rosenthal, Max J., and David Conrad. 2014. "At the World Cup, There Are More French-Born Players Playing against France than for It." Sports. *PRI* (blog). 30 June 2014. https://www.pri.org/stories/2014-06-30/frances-cosmopolitan-society-shines-world-cup-other-countries-too

Schinkel, Willem. 2017. *Imagined Societies. A Critique of Immigrant Integration in Western Europe.* 1st ed. Cambridge: Cambridge University Press.

Seiberth, Klaus, Ansgar Thiel, and Ramon Spaaij. 2019. "Ethnic Identity and the Choice to Play for a National Team: A Study of Junior Elite Football Players with a Migrant Background." *Journal of Ethnic and Migration Studies* 45 (5): 787–803. doi:10.1080/1369183X.2017.1408460.

Skey, Michael. 2010. ""A Sense of Where You Belong in the World": National Belonging, Ontological Security and the Status of the Ethnic Majority in England." *Nations and Nationalism* 16 (4): 715–733. doi:10.1111/j.1469-8129.2009.00428.x.

Skey, Michael. 2011. *National Belonging and Everyday Life. The Significance of Nationhood in an Uncertain World*. 1st ed. Houndmills: Palgrave Macmillan Ltd.

Van Amersfoort, Hans, and Mies Van Niekerk. 2006. "Immigration as a Colonial Inheritance: Post-Colonial Immigrants in The Netherlands, 1945-2002." *Journal of Ethnic and Migration Studies* 32 (3): 323–346. doi:10.1080/13691830600555210.

Van Campenhout, Gijs, Jacco Van Sterkenburg, and Gijsbert Oonk. 2018. "Who Counts as a Migrant Footballer? A Critical Reflection and Alternative Approach to Migrant Football Players in National Teams at the FIFA World Cup, c. 1930-2018." *The International Journal of the History of Sport* 35 (11): 1071–90. doi:10.1080/09523367.2019.1581769.

Van Campenhout, Gijs and Jacco Van Sterkenburg. 2019. "The Diversification of National Football Teams: Using the Idea of Migration Corridors to Explore the Underlying Structures of Nationality Changes amongst Foreign-Born Players at the Football World Cup." *International Review for the Sociology of Sport*, 1–26. doi:10.1177/1012690219892849.

Van Houtum, Henk. 2010. "The Janus-Face: On the Ontology of Borders and b/Ordering." *Simulacrum - Tijdschrift Voor Kunst En Cultuur*.Van Sterkenburg, Jacco, Rens Peeters, and Noortje Van Amsterdam. 2019. "Everyday Racism and Constructions of Racial/Ethnic Difference in and through Football Talk." *European Journal of Cultural Studies* 22 (2): 195–212. https://doi.org/10.1177/1367549418823057journals.sagepub.com/home/ecs. doi:10.1177/1367549418823057.

Van Houtum, Henk, and Frank Van Dam. 2002. "Topophilia or Topoporno? Patriotic Place Attachment in International Football Derbies." *HAGAR* 3 (2): 213–48.

Van Houtum, Henk, and Ton Van Naerssen. 2002. "Bordering, Ordering and Othering." *Tijdschrift Voor Economische En Sociale Geografie* 93 (2): 125–36. doi:10.1111/1467-9663.00189.

Wimmer, Andreas, and Nina Glick Schiller. 2003. "Methodological Nationalism, the Social Sciences, and the Study of Migration: An Essay in Historical Epistemology." *International Migration Review* 37 (3): 576–610. doi:10.1111/j.1747-7379.2003.tb00151.x.

Yuval-Davis, Nira. 2011. *The Politics of Belonging: Intersectional Contestations*. 1st ed. London: Sage.

Yuval-Davis, Nira, Georgie Wemyss, and Kathryn Cassidy. 2019. *Bordering*. Cambridge: Polity Press.

Building American Supermen? Bernarr MacFadden, Benito Mussolini and American fascism in the 1930s

Ryan Murtha, Conor Heffernan and Thomas Hunt

ABSTRACT

In 1931, Bernarr MacFadden, America's self-proclaimed prophet of physical culture joined forces with Italian dictator Bennito Mussolini in an attempt to train a new generation of Italian soldiers. Done as part of MacFadden's own attempts to secure a position within President's Roosevelt's cabinet, MacFadden's trip has typically been depicted as an odd quirk of Italian-American relations during this period. Italian historians have viewed the collaboration as an indication of Mussolini's commitment to strength and gymnastics for nationalist ends. For MacFadden's biographers the trip is depicted as a new turn in MacFadden's business enterprise which sought to heighten MacFadden's socio-political importance. Building on previous studies, the proposed article depicts MacFadden's fascist flirtation as a new turn in American nationalism which both admired, and sought to emulate, European fascism. Touching on issues of gender, race, and transnationalism, MacFadden's trip exemplifies the well-established relationship between sport and nationalism.

The old-time concept of ideal manhood is by far the best ... the master mind, the self-reliance and dependability that insure success and happiness - the great prizes for which we are all seeking ...

Bernarr Macfadden (1931)

Described by contemporaries as everything from a quack, to 'Body Love', Bernarr Macfadden remains one of the most intriguing health entrepreneurs in American history (Hunt 1989). In 1899, he established *Physical Culture* magazine, a periodical related to health and fitness which, by 1910, boasted a readership totalling over one hundred thousand (Fabian 1993). Impacted financially by the Great War, Macfadden's business interests recovered during the 1920s as evidenced by his creation of several other successful periodicals, such as a *True Crime* series. Characterised by biographers as a staunch believer in alternative medicine (Ernst 1991; Adams 2009), Macfadden was defined by the success of his magazine and book empire, as well as his, often unconventional, beliefs.

Macfadden's beliefs underscore this article. From the early 1900s, Macfadden preached a gospel of soft eugenics - that strong and healthy parents would naturally produce strong and healthy children. Often relying on a misguided understanding of evolution, Macfadden promised that his physical culture systems could improve future generation's health (Todd 1987). He claimed that his methods protected customers from the scourges of modernity. Modernity, as understood by Macfadden, meant devitalized diets, sedentary behaviour and unfit living conditions. Distrustful of conventional medicine, Macfadden railed against purgative drugs and doctors' 'misguided' efforts to cure illnesses. The closer one lived to nature, the better one's health. In the post-War period, Macfadden returned to his soft eugenic ideals.

As retold by Ina Zweiniger-Bargielowska (2006), Joan Tumblety (2012) and Charlotte Macdonald (2013), the interwar period saw an increased interest among the masses in eugenics and physical activity. Governments took a greater interest in physical activity, specifically, institutional physical activity. Likewise, it was during this time physical education in schools, military training and voluntary government training centres emerged in Great Britain, Italy, France, Germany and a host of other countries (Bolz 2012). In regions, like Italy and Germany, this move towards physical training, as underpinned by the state, was intensified under fascist regimes (Hau 2003). On rising to power in 1922, Italian fascist leader Benito Mussolini privileged sport and physical culture as a means of encouraging and advertising Italian vigor (Gori 2012). Under this system of physical training, strong and fit male bodies became an emblem for the strength of the Italian nation itself. In Germany, Adolf Hitler and the National Socialist Party employed similar tactics during the 1930s.

Studies of European fascism during this period have emphasised the importance of physical culture in the validation of regimes. In Italy, physiques of Italian soldiers performing mass gymnastics were used as a means of rallying the nation around the idea of a prosperous Italy (Tunis 1936). Like soccer (Martin 2004), physical training became an embodied advertisement for the nation's government. In Germany, mass physical training displays were taken as physical proof of the nation's renewed strength. What differentiated Germany from Italy was the former's ability to convert fringe interests in naturalism and physical culture into rigid forms of state pageantry (Kant 2016). Germany and Italy led the way in this regard but they inspired other European nations to undertake similar forms of physical culture as a nation building exercise (Bolz 2012). European physical culture and its relation to nationalism has been well covered by historians. Similarly, attention has been given to short-lived fascist movements in the United States, like the *Amerikadeutscher Volksbund* and Silver Legion of America (Remak 1957). What is currently missing from such studies is a thorough discussion of mass gymnastics and embodied nationalism within these discourses. As was the case in Italy and Germany, open athletic displays of fit and muscular bodies were a cornerstone of eugenic and fascist thinking in the United States.

The focus of this article, Bernarr Macfadden, is a prime example. In the early 1930s Macfadden made two trips to Europe, one to Mussolini's Italy and another to Salazar's Portugal, with two goals in mind. First, Macfadden hoped to strengthen bonds between the United States and these countries, a goal motivated by his own political ambitions. Additionally, and aware of the primacy placed on the body by both leaders, Macfadden planned to demonstrate the value that his unique brand of physical culture had for nation-states. Over the course of several months, Macfadden trained troops from both Italy and Portugal in the hope of improving their physical strength and fitness, a goal he ultimately achieved. Publicising his 'experiments' and results over several articles and monographs, Macfadden's beliefs were founded on nationalist principles infused with a fascist respect for authority and a stress laid on the muscular body. Macfadden would, in time, come to disavow his fascist links and, during the Second World War, became an ardent supporter of American involvement.

What never left Macfadden's thinking, however, was the importance of the muscular, male physique as an embodiment of one's national patriotism. Nationalism was manifested as an embodied trait, made evident by one's muscles and strength. The emphasis Macfadden placed on the body as a cornerstone of national pride is the focus of this article. First attention is given to the idea of 'embodied nationalism' - what it means in practice and how it existed in the liminal space between nationalism and fascism. Here Benedict Anderson's (2006) theory of 'imagined communities' is combined with works on public display and embodiment to examine the rhetoric created by Macfadden and reiterated by his writers. While the article is limited in examining writers', rather than readers', perceptions, it highlights the existence of such ideals in the United States. Following this, the article delves into Macfadden's trips to Italy and Portugal. In the aftermath of these trips, Macfadden expressed a deep admiration for both dictators, that is Salazar and Mussolini. This admiration relented in the immediate period before the Second World War. The shift from admiration to a distinctly 'America first' ethos is discussed in the final section. Taken together, this paper shows that Macfadden attempted to create a form of American nationalism which began with the physique and came to represent patriotic traits such as fighting and dying for one's country. Put another way, the article argues that a distinctly embodied form of nationalism was promoted during these years, one inspired by European nations and appropriated to the American landscape.

Defining embodied nationalism

Despite years pondering over nationalism, concepts as basic as what constitutes a nation still engender much debate (Finkel 2016). Sociologist Anthony Smith (1995, 57) defined it as 'a named population sharing a historic territory, common myths and historical memories, a mass public culture, a common economy and common legal rights and duties for its members'. Historian Eric Hobsbawm dismissed this idea (Elliott and Hobsbawm 2010, 43), declaring that 'Nations as a natural, God-given way of classifying men, as an inherent [...] political destiny, are a myth' (Elliott and Hobsbawm 2010, 43). He claimed that nations were not complex – they were 'any sufficiently large body of people whose members regard themselves as members of a nation'. Though innumerable other views on the nation exist, these views can be understood as representative of the major camps in nationalism studies: one that views the national as constructed, and the other as natural. Transcending the modern liberal-conservative binary, these schools argue over whether modern nations are rooted in antiquity in some form, or if their basis for legitimacy is the belief of its members.

The standard-bearers for the latter school include Benedict Anderson and Ernst Gellner. Anderson and Gellner both released texts in 1983 that shaped nationalist theory. Anderson and Gellner viewed nations as recent phenomena, accidents of history or culture, respectively. For Anderson, the roots of nationalism were found in eighteenth century Europe. Contrary to Smith, Anderson suggests that it was the erosion of powerful religious and governmental institutions, not their presence, that sparked the rise of nations. Nationalism took the place of, rather than built on, these bonds. It spread through books and other media, which

Anderson classified as print capitalism. For Anderson, this created an imagined community, where a nation came into existence strictly because its members believe that it exists, and that they belong to it. As Anderson (1991, 7) writes, 'Members of even the smallest nation will never know most of their fellow-members, meet them, or even hear of them, yet in the minds of each lives the image of their communion'. Anderson and Gellner differed in that Gellner saw modern nations as inauthentic communities. Per Gellner (1983, 6), 'Nationalism is not the awakening of nations to self-consciousness: it invents nations where they do not exist'.

Oftentimes, symbols are used to make physical the imagined community (Hobsbawm and Ranger 1983). The form such symbols take vary greatly beyond flags or monuments, and include the bodies of a nation's citizenry. Anthropologist Oluwakemi Balogun, in a study of beauty pageants, explained how the bodies of contestants became reflections of Nigeria's idealized nationhood. 'Bodily practices and markers of appearance', Balogun (2012) wrote, 'are vehicles of collective identity'. Athletes' bodies function similarly, as numerous sport historians have discussed instances in which sporting events, and famous athletes have come to become ambassadors, and symbols, for their respective nations (Guinness and Besnier 2016). Their strong, healthy bodies are seen as reflections of the strength and health of the nation, and their performances (especially in international competitions) become referenda on a nation's international standing. This was the position taken by Macfadden and his *Physical Culture* magazine, albeit with reference to ordinary citizens. Macfadden, and his writers, ascribed to the idea that strong citizens led to strong nations, and used his pulpit to attempt to increase the nation's strength.

The connections between body and nation were also explored in anthropologist Meira Weiss study of military bodies. Weiss (2001) explained that, with soldiers, 'The national territory becomes equivalent to the personal body; the body politic and the citizen become one'. Weiss found that, in Israel, dead soldiers received special preparation for burial. They were never dissected, as part of a larger 'ideological mission of preserving the wholeness of the soldier's body'. Israel, in this respect, is not unique. Historian Avner Ben-Amos found a similar pattern in France, where he argued national monuments stand in for the bodies of French icons and saints (Weiss 2001, 38–48).

According to those who preach an embodied nationalism, stronger bodies help build, and maintain, a nation. These bodies are seen as more worthy sacrifices. Political philosopher Jean Benthke Elshtain (1991) went further, saying that not only was there a relationship between body and nation, the individual is actively subsumed by the nation. Likewise, Elshtain (1991, 398) reported that Spartan communities marked the graves of two groups of people: men who died in battle, and women who died in childbirth. Both, she wrote, 'embodied the sacrificial moment of civic identity'. Anthropologist Allen Feldman (1991), looking at the 1981 Irish hunger strike, came to a similar conclusion, deeming the body to be a sacrifice and weapon for the nation. Turning to the present paper, 'embodied nationalism', it is clear that many nations, and cultures, have ascribed to the idea that the soldier's, or at times citizen's, body can be representative of the state itself. Where Macfadden differed was in stressing the importance of the muscular body.

Macfadden's embodied nationalism was only as powerful as the organ he had to propagate it. *Physical Culture* gave him a powerful voice. Through it, he was able to build a community spread across the United States who were joined through their shared experience of magazine. At a time which historian Joseph Morneau (2004) believed had weakened family ties, Americans were drawn to alternative forms of community. For thousands, Macfadden and *Physical Culture* helped fill that vacuum. This brings us back to Anderson, and print capitalism. Anderson (1991) explained that a shared print media can build a common level of cultural literacy, which is a key component of nation construction. This is what Macfadden strived to achieve. Macfadden's armies of readers shared in this experience. By reading the same interpretations, they developed similar understandings of the world. While Macfadden's readership was perhaps unique in its scope, his impact was substantial, and indeed, transnational.

This is not the first paper to suggest sporting magazines could be used for nationalistic ends. Sociologist Tamir Sorek's study of Palastinian sports writing in the 1940s found that it was a powerful tool for spreading such ideology. Many colonies of European empires across Asia and Africa gained their independence in the twentieth century, and it was the vernacular presses that gave these newly freed regions a nationalist conscience. Sorek (2007) echoed Anderson, writing that 'The newspaper allows one to imagine comradeship with a large number of fellow readers, most of whom had never met and would never meet over the course of their lifetimes'. The unity of cultural experiences like sport, he argued, were key. In the pages of the paper, sport was presented as a mechanism that strengthens the national body through strengthening the individual body (Sorek 2007). Physical fitness in this regard was not an individualistic pursuit, but one done for the 'good' of the community.

Macfadden's trips to Italy & Portugal

In 1932, readers of *Physical Culture* magazine, then with a circulation in the hundreds of thousands, were greeted with an unusual interview. Past magazine issues featured everyone from George Bernard Shaw to Upton Sinclair, but this was the first time a self-proclaimed fascist appeared. The man was Bennito Mussolini, the leader of Italy (Mussolini 1932, 14–15). Since Mussolini's rise to power in 1922, Macfadden had kept a close eye on *Il Duce's* love of sport (Martin, 2004). Mussolini's detailed a subject deemed to be of utmost national importance, physical culture (Bolz 2016). On this point, Mussolini found a captive audience. Throughout the 1930s Bernarr Macfadden attempted, ultimately in vain, to enter American politics through a presidential bid and, later, as a member of a president's council. His guiding focus was a belief in the importance of personal hygiene, health and strength. This quest, which ultimately proved unsuccessful, explained Mussolini's appearance in *Physical Culture* magazine. Months prior to *Il Duce's* article, Macfadden travelled to Europe as part of President Hoover's Conference on Child Health and Protection (Little 2002, 58). MacFadden himself appears to have had no solid set of political beliefs (Hunt 1989), focusing primarily on issues of health above all else. He unsuccessfully ran as a Republican presidential candidate in 1936 but later attempted to gain a position in Democratic President Franklin Delano Roosevelt's office. It was during his trip that to Europe that Macfadden crossed paths with Mussolini. United, it seemed, in their appreciation for fitness, a deal was struck, the contents of which were revealed *Physical Culture's* readers.

Through Mussolini's article, and a later piece penned by Macfadden entitled, 'What Bernarr Macfadden did for Italian Physical Culture', it was reported that Macfadden took personal responsibility for training forty Italian naval cadets, ranging in age from their late teens to early thirties (Morgan 1932, 1–12). Cadets were brought to New York, trained under Macfadden and introduced to American culture. The experiment, which lasted six months, was recorded by Thomas Morgan on behalf of the Macfadden publishing company. Between Macfadden's articles in *Physical Culture* and Morgan's 1932 writings, two messages emerged. First that Italian fascists had an appreciation of the body surpassing anything found in the United States. Mussolini's article in *Physical Culture,* which contained musings from Macfadden on the Dictator's writing, stressed the value of strength and athleticism in undertaking hard work. 'A whole country organized for work' was presented as the cornerstone of fascism (Mussolini 1932). Training men so they could undertake even greater labours was part of this project. As part of the great 'Italianization' of citizens undertaken the Fascists, men and women were trained to take civic pride in their surroundings. Macfadden later contrasted this with the selfish individualism he believed rampant in America.

Relaying his experiences, Macfadden spoke of the 'sports and athletic revival' undertaken in Italy (Morgan 1932, 33–45). Macfadden perceived this to be an extension of Italian nationalism that he wished to replicate in America. Owing to Macfadden's strict dietary regimen, cadets were fed a vegetarian diet. This, combined with a heightened attention to hygiene, was taken by Macfadden as an indication of their moral strength and virtuous living. Once more they were contrasted with American counterparts deemed to live a hedonistic and sedentary lifestyle, one defined by individualism and disregard for the nation-state. Italian cadets were presented as a benchmark through which Macfadden had the means to simultaneously criticise American lifestyles while also promoting a Fascist zeal for exercise (Morgan 1932, 100–110). The cadets were called true 'students of physical culture' who, it was hoped, would serve as inspiration for fellow countrymen and women.

Over six months, each man claimed increased strength and musculature. The transformation's aftermath this served as the foundation for Macfadden's second claim - that American politics and physical culture could, and should, develop a similar appreciation for training. Throughout his reminiscences, Macfadden spoke the 'unbounding energy' and 'dynamism' in the United States which, in the mid-1930s, had yet to be cultivated (Morgan 1932, 55–70). American athleticism and sporting prowess were praised, as were the physiques of those few American men and women who dedicated themselves to the cause of physical culture. The problem was that too few understood and appreciated the value of physical culture to either the nation or to their personal selves.

On coming to power in 1922, it was said that Mussolini believed 'the safeguarding of the people's health was one of the first responsibilities of the fascist government' (Mussolini 1932). Macfadden's expressed desire to find a similar situation in the United States. Robert Ernst, Macfadden's biographer, claimed that a combination of personal vanity and political ambition motivated Macfadden's reporting (1991, 103–105). Equally important was his unique understanding of a national sentiment expressed through the body. This assessment was reiterated in historian Charles Kupfer's (2000) appraisal of the Italian trip. Regardless of his motives, Macfadden's written accounts praised Mussolini's government and its appreciation of physical culture. The primacy placed on physical fitness and the willingness to trial Macfadden's exercises separated fascist Italy from a democratic America. Macfadden stopped short of saying Italy was superior to the United States but his writings included wishful appraisals of the Italian state and claims that America had much to learn.

According to Macfadden, his Italian sojourn was a success. This explained, or so it was claimed, why the Portuguese government extended a similar invitation to Macfadden in 1932, the same year António de Oliveira Salazar assumed control of the state (De Meneses 2013). A military dictatorship existed in Portugal from 1926 but Salazar's rise to power marked an intensification of authoritarianism alongside a growing cult of personality around Salazar (Pinto 2006). Salazar's dictatorial control differed from Mussolini's Italy in several respects, most notably Salazar's expressed and continued distancing from fascist regimes (De Meneses 2013). That withstanding, Salazar's government shared, at least somewhat, Mussolini's admiration of strong and healthy bodies. Maurício Drumond's study of sport in Salazar's regime explained that although Salazar rarely expressed an interest in sport, he used it for political purposes (Drumond 2013). Salazar saw sport as a means of mobilizing subjects around a common Portuguese identity. That Salazar's government expressed an interest in collaborating with Bernarr Macfadden is not too surprising.

Governing with an expressed interest in maintaining Portugal's agrarian economy, the promotion of strong and youthful bodies fit with Salazar's emphasis on 'returning to the soil' (Sapega 2008). His regime's efforts to distance the Portuguese leader from Mussolini and Hitler, which began soon after his appointment as Prime Minister in 1932, were well served by an alliance with the American Bernarr Macfadden. Where Mussolini asked Macfadden to train navy cadets, the Portuguese government instead asked Macfadden to devise a means of training for schoolchildren (Dixon 1934). Captain Claude de Vitalis (1932), writing in *Physical Culture* magazine in 1932, explained his country's motivations for approaching Macfadden. According to de Vitalis, his government chose fifty untrained boys, aged between ten and fifteen, from a range of different schools. Schoolchildren represented the future of the regime and securing their health was of national importance (de Vitalis 1932). It was hoped that reforming those perceived as physically weak would become a testament to Salazar's Portugal (Cairo 2006). Much like Macfadden's Mussolini experiment, the children were put into an exclusive training camp where they could eat pure food, 'devote' themselves to physical culture and improve their physiques. Like the cadets, children trained using MacFadden's unique callisthenic system of exercise. In time, the boys' 'dull and stupid little faces' became 'alert and interested' (de Vitalis 1932). As was the case with Italy, the European's zeal for exercise, and appreciation of its national implications, was contrasted with a lethargic America (Dixon 1934, 12–44). After their time in 'Macfadden Children's Colony', pupils returned to schools transformed.

Capitalizing on his successes, Macfadden co-authored another book, this time with Thomas Dixon. Dixon appeared an odd choice. Better known for his 1905 play *The Clansman*, which inspired D.W. Griffith's controversial 1915 film, *The Birth of a Nation*, Dixon seemed to possess little interest in fitness. Macfadden, although interested in the white male physique, displayed few of Dixon's overt racial ideas. Commenting on this partnership, Anthony Slide (2004) speculated that it was Dixon's sister, May Dixon Thacker, then editor with Macfadden Publications, that facilitated the connection. Beginning with Macfadden's assertion that he 'never' works but rather enjoys every moment in life (Dixon 1934, 1–3), the book reiterated physical culture's importance, and strong bodies, for a nation. Macfadden purposely sought fifty boys from working class schools or orphanages that he could mould to be upstanding citizens. On 'a crusade for the health and happiness', Macfadden claimed to have been shocked by the enthusiasm given to health in both nations (Dixon 1934, 5–9).

110 SPORT AND NATIONALISM

Portugal was chosen by Macfadden because it was the 'weakest of the great historical nations' (Dixon 1934, 7–9). Its people were malnourished and its, once lauded, empire had faded. Macfadden cited luxury, comfort and lethargy in Portugal's weaknesses. Despite such problems, the Portuguese government, at least in Macfadden and Dixons' writings, was attempting to rebuild the nations' glory through a rebuilding of its budding generation's health. Macfadden envisioned himself as a catalyst in this transformation. Accordingly, it was claimed

> He would take fifty weaklings ... and build them into perfect specimens of physical boyhood. If it could be done he would thus proclaim to Portugal a gospel through which she might regain an empire lost by neglect (Dixon 1934, 44).

Reporting on Portugal contained the promise that nations could be rebuilt through physical culture, and a warning that inactivity led to national decline. Portugal's geo-political decline was framed as a natural consequence of its growing opulence. Macfadden's experiment sought to rectify this matter, thus turning the tides of history (Dixon 1934, 12–22). On the completion of this trial, which Macfadden and Dixon were keen to note resulted in improved physical measurements, Macfadden declared that 'powerful physiques' had been attained by all (Dixon 1934, 32). This, he stressed, would help Portugal's revival. It would act as the very foundation of it.

Macfadden's two experiments were exceptional in their scope and international reach. In reporting, both during and after the trials, the message that a nation needed strong and healthy generations was continuously reiterated. Reframed slightly, Macfadden adopted and expanded on a growing European authoritarian school of thought which linked athleticism and strength to patriotism. An individual's or group's nationalism included a commitment to their health. When Macfadden returned to the United States in 1932, and it became apparent that the incumbent president, Franklin Roosevelt was not forthcoming with an offer of a government position, Macfadden's interest in this message grew (Hunt 1989, 188). Over the next several years, *Physical Culture* magazine featured articles on the need for government programs, the benefits of eugenic programs and personal responsibility in health.

The aftermath of Macfadden's experiments saw him further his admiration for fascist body cultures. Reflecting on fifty years as a physical culturist soon after he returned from Portugal, Macfadden told readers of the joy of dedicating one's life to fitness (1933a, 4–16). Bitter about the manner he had been treated in the United States, especially by physicians, he expressed a longing for health fanaticism in all citizens. This, he stated, helped the individual and the nation maintain prosperity (1933a, 10–15). Later articles claimed that 'Great Men' of recent times, like Calvin Coolidge or Theodore Roosevelt, understood the importance of keeping strong, fit and healthy (Macfadden 1933b, 4–12). The focus on strong men and men of destiny was very much in keeping with the rhetoric of people like Mussolini, Hitler and Salazar (Gori 1999). The consequence of physical weakness was made apparent in later discussions of criminality, and especially in claims that 'criminals are all abnormal' and physically wanting. Weakness at an individual level bred criminality. At a state-level, it bred decadence and downfall. Macfadden was an outspoken proponent of the body regimes fostered in fascist regimes but he was not the only one. Equally important were contributors, like Albert Edward Wiggam, the American psychologist and eugenicist, who published several articles in *Physical Culture* on potential eugenic programs in the United States (Selden 2000).

Wiggam's articles which ran until 1935, discussed both positive eugenics, such a national welfare program, and negative eugenics, like selective breeding. Like Macfadden, Wiggam (1934a) was a strong proponent of positive eugenics, especially the belief that parents improve future generations by making themselves strong. Showcasing the influence that fascist body cultures had on Macfadden's magazine was Wiggam's more stringent belief that negative eugenics, in the form of forced sterilization, may be necessary to improve America's racial stock (Wiggam 1934a). In 1933, roughly 16,000 sterilizations had been recorded across the United States among the 'insane, feeble-minded, criminals' (Wiggam 1934b). For Wiggam, continued progress in this vein would further America's strength.

Wiggam's support for sterilization was not unique to the United States, indeed Christina Cogdell (2010) highlighted the popularity of eugenics at this time, but his articles stressed the intense focus given to these concerns in *Physical Culture*. As a final point in this regard, it is important to note the national component given over to physical culture and eugenics. Another Wiggam (1934c) article from the mid-1930s stressed the two paths facing the United States. The first, which supported physical culture, meant individual and national prosperity. The other, which eschewed eugenics and physical culture, meant ruin. Between Macfadden's experiments and articles in *Physical Culture*, a clear appreciation of fascist body cultures existed. This admiration and appreciation stressed the link between body and nation. *Physical Culture* became an arena to propagate this European styled nationalism and Macfadden's appreciation of nationalist physiques, which intensified in the late 1930s, was born.

A turning tide? Bernarr Macfadden and wartime nationalism

As the 1930s wore on and war in Europe became an increasingly likely possibility, Macfadden turned his magazine's attention even more to the physical health of the American public. He would use the late 1930s and early 1940s to champion an embodied nationalism, drawing connections between individual and national health. Sometimes these articles came from Macfadden himself, or one of his writers, but oftentimes he used elected or military officials to make the same point. Thus, *Physical Culture* worked to spread his nationalist ideology to a wide range of readers. 'Every man, woman and child should endeavor to maintain the highest possible degree of vital vigor', he declared in a 1935 article titled 'War is an Ugly Word' (Macfadden 1935, 4). Macfadden (1936, 9) later told readers that 'life and health means more during war time than at any other period', drawing explicit connections between personal wellness and the wellness of the nation. He blamed the losses suffered in the First World War on the lack of physical fitness among Americans, and believed they would mitigate this issue with proper preparation. A few issues later, he again called for fitness to take a roll of greater import among the public. 'I would like to see every reader a fine upstanding specimen of humankind', he wrote. 'Men should be men – square-shouldered, bright-eyed, with the form of an Apollo or a Hercules and with the power of a giant in a muscular body'.

In this way, Macfadden's printing helped to generate nationalism in the process later described by Anderson – while also helping to define exactly what that nationalism would look like. Anderson suggested that creating a shared literacy about anything would help forge a national identity. Macfadden made sure there was a shared literacy around the nation itself, which allowed him to spread his belief about the body and connect it to that of the nation.

In fall 1936, Macfadden's magazine published an impassioned plea for the country to stay out of another war, writing that the previous conflict was not a war to make the world safe for democracy, but rather an opportunity for rich individuals to become richer at the cost of millions of lives: a 'War to Make the World Safe for DuPontcracy' (Haig 1936, 16). By the start of 1938, Macfadden changed his mind, and for the remainder of the conflict he and his publication were firmly in the pro-war camp. His magazine became for readers a monthly call to increase their fitness to defend the nation. Macfadden enlisted Ernest Lundeen (1938, 34), then junior senator from Minnesota, to write an article titled 'Why I Am Sending My Boy to Military School'. Lundeen, who famously voted against declaring war against Germany in 1917, admitted that 'Probably sooner than later, the Second World War will be upon us'. In the spirit of preparation, he said he would send his teenage son to a military academy to learn the finer points of soldiering. Lundeen admitted that not only is it better to kill than to be killed, but also that 'If our life must be forfeit, it is better to die fighting an enemy, than to fall prey to the 'flu', or to be self-slain on the altar of inefficiency'.

Macfadden also commissioned an article from Dr. George Calver (1938, 13), medical director of the US Navy, who used his column space to bemoan the general lack of physical preparedness for war among the citizenry. He looked enviously upon the European powers that 'have well learned more clearly than we have how necessary it is to take compulsory steps to keep their youth healthy, to build them up into the type of man who can become of use to his country both in, and out, of the fighting forces'. Subsequently, articles arguing for national fitness appeared in many issues of *Physical Culture*. In April that year, Macfadden (1938, 8) took up the pen, writing that 'Only spirited health can save the nation', which would soon need soldiers who were 'strong, vigorous specimens of manhood'. He worried that the United States was following behind its soon-to-be-fellow combatants. Whereas previously Macfadden linked muscular and strong physiques to a nation's overall prosperity, they now became an issue of national importance.

Two years later Macfadden was fixated with this issue. He repeated his previous call for a domestic program similar to 'the carefully planned health program of the Nazi regime;' something, he said, that would become 'America's first line of defense' (Heiser 1940, 7) Likewise, Macfadden (1941a, 4) predicted that masses of men would get rejected by the draft board, which he called 'a scathing arraignment of the youth of this nation'. It was not just the frontline grunts he was concerned about, but also 'the men behind the guns, the men behind the army', he warned, 'they cannot be too vital, too vigorous'. In Macfadden's eyes, the United States had become 'a race of weaklings' who 'are in no way prepared to meet such fiendish savagery as that unleashed by Hitler's legions' because of how the country had neglected general physical fitness. In February of 1941, Macfadden put the onus on the reader, commissioning an article from Warner (1941, 6–7), the National Commander of the American Legion, which trumpeted in bold headlines splashed across two pages: 'Vital Health – Your Patriotic Duty'. And two months later, in April, Macfadden put a man on the cover of his magazine: a soldier, before and after six months of training (Front Cover 1941).

In the weeks preceding the bombing of Pearl Harbor, Macfadden (1941b, 3) launched what he labelled 'America's Own V Campaign', encouraging readers to consume 'vitamins for national health and national defense, vitamins for victory!' To further cajole readers, Macfadden quoted Surgeon General Thomas Parran's claim that 'We shall need in the days to come rugged health and coverage such as the world has never seen. The magnitude of our effort for this war is only the beginning of our historic task. […] All the strength and courage that America can muster will be needed for the rebuilding of a shattered world. We Americans must be conscious of our destiny, for America is the last great hope on earth'. The success of the war effort was said then, to be dependent on how well they took care of their bodies.

Even in 1943, two years into the United States' involvement in the war, Macfadden continued to draw connections in the minds of his readers between the military and *Physical Culture*. He ran advertisements containing what were likely fictional conversations between WWI heroes Generals Bullard and Pershing. The military men fawned over Macfadden's fitness system, with Colonel Pershing (1944, 4) exclaiming that it had 'done much good to the Army', and Bullard stating that he had retired to teach at 'a military school of the Bernarr Macfadden Foundation'. Macfadden also began to include stories about how his system helped prepare women as well as men to participate in the war effort, with articles like 'A 'Softie' Becomes an Air Raid Warden' (Morosco 1944, 14) and 'I Passed my Army Physical With Flying Colors!' (Godek 1944, 25). He took to printing letters from soldiers, which disparaged enemy states and glorify America with statements like 'We Americans are a nation of giants who will assure our place in the sun' (Haigh 1944, 86). If nothing else, this type of rhetoric evidenced the kind of imagined community envisioned by Macfadden, one in which the strong body was the patriotic one.

Macfadden used his platform to trumpet the positives of the war. Nowhere were there stories of soldiers suffering from gruesome injuries. Enlisting, for *Physical Culture*, meant health, confidence, and happiness. One soldier reported how the army 'taught him to keep clean'. Others had even more impactful experiences. In May 1945, near the end of the War, Macfadden published a story explaining how a husband getting drafted ended up saving his wife from unnecessary surgery. In the same issue, a sailor explained how he had been 'a coward and a weakling [who] lived a miserable life' (Gottlieb 1945). 'I hated myself', he wrote, 'and all that I stood for'. Basic training made him 'a new man', who 'can now look forward to a future of unsurpassed happiness and health'. In fact, the only negative story printed about the War during this time was a commentary against war rations, which might threaten the collective physical health of the citizenry (Chidester 1940). Macfadden's emphasis on physical health during wartime may not have tipped the balance of the conflict, but it attempted to inform his readers' actions. What may have previously been seen as a personal hobby or lifestyle choice was reframed as a deeply patriotic act. Exercising was not about strengthening yourself, it was about strengthening the nation. As Macfadden repeated this message of embodied nationalism issue after issue, he forged a distinct, but very real, imagined community.

Conclusion

Throughout the entirety of the Second World War, Macfadden made sure readers received monthly missives reminding them not just of the righteousness of the war, but also of the important role they played staying fit and staying ready. He was not alone in this effort. Sociologist Dahn Shaulis (1997) noted that a number of prominent publications, like *Time* and *Reader's Digest*, published articles drawing similar connections, but none banged the drum as consistently and forcefully as did *Physical Culture*. Likewise no other publication proved as intensely committed to the ideal of muscular nationalism as Macfadden and his writers. It is difficult to quantify the impact of Macfadden alone at a time when the entire country was transforming in the face of the war, but his message did seem to find an audience. A 1940 Gallup poll found that over two thirds of Americans did not exercise, but two years later a similar poll suggested that the number fell to 42% (Shaulis 1997, 112). This evidences the theory of print capitalism that Anderson put forth many years later. Anderson believed that different people would come to see themselves as one when exposed to the same media and indoctrinated into the same belief system. Macfadden turned his popular magazine into an organ to do just that, spreading an embodied nationalism. He found success in doing so, providing ample evidence for Anderson's thesis. Whether or not his readers realized it, by consuming *Physical Culture* every month, they were part of a community that was developing a common level of cultural literacy. Readers acquired a shared understanding of the importance of personal fitness and how it related to the defense and wellbeing of the nation, and through them the idea spread beyond *Physical Culture*'s niche market. Historians then should take note of the usefulness of applying theories of nationalism to sporting publications, and the way that it can expand our understanding of both the role the role of media and its relationship to the state.

From the early 1930s Macfadden used *Physical Culture*'s wide readership to advance his theories on strength and citizenship. During the decade's opening years Macfadden promoted, and indeed aided, the role of exercise in fascist regimes. Macfadden was not alone, of course, in expressing an admiration in Benito Mussolini's shrewd use of physical culture for political gain but was unique in actively helping to advance it. Similarly, Macfadden played a small, but nevertheless significant, role in helping to bulwark António de Oliveira Salazar's regime in Portugal. Done in peacetime, Macfadden's trumpeted successes, as expressed in magazine and monographs, spoke to the foundational link he saw between the body and the nation. Where other Americans expressed admiration for the physical health initiatives found in these regimes and, at times, linked them to a nation's military prowess, Macfadden instead linked exercise to the very functioning of the state. Under this rubric an efficient, loyal and hardworking citizen was a trained citizen. This meant then that a dedication to one's body was, in effect, a patriotic act one which passed through the generations.

This was an implicit, but nevertheless attractive form of nationalist rhetoric, one which intensified in the coming years. When it became apparent that American was destined for war, or at the very least, preparing for conflict, Macfadden became even more vocal in his writings. In wartime the trained body was examined with reference to sovereignty, protection and violence. Strong male bodies were of utmost importance, but so too were those of the regular citizenry. The previous relationship between efficient citizens and strong bodies was expanded to include military prowess. Macfadden changed his focus, but only at a superficial level. He still linked strong and muscular bodies to the nation-state and to one's nationalist duties. What changed was instead the focus of what these duties entailed.

What then, can be learned from Macfadden's magazine and writings? First that the well-studied European commitment to physical fitness for nationalist ends was not confined to one side of the Atlantic. It could, and did, find ardent supporters in North America, some of whom went to great lengths to promulgate it. This suggests a transnationalism in American physical fitness, and an embodied transnationalism, that has rarely been explored. Second, that print communities, even recreational ones like Macfadden's, had a leading role to play in debating, critiquing, and creating new ideas of American nationalism. The kind of nationalism promoted by Macfadden was in many ways a palimpsest, one which built on prevailing trends linked to fitness, eugenics, nationalism, and American identity. Macfadden created, promoted, and sustained, an American sense of nationalism that began first and foremost with the body. Despite the changing geopolitical circumstances, Macfadden's focus remained the same – built bodies were patriotic ones. Macfadden's enterprise serves then as a reminder that nationalism is both an ideological construct, but also a physical, breathing, and living reality.

Disclosure statement

No potential conflict of interest was reported by the authors.

References

Adams, Mark. 2009. *Mr. America: How Muscular Millionaire Bernarr Macfadden Transformed the Nation through Sex, Salad, and the Ultimate Starvation Diet*. New York: Harper.
Anderson, Benedict. 1991. *Imagined Communities: Reflections on the Origin and Spread of Nationalism*. London: Verso.
Anderson, Benedict. 2006. *Imagined Communities: Reflections on the Origin and Spread of Nationalism*. New York: Verso books.
Balogun, O.M. 2012. "Cultural and Cosmopolitan: Idealized Femininity and Embodied Nationalism in Nigerian Beauty Pageants." *Gender & Society* 26 (3): 357–381.
Bolz, D. 2012. "Creating Places for Sport in Interwar Europe. A Comparison of the Provision of Sports Venues in Italy, Germany and England." *The International Journal of the History of Sport* 29 (14): 1998–2012. doi:10.1080/09523367.2012.677825.
Bolz, D. 2016. "Sport and Fascism." In *The Routledge Handbook of Sport and Politics*, edited by Alan Bairner, John Kelly, and Jung Woo Lee, 55–65. London: Routledge.
Cairo, H. 2006. ""Portugal Is Not a Small Country": Maps and Propaganda in the Salazar Regime." *Geopolitics* 11 (3): 367–395. doi:10.1080/14650040600767867.
Calver, George W. 1938. "Is the Nation Fit If We Should Go to War?" *Physical Culture* 79 (3): 13.
Chidester, F.E. 1940. "War Rations–the Destruction of Unborn Children." *Physical Culture* 83 (2): 10.
Cogdell, C. 2010. *Eugenic Design: Streamlining America in the 1930s*. Pennsylvania: University of Pennsylvania Press.
Colonel Pershing. 1944. "A Great Soldier's Opinion." *Physical Culture* 88 (4): 4.
De Meneses, F.R. 2013. *Salazar: A Political Biography*. Kentucky: Enigma books.
de Vitalis, Claude. 1932. "Physical Culture Transforms Portuguese Children." *Physical Culture* 68 (2): 17–19.
Dixon, Thomas. 1934. *A Dreamer in Portugal: The Story of Bernarr Macfadden's Mission to Continental Europe*. New York: Macfadden Publishing.
Drumond, M. 2013. "For the Good of Sport and the Nation: Relations between Sport and Politics in the Portuguese New State (1933-1945)." *Revista Estudos Politicos* 4 (8): 319–340.
Elliott, Gregory, and Eric Hobsbawm. 2010. *History and Politics*. London: Pluto.
Elshtain, J.B. 1991. "Sovereignty, Identity, Sacrifice." *Millennium: Journal of International Studies* 20 (3): 395–406. doi:10.1177/03058298910200031301.
Ernst, R. 1991. *Weakness is a Crime: The Life of Bernarr Macfadden*. New York: Syracuse Univ Pr.

Fabian, A. 1993. "Making a Commodity of Truth: Speculations on the Career of Bernarr Macfadden." *American Literary History* 5 (1): 51–76. doi:10.1093/alh/5.1.51.

Feldman, Allen. 1991. *Formations of Violence: The Narrative of the Body and Political Terror in Northern Ireland*. Chicago, IL: University of Chicago Press.

Finkel, M. 2016. "Theories of Nationalism: A Brief Comparison of Realist and Constructivist Ideas of the Nation." *Inquiries Journal* 8 (10): 1–12.

Front Cover. 1941. "Physical Culture Magazine." *Physical Culture* 85 (4): 36–37.

Gellner, Ernest. 1983. *Nations and Nationalism*. Ithaca, NY: Cornell University Press.

Godek, Lillian L. 1944. "I Passed My Physical with Flying Colors!" *Physical Culture* 88 (4): 25.

Gori, G. 1999. "Model of Masculinity: Mussolini, the "New Italian" of the Fascist era." *The International Journal of the History of Sport* 16 (4): 27–61. doi:10.1080/09523369908714098.

Gori, G. 2012. *Italian Fascism and the Female Body: Sport, Submissive Women and Strong Mothers*. London: Routledge.

Gottlieb, Alfred. 1945. "Cowardly Weakling Lauds Navy–Results." *New Physical Culture* 89 (8): 36.

Guinness, D., and N. Besnier. 2016. "Nation, Nationalism, and Sport: Fijian Rugby in the Local-Global Nexus." *Anthropological Quarterly* 89 (4): 1109–1141. doi:10.1353/anq.2016.0070.

Haig, John Angus. 1936. "So We'll Have No More War." *Physical Culture* 76 (3): 16.

Haigh, Arthur. 1944. "U.S. Citizen Answers Jap." *New Physical Culture* 88 (4): 86.

Hau, M. 2003. *The Cult of Health and Beauty in Germany: A Social History, 1890-1930*. Chicago: University of Chicago Press.

Heiser, Victor G. 1940. "Why We Should Build National Health." *Physical Culture* 84 (5): 7.

Hobsbawm, Eric, and T.O. Ranger. 1983. *The Invention of Tradition*. Cambridge: Cambridge University Press.

Hunt, W.R. 1989. *Body Love: The Amazing Career of Bernarr Macfadden*. Chicago: Popular Press.

Kant, M. 2016. "German Gymnastics, Modern German Dance, and Nazi Aesthetics." *Dance Research Journal* 48 (2): 4–25. doi:10.1017/S0149767716000164.

Kupfer, Charles. 2000. "Il Duce and the Father of Physical Culture." *Iron Game History* 6 (2): 3–9.

Little, W.G. 2002. *The Waste Fix: Seizures of the Sacred from Upton Sinclair to the Sopranos*. New York: Psychology Press.

Lundeen, Ernest. 1938. "Why I Am Sending My Boy to Military School." *Physical Culture* 79 (1): 34.

Macdonald, C. 2013. *Strong, Beautiful and Modern: National Fitness in Britain, New Zealand, Australia and Canada, 1935-1960*. Vancouver: UBC Press.

Macfadden, Bernarr. 1931. "Ideal Manhood." *Physical Culture* 65 (12): 4–7.

Macfadden, Bernarr. 1933a. "Celebrating Fifty Years of Physical Culture." *Physical Culture* 68 (3): 4–16.

Macfadden, Bernarr. 1933b. "Premature Death of Great Men." *Physical Culture* 68 (4): 4–15.

Macfadden, Bernarr. 1935. "War is an Ugly Word!" *Physical Culture* 73 (2): 4.

Macfadden, Bernarr. 1936. "Dynamic Manhood–Unfading Beauty." *Physical Culture* 75 (5): 9.

Macfadden, Bernarr. 1938. "Only Spirited Health Can Save the Nation." *Physical Culture* 79 (4): 8.

Macfadden, Bernarr. 1941a. "Physical Preparedness an Imperative Duty." *Physical Culture* 85 (1): 4.

Macfadden, Bernarr. 1941b. "America's Own V Campaign." *Physical Culture* 86 (6): 3.

Martin, S. 2004. *Football and Fascism: The National Game under Mussolini*. Oxford: Berg.

Martin, Simon. 2004. *Football and Fascism: The National Game under Mussolini*. Oxford: Berg.

Morgan, T.B. 1932. *Italian Physical Culture Demonstration: A Report of the Visit, Training and Accomplishments of the Forty Italian Students Who Were Guests of Bernarr Macfadden during a Stay of Six Months in the United States Studying His Methods of Physical Culture*. New York: Macfadden Book Company.

Morneau, Joseph. 2004. *School book Nation*. Ann Arbor, MI: University of Michigan Press,

Morosco, Beatrice. 1944. "A Softie Becomes an Air Raid Warden." *Physical Culture* 88 (4): 14.

Mussolini, Benito. 1932. "Building a Nation's Health." *Physical Culture* 7: 14–15. 64, 68.

Pinto, A.C. 2006. "'Chaos' and 'Order': Preto, Salazar and Charismatic Appeal in Inter-War Portugal." *Totalitarian Movements and Political Religions* 7 (2): 203–214. doi:10.1080/14690760600642222.

Remak, J. 1957. "'Friends of the New Germany': The Bund and German-American Relations." *The Journal of Modern History* 29 (1): 38–41. doi:10.1086/237964.

Sapega, E.W. 2008. *Consensus and Debate in Salazar's Portugal: Visual and Literary Negotiations of the National Text, 1933–1948*. Pennsylvania: Penn State Press.

Selden, S. 2000. "Eugenics and the Social Construction of Merit, Race and Disability." *Journal of Curriculum Studies* 32 (2): 235–252. doi:10.1080/002202700182736.

Shaulis, D.E. 1997. "Exercising Authority: A Critical History of Exercise Messages in Popular Magazines, 1925-1968." PhD dissertation, University of Nevada, Las Vegas.

Slide, A. 2004. *American Racist: The Life and Films of Thomas Dixon*. Kentucky: University Press of Kentucky.

Smith, Anthony D. 1995. *Nations and Nationalism in a Global Era*. Cambridge: Polity.

Smith, Anthony D. 2009. *Ethno-Symbolism and Nationalism: A Cultural Approach*. London: Routledge.

Sorek, T. 2007. "The Sports Column as a Site of Palestinian Nationalism in the 1940s." *Israel Affairs* 13 (3): 605–616. doi:10.1080/13537120701531692.

Todd, J. 1987. "Bernarr Macfadden: Reformer of Feminine Form." *Journal of Sport History* 14 (1): 61–75.

Tumblety, J. 2012. *Remaking the Male Body: Masculinity and the Uses of Physical Culture in Interwar and Vichy France*. Oxford: Oxford University Press.

Tunis, J.R. 1936. "The Dictatorship Discover Sport." *Foreign Affairs* 14 (4): 606. doi:10.2307/20030762.

Warner, Milo J. 1941. "Vital Health–Your Patriotic Duty." *Physical Culture* 85 (2): 6–7.

Weiss, M. 2001. "The Body of the Nation: Terrorism and the Embodiment of Nationalism in Contemporary Israel." *Anthropological Quarterly* 75 (1): 37–62.

Wiggam, Albert Edward. 1934a. "Shall we Breed or Sterilize Defectives?" *Physical Culture* 68 (6): 16–18.

Wiggam, Albert Edward. 1934b. "Wanted: Eugenics Conscience." *Physical Culture* 68 (7): 16–18.

Wiggam, Albert Edward. 1934c. "Will the Future American Be a Weakling?" *Physical Culture* 72 (6): 12–14.

Zweiniger-Bargielowska, I. 2006. "Building a British Superman: Physical Culture in Interwar Britain." *Journal of Contemporary History* 41 (4): 595–610. doi:10.1177/0022009406067743.

Sport and the 'national Thing': exploring sport's emotive significance

Jack Black

ABSTRACT
This article critically details how the work of Slavoj Žižek theoretically elaborates on the links between nationalism and sport. Notably, it highlights how key terms, drawn from Žižek's work on fantasy, ideology and the Real (itself grounded in the work of Jacques Lacan), can be used to explore the relationship between sport, nationalism and enjoyment (*jouissance*). In outlining this approach, specific attention is given to Žižek's account of the 'national Thing'. Accordingly, by considering the various ways in which sport organizes, materializes and structures *our* enjoyment, the emotive significance of sport during national sporting occasions is both introduced and applied. Moreover, it is argued that such an approach offers a unique and valuable insight into the relationship between sport and nationalism, as well as an array of social and political antagonisms.

Introduction

Despite many politicians, entrepreneurs and journalists hailing the 'end of the nation-state', today, the nation undoubtedly upholds a particular importance in the practices and imaginations of large swathes of the world's population. As evident in recent political movements, which promise a national restoration (fueled by xenophobia, racial politics and a litany of national myths, fantasies and traditions), 'the nation' maintains a certain emotive and contested significance – but also, a theoretical importance.

In view of this importance, this article will critically detail how the work of Slavoj Žižek can provide a unique approach to detailing the links between nationalism and sport (Žižek 1993). Notably, it will highlight how key terms, drawn from Žižek's (1992, 2008a, 2008b) work on fantasy, ideology and the Real (itself grounded in the work of Jacques Lacan), can prove useful for examining the extent to which examples of nationalism are underscored by forms of enjoyment (*jouissance*). Though critical discussions on the apparent 'decline' of the nation have sought to trace its descendance in relation to technological and capital advancements, this article will argue that the nation continues to procure a unique significance in forms of enjoyment and desire – of which, sport provides an important locus of examination. Nonetheless, while theoretical discussions of enjoyment remain largely ignored in theories of nationalism and sport (the work of Kingsbury [2011] provides a notable exception), this article will assert that sport provides a shared cultural practice that serves to materialize and maintain relations with one's 'national Thing'.

In following this path, it will be highlighted how sport presents a key opportunity for sustaining national sentiments via a mediated consumption that proffers intense enjoyment (and pain) for national communities. Specifically, this discussion will be grounded in an explanation of how the role of the 'Other/other', as well as the effects of fantasy and the Real, can help to critically explore the antagonisms and impasses embedded in sporting nationalisms. These non-discursive practices are, according to Žižek (1993), what constitute the subject's nationalization and, for the purposes of this article, will subsequently be used to outline, critique and evaluate the ideological significance of sport, nationalism and national identity. Ultimately, by examining the various ways in which sporting spectacles organize, materialize and structure our enjoyment, this article will highlight the emotive significance of sporting occasions, such as, international sporting mega-events.

Myth, history and loss: a return to 'national origins'

It is evident that the study of nationalism poses just as many theories as it does contentions regarding the historical significance, socio-political emergence and cultural particularity of the nation and its associated population. Other accounts have sought to examine how the individual becomes embroiled as part of the 'national popular' (Gramsci 1972), as well as those which seek to locate the nation in banal, everyday routines (Billig 1995; Edensor 2002; Skey 2011), which help to aver its 'presence' in a collection of lived performances. Indeed, many of these practices prove constitutive of a community whose 'national' character remains largely 'imagined' (Anderson 2006). It is through these taken-for-granted performances that differences between the national 'us' and the foreign 'they' become socially learned (Elias 2001).

However, for many, these differences reveal wider contentions with regards to the literature on globalisation and the apparent homogenization or heterogenization of national cultures (Bairner 2001; Maguire 1999). These trends seek to delineate the various ways in which national cultures have been extended and inhibited by global transformations, including the post-1989 expansion of a liberal democratic order, based on the free movement of capital (Jameson 1991), as well as earlier forms of imperial expansion and decline (Black 2018). Nevertheless, despite what has been celebrated as the 'global village', the proliferation of nations post-World War Two, has continued to result in examples of xenophobia, ethnic violence and, more recently, a revival in far-right politics fueled by anti-immigration rhetoric. For many of these movements, the return to some form of previous 'greatness' (note, Trump's 'Make America Great Again') has merely served to accentuate and ultimately propagate tensions *within* globalization (Žižek 1992).

To this extent, a return to the *historical emergence* of the nation can help to elaborate upon these tensions, with examples of national traditions, myths and collective historical narratives proving to have a continuing importance in contemporary national movements and sporting occasions. Here, modernist approaches, such as the work of Gellner (2006), have turned to the industrial revolution in order to identify the complex ways in which capitalism helped to establish an economic and political elite, whose authority became

120 SPORT AND NATIONALISM

embroiled with a distinct sense of national purpose. By artificially creating the nation, a proliferation of national traditions – largely 'invented' (Hobsbawm and Ranger 1983) – were established

These 'modernist' approaches stand in contrast to primordial conceptions of the nation, which see its significance and importance in national myths that are not simply constructed, but also culturally transmuted. This latter approach underscores 'ethno-symbolic' conceptions of the nation, which realign attention to the historical timeliness of national historical narratives. Smith (2012, 193) explains:

> Even it elements of ethnicity are 'constructed' and 'reconstructed' and sometimes plainly 'invented', the fact that such activities have been operating for centuries, even millennia, and that several ethnies while changing their cultural character have nevertheless persisted as identifiable communities over long periods, suggests that we ignore the presence and influence exerted by such communities on the formation of modern nations at our peril.

Smith's (2012) ethnic approach has been extended in work by Bell (2003), which has continued to examine the effects of these myths in forms of national collective memory.

Indeed, what underlies these approaches, however, is the assertion that the 'deep ties' that nationalism seems to evoke go beyond any mere 'invention'. As Smith (2012, 191) asserts, 'there is more to the formation of nations than nationalist fabrication, and "invention" must be understood in its other sense of a novel recombination of existing elements'. Smith's (2012) reference to a 'recombination of existing elements' helps to shed light on the 'social bonds' that nationalism adeptly provides. While historical accounts of the nation's past can be used to procure a collective sense of 'national destiny' (Anderson 2006), much of the 'meaning' which is attributed to this history relies primarily on 'existing elements' that retroactively define the nation (Žižek 2014). This retroactive construction of the national past can expose the socio-political tensions of the moment and how current forms of national culture and identity remain forged through historical debates.

What is clear, therefore, is that such debates are not forged with the *past*, but with political tensions in the *present*. This can be seen in periods of 'national reconciliation', where the capacity to define what counts as 'reconciliation', relies upon an antagonistic struggle between various group, each vying for political hegemony (Laclau and Mouffe 2001). Such contestation bears witness to a *formal* significance, which brings together forms of postcolonial struggle, alongside far-right assertions to 'reclaim' the nation. Despite their varying political motivations, in both cases, we see a 'return to origins' fueled by 'processes of lost and regained national identity' (Žižek 2014, 136). Žižek (2014, 136-137) asserts:

> In the process of its revival, a nation-in-becoming experiences its present constellation in terms of a loss of precious origins, which it then strives to regain. In reality, however, there were no origins that were subsequently lost, for the origins are constituted through the very experience of their loss and the striving to return to them. ... This holds for every return to origins: when, from the nineteenth century onwards, new nation-states popped up across Central and Eastern Europe, their returning to 'old ethnic roots' generated these very roots, producing what the Marxist historian Eric Hobsbawm calls 'invented traditions'.[1]

It is in this way that 'a nation finds its sense of self-identity by means of such a tautological gesture, i.e., by way of discovering itself as already present in its tradition' (Žižek 1993, 148). This gesture brings together both 'past' and 'present' through a consideration of the significance of ideology and fantasy in both constructing the nation as well as 'freeing' it from those antagonisms (threats from 'the other'), which, in some form or another, seek to undermine the nation's unity. Such unity is what fuels liberation struggles, underscored by a desire to 'return' to some former existence (Collins and Hanafin 2001).

As noted, this 'return' proves indicative of postcolonial, liberation and far-right narratives as well as helping to define and make sense of traumatic national events, such as 9/11. In the case of the US, Solomon (2014, 675) identifies how post-9/11 political rhetoric revealed examples of a 'retroactive temporality and desire'. Accordingly:

> In the war on terror, the ideal of a complete and unified nation free of threats and antagonisms is an image that covers over the constitutive ambiguities and divisions of such an entity. A unified 'America' is posited as lost, yet, such an 'America' did not, in fact, exist before 9/11. (Solomon 2014, 678).

It is in this regard that we can begin to ascertain the role of fantasy in helping to maintain and construct the nation. While these fantasies remain predicated upon some 'missing part', that subsequently needs 'returning', further connections can be made towards the significance of these fantasies for sport and nationalism.[2]

The relationship to sport and nationalism will be returned to shortly; for now, what the above discussion has sought to trace is how our understandings of the nation and nationalism can become enveloped through national myths which seek to obscure a sense of national loss. There is, in this respect, an ongoing need 'to account for the agency that is evidently a part of nationalism and for the fervour, loyalty and passion that it can inspire' (Finlayson 1998, 146). If examples of 'national heritage' and 'national myths' reveal a retroactive significance that allows both ideology and fantasy to mask present antagonisms (Žižek 1993, 2014), and, if the enjoyment which these myths can aver proves integral to assuring one's belief, trust and relation to 'the nation'; then, extending these assertions to the analytical importance and sense of enjoyment that sport provides, can be theoretically useful in detailing sport's social, political and national significance. In what follows, this significance will be considered from a psychoanalytic approach, drawing primarily from the work of Slavoj Žižek and his reference to the national Thing (Žižek 1993). The benefits of this approach will be concluded with an examination on the significance of the national Thing for sport.

Sport and the nation – 'identification with the very gesture of identification'

There is no doubt that individuals are in some way tied to the nation through intangible dynamics. Here, national symbols and beliefs, often resonate with a variety of individuals who feel a clear sense of affiliation and identification (Giddens 1987). Yet, as noted by Finlayson (1998), it is also apparent that understandings of nationalism go beyond a simple individual-society causality (and vice versa), towards a process of identification, whereby both the subject and object (the nation) are simultaneously defined. Importantly, this process 'is not an identification with any concrete thing; it is rather *identification with the very gesture of identification*' (Hook 2008, 65 see also Žižek 2006).

The previous section sought to locate this 'gesture' in relation to the retroactive significance of the nation; a significance fueled by a return to 'ethnic roots'. However, the importance of this significance is not one that is simply achieved through the power of political discourse, but, rather, points to a specific form of enjoyment that helps to outline the particularities of a group's 'way of life'. It is on these grounds that we can begin to trace the unique sense of personal sacrifice that the nation seems to evoke, as well as the less violent manner in which large populations literally 'stop' what they are doing in order to watch and support their nation in sport (Black 2020). In fact, amidst 'All the different forms of a passionate "return" to ethnic, cultural, religious or nationalist "roots"' it is 'the violent-emotional moment of "recognition", of becoming aware of one's "true" belonging' which seems to offer, for many, a unique 'answer to the experience of social life as fleeting and non-substantial, of being "adrift in the world"' (Moolenaar 2004, 286).

Here, sport offers an opportunity for such recognition to be displayed, often in coded forms of national support that allow one to delineate oneself from neighboring nations and competitors (Whigham 2014). In reality, however, sport never provides any 'complete' rendering of such affiliation, but, instead, remains embroiled in its own complications and antagonisms related to the use of 'foreign' athletes for international competitions (Black, Fletcher, and Lake 2020; Whigham and Black 2020), as well as multi-national state formations, where various nations compete as 'one' team (the United Kingdom being a unique example) (Black and Whigham 2020; Whigham and Black 2018). If anything, these antagonisms point to the fact that 'establishing a definitive conception of the nation is never completed, just as the process of establishing a permanent, fixed, subjectivity is ever incomplete' (Finlayson 1998, 158). What is more, it is this lack of permanence that sport seems to encourage, through its competitive, unpredictable form. Commenting upon the sport of football, Kingsbury (2011, 730, italics added) notes how:

> Football's numerous lacks, that is, the unpredictability of the outcome of a football match ... and its panoply of 'negative' experiences that range from mild half-expected disappointment to crushing depression in defeat are not so much obstacles as *the very stuff of the national Thing*.

It is to an understanding of this 'very stuff' that we now turn.

The national Thing

Žižek's (1993) conception of the national Thing is one closely aligned with the contention that any recourse to nationalism serves to obfuscate some form of trauma and/or social antagonism which surrounds a sudden sense loss (this is evident in his account of ethnic nationalism during the disintegration of Yugoslavia). Indeed, the significance of this loss is not held solely by former Communist states, but by any nation/nation-state (East or West) which resorts to a narrative of decline or inhibited development. For example, while references to the apparent decline of US society have permeated throughout its history, equally, in England, 'political discourse ... regularly revolves around some supposed crisis of the nation and national values' (Finlayson 1998, 156 see also Black 2019a).

Notably, it is the sense in which something has been 'lost' which gives support to the suggestion that there is a certain set of, albeit contested, national characteristics that are believed to constitute the nation. Though these characteristics are encapsulated in national activities –which, in most cases, tend to be shared across a variety of nations – they nonetheless maintain an 'indefinable "Thing"': indeed, 'a belief that there is more to these activities than what appears on the surface' (Finlayson 1998, 155). Finlayson (1998, 155) continues:

rather than being thought of as adding up to some gestalt, some way of life greater than the parts of which it consists, the Thing is thought of as producing these rituals. Thus it is imagined that there is something behind them that gives them consistency. That something is the nation imagined as an essence which produces all these practices and makes them cohere into a universal yet particular way of life.

This imagined sense of 'consistency' is reflected in the various attempts to define or even construct the nation. When delineating any specific characteristic, one is 'inevitably circl[ing] around the Thing, rather than capturing its "essence" directly' (Solomon 2014, 678). Accordingly, while a variety of signifiers are used to 'pin down' the nation and its values (Black 2019b); what becomes clear, however, is that this proliferation speaks more to an attempt to cover-over the 'constitutive lack' which underscores 'the nation' (Solomon 2014). To this extent, Kingsbury (2011, 722, italics added) highlights how 'the national Thing is not an ultimate truth or authentic reality that is blocked or hidden by discourse', instead, 'the Thing emerges out of the *limits, inconsistencies, and impasses of discourses*'. Solomon (2014, 678) helpfully summarises this significance, when he notes that any discursive construction, and any attempt to conceive of the nation's essence, bears no objective correlate, but instead reveals the various 'ways of covering over the incompleteness – the lack – of a "whole" nation'.

This inability to name the 'Thing' suggests an inherent tautology (Žižek 1993). Though the Thing refers to a certain set of features, which are believed to constitute a specific national 'way of life':

> The Thing is not directly a collection of these features; there is 'something more' in it, something that *is present* in these features, that *appears* through them. Members of a community who partake in a given 'way of life' *believe in their Thing*, where this belief has a reflexive structure proper to the intersubjective space: 'I believe in the (national) Thing' is equal to 'I believe that others (members of my community) believe in the Thing'. The tautological character of the Thing – its semantic void, the fact that all we can say about it is that it is 'the real Thing' – is founded precisely in this paradoxical reflexive structure. The national Thing exists as long as members of the community believe in it; it is literally an effect of this belief in itself. (Žižek 1993, 202).

This supports the contention that one's relation to a specific nation is itself a relation to the process of identification. Moreover, it reveals how the 'impossible fullness of meaning' underscores what Lacanian analysis refers to as the Master-Signifier (Žižek 2000, 370). Notably, the Master-Signifier represents an empty form, so that 'its meaning is "imaginary" in the sense that its content is impossible to positivize' (Žižek 2000, 370). While Master-Signifiers can vary, the nation represents such a signifier in that 'when you ask a member of the Nation to define in what the identity of his Nation consists, his ultimate answer will always be: "I can't say, you must feel it, it's *it*, what our lives are really about"' (Žižek 2000, 370).

It is this strange sense of 'absence', which undoubtedly underscores the nation's felt 'presence'. Furthermore, it is this absence which provides a sense of objectivity – a belief which goes beyond the individual subject – from which the nation's empty form can evoke great feelings of pleasure and pain, most notable during moments of sporting competition (Kingsbury 2011). These sporting moments serve to reveal how the national Thing maintains a level of sublimity that is 'permeated and sustained by unusually intense outbreaks of enjoyment' (Kingsbury 2011, 722). Outside of sport, this 'intense enjoyment' is evoked during violent moments of ethnic conflict that bear witness to nationalism's transcendent quality. In effect, however, one's utter fanaticism for the nation, reveals an illusion that one can gain 'direct access to the Thing' (Žižek 1993, 222). Though such access is not possible, the immaterialism of the Thing nonetheless *materializes* in intense forms of enjoyment which can be evidenced in examples of popular nationalism (Wood 2012). It is in this respect that we can begin to trace the relation between the national Thing and Lacan's account of *jouissance*. Untranslated, the term *jouissance* denotes a form of enjoyment characterized by pleasure in pain. Lacan draws upon the Freudian notion of '*das Ding*' (the Thing) in order to locate 'the Thing as an incarnation of the impossible *jouissance*' (Cohen 1995, 351).[3] In sum: 'the "Thing" is "enjoyment incarnated"' (Finlayson 1998, 155).

In what follows, it will be argued that 'a nation exists insofar as it is a national Thing that is materialized through social practices of enjoyment' (Kingsbury 2011, 722); with sport providing one notable social practice. To do so, however, will require a brief recourse through some key characteristics which help to elucidate upon the significance of the national Thing as well as provide it a certain analytical importance. This will include a discussion of fantasy, the Other/ other, and the Real. A specific consideration on sport and the national Thing will conclude.

Fantasy

As evident in Žižek's (2008a, 2008b) work on ideology and fantasy, it is through fantasy that our relation to reality achieves a form of ontological consistency: it is not that we have reality then fantasy, but that our capacity to conceive of reality requires fantasy. To this end, the role of the Thing can help supplement the work of fantasy, by providing the substance that establishes a sense of national unity. The national Thing serves as a fantasy-object which masks the lack in 'reality' as well as those antagonisms which are believed to befall the national community. We can see this in the resort to racist fantasies that reveal a desire to mask social antagonisms which undermine the national community or bring it into disrepute. As seen in the 'Jew', under Nazi Germany, it was the racist fantasies within the Nazi regime which conceived of the Jew's 'removal' as justified in helping to maintain society's 'natural' hierarchy.

What is apparent, however, is that the 'The Thing is ... an impossible object of fantasy' (Dean 2005, 161), forever unobtainable and always out of reach. Again, this is not to ignore or downplay the fantasies that constitute and give life to the nation; rather, it is to highlight how the recourse to fantasy underscores the nation's non-existence. Bentley (2007, 486) provides further clarification with regard to Englishness: 'Englishness does not exist in reality; it is constructed in our fantasy space. This means, ... that it does have a form of symbolic existence and can be recognized as a chain of signifiers', conceived as 'a cycle of open symbols that do not have referents in the real world but are in a continuous *glissement* with each other'. Notably, this 'fantasy space' proves useful in obscuring or even downplaying those real antagonisms which remain inherent to society (and not just those within former fascist regimes).

For example, if we consider the 'Keep Calm and Carry On' message, which adorned a whole range of paraphernalia (mugs; posters; t-shirts; internet memes) following the 2008 financial crash, then it becomes apparent that the significance of the 'war-time slogan' was one that appeared to 'tap[p] into an already established narrative about Britain's "finest hour"' (Hatherley 2017, 17). Hatherley (2017, 17) asserts how, post-2008:

> The 'Keep Calm and Carry On' poster seemed to embody all the contradictions produced by a consumption economy attempting to adapt itself to thrift, and to normalize surveillance and

security through an ironic, depoliticised aesthetic. Out of apparent nowhere, this image – combining bare, faintly modernist typography with the consoling logo of the Crown and a similarly reassuring message – spread everywhere.

What is significant about the message is that the slogan, and its accompanying poster, were never used during the Second World War, but, rather, were rediscovered in 2000, before being privately reproduced (Hughes 2009). As evident in Hatherley's account (2017), its subsequent use meant that any real antagonism brought by the financial crisis was neatly obscured amidst a prevalent and reoccurring Second World War national fantasy. Indeed, one notable way in which these fantasies are maintained is through our relations with the Other/other.

The Other/other

As evident from the previous section, our recourse to fantasy allows us, on the one hand, 'to convince subjects that they once had the lost object that they never had', while, on the other, 'provid[ing] a narrative for explaining the absence that exists within every signifying structure' (McGowan 2015, 51-52). Notably, the 'the Nation-Thing as enjoyment is produced by the continual fear of its loss' (Finlayson 1998, 155), from which this 'fear' becomes embroiled in fantasies that perceive this loss as residing in the Other or as stolen by the other. The capitalization/non-capitalization of the Other/other, in this instance, refers to two forms of 'other' which underscore Lacanian theory. While 'the Other' refers to the 'big Other', a naïve 'third person' that maintains and upholds the 'Law' of social interaction (insofar as subjects believe in the Law);[4] 'the other' refers to another subject – i.e. an individual or group. What is unique to both accounts, however, is the extent to which we enjoy fantasizing about the Other/other's enjoyment (Dean 2007). For the subject, fantasy can provide some sense of 'completeness', via one's enjoyment *through* an 'other'.

For example, if we consider the Holocaust, it is apparent that one's capacity to follow through with prescribed orders, as evident in Arendt's (2006) account of Adolph Eichmann, relied upon one's allegiance to the Other – in this case, the Führer, head of the symbolic Law (Adolph Hitler). Yet, in contrast to Arendt (2006), we can assert that one's capacity to follow the Law was not attributable to the apparent sincerity of one's 'banal' actions (merely following orders), but by the *disavowed* enjoyment that occurred through the fantasy that permitted the individual to unquestionably follow the declarations of the Other, i.e. 'the Führer/Nazi ideology' (a similar process can be identified by those who kill in the name of 'God'). The ideological significance of this disavowal is that it maintains a level of enjoyment that allows one to commit and partake in certain actions that they may later admonish or even regret. In fact, such disavowal helps to point to those examples of national mobilization, exuberance and even violence, that collectively embodies a group of individuals.

Nevertheless, the success of this fantasy relies upon identifying those others who seek to steal our enjoyment, i.e. our national Thing. Here the 'essence' which underscores our 'way of life' – the national Thing which only *we* can possess and the subsequent enjoyment that can be gained from this 'access' – is an enjoyment that is routinely under threat from the other (equally, the other can expel too much 'enjoyment', thus leading to the derision of *their* enjoyment, which they unashamedly flaunt). Dean (2005, 163) elaborates:

> Others are always trying to take our Thing. Or, that's what we think because this is the only way we have a Thing in the first place. … National myths organize a community with reference to external threats. These threats threaten our national Thing. To this extent, we need others:

they provide the mechanism through which, via fantasy, we organize our enjoyment. If others don't steal our enjoyment, we won't have it. In this way, the others are actually part of us.

Dean's (2005) final sentence offers a neat conclusion to the relation between fantasy and the other: that is, it is in accordance with the other that the fantasies we create serve to speak to our own inherent antagonisms, and their subsequent obfuscation.

The real

If the Thing is always circled and never found; if the Thing forever eludes symbolization, but, nonetheless, continues to evoke the process of symbolization; and, if it is under the rubric of the national Thing that some of our most enjoyable experiences are orchestrated, then, it is clear that we are always dealing with 'The Thing [as] an enigmatic leftover or stain of the Real that lacks determinate existence and eludes straightforward interpretation' (Kingsbury 2011, 717). Certainly, the notion of the Real remains one of Lacan's most unique and important conceptions. Though indefinable, the Real is that which always returns; it is a disruptive phenomenon that disturbs any social or phantasmatic arrangement. In the case of the national Thing, this is further reflected by the fact that:

> The mythic point of origin around which nationalism revolves is actually nothing but a gap or void that is positivized through the actions of believers. Fantasy functions so as to camouflage the Real antagonism that ruptures any (allegedly) organic, social unification. (Wood 2012, 37).

As evident in Wood's (2012) account, the Real is not an outside force impeding on our symbolic and imaginary constructions, but, rather, part of them. It is the Real rupture of any nationalism, which reveals its constructed precarity (Black, Fletcher, and Lake 2020) and it is the Real which undermines and dislodges the myths that the nation is founded upon. Bentley (2007, 487) continues:

> Žižek goes on to talk of the 'Nothingness' that Lacan identifies at the moment when the Real surfaces as the radical threat to the Symbolic scaffolding upon which the structure hangs. Because the Real is that which is 'impossible to symbolize', then it appears as a hole or lack in the fabric of the symbolic network of signifiers that make up the nation.

By examining the effects of the Real in relation to England's imperial past, Bentley (2007) notes how the violence of this imperial history can be traced in the ongoing contestations that underscore (British) multiculturalism. Here, multiculturalism becomes a repetitive event that continually struggles with the horrors of the Real (the Real of England's imperial past).

However, while the Real can serve to dislodge national myths – exposing the nation's inherent emptiness – it can also disturb and ignite the 'strong economy of *jouissance* [which] is at work in the identification with one's own "way of life"' (Žižek 2020, 59). Žižek (2005, 597-598) confirms:

> Perhaps the most notable case was the disastrous collapse of international solidarity within the worker's movement in the face of 'patriotic' euphoria at the outbreak of the First World War. Today, it is difficult to imagine what a traumatic shock it was for the leaders of all currents of social democracy and socialism, ... when the social-democratic parties of all countries (with the exception of the Bolsheviks in Russia and Serbia) gave way to chauvinist outbursts, and stood 'patriotically' behind 'their' respective governments, oblivious of the proclaimed solidarity of the working class 'without country'. This shock, the *powerless fascination* felt by its participants, bears witness to an encounter with the Real of enjoyment.

In the final part of this article, consideration will be given to expanding upon the above characteristics in the context of sport.

Sport and the national thing

It is important to assert that the Thing should not be reduced to the individual and their own private psyche (Kingsbury 2011). As Kingsbury (2011, 721) explains, 'the Thing is first and foremost intersubjective, that is, a social phenomenon'. Yet, it is a unique social phenomenon; one akin to the unique brand of dialectical materialism that Žižek's (2014) philosophical outlook provides: a materialism without matter. This outlook underscores Sharpe and Bouchers's (2010, 59) assertion that 'People *enjoy* their ideological commitments in such 'ineffable' moments – and this is a visceral, passionate Thing'. In fact, if the remark: '"You had to be there" is something a political subject often says to an uncomprehending outsider' (Sharpe and Boucher 2010, 56); equally, we can begin to see how such remarks are given an added significance in the context of national sporting moments. Ultimately, the national Thing allows us to pay closer attention to such ineffable moments in sport, shedding further light on how the significance of enjoyment (*jouissance*) helps to maintain and uphold an ethnic community.

To this end, while we can all imagine the various ways in which sport's sense of collective enjoyment is experienced – cheering in crowded pubs during international competitions; watching the clock countdown during the final round of our favourite boxer; or, anxiously awaiting the medical update on our nation's 'star' player – the qualities that underscore such practices pay homage to the fragmentary, yet Real, nature of the Thing.

That is, the national Thing cannot be enjoyed individually, but is 'sustained by shared practices of belief' (Kingsbury 2011, 728). This belief – the belief in our national team, for example – is what 'becomes inscribed within' the practice of sports fans: it is the fan's 'pre-suppositions of the existence of other passionate fans that share an enjoyment of and belief in the national team' (Kingsbury 2011, 721). Conceived as 'materialized enjoyment', we can begin to ascertain 'why it is precisely "nationalism" that is the privileged domain of the eruption of enjoyment into the social field' (Žižek 1992, 165). While Žižek (1992, 165) asserts that it is 'the national Cause [which] is ultimately the way subjects of a given nation organize their collective enjoyment through national myths', we can expand upon such comments by considering how these 'Causes' become collectively enacted during national sporting moments. Here, 'the objects, practices, and relations of sports' (Kingsbury 2011, 720), play a unique role in organizing this collective enjoyment, with the sublime object of ideology being emotionally displayed during national sporting successes. But how does this enjoyment emerge in examples of sport, and, more importantly, how does the national Thing allow us to explore the 'national' enjoyment that sport provokes? To answer these questions, we can return to our previous characteristics.

Sport and the national thing: the role of fantasy, the Other/other and the real

Certainly, the globalization of sport has not hindered the development of sporting nationalisms. In fact, as evident in the array of developing nations, who have hosted international sporting mega-events, sporting success suggests one way in which sport can be used to express one's 'national' status on an international stage. Moreover, this process proves amiable to promoting a number of 'ethnic fantasies' concerning the nation, as highlighted in media coverage (Black 2019b). Indeed, the relation between national fantasies and sport serves to reveal 'the kernel of enjoyment at the heart of nationalist discourse (a "piece of the Real")' with 'official' events and sporting occasions being 'mediated through fantasy' (Collins and Hanafin 2001, 69). Here, the unique way that sport evokes national fantasies – often centering around past sporting successes – highlights the extent to which the nation's ontological consistency remains tied to a fantasmatic support that upholds and maintains nationalist ideology.

Consequently, sport remains a unique platform for these national fantasies to be produced and maintained; yet, such fantasies (such as, sport's inherent meritocracy, sense of 'fair play', and declared professionalism) are, in the case of the nation, neither consistent nor infallible. Instead, they remain under continual negotiation and resistance. Kingsbury (2011, 722) notes:

> Sport, ... is the global activity par excellence that offers people social fantasies that coordinate people's desire for objects teeming with sublimity and cosmic relevance. Crucially, the national Thing is not an ultimate truth or authentic reality that is blocked or hidden by discourse. Rather, the Thing emerges out of the limits, inconsistencies, and impasses of discourses.

It is these 'limits, inconsistencies, and impasses' which are frequently highlighted in critical analyses of sporting mega-events. It is amidst such inconsistency that the relation between sport's projected desires and the national Thing can be found.

Furthermore, to support one's nation immediately places one in contrast to a national opposition; an opposition that is usually marked by fierce rivalries and a 'more than just a game' incentive (Whigham 2014). Accordingly, sport's ability to distinguish between the national 'us' and 'them' remains a widely recited theme in political as well as media discourses of sporting events. However, while these discourses, 'help to define who "we" are in contrast to "them"', Solomon (2014, 678) emphasizes how the construction of these boundaries can serve to 'function as the signifiers of a national subject'. Echoing Dean's (2007) previous contention, the contrast delineated between the self and other, emphasizes how the act of 'describing who "we" are' helps to 'construct a fantasy that covers over the subject's lack of full presence' (Solomon 2014, 678). In other words, it is *through the other* that the national collective and national subject achieve a sense of 'full presence' in the face of an inherent absence. This lack is accentuated when one considers the contentions that abound those 'national athletes', who are considered as not 'belonging' to the nation (Black, Fletcher, and Lake 2020). Ultimately, these contentions reveal more about the forms of 'circling' that mark the Thing's periphery: the lack at its heart.

Equally, this 'lack' is neatly 'covered over ... through phantasmatic assumptions of fullness, closure and resolution, which is achieved through the "'organisation of enjoyment" through an Other' (Finlayson 1998, 155). Again, sport offers a unique setting for the organisation of such enjoyment. In particular, what we observe during sporting occasions is how such events can, paradoxically, have nothing to do 'with [one's] conscious awareness', but instead, reveal a 'truth' which occurs through the sporting event itself (Žižek 2006, 66).[5] In effect, sport projects a collective form whose tangible significance bears no relation to the inherent logics of the practice itself, but which, nonetheless, gain some level of significance from the sense of belief that is externalized *via the practice* (Black 2020a). Such a contention follows Žižek's (2001) countering of the 'psychological' assumption that belief 'takes place inside people's heads or psyches', arguing instead that 'belief is materially externalized in material social practices' (Kingsbury 2011, 729). These 'material social practices' highlight how 'The national Thing is concretized through the effects of belief via the social practices of loyalty, service, and even sacrifice for a nation' (Kingsbury 2011, 729). This externalization of belief is maintained *in* the belief that one holds for their national team/performer (Kingsbury 2011), but also in the sense of obligation that one must 'watch' their national team. In doing so, belief is externalized through an Other, such as, the symbolic 'patriots at play', who come to represent and embody the nation's sporting desires (Tuck and Maguire 1999). Ultimately, our relation to sport – and the nation – bears a certain ex-timacy.[6]

Finally, though sport and the national Thing display clear fantasmatic elements, grounded in relations with the Other/other, they also bear an advertence of the Real. The Real in sport can be identified in those moments of excessive *jouissance*; in the agony, but also the utter astonishment that sporting moments can invigorate. It is also there in those moments of disruption, evident in Kingbury's (2011) reference to the injury suffered by Wayne Rooney before the 2006 World Cup. He notes:

> six weeks before the start of England's 2006 World Cup campaign, Wayne Rooney – an integral part of England's chances of winning the World Cup – fractured a metatarsal bone in his right foot. In the following hours and days, an estimated 3000 articles in newspapers, on the Web, and even academic medical journals focused on Rooney's metatarsal by speculating on whether or not he would be fit to play, and, if so, whether he would be effective or not. Media speculation even incited the creation of healrooney.com, a website established to expedite Rooney's recovery. Users were invited to move their cursor arrow over an image of Rooney's foot and tap into the "power of positivity". In this example, Rooney's metatarsal occupies the place of the Thing and becomes a sublime object because of all the fuss and panic. (Kingsbury 2011, 722).[7]

Though Kingsbury's (2011) example relates the significance of Rooney's injury in relation to the national Thing (with Rooney's metatarsal itself occupying the sublime object), it is important to frame these actions in relation to that excessive *jouissance* which seems to accompany the bizarre array of mediated activities that the injury evoked. Such excesses underscore the inherent lack which occupies the national Thing: the unremitting concern that to do 'something' is better than nothing.

Conclusion

The underlying aim of this article has been to introduce a psychoanalytic approach to the study of sport and nationalism, as described in Žižek's conception of the national Thing. Notably, it has been argued that this Thing bears a unique relation to the sense of enjoyment that is procured through sport and sporting events that involve the nation. Indeed, as noted by Kingsbury (2011), for many, the relationship between sport, nationalism and enjoyment remains an understudied relationship, which, at its worst, simply views sport's enjoyable moments as a form of 'ideological delusion'. To this end, Žižek's conception of the national Thing offers a unique path for navigating these 'delusions'.

In part, we can observe this navigation via the clear reason that, despite our 'postmodern epoch' which remains indebted to global infrastructures and intra-state organisations, nationalism maintains a unique and passionately defended importance. Here, sport continues to provide an essential context for one's enjoyment in their nation to be expressed and shared. Central to this enjoyment is the extent to which the national Thing offers both a subjective and intersubjective relevance in examining the ongoing significance of national myths, fantasies and ideology. If there is, as Whigham (2014) asserts, the potential to 'over-politicse' one's political attachments in the context of national sport; then, evidently, such national attachments can reveal other forms of enjoyment that encourage one to watch, support and partake in national sporting spectacles and associated 'national' rivalries.

In fact, though it is widely noted that the nation maintains some form of connection with particular groups – which, in light of the nation's history (Smith 2012), frequently draws upon contingent elements (Anderson 2006; Gellner 2006; Hobsbawm and Ranger 1983) that both frame and limit how one is to belong and/or perform the nation (Edensor 2002; Billig 1995; Black, Fletcher, and Lake 2020) – Žižek's use of the national Thing posits no definite center and no objective correlate to defining what the nation 'is'. However, though we may assert the inherent incompleteness which constitutes the nation, it is through a 'temporally bound incompleteness and consequent sparking of desire' that sport's mediated enjoyment can allow us to see how 'The social construction of the "nation" is always "distorted by desire" channeled through the various discourses in which it is named' (Solomon 2014, 678). In the case of this article, such construction has been related to the experiences that constitute inter*national* sport.

To conclude, future research can continue this line of inquiry in relation to sporting spectacles, that so often provide a 'sit[e] for the assertion and affirmation of particular discursive constructions of nation' (Silk and Falcous 2005, 454). While these 'constructions' offer carefully choreographed and performative segments, which seek to highlight the nation's past in accordance with its present, equally, these spectacles can be examined for their retroactive staging of 'the nation's' past. Here, the evocation of national myths and the nation's 'origin' – key themes in any opening ceremony – can be examined for the various ways in which they retroactively obfuscate the nation's contingent underpinnings. This contingency is laid bare by observing the 'imagined' origins and sense of consistency which the national Thing requires. Ultimately, by drawing upon the national Thing, one can offer unique and valuable insights into the relationship between sport and nationalism as well as an array of social and political antagonisms, which, despite the well-rehearsed proclamation that sport and politics do not mix, continue to exhibit sport's political significance.

Notes

1. Comparably, this 'return' to some form of 'origin' – however tenuous – is identified in Collins and Hannifin's comments on the founding of the Irish Constitution. They highlight how 'The Irish Constitution admirably performs this task by "founding" the Nation through the very act of "officially" announcing its existence. As the country had enjoyed neither national unity nor political independence at any period in the modern age, the declaration of nationhood had to be grounded in an appeal to an idyllic "Golden Age" of the Gaels' (Collins and Hannifin, 2001, 61).
2. Admittedly, the desire for the World Cup can be transferred to the English national team bringing any sort of trophy 'home'.
3. Daly (2014, 80) elaborates 'Enjoyment can be characterized as a kind of existential electricity that not only animates the subject but also threatens to destroy them. ... If the body of Frankenstein's monster is the intelligible symbolic structure, then lightning is the raw substance of enjoyment that reflects the primordial character of human drives and obsessions'.
4. Notably, the big Other is also 'split', with cynics often resorting to paranoid conspiracies revealing an 'Other of the (big) Other', who, secretly, 'pulls the strings'.
5. This contention is drawn from Žižek's (2006) account of Hegel's comments on the 'marriage ceremony'.

SPORT AND NATIONALISM

6. Extimacy (*extimité*) refers to the problematization of a clear 'inside' and 'outside' for the subject.
7. Similar examples were also evident in a previous injury sustained by England 'golden boy' David Beckham before the 2002 World Cup.

Disclosure statement

No potential conflict of interest was reported by the author.

References

Anderson, Benedict. 2006. *Imagined Communities*. London, UK: Verso.

Arendt, Hannah. 2006. *Eichmann in Jerusalem*. London, UK: Penguin.

Bairner, Alan. 2001. *Sport, Nationalism, and Globalization*. New York: State University of New York Press.

Bell, Duncan S. A. 2003. "Mythscapes: Memory, Mythology, and National Identity." *The British Journal of Sociology* 54 (1): 63–81. doi:10.1080/0007131032000045905.

Bentley, Nick. 2007. "Re-Writing Englishness: Imagining the Nation in Julian Barnes's *England, England* and Zadie Smith's *White Teeth*." *Textual Practice* 21 (3): 483–504. doi:10.1080/09502360701529093.

Billig, Michael. 1995. *Banal Nationalism*. London, UK: Sage.

Black, Jack. 2018. "The United Kingdom and British Empire: A Figurational Approach." *Rethinking History* 22 (1): 3–24. doi:10.1080/13642529.2017.1419446.

Black, Jack. 2019a. "From Mood to Movement: English Nationalism, the European Union and Taking Back Control." *Innovation: The European Journal of Social Science Research* 32 (2): 191–210.

Black, Jack. 2019b. "The Subjective and Objective Violence of Terrorism: Analyzing 'British Values' in Newspaper Coverage of the 2017 London Bridge Attack." *Critical Studies on Terrorism* 12 (2): 228–249. doi:10.1080/17539153.2018.1498191.

Black, Jack. 2020. "Football is 'the Most Important of the Least Important Things': The Illusion of Sport and COVID-19." *Leisure Sciences*. doi: 10.1080/01490400.2020.1773989

Black, Jack, Thomas Fletcher, and Robert J. Lake. 2020. "Success in Britain Comes with Awful Lot of Small Print': Greg Rusedski and the Precarious Performance of National Identity." *Nations and Nationalism*. doi:10.1111/nana.12614

Black, Jack, and Stuart Whigham. 2020. "'Team GB' or 'Team Scotland'? Media Representations of 'Britishness' and 'Scottishness' at London 2012 and Glasgow 2014." *Journalism* 21 (10): 1450-1467.

Cohen, Tom. 1995. "Beyond 'the Gaze': ŽIžek, Hitchcock, and the American Sublime." *American Literary History* 7 (2): 350–378. doi:10.1093/alh/7.2.350.

Collins, Barry, and Patrick Hanafin. 2001. "Mothers, Maidens and the Myth of Origins in the Irish Constitution." *Law and Critique* 12 (1): 53–73. doi:10.1023/A:1011245400526.

Daly, Glyn. 2014. "Enjoyment/*Jouissance*." In *The Žižek Dictionary*, edited by Rex Butler, 80–83. London, UK: Routledge.

Dean, Jodi. 2005. "Žižek against Democracy." *Law, Culture and the Humanities* 1 (2): 154–177. doi:10.1191/1743872105lw012oa.

Dean, Jodi. 2007. "Why ŽIžek for Political Theory?" *International Journal of Žižek Studies* 1 (1): 18–32.

Edensor, Tim. 2002. *National Identity, Popular Culture and Everyday Life*. Oxford, UK: Berg.

Elias, Norbert. 2001. *The Society of Individuals*. New York: Continuum.

Finlayson, Alan. 1998. "Psychology, Psychoanalysis and Theories of Nationalism." *Nations and Nationalism* 4 (2): 145–162. doi:10.1111/j.1354-5078.1998.00145.x.

Gellner, Ernest. 2006. *Nations and Nationalism*. Ithaca, NY: Cornell University Press.

Giddens, Anthony. 1987. *The Nation-State and Violence*. Berkeley, CA: University of California Press.

Gramsci, Antonio. 1972. *Selections from the Prison Notebooks*. New York: International Publishers.

Hatherley, Owen. 2017. *The Ministry of Nostalgia*. London, UK: Verso.

Hobsbawm, Eric, and Terence Ranger, eds. 1983. *The Invention of Tradition*. Cambridge, UK: Cambridge University Press.

Hook, Derek, 2008. "Absolute other: Lacan's 'big Other' as adjunct to critical social psychological analysis? Social and Personality" *Psychology Compass* 2 (1): 57–73.

Hughes, Stuart. 2009. "The Greatest Motivational Poster Ever?" *BBC News*, February 4. http://news.bbc.co.uk/1/hi/magazine/7869458.stm

Jameson, Fredric. 1991. *Postmodernism, or, the Cultural Logic of Late Capitalism*. Durham, NC: Duke University Press.

Kingsbury, Paul. 2011. "The World Cup and the National Thing on Commercial Drive." *Environment and Planning D: Society and Space* 29 (4): 716–737. doi:10.1068/d4410.

Laclau, Ernesto, and Chantal Mouffe. 2001. *Hegemony and Socialist Strategy*. London, UK: Verso.

Maguire, Joseph. 1999. *Global Sport: Identities, Societies, Civilizations*. Cambridge, UK: Polity.

McGowan, Todd. 2015. *Psychoanalytic Film Theory and The Rules of the Game*. New York, NY: Bloomsbury.

Moolenaar, R. 2004. "Slavoj Žižek and the **Real** Subject of Politics." *Studies in East European Thought* 56 (4): 259–297. doi:10.1023/B:SOVI.0000043003.05995.3d.

Sharpe, Matthew, and Geoff Boucher. 2010. *Žižek and Politics*. Edinburgh, UK: Edinburgh University Press.

Silk, Michael, and Mark Falcous. 2005. "One Day in September/a Week in February: Mobilizing American (Sporting) Nationalisms." *Sociology of Sport Journal* 22 (4): 447–471. doi:10.1123/ssj.22.4.447.

Skey, Michael. 2011. *National Belonging and Everyday Life*. Basingstoke, UK: Palgrave Macmillan

Smith, Anthony D. 2012. "Nationalism and the Historians." In *Mapping the Nation*, edited by Gopal Balakrishnan, 175–197. London, UK: Verso.

Solomon, Ty. 2014. "Time and Subjectivity in World Politics". *International Studies Quarterly* 58 (4): 671–681.

Tuck, Jason, and Joseph Maguire. 1999. "Making Sense of Global Patriot Games: Rugby Players' Perceptions of National Identity Politics." *Football Studies* 2 (1): 26–54.

Waterson, Jim. 2018. "'It's Not Coming Home': England's Anthem Returns to Haunt Them." *The Guardian*, July 17. https://www.theguardian.com/football/2018/jul/17/its-not-coming-home--englands-anthem-returns-to-haunt-them

Whigham, Stuart. 2014. "Anyone but England?' Exploring anti-English Sentiment as Part of Scottish National Identity in Sport." *International Review for the Sociology of Sport* 49 (2): 152–174. doi:10.1177/1012690212454359.

Whigham, Stuart, and Jack Black. 2018. "Glasgow 2014, the Media and Scottish Politics: The (Post) Imperial Symbolism of the Commonwealth Games." *The British Journal of Politics and International Relations* 20 (2): 360–378. doi:10.1177/1369148117737279.

Whigham, Stuart, and Jack Black. 2020. "London 2012, Glasgow 2014 and Athletes as Political Symbols – the Precarious Positioning of Athletes within the Evolving Contemporary Politics of the United Kingdom." *European Journal for Sport and Society* 17 (1): 47–65. doi:10.1080/1613817 1.2019.1706249.

Wood, Kelsey. 2012. *Žižek: A Reader's Guide*. Chichester, UK: Wiley-Blackwell.

Žižek, Slavoj 1993. *Tarrying with the Negative*. Durham, NC: Duke University Press.

Žižek, Slavoj. 1992. *Looking Awry*. Cambridge, Mass: MIT Press.

Žižek, Slavoj. 2000. *The Ticklish Subject*. London, UK: Verso.

Žižek, Slavoj. 2001. *On Belief*. Abingdon, UK: Routledge.

Žižek, Slavoj. 2005. "Enjoy Your Nation as Yourself!" In *Theories of Race and Racism: A Reader*, edited by Les Back and John Solomos, 594–606. Abingdon, UK: Routledge.

Žižek, Slavoj. 2006. *The Parallax View*. Cambridge, Mass: MIT Press.

Žižek, Slavoj. 2008a. *The Sublime Object of Ideology*. London, UK: Verso.

Žižek, Slavoj. 2008b. *The Plague of Fantasies*. London, UK: Verso.

Žižek, Slavoj. 2014. *Absolute Recoil*. London, UK: Verso.

Žižek, Slavoj. 2020. *A Left That Dares to Speak Its Name*. Cambridge, UK: Polity.

Everyday bordering. Theoretical perspectives on national 'others' in sport and leisure time physical activity

Sine Agergaard (iD) and Verena Lenneis

ABSTRACT
While it is well documented that sports events can reinforce nationalism, less attention has been given to how borders are drawn to mark off groups whose national identity is questioned in connection with their everyday sports and leisure practices. This article aims to develop a conceptual framework for studying such collective identification processes that not only include some but also exclude 'others' from the nation. To do so, we draw on postcolonial and transnational feminist scholars' descriptions of politics of belonging and everyday bordering that place non-western women in a position as 'others'. The utility of such a conceptual framework is illustrated in analysing current political and public discourses about Muslim women's sports and leisure practices that demarcate this group from belonging to the nation. Further, we discuss the contributions and limitations of this conceptual framework and point towards related perspectives that can further develop research with national 'others' in sport.

Introduction

In contemporary societies, sports competitions between nations have been described as the essence of international sports events (Bairner 2015). Indeed, sport has become one of the most powerful ways to reinforce nationalism (Edensor 2002). Yet, not only as mega events but also as everyday leisure practices, sport produce and activate stories about who we are as a nation (Seippel 2017). For instance, specific narratives about how 'Danes' organise sport in local clubs or how handball was invented in Denmark do not only contribute to the national identity, but also often involve a comparison with 'others' who are not seen to organise sport or not know of/play handball in the same way as 'we' ('Danes'). In other words, sports-related nationalism is defined both with reference to internal traits as well as in comparison with 'strangers' (Armstrong 1982).

In this article, we argue that sport does not only contribute to the national identification but is also involved in drawing borders to detach some groups and individuals from the nation. We find it highly relevant to conduct research of such boundary-making processes since nationalism flourishes in many Western societies in combination with populist movements that draw distinctions; both vertically between a political elite and the people as well as horizontally between insiders and outsiders within national communities (Brubaker 2017). While belonging to modern nations often has been linked with civic traits such as citizenship and shared institutions, Europe is currently witnessing a resurgence of ethno-nationalism according to which members of a nation must have shared ethnic and cultural heritage (Elgenius and Rydgren 2019). As a result, migrants and descendants who may have been attributed asylum or citizenship in a nation are often perceived as 'internal outsiders' threatening the unity of a nation (Thangaraj et al. 2018).

Thus, at heart of the nationalism that seeks to preserve ideas about the sovereignty of the nation and a uniform national identity is the 'problem of the other' (Spencer and Wollman 2002). In other words, for nations to appear integrated as a unity some must be included and others excluded (Simonsen 2018). In line with Alan Bairner's call for the use of a wider range of theoretical (and methodological) perspectives in studies of sport and nationalism (Bairner 2015), this article aims to develop a conceptual framework that will help draw our attention to such boundary-making processes in connection with sports and leisure time physical activity. Thus, the research question that drives this article is, 'How may sports and leisure time physical activity contribute to not only including but also excluding groups and individuals from belonging to the nation state?'

In answering this question, we will move away from primordial theories that describe nationalism as a naturally occurring phenomenon and supplement ethno-symbolist descriptions of nationalism as a historically evolving phenomenon with attention to modernist and constructionist perspectives. Thus in our understanding, nations are not merely historical but also socially constructed communities as identified in Benedict Anderson's seminal work on imagined communities (Anderson 1991). As a further evolvement of Anderson's work, postcolonial feminist scholars, specifically Nira Yuval-Davis' work on current politics of belonging and bordering, will serve as our conceptual framework to expand the theoretical approaches used in studies of sport and nationalism. As such, this article will remind us about some of the dark sides of nationalism and the ways in which sports and leisure time physical activity contribute to not only marking who belongs but also who does not belong to the nation.

Postcolonial and transnational feminist perspectives on boundary-making

Together with the postcolonial theory, a so-called third-wave feminism emerged in the North American scholarship in the 1980s (Diaz 2003). In comparison with the first and second waves of feminism, the third wave involved a critique of Western feminist studies for their claim to universalism and for misrepresenting non-western women as a homogenously oppressed group (Brown 2018). Influential studies like Chandra Mohanty's *Under western eyes* point out how western feminist scholars represented third-world women as poor and uneducated as well as victimised through domestic obligations such as caring for family and traditions (Mohanty 1988). Such descriptions reproduce colonial representations and also contribute to the self-representations of western women as educated, liberated and modern. Moreover, Mohanty points out a tendency in feminist studies to focus on gender and presuppose a shared sisterhood, while making differences in race, class, ethnicity, etc. invisible (Mohanty 1988).

Closely related to postcolonial feminism is the work of transnational feminist scholars who also seek to destabilise the global feminist ideas that women around the world share the same experiences while pointing to differences and inequalities which arise from power differences influencing life across nation state borders (Nagar and Swarr 2010). The transnational feminists attempt to support transnational solidarity and collaboration in recognizing power differences and listening to the voices of women who tend to be silenced (Enns, Díaz, and Bryant-Davis 2020). Due to the transnational perspective, particular attention is paid to interaction across borders and to the lives of people who are particularly affected by shifting borders. 'Borderland thinking' is suggested as a useful way of turning attention to hybrid identities, challenges and resistance among such groups (Enns, Díaz, and Bryant-Davis 2020, 7).

A scholar occupied with describing such processes is Nira Yuval-Davis. Supplementing the modernist and constructionist understanding of nations as 'imagined communities' (Anderson 1991), Yuval-Davis points out how such identification processes draw boundaries between the ones that stand inside and the ones that stand outside 'the imaginary boundary line of the nation and/or other communities of belonging' (Yuval-Davis 2006, 204).

The ways in which groups and individuals are able to develop belonging to different communities are related to the processes that Yuval-Davis (2006, 197) has termed the 'politics of belonging':

> The politics of belonging comprises specific political projects aimed at constructing belonging in particular ways to particular collectivities that are, at the same time, themselves being constructed by these projects in very particular ways.

Thus, Yuval-Davis alerts attention to the political interests involved in collective identification processes. Accordingly, the politics of belonging is also described as 'the dirty work of boundary maintenance' (Crowley 1999 cited in Yuval-Davis 2006, 204). The boundaries worked on are those of specific political communities such as nation states, which through regulation of their territorial borders, immigration laws, etc. – but also through symbolic boundary making – include some and exclude 'others' (Yuval-Davis 2006, 204). As such, political communities have the hegemonic power to identify who belongs and who does not belong to a nation, even if these boundaries are also contested by other political agents and the excluded groups themselves.

In her most recent work Yuval-Davis has supplemented her studies of politics of belonging with the concept of border*ing* which is used to stress the interplay between the concept of ordering and the active processes of creating and recreating socio-cultural borders (Yuval-Davis 2011; Yuval-Davis, Wemyss, and Cassidy 2018). In a historical period in which nation states conduct increasing control of their external territorial boundaries Yuval-Davis points to the subtle ways in which borders are also constructed in everyday life by way of ideology and attitudes as well as political regulations that expand into healthcare institutions, schools, workplaces, etc. (Yuval-Davis, Wemyss, and Cassidy 2019). As such, bordering is defined as practices that are intimately linked to political projects of belonging and performed in everyday life in ways that shape subjectivities of individuals and groups, who also contest such processes (Yuval-Davis, Wemyss, and Cassidy 2019).

Even if bordering shapes the lives of all people, particular attention has been paid to how processes of everyday bordering reach into the daily lives of both irregular and regular migrants and shape their subjectivities (Tervonen, Pellander, and Yuval-Davis 2018).

Further, such bordering practices are described as 'differentiating machines' (Rigo 2009, 51 cited in Tervonen, Pellander, and Yuval-Davis 2018) that distinguish between 'us and them' and produce complex hierarchies, for instance between migrants and the population as such. Yuval-Davis (2006) points out that such collective identification processes are often made with reference to one identity marker such as national identity or ethnicity, but it is critical to consider belonging in relation to the intersecting social locations such as gender, race, religion, class, etc. This perspective is taken up in the work on 'everyday intersectional bordering' (Yuval-Davis, Wemyss, and Cassidy 2019, 24) that points out that the current political regulation of national belonging shapes everyday practices of migrant groups in particular.

While the nation is a central community of belonging accompanied by political regulations of citizenship and the rights and obligations that ensue, it is not the only identity marker at play. Thus, Yuval-Davis also builds on Black feminists' work on intersectionality (Crenshaw 1991; Collins and Bilge 2016). Originally, Crenshaw used the concept to describe how gender as well as race and social class make up multiple sources of identity but also social structures that oppress Afro-American working class women. Later, the concept of intersectionality has been used widely in the social sciences not only to describe intersecting structures that oppress certain groups and individuals but also to point to the intersecting layers of identities such as gender, race, ethnicity, class, etc. that relate with each other in diverse ways. In fact, intersectionality has been described as the most important contribution from the feminist theory to the broader social sciences (McCall 2005).

In the wake of this theoretical development, it has been discussed whether wider studies of intersecting layers of identity encompassing age, class, gender, ethnicity, nationality, race, etc. have become detached from attention to the oppressive structures of power (Tomlinson 2013). Scholars using the intersectionality perspective argue for the non-additive principle according to which multiple identities and structures may at times enforce each other but also sometimes reduce the oppression arising from each other (Christensen and Jensen 2012). Yet, the intersectionality perspective does not simply encourage researchers to describe the complexity of intersecting identities but also to point out how such identities combine with social structures in ways that shape the subjectivities of the groups and individuals involved (Davis 2008).

Below we will focus on how the position of ethnic 'other' women in sports and leisure time physical activity is shaped by the political and public debate about national belonging. Before doing so, we will outline former studies that have more or less explicitly applied postcolonial and transnational feminist perspectives.

Postcolonial and transnational feminist studies of ethnic 'other' women in sport

While a couple of studies of sport have directly referred to Yuval-Davis' concept of belonging (Spaaij 2015; Stone 2018), to our knowledge no studies (besides our own) have yet used these perspectives to study sport and nationalism. Notwithstanding, the postcolonial and transnational feminist perspectives are not new to studies of sports and leisure time physical activity. A number of studies have more or less explicitly applied such perspectives to study ethnic 'other' and particularly Muslim women's relationship to sports and leisure time physical activity. Below, we outline such studies to build on their insights and to point out how

Yuval-Davis' concepts may add attention to the ways in which Muslim women are turned into national 'others' in connection with their sports and leisure time physical activity.

In her study from 2000, Jennifer Hargreaves did not explicitly term her approach post-colonial feminist but delivered a sharp critique of the ways in which western feminists have contributed to homogeneous representations of ethnic 'other' women, without describing the mechanisms that shape the identification of specific sporting females (Hargreaves 2000). Another classic text within this field is the book *Muslim women and sport* (Benn, Pfister, and Jawad 2012), which is breaking away from the western perspective on 'others' by including chapters not only about but also by Muslim women.

Notwithstanding, several studies have demonstrated that orientalist thinking is highly prevalent in political and public discourses that among others describe Muslim women as uniformly constrained from sports participation due to their religion and culture (Ahmad 2011; Ratna 2011; Walseth and Strandbu 2014). Studies have also demonstrated that Muslim women are often invisible or depicted as 'strange, incompetent, and out of place' in sporting institutions and media (Samie 2013; Samie and Sehlikoglu 2015). Furthermore, as identified in their edited collection on the politics of ethnic 'other' girls and women (Ratna and Samie 2018), some of the critical literature may also unwittingly contribute to reproducing stereotypes about ethnic 'other' women as a group in particular need of scrutiny or interventions.

As pointed out by sport for development scholars, western images of 'others in need of saving' often form the basis for the current sports policies and programmes (Darnell 2010; Spaaij and Jeanes 2013). Among others, such an approach is prevalent in the policies and programmes in which sport is considered a means to integrate ethnic 'other' groups into their new nation states (Agergaard 2018). Notwithstanding, studies have demonstrated that while sport is assumed to lead to belonging to the nation state, belonging is multi-facetted and evolve at different levels ranging from the team and the sports discipline to free and individualised sporting spaces (Walseth 2006).

In order to move beyond the one-sided attention to Muslim women in sport as shaped by the receiving nations' political focus on, among others, integration, Kim Toffoletti and Cathrine Palmer argue for the usefulness of a transnational feminist approach (Toffoletti and Palmer 2017). The authors criticize the sports development approach in which ethnic 'other' groups and individuals are described as in deficit (e.g. in need of integration and/or health promotion). Further, they argue that sports narratives largely fail to take into account the varied ways in which Muslim women engage in and take pleasure from participating in and consuming sport with diverse approaches (Hamzeh and Oliver 2012; Toffoletti and Palmer 2017).

We agree with the long-standing call for studies of the diverse lives of women of colour and their experiences of sport (Birrell 1990; Scraton 2001; Scraton and Flintoff 2013). However, at present we find it particularly relevant to display the shortcomings in the political and public representation of ethnic 'other' women in a time where rising nationalism and populism influence sports policies and programmes (Agergaard 2018; Spaaij et al. 2019; Thangaraj et al. 2018). Already in 2014, Aarti Ratna described how the national identity of British Asian groups intersects with their gender, race, ethnicity and religion in contradictory inclusion and exclusion processes related to sport. Thus, some British Asians manage to be included by displaying the 'right' attitudes to football while particularly young Muslim British Asian men remain 'outsiders' (Ratna 2014). Below we will make explicit use of a postcolonial and transnational feminist framework to analyse how current political and public discourses only conditionally include and rather exclude Muslim women from belonging to the national community in connection with their sports and leisure practices.

Applying Yuval-Davis to studies of sport and nationalism

In our own studies, we have been making use of the conceptual framework of Yuval-Davis to analyse the politicisation of sports and leisure practices of various groups of Muslim women in Denmark (Lenneis and Agergaard 2018; Agergaard 2019; Lenneis, Agergaard, and Evans 2020; Agergaard et al. 2021). As other European countries, the Danish state has enacted increasingly restrictive immigration and asylum policies (Bergmann 2017; Stainforth 2009), while a growing political and public attention is also paid to immigrants' and descendants' civic integration into their new nation states (Mouritsen and Olsen 2013; Mouritsen, Jensen, and Larin 2019). Thus, we assume that the tendencies identified in our studies towards nationalism as a political ideology and as public attitudes interfering with the sports and leisure practices of ethnic 'other' groups and individuals are not unique to Denmark, but may also deserve attention elsewhere.

Firstly, we will describe how Yuval-Davis' concept politics of belonging may be used in analysing the current nationalism as evident in the lengthy political debate about the 'Danishness' (or rather non-Danishness) of women-only swimming (Lenneis and Agergaard 2018; Lenneis, Agergaard, and Evans, 2020). Secondly, we will demonstrate how the concept of everyday bordering contributes to analyse the ways in which novel political regulations and public attitudes shape Muslim women's options for engaging themselves in leisure time physical activity (Agergaard et al., 2021). Thirdly, in order to further demonstrate the utility of postcolonial and transnational feminist theory we will also pay attention to the agency of ethnic 'other' women to negotiate current politics of national belonging (Agergaard 2019). Across the three case studies, the framework of Yuval-Davis will contribute to point out how national identity is key in current collective identification processes, while more complex intersecting structures and identities are also at play.

Politicizing Danish Muslim women's leisure time physical activity

Despite the often problematised low degree of physical activity among minority ethnic women in western societies (Agergaard 2016; Lenneis and Pfister 2016), women-only swimming sessions, which are popular among Muslim women, have caused great debate in several European countries (Almila 2019; Shavit and Wiesenbach 2012). In the spring of 2016, the debate also arose in nationwide newspapers and among national and local politicians in Denmark. Before then women-only swimming programmes had received governmental and private funding, among others, from the Fund of the Crown Prince and Crown Princess of Denmark and had been praised by the participating women, the organisations involved and by politicians for promoting well-being and civic participation of Muslim women (Agergaard 2018).

However, women-only swimming attracted political and public attention in Denmark at a time when the 'threat' of refugees and immigrants had become important in the current formulations of Danish identity and values (Bergmann 2017; Stainforth 2009). Politicians ranging from the right wing to the central left wing were now keen to utter their critique of Muslim girls and women's participation in such activities (Agergaard 2018). For instance, the political spokesperson and current political leader of the liberal party 'Venstre' was quoted for saying, 'It is not Danish to gender-segregate in swimming pools, and if you do not want to accept the Danish culture, you should find another country to live in' (author's translation, Jakob Ellemann-Jensen, *Berlingske*, 27 April 2016).

In the city council of Aarhus (Denmark's second biggest city) a variety of arguments were expressed during a one-year-long political debate that was initiated by a proposal 'to end women-only swimming' tabled by city councillors of the Liberal Party (Lenneis and Agergaard 2018). Thus, women-only swimming was presented as a non-Danish leisure time physical activity, making it relevant to use Yuval-Davis' understanding of politics of belonging to analyse the line of argumentation about what (and who) belongs to a Danish way of practising sports and leisure time physical activity. This argumentation evolved around four major city councils.

The first city council discussion described women-only swimming as an activity making the participants part of a segregated community. This was reflected in the fact that the concept 'parallel society' was used 29 times (Lenneis and Agergaard 2018). As such, women-only swimming was linked to an ongoing political debate about ethnic 'other' norms and values in politically designated ghetto areas which uniformly makes living there incompatible with the Danish society (von Freiesleben 2016). Moreover, politicians made links between women-only swimming and coercive control in Muslim families portraying the participating all of the women as mothers who hand over norms to their children that are 'non-desirable' in Denmark (Lenneis and Agergaard 2018). In other words, Muslim women's leisure practices had become part of a wider political debate that draws boundaries between who belongs and who does not belong to the nation.

In the second discussion, a city councillor from the Danish People's Party, described gender segregation as a non-Danish practice; thus adding to the general line of argumentation in which nationalism is reinforced through negations of what (and who) is excluded therefrom (Simonsen 2018). Furthermore, the politicians presented gender equality as a core value in the Danish society with the assumption that white Danes have achieved gender equality while ethnic 'others' lack behind. Through such 'nationalizing of gender equality' (Andreassen and Lettinga 2012 cited in Lenneis and Agergaard 2018, 712) the politicians were creating a binary division between the progressive West and the backward Islam. As described by postcolonial feminist scholars (Mohanty 1988), the political debate contributed to represent ethnic 'other'women as a homogeneous group without agency. Notwithstanding, a survey reported the variety in age, ethnicity, religion, citizenship and language proficiency of attendees in women-only swimming sessions and a protest group was formed to claim agency and the right to participate in leisure practices of your own choice (Lenneis and Agergaard 2018).

In the third city council discussion, the Social Democratic Party started supporting the proposal against women-only swimming while also expressing their concern about abolishing club-organised women-only swimming, which they portrayed as a leisure activity that was not religiously motivated (Lenneis and Agergaard 2018). Thus, these politicians reinforced a widespread political belief that ethnic 'others' will obtain civic integration into Denmark through sports clubs (Agergaard 2011), while the participants' religious identity was detached from the debate. As pointed out by Yuval-Davis (2006), national or ethnic identity is often the single predominant characteristic in collective identification processes, which leaves out the intersecting social locations such as gender, race, religion, class, etc. that shape Muslim women's sports and leisure practices.

In the last political discussion, the Social Democrats did criticise the Liberal Party for categorically describing women-only swimming as a uniform practice that leads to women's oppression (Lenneis and Agergaard 2018). Yet, councillors from the two political parties agreed that women-only swimming violated the options for men and women to have equal access to sports facilities in Denmark. Thus, in February 2017 a large majority of the city councillors voted for a ban that closed the single weekly session designated to women-only swimming in one municipal swimming pool located in a socially deprived neighbourhood.

Throughout the debate, 'Danishness' appeared as an overarching theme that intersected with changing arguments linking women-only swimming to, among others, segregation, gender, religion, equality (or not) in ways that drew attention to single dimensions of the participating women's multiple identities. Below, we will point further to the intersecting structures that shape specific groups of Muslim women's leisure practices.

Everyday bordering shaping newcomer women's leisure time physical activity

As a further development of politics of belonging, Yuval-Davis points to everyday bordering in the shape of political regulations, ideologies and public attitudes that extend into various societal institutions and shape the daily practices of particularly migrant groups (Yuval-Davis, Wemyss, and Cassidy 2019). Such political regulations may act as 'differentiating machines' (Rigo 2009, 51 cited in Tervonen, Pellander, and Yuval-Davis 2018) that distinguish between the ones who belong to the nation and the ones who do not.

In 2019, a so-called paradigm shift took place in the Danish immigration policy that had consequences for newcomers in particular. Accordingly, the introduction programme for refugees and family reunified persons was renamed 'the self-support and repatriation programme'.[1] Besides the current emphasis that persons with refugee and family reunified background should become self-supporting within the first years during which they are also learning the Danish language, it has been explicated that the residence permit is temporary and has to be re-evaluated every year or every second year.[2]

The first author and colleagues have conducted a qualitative study with Syrian newcomer women who were part of such an introduction programme in a Danish municipality (Agergaard et al. 2021). Asking these women about their relationship to physical activity, we found that most of the women had been physically active as children and had been engaged in everyday physical activity in their country of origin. Yet, the transition to Denmark had changed their everyday lives, among others, by political regulations for job training and language education. All of the women expressed their desire to be more physically active, while also expressing that they did not have the time and resources needed to participate in sports and leisure time physical activity.

Moreover, the women expressed their feelings of otherness in relation to what they described as active (white) Danish women. For instance, one of the Syrian women newcomers described that it looks right when 'white' Danish women are running, while it would look completely wrong and strange to Danish women if Muslim women were running (Agergaard et al. 2021). As described by Yuval-Davis, everyday bordering includes ideology and attitudes, such as the public attention to veiled Muslim women in public spaces. Such attention has been sharpened with the passing of a law in Denmark against masking directed towards preventing Muslim women from wearing a burka and niqab.[3] As Yuval-Davis and colleagues point out, such political and public debates are moving into the everyday lives of the migrant population. The othering of women that wear Muslim attire also appears to regulate Muslim women's sports and leisure practices. Besides the Syrian women newcomers' utterances, the participants in women-only swimming also described that they refrained from going to the beach or went to beaches in remote places to avoid the public gaze on them as 'others' (Lenneis, Agergaard, and Evans 2020). Thus, even if some of the Muslim women negotiate their options for going to the beach, political regulation and public attitudes appear to increasingly shape the options for Muslim women to participate in leisure time physical activity in Denmark.

Such processes of everyday bordering also evolve around intersecting structures and identities (Yuval-Davis, Wemyss, and Cassidy 2019). In our study with the Syrian women newcomers to Denmark, we identified an entanglement of intersecting structures that shapes these Muslim women's access to leisure time physical activity. Such structures included limited financial resources, obligations following the introduction programme together with household and family obligations. Moreover, Muslim women's engagement in sports and leisure practices did also appear to be limited by pain and worries about the political situation both in their country of origin and in Denmark. This appeared as an interrelated pressure structured both by an increasingly restrictive asylum policy on the one hand and by political conflicts and regimes in their country of origin on the other hand (Agergaard et al. 2021).

Thus, it is relevant to develop a transnational feminist perspective on the power differences that influence life across nation state borders (Nagar and Swarr 2010) and to listen to the voices of newcomer women to shed light on their hybrid identities, challenges and resistance (Enns, Díaz, and Bryant-Davis 2020, 7). Some of the Syrian women attempted to resist challenges arising from processes of everyday bordering, e.g. through jogging in the public domain or through attending leisure time physical activity in closed-off spaces, such as women-only swimming. Below we will elaborate further on the ways in which Muslim women may also negotiate nationalistic politics of belonging and everyday bordering.

Resisting the position as national 'others'

As pointed out by postcolonial and transnational feminist scholars, the lives of national 'other' women are not merely shaped by political discourses but also negotiated and resisted in various ways by the women themselves. This has already been described in studies of how Muslim women use social media to challenge stereotypical and dominant portrayals of ethnic 'other' women as in need of saving, among others, through displaying their participation in sport (Ahmad and Thorpe 2020; Hamzeh 2011).

Muslim women who are successful professional athletes appear to be positioned so that they are better capable of negotiating current politics of belonging. The first author's study of Danish newspapers' representation of Nadia Nadim around the Euro 2017 shed light on such processes using Yuval-Davis conceptual framework and in particular her inspiration from the intersectionality theory to analyse how some groups and individuals are included while others are excluded from belonging to the nation state (Agergaard 2019).

Up through the years when Nadim became one of the most popular players of the Danish national team in women's football, Nadim was described several times in the media as the exemplary ethnic 'other'; a 'poor' girl with refugee background who through sport had become integrated into the Danish society. However, in the wake of an evolving political and public debate about 'Danishness' in 2016–2017, Nadim used the position she had obtained to utter that she had followed the debate on Danishness and had a feeling that it was moving away from the humanity, solidarity and tolerance she and her family had experienced when first coming to live in Denmark. In the run-up to Euro 2017, she participated in a TV documentary in which she raised her concern about the tone and rhetoric of the immigration debate that she described as xenophobic and as detrimental for the part of the Danish population that has a different ethnic background than Danish. Directly questioned by journalists she admitted that she might not have chosen the Danish national team if she still had the choice to play for the Afghan national team. Particularly, the last utterance was discussed fiercely among politicians and media reporters who, among others, argued that as a national team player Nadim could not hesitate in 'fully calling herself Danish' (cited in Agergaard 2019).

Despite Nadim's resistance to such political debate and public attitudes, Nadim's performance and self-presentation at the Euro 2017 contributed to re-awarding her Danishness. As Nadim contributed to the success of the Danish national team in women's football, she was again made Danish to the public. She figured in nation-wide newspapers after the Euro games in embracement with the Crown Prince of Denmark, and she contributed to a joking relationship between nations in stating to the media that her favourite song is 'Deutschland, Deutschland, alles ist vorbei' (Germany, Germany, Germany, it's all over). Thus, a shared national 'other' (Germany) contributed to including Nadim into the nationalism uttered around the women's football team.

Later the same year, Nadim was voted 'Dane of the Year' by the conservative national newspaper, Berlingske. The media reported that Nadim was very happy and honoured to win this price, while Nadim's concern about the minority ethnic population affected by the same political and public attention to Danishness seemed to be silenced (Agergaard 2019). Rather, Nadim was praised for not only being a very skilled female football player, but also for her concurrent training as a medical doctor. Thus, while Nadim's intersecting national, gendered and educational identities were pointed out, the intersecting structures facilitating her trajectories such as the fact that she had grown up in an Afghan upper class family were not pointed out, and neither was her identity as a Muslim.

Thus, popular athletes like Nadim may be included into the national community but on the condition that they embrace ideas about 'Danishness'. Nevertheless, in the run-up to Euro 2017 Nadim did use her position to express her hybrid identity (as Danish and Afghan) and to connect with the minority ethnic population that is excluded from the national community by the debate about Danishness. Despite politician and media reporters' critique of her resistance, Nadim was reintegrated into a Danishness that pointed out that she is successful, well-educated, sports-active, etc. In other words, Nadim is everything that the group of homogenously represented Muslim women is not in Western eyes (Mohanty 1988).

Muslim women who are professional athletes appear to have a platform from which they can utter their resistance towards nationalist discourses. A postcolonial and transnational feminist framework helps to point out that media representations of Nadim are shaped by political and public attitudes that ascribe belonging on the condition of certain intersecting identities while leaving out other aspects of Nadim's hybrid identity. In addition, the political and public debate did not pay attention to the structures that contribute to keeping the large majority of Muslim women in positions as national 'others'.

Discussion

After demonstrating how the postcolonial and transnational feminist perspectives can be applied in studies of sport and nationalism, it is relevant to discuss the contributions and limitations of this theoretical framework. Below we will also point to a possible further development of related theoretical and methodological perspectives that will help research-ers to pay more attention to how sport not only includes but also excludes groups and individuals from belonging to the crucial political community of the nation.

While it is well-described that sports events may contribute to reinforce the national identity of the members of the competing nations, Yuval-Davis' conceptual framework contributes to analysing how groups and individuals that are marked as 'others' may be excluded from belonging to the nation in connection with their sports and leisure practices. While postcolonial and transnational feminism critique the othering of particular groups and individuals as well as western ethnocentric perspectives on national 'others', the question remains whether this conceptual framework allows us to break away from such categories. Paying attention to politics of belonging and everyday bordering, this article describes political regulations and public attitudes that reproduce stereotypical categories of Muslim women as a homogeneous and oppressed group. While we do critique such nationalist policies and public attitudes and also point out how the participating women negotiate and resist such discourses, we may not give sufficient attention to the diverse experiences of sports and leisure practices of Muslim women in their own right.

Postcolonial and transnational feminist theories may be used to analyse how political and public debates about sports and leisure time physical activity are not innocent pastime activities but rather form a part of everyday bordering activities that shape the daily lives of migrant groups in particular. Moreover, the conceptual framework points out that sports and leisure practices of some groups and individuals may be politicized in ways in which nationality (in the shape of ethnic belonging rather than citizenship) become the dominant marker for intersecting identities and structures, while other aspects of migrants' hybrid identities are silenced.

In future research, postcolonial and transnational feminist perspectives could be linked more closely to a social justice perspective so that more attention can be paid to identifying and transforming the inequalities at play. In a position statement, Darnell and Millington (2019) argue that sport may contribute to social justice, but only when efforts are made to distinguish between justice and charity. While many sports and leisure programs are directed towards providing the popular activity of sport to marginalised groups, often no efforts are made to influence the power dynamics and change the existing inequalities. To work towards such a change, the stakeholders must move away from the dominant model of sports devel-opment and instead towards a transformative model (Darnell and Millington 2019). Within the dominant model, the focus is on providing sport as charity to people 'in need', while the structures that reproduce social inequality are often seen as secondary. In contrast, the transformative model for sports and leisure programs is directed towards pursuing social change and initiatives are shaped to support people in their struggle for justice, for instance through linking their sports and leisure practices with social movements (Darnell and Millington 2019).

This also points to the relevance of further developing the postcolonial and transnational feminist approaches and matching them with appropriate methodological perspectives. Pursuing the transformative model for sports and leisure programs involves a shift from simply describing and analysing sports and leisure activities towards contributing to designing, implementing and evaluating sports and leisure activities that are directed towards social change (Long, Fletcher, and Watson 2017). Thus, it appears relevant to develop further attention to participatory approaches and action research in which researchers are involved together with relevant stakeholders and, not least, the marginalized groups and individuals themselves (Hayhurst, Giles, and Radforth 2015). More attention should be paid to how such methodological approaches could be applied in order to give voice, among others, to Danish Muslim women's concerns and resistance against the collective identification processes that demarcate them as national 'others'.

Conclusion

In this article, we set out to develop a conceptual framework for analysing sport and nationalism that is not limited to sports events but move into the processes evolving around everyday sports and leisure activities. Based on a postcolonial and transnational feminist approach – and more particularly Nira Yuval-Davis' concepts of politics of belonging and everyday bordering – we enquired into the processes through which sports and leisure practices do not only include but also exclude groups and individuals from belonging to the nation state.

While postcolonial and transnational feminist perspectives have been applied (implicitly or explicitly) in previous studies of ethnic 'other' women, we have identified a continuous need for critical studies of the ways in which the current nationalist political and public debate shape Muslim women's sports and leisure practices. To be more specific, we found that such political regulations and public attitudes are part of everyday bordering processes that interfere with Muslim women's leisure practices but also their clothing and their movements in public space. Furthermore, we found that Muslim women do also negotiate and resist such political and public regulations and that some individuals and groups are better positioned to do so than others.

Finally, we suggest that related theoretical perspectives such as the social justice perspective and methodological approaches such as participatory and action research can further support research not only on but also with national 'others' in sport. Thus, we point out the relevance of working with groups like Danish Muslim women in claiming to belong to and have equal access to sports and leisure time physical activity.

Notes

1. Information retrieved 01.06.2019 from: https://uim.dk/arbejdsomrader/Integration/ Selvforsorgelses-og-hjemrejseprogrammet-og-introduktionsprogrammet

2. Information retrieved 01.07.2020 from: https://www.nyidanmark.dk/en-GB/Applying/Asylum/Adult%20asylum%20applicant
3. Information retrieved 01.10.2020 from: https://www.retsinformation.dk/eli/ft/201712L00219

Disclosure statement

No potential conflict of interest was reported by the authors.

Funding

The studies described in this article were supported by the Danish Cultural Ministry, Committee of Research as well as Region Midtjylland.

ORCID

Sine Agergaard ⓘ http://orcid.org/0000-0003-2658-8933

References

Agergaard, S. 2011. "Development and Appropriation of an Integration Policy for Sport. How Danish sports clubs have become arenas of ethnic integration." *International Journal of Sport Policy and Politics*, 3 (3): 341–353.

Agergaard, S. 2016. "Religious culture as a barrier? A counter-narrative of Danish Muslim girls' participation in sports." *Qualitative Research in Sport, Exercise and Health*, 8 (2): 213–224.

Agergaard, S. 2018. *Rethinking Sports and Integration*. London and New York: Routledge.

Agergaard, S. 2019. "Nationalising Minority Ethnic Athletes: Danish Media Representations of Nadia Nadim around the UEFA Women's Euro 2017." *Sport in History*, 39 (2): 130–146.

Agergaard, S., Lenneis V., Bakkær Simonsen C., and Ryom K. 2021. "Granted asylum and healthy living? Women newcomers' experiences of options for accessing leisure time physical activity in Denmark." In: Caudewell, J., and Ugolotti, N. De Martini (eds.), Leisure and forced migration. Reframing critical analysis of lives lived in the asylum system. Routledge Advancing Leisure Series.

Ahmad, Aisha. 2011. "British Football: Where Are the Muslim Female Footballers? Exploring the Connections between Gender, Ethnicity and Islam." *Soccer & Society* 12 (3): 443–456. doi:10.1080/14660970.2011.568110.

Ahmad, Niha, and Holly Thorpe. 2020. "Muslim Sportswomen as Digital Space Invaders: Hashtag Politics and Everyday Visibilities." *Communication & Sport* 8 (4-5): 668–691. doi:10.1177/2167479519898447.

Almila, Anna-Mari. 2019. *Veiling in Fashion: Space and the Hijab in Minority Communities*. London: I.B Tauris.

Anderson, Benedict. 1991. *Imagined Communities: Reflections on the Origin and Spread of Nationalism*. London: Verso.

Armstrong, John A. 1982. *Nations before Nationalism*. Chapel Hill: University of North Carolina Press.

Bairner, Alan. 2015. "Assessing the Sociology of Sport: On National Identity and Nationalism." *International Review for the Sociology of Sport* 50 (4-5): 375–379. doi:10.1177/1012690214538863.

Benn, Tansin, Gertrud Pfister, and Haifaa Jawad, eds. 2012. *Muslim Women and Sport*. London: Routledge.

Bergmann, Eirikur. 2017. "Denmark: From Multi-Ethnic and Supra-National Empire to Little Denmark." In *Nordic Nationalism and Right-Wing Populist Politics*, edited by Eirikur Bergmann, 33–69. London: Palgrave Macmillan.

Birrell, Susan. 1990. "Women of Color: Critical Autobiography and Sport." In *Sport, Men and the Gender Order*, edited by Michel A. Messner and Donald F. Sabo, 185–200. Champaign, IL: Human Kinetics.

Brown, Letisha Engracia Cardoso. 2018. "Post-Colonial Feminism, Black Feminism and Sport." In *The Palgrave Handbook of Feminism and Sport, Leisure and Physical Education*, edited by Louise Mansfield, Jayne Caudwell, Belinda Wheaton, and Beccy Watson, 479–495. London: Palgrave Macmillan.

Brubaker, Rogers. 2017. "Between Nationalism and Civilizationism: The European Populist Moment in Comparative Perspective." *Ethnic and Racial Studies* 40 (8): 1191–1226. doi:10.1080/01419870.2017.1294700.

Christensen, Anne-Dorthe, and Sune Qvortrup Jensen. 2012. "Doing Intersectional Analysis. Methodological Implications for Qualitative Research." *NORA - Nordic Journal of Feminist and Gender Research* 20 (2): 109–125. doi:10.1080/08038740.2012.673505.

Collins, Patricia H., and Sirma Bilge. 2016. *Intersectionality*. Malden: Polity Press.

Crenshaw, Kimberlé. 1991. "Mapping the Margins: Intersectionality, Identity Politics, and Violence against Women of Color." *Stanford Law Review* 43 (6): 1241–1299. doi:10.2307/1229039.

Darnell, Simon. 2010. "Sport, Race, and Bio-Politics: Encounters with Difference in 'Sport for Development and Peace' Internships." *Journal of Sport and Social Issues* 34 (4): 396–417. doi:10.1177/0193723510383141.

Darnell, Simon C., and Rob Millington. 2019. "Social Justice, Sport, and Sociology: A Position Statement." *Quest* 71 (2): 175–187. doi:10.1080/00336297.2018.1545681.

Davis, Kathy. 2008. "Intersectionality as Buzzword. A Sociology of Science Perspective on What Makes a Feminist Theory Successful." *Feminist Theory* 9 (1): 67–85. doi:10.1177/1464700108086364.

Diaz, Angeli R. 2003. "Postcolonial Theory and the Third Wave Agenda." *Women and Language* 26 (1): 10–17.

Edensor, Tim. 2002. *National Identity, Popular Culture and Everyday Life*. Oxford: Berg.

Elgenius, Gabriella, and Jens Rydgren. 2019. "Frames of Nostalgia and Belonging: The Resurgence of Ethno-Nationalism in Sweden." *European Societies* 21 (4): 583–602. doi:10.1080/14616696.2018.1494297.

Enns, Carolyn Zerbe, Lillian Comas Díaz, and Thema Bryant-Davis. 2020. "Transnational Feminist Theory and Practice: An Introduction." *Women & Therapy*, 44 (1-2), 11–26. doi:10.1080/0270314 9.2020.1774997.

Hamzeh, Manal. 2011. "*Deveiling* Body Stories: Muslim Girls Negotiate Visual, Spatial, and Ethical *Hijabs*." *Race Ethnicity and Education* 14 (4): 481–506. doi:10.1080/13613324.2011.563287.

Hamzeh, Manal, and Kimberly L. Oliver. 2012. "Because I Am Muslim, I Cannot Wear a Swimsuit." *Research Quarterly for Exercise and Sport* 83 (2): 330–339. doi:10.5641/027013612800745167.

Hargreaves, Jennifer. 2000. *Heroines of Sport: The Politics of Difference and Identity*. London: Routledge.

Hayhurst, Lyndsay M. C., Audrey R. Giles, and Whitney M. Radforth. 2015. "'I Want to Come Here to Prove Them Wrong': Using a Post-Colonial Feminist Participatory Action Research (PFPAR) Approach to Studying Sport, Gender and Development Programmes for Urban Indigenous Young Women." *Sport in Society* 18 (8): 952–967. doi:10.1080/17430437.2014.997585.

Lenneis, Verena, and Gertrud Pfister. 2016. "Health, Physical Activity and the Body: An Inquiry into the Lives of Female Migrant Cleaners in Denmark." *International Journal of Sport Policy and Politics* 8 (4): 647–662. doi:10.1080/19406940.2016.1220408.

Lenneis, V., and Agergaard S. 2018. "Enacting and Resisting the Politics of Belonging Through Leisure. The Debate About Gender-segregated Swimming Sessions Targeting Muslim Women in Denmark." *Leisure Studies* 37 (6): 706–720.

Lenneis, V., Agergaard, S., and Evans, A.B. 2020. *Women-only swimming as a space of belonging, Qualitative Research in Sport, Exercise and Health*. doi:10.1080/2159676X.2020.1844790.

Long, Jonathan, Thomas Fletcher, and Beccy Watson, eds. 2017. *Sport, Leisure and Social Justice*. Abingdon: Routledge.

McCall, Leslie. 2005. "The Complexity of Intersectionality." *Signs: Journal of Women in Culture and Society* 30 (3): 1771–1800. doi:10.1086/426800.

Mohanty, Chandra. 1988. "Under Western Eyes: Feminist Scholarship and Colonial Discourses." *Feminist Review* 30 (1): 61–88. doi:10.1057/fr.1988.42.

Mouritsen, Per, Kristian K. Jensen, and Stephen J. Larin. 2019. "Introduction: Theorizing the Civic Turn in European Integration Politics." *Ethnicities* 19 (4): 595–613. doi:10.1177/1468796819843532.

Mouritsen, Per, and Tore Vincents Olsen. 2013. "Denmark between Liberalism and Nationalism." *Ethnic and Racial Studies* 36 (4): 691–710. doi:10.1080/01419870.2011.598233.

Nagar, Richa, and Amanda Lock Swarr. 2010. *Critical Transnational Feminist Praxis*. Albany: State University of New York Press.

Ratna, Aarti. 2011. "'Who Wants to Make Aloo Gobi When You Can Bend It Like Beckham?' British Asian Females and Their Racialised Experiences of Gender and Identity in Women's Football." *Soccer & Society* 12 (3): 382–401. doi:10.1080/14660970.2011.568105.

Ratna, Aarti. 2014. "'Who Are ya?' The National Identities and Belongings of British Asian Football Fans." *Patterns of Prejudice* 48 (3): 286–308. doi:10.1080/0031322X.2014.927603.

Ratna, Aarti, and Samaya F. Samie, eds. 2018. *Race, Gender and Sport. The Politics of Ethnic 'Other' Girls and Women*. New York: Routledge.

Samie, Samaya Farooq. 2013. "Hetero-Sexy Self/Body Work and Basketball: The *Invisible* Sporting Women of British Pakistani Muslim Heritage." *South Asian Popular Culture* 11 (3): 257–270. doi:10.1080/14746689.2013.820480.

Samie, Sumaya Farooq, and Sertaç Sehlikoglu. 2015. "Strange, Incompetent and out-of-Place." *Feminist Media Studies* 15 (3): 363–381. doi:10.1080/14680777.2014.947522.

Scraton, Sheila. 2001. "Reconceptualizing Race, Gender and Sport: The Contribution of Black Feminism." In *Race, Sport and British Society*, edited by Ben Carrington and Ian McDonald, 170–187. London: Routledge.

Scraton, Sheila, and Anne Flintoff. 2013. "Gender, Feminist Theory and Sport." In *A Companion to Sport*, edited by David L. Andrews and Ben Carrington, 96–111. Oxford: Blackwell Publishing.

Seippel, Ørnulf. 2017. "Sports and Nationalism in a Globalized World." *International Journal of Sociology* 47 (1): 43–61. doi:10.1080/00207659.2017.1264835.

Shavit, Uriya, and Frederic Wiesenbach. 2012. "An 'Integrating Enclave': The Case of Al-Hayat, Germany's First Islamic Fitness Center for Women in Cologne." *Journal of Muslim Minority Affairs* 32 (1): 47–61. doi:10.1080/13602004.2012.665621.

Simonsen, Kristina Bakkaer. 2018. "What It Means to (Not) Belong: A Case Study of How Boundary Perceptions Affect Second-Generation Immigrants' Attachments to the Nation." *Sociological Forum* 33 (1): 118–138. doi:10.1111/socf.12402.

Spaaij, Ramón. 2015. "Refugee Youth, Belonging and Community Sport." *Leisure Studies* 34 (3): 303–318. doi:10.1080/02614367.2014.893006.

Spaaij, Ramón, and Ruth Jeanes. 2013. "Education for Social Change? A Freirean Critique of Sport for Development and Peace." *Physical Education & Sport Pedagogy* 18 (4): 442–457. doi:10.1080/17408989.2012.690378.

Spaaij, Ramón, Broerse Jora, Oxford Sarah, Luguetti Carla, McLachlan Fiona, McDonald Brent, Klepac Bojana, Lymbery Lisa, Bishara Jeffrey, and Pankowiak Aurélie. 2019. "Sport, Refugees, and Forced Migration: A Critical Review of the Literature." *Frontiers in Sports and Active Living* 1: 47. doi:10.3389/fspor.2019.00047.

Spencer, Philip, and Howard Wollman. 2002. *Nationalism. A Critical Introduction*. London: Sage.

Stainforth, Thorfinn. 2009. "The Danish Paradox: Intolerance in the Land of Perpetual Compromise." *Review of European and Russian Affairs* 5 (1): 83–106. doi:10.22215/rera.v5i1.204.

Stone, Chris. 2018. "Utopian Community Football? Sport, Hope and Belongingness in the Lives of Refugees and Asylum Seekers." *Leisure Studies* 37 (2): 171–183. doi:10.1080/02614367.2017.1329336.

Tervonen, Miika, Saara Pellander, and Nira Yuval-Davis. 2018. "Everyday Bordering in the Nordic Countries." *Nordic Journal of Migration Research* 8 (3): 139–142. doi:10.2478/njmr-2018-0019.

Thangaraj, Stanley, Aarti Ratna, Daniel Burdsey, and Erica Rand. 2018. "Leisure and the Racing of National Populism." *Leisure Studies* 37 (6): 648–661. doi:10.1080/02614367.2018.1541473.

Toffoletti, Kim, and Cathrine Palmer. 2017. "New Approaches for Studies of Muslim Women and Sport." *International Review for the Sociology of Sport* 52 (2): 146–163. doi:10.1177/1012690215589326.

Tomlinson, Barbara. 2013. "Colonizing Intersectionality. Replicating Racial Hierarchy in Feminist Academic Arguments." *Social Identities. Journal for the Study of Race, Nation and Culture* 19 (2): 245–272.

von Freiesleben, Anna Mikaela. 2016. "Et Danmark af Parallelsamfund [a Denmark of Parallel Societies]." PhD diss., University of Copenhagen.

Walseth, Kristin. 2006. "Sport and Belonging." *International Review for the Sociology of Sport* 41 (3-4): 447–464. doi:10.1177/1012690207079510.

Walseth, Kristin, and Aase Strandbu. 2014. "Young Norwegian-Pakistani Women and Sport: How Does Culture and Religiosity Matter?" *European Physical Education Review* 20 (4): 489–507. doi: 10.1177/1356336X14534361.

Yuval-Davis, Nira. 2006. "Belonging and the Politics of Belonging." *Patterns of Prejudice* 40 (3): 197–214. doi:10.1080/00313220600769331.

Yuval-Davis, Nira. 2011. *The Politics of Belonging : Intersectional Contestations*. London: Sage.

Yuval-Davis, Nira, George Wemyss, and Kathryn Cassidy. 2018. "Everyday Bordering, Belonging and the Reorientation of British Immigration Legislation." *Sociology* 52 (2). 228–244. doi:10.1177/0038038517702599.

Yuval-Davis, Nira, George Wemyss, and Kathryn Cassidy. 2019. *Bordering*. Cambridge: Polity Press.

Analysing British Asian national sporting affiliations post-London 2012

Alison Forbes

ABSTRACT
London's selection as hosts for the 2012 Olympic Games was a significant moment for Britain. It was a chance to reinforce, through sport, a collective and inclusive British national identity. Most international sporting contests draw on *English* rather than British loyalties and identity constructions. This might have been especially important for members of the large British Asian diaspora, many of whom feel excluded from ethnically exclusive and narrowly White notions of 'Englishness'. This paper is framed within a post-London 2012 period and examines the role of sport in constructing and negotiating British Asian national identities. Semi-structured interviews were conducted with young British Asians in two English cities. For those who rejected an English national identity through sport, the Games presented an opportunity to connect with a more inclusive British version of sporting allegiance.

Introduction

Britain's diverse and multi-ethnic communities were strategically placed at the heart of London's successful bid to host the 2012 Olympic and Paralympic Games. The subsequent promotional build up to the Games continued to celebrate Britain's diversity, and a group of athletes, from a variety of different ethnic and faith backgrounds, represented Great Britain at the London 2012 Olympic Games. The continued public promotion in the United Kingdom (UK) of ethnic and cultural diversity around the Games prompted media claims that Great Britain's Olympic Team (hereafter Team GB) was symbolic of an inclusive and authentic national pride (Black 2016).

The rhetoric of an inclusive national pride, to be celebrated by Team GB at London 2012, was very much in contrast to Conservative MP Normal Tebbit's controversial comments in 1990 regarding the loyalties and citizenship of British Asians. He purported that Britain's migrant communities must be willing to publically demonstrate an allegiance to the English national cricket team, to signal their commitment to fully assimilate into a 'British way of life':

> Which side do they cheer for? Are you still harking back to where you came from - or where you are? (Norman Tebbit as quoted in Farrington et al. 2012, 87)

Tebbit's controversial comments – that sparked widespread debate in the UK about the relationship between national identity and sport, especially in relation to Britain's minority ethnic communities - have been criticised as representing an essentialist interpretation of 'Britishness' and 'Asianness'. Such narrow interpretations 'demonstrate a lack of sensitivity to the concepts of diaspora, hybridity and multiple identities' (Fletcher 2012, 620). These concepts have proven useful theoretical tools for debates concerning British Asian identities and sporting loyalties. Exploring ways in which notions of belonging, 'Englishness' and 'Britishness' are constructed, contested and in some cases resisted by British Asians has helped to articulate the complexity of British Asian diasporic identities (Burdsey 2006; Fletcher 2012; Ratna 2014). As Fletcher (2012, 619) asserts, questioning whether British Asians should be supporting England in sporting contests involving teams from the Indian subcontinent presumes that a correct answer exists. Instead, he advocates that a more pertinent question is, 'if British Asians are not supporting England, why not?'

A developing body of literature has started to explore the relationship between British Asians and English national identities (see Fletcher 2012; Raman 2015; Ratna 2014). However, the impact of the 2012 Olympic Games on experiences of a wider (and potentially more inclusive) British identity has hitherto been excluded from these explorations. The unique structure of international competition in the Olympic Games - where athletes from England, Wales, Scotland and Northern Ireland come together to compete as Great Britain – offers a sociologically significant lens via which to explore 'Britishness', national identity and sport. Framed within a post-London 2012 period, this article utilises diaspora and hybridity as conceptual tools to provide a framework for the analysis of British Asian national sporting affiliations.

Literature review

Diaspora and hybridity as conceptual tools

The concept of diaspora describes groups of people who share some form of collective history from a place of origin, but who have now dispersed. Kalra, Kaur, and Hutnyk (2005, 29) usefully describe this as being *from* one place, but *of* another'. The British Asian diaspora, then, is a collective of migrant communities in Britain who are connected to a specific place of origin – in this case, the Indian subcontinent (comprised of India, Pakistan, Bangladesh and Sri Lanka). Exploring national identity through a diasporic lens is useful because the idea of diaspora acknowledges that national identity exists across the boundaries of nation states, instead of within them (Anthias 2001; Fletcher and Lusted 2017). For Carrington (2015, 394), the concept of diaspora provides a framework that has redefined notions of place and identity, encouraging us to think 'less in terms of fixity and rootedness but instead through notions of flow and routes.' Place of residence and intimate or material connections to other places characterise the concept of diaspora, meaning that belonging is 'never a simple question of affiliation to a singular idea of ethnicity or nationalism, but rather about the multivocality of belongings' (Kalra, Kaur, and Hutnyk 2005, 29).

The concept of diaspora has been widely drawn upon within sociological studies to help analyse the negotiation of identity in several different social fields. Brah (1996, 16), highlights the usefulness of diaspora as 'an interpretive frame for analysing the economic, political and cultural modalities of historically specific forms of migrancy.' Whilst sport, in the post-migration era, has become a useful analytical framework for theorising the notion of being part of a diaspora, the concept is still regarded as in its infancy within the sociological study of sport and identity (Carrington 2015). The relationship between British Asians and national sporting identity is one area where theories of diaspora have been explicitly used, although, as detailed in the upcoming literature review, this scholarship has focused almost exclusively on the sports of cricket and football. These debates concerning British Asian identities and sporting loyalties have typically drawn on the concept of diaspora to account for the multifarious ways in which British Asians connect with each other and with their homelands (Burdsey 2007; Fletcher 2015; Ratna 2014). With this in mind, diaspora is a particularly useful concept in thinking about how young British Asians experience sport and how sport contributes to their understanding of a British Asian identity, especially in the context of the Olympic Games.

Notably, diasporic identities are not fixed, and instead should be conceived as fluid and hybrid. When adopting a diasporic lens, it is insufficient to think in terms of either/or identities. As Fletcher and Lusted (2017, 14) argue, 'it Is not the case that being English translates to not being South/British Asian, Black etc., and vice versa. Rather a diasporic lens encourages us to accept the possibility of a third space of hybrid identities.' Bhabha developed this notion of a third space as a place for negotiation:

> Where power is unequal but its articulation may be equivocal. Such negotiation is neither assimilation nor collaboration. It makes possible the emergence of an 'interstitial' agency that refuses the binary representation of social antagonism. Hybrid agencies find their voice in a dialectic that does not seek cultural supremacy or sovereignty. (Bhabha 1996, 58)

Similarly, in his work on diaspora in the context of sport, Carrington (2015, 394) suggests that migration does not necessarily result in the loss of a home identity, and nor does it mean an unproblematic assimilation into the new host country. Instead, he conceives this process as a 'continual (re)negotiation of identities, understood as hybrid and contingent through a process of contestation that ultimately reshapes the imaginary, both the "sending" and "host" countries'.

Hybridity then, is a relevant conceptual tool to explore British Asian identities: 'British' and 'Asian' are not exclusive cultural categories but dynamic and fluid identities that can fuse in sporting and other arenas to form hybridised identities (Fletcher 2012). Thus, British Asians can be *both* British (or English) and Asian and be comfortable with more than one sense of ethnic identity. Indeed, Fletcher (2012) suggests that it would be naïve to try to simplify what is clearly a complex process of identity negotiation. Such simplicity risks leading us back to the narrow understanding of 'Britishness' that Norman Tebbit once propagated regarding British Asians and their cricketing allegiance.

'Britishness', 'Englishness' and contested concepts of national identity

Sport has been described as a microcosm through which problems surrounding English national identity can be observed. For example, in their edited collection on sport and English national identity, Gibbons and Malcom (2017, 1) demonstrate that 'current debates regarding Englishness are manifest in sport in diverse, and at times contradictory, ways'. Post-modernist approaches to nationalism identify a need to extend the focus of the modernist paradigm to include how post-colonial perspectives and the influence of globalisation have impacted upon traditional ways of theorising the nation (Smith 2010). When aligned to the heterogenisation perspective, globalisation is considered as providing opportunities for interaction between different cultures across the world, enabling the development of hybrid practices and identities (Gibbons and Malcolm 2017). Thus, the global migration of individuals, such as those who trace their ancestry back to the Indian subcontinent, has led to the possibility of hybrid cultural identities operating within nation-states.

Nationalism has been examined, amongst other things, as a cultural construct of collective belonging, and as a site for material and symbolic struggles over the definition of national inclusion and exclusion (Fox and Miller-Idris 2008). The context of sport is perhaps one of the most significant means through which notions of 'Englishness' and 'Britishness' are constructed, contested and resisted (Black, Fletcher, and Lake 2020). International sporting events – such as the Olympic Games - provide important contexts for everyday articulations of the nation because sport can capture the national imagination in ways that other cultural events do not. As Fox and Miller-Idris (2008) identify, during international competitions fans become a physical embodiment of their nation. With their faces painted, flags draped over shoulders and clothing emblazoned in national colours, fans physically encapsulate and communicate national allegiance.

Debates around the conflation of 'Englishness' and 'Britishness' tend to resurface in the build-up to any Olympic Games. At the centre of this debate in the run up to London 2012 was a dispute about whether there would be a Great Britain team playing in the Olympic football tournament. The constituent nations of the UK have a long tradition of being represented by separate football teams, and have voting rights with FIFA to match. There were concerns that the independent status that the home nations enjoy in world football might be compromised if they combined to play as Great Britain in the Olympic Games (Ewen 2012).

The contested concept of a British national identity in sport was bought to the fore in public debate at the London Games when the male Welsh footballers Ryan Giggs, Craig Bellamy, Joe Allen and Neil Taylor and the female Scottish players Kim Little and Ifeoma Dieke, all representing Team GB, elected not to sing the shared English and British national anthem, God Save the Queen, before their respective matches. Vincent et al. (2018) have noted that many Scottish and Welsh players and fans regard their primary Scottish or Welsh national identity as more important than a much less meaningful British identity. To further complicate matters, English and British national identities are ambiguous, contested and often applied interchangeably (Fletcher and Lusted 2017; Gibbons and Malcolm 2017), perhaps contributing to the weaker connection to a British identity for many citizens of the other UK home nations.

The Olympics, success narratives and British multiculturalism

The London 2012 Olympic Games bid (and its successful staging in London) was based on the premise that by hosting the Games, London (and the UK) could engage, celebrate and cohere its diverse and multi-ethnic communities. Such seductive narratives were uncritically accepted by many: it was widely stated that London 2012 would '*inevitably* create lasting legacy benefits' by ensuring that sport was accessible for everybody, regardless of their background (Hylton and Morpeth 2012, 379). Despite the hyperbole of multiculturalism around the London 2012 'back the bid' campaign, not all sections of the host population would be the beneficiaries of a so-called Olympic legacy. Billing London 2012 as an inclusive and multicultural project to celebrate a diverse and harmonious Britain was, according to Winter (2013), a 'projected fantasy' that distracted from the social, political and economic realities of many disenfranchised communities. As Hylton and Morpeth (2012) argue, race 'matters' in Olympic legacy discourses and single mega-event policies seemingly neglect the micro-details of accumulated historical factors, such as entrenched racial inequalities in sport.

The successes of British athletes Mo Farah and Jessica Ennis at the London Games were widely regarded as validation of the rhetoric of ethnic and cultural diversity and inclusion that had been promoted in London's successful Olympic bid, and in the subsequent build up to the games. Farah, a Black Muslim of Somalian heritage and Ennis, born in Britain to a Jamaican father and English mother, were lauded for their Olympic successes (both winning gold medals in their respective athletic disciplines) and portrayed as positive role models for Britain's diverse and multi-ethnic communities (Black 2016; Burdsey 2016). The narratives surrounding Farah's achievements at the London 2012 Olympic Games have been presented as an affirmation of Britain's achieved multiculturalism, and thus the perceived validation that sport is 'meritocratic' and that ethnic and religious backgrounds are no barriers to sporting success (Burdsey 2016; Black 2016). This rhetoric of multiculturalism was largely appropriated due to the assorted ethnic backgrounds of representatives of Team GB, which were used as evidence that racial inequality in elite sport in the UK no longer exists. However, as Burdsey (2016) emphasises, the biographies of the participating British athletes actually highlighted ethnic, class and educational backgrounds that were still largely unrepresentative of multicultural Britain. Critical readings of the media representations of Farah have led to conclusions that his British acceptance was something that needed both to be achieved and performed (Black 2016), and that 'the wider multicultural ramifications of his achievements are more conditional, ephemeral and limited than is widely suggested' (Burdsey 2016, 22).

The academic literature that has explored the successes of Mo Farah in the context of his Britishness and belonging to the nation has mainly focused on analysing media representations. What is still unclear is how these successes of British athletes with multi-ethnic backgrounds might have impacted on young British Asians' interest in and consumption of the 2012 Olympic Games, and on their identity construction and national affiliations. This article therefore aims to make a contribution to the literature by exploring the significance of the London 2012 Olympic Games – with its alternative structure of international competition - in constructing British Asian national identities through sport.

The importance of sport for diasporic groups

An emergence of sport sociologists have begun to explore the role and importance of sport for diasporic groups. Within these studies the concept of diaspora has provided a framework to illustrate how sport can connect geographically dispersed groups (Carrington 2015). Whigham's (2015) work focused on the Scottish diaspora in England to explore the role of sport in maintaining cultural attachments to their homeland. Similarly, Joseph's (2014) empirical study of the Caribbean diaspora in Canada identified the importance of cricket for generating and maintaining diasporic communities, and a connection with their

Caribbean heritage. In their systematic literature review of sport and diaspora, McSweeny and Nakamura (2020) identified that 'nation' and 'homeland' were both key constructs within many examinations of diaspora, which provides insights into how identities are negotiated, often unstable and hybrid in their formation. Importantly, those that have conducted studies with ethnic minority diasporic groups have frequently identified how fostering a sense of diasporic connectivity through sport can help challenge and resist institutionalised white privilege and reject aspects of the host nation that are exclusionary or oppressive (Burdsey 2007; Fletcher and Lusted 2017; Fletcher and Walle 2015). The final section of this literature review revisits debates about sport and British Asian identities, focusing on the role that cricket and football play for the British Asian diaspora in the UK.

The role of cricket for the british asian diaspora

The role that cricket plays in fostering a sense of diasporic connectivity for a number of diasporic groups has been well documented. In their work on Asian-specific cricket teams in the UK and Norway, Fletcher and Walle (2015) identify the significant social network that cricket represents for Pakistani heritage Muslim men. Many South Asian migrants experienced alienation upon their arrival to Britain, with many historically White cricketing spaces prohibiting South Asian heritage players from entering the social spaces of established English cricket clubs (Raman 2015; Fletcher 2012). Cricket then, became a cultural location for those that had migrated from the Indian subcontinent to display resistance to British cultural norms and values. By creating their own domestic cricketing networks in England, South Asian arrivals played cricket together and watched and supported their homeland national teams, thus creating spaces of diasporic connectivity while maintaining meaningful links with 'home' (Devan 2012; Fletcher 2012; Raman 2015). Playing cricket within their own networks, and displaying allegiance and support for the national cricket teams of their ancestral roots was a symbolic way of emancipating South Asians from the struggles of everyday life.

Affiliation with national teams of the homeland is frequent and perhaps expected amongst the older generations of migrants from the subcontinent. These loyalties have been forged over time and, despite acculturation into English ways of life, they are unlikely simply to dissolve (Raman 2015). However, generational difference in relation to national affiliation and belonging is becoming more apparent, especially for those British Asians who have been born, brought up and educated in Britain and feel very closely aligned with British culture. As Fletcher (2012, 617) notes: 'The lives of young British Asians are grounded through a combination of the cultures and traditions of their parents and the Indian subcontinent, and in the culture and social practices of Britain'. Consequently, despite Raman's (2015) assertion that even amongst very young British Asians support for the homeland teams was undisputed, she also reported an emerging and growing separation between younger and elder generations, as the former's dual ethnicities and cultural hybridity comes between them.

Within their work on sports fandom and national affiliation in the context of the 2014 Football World Cup, Stanfill and Valdivia (2017) illustrated how sports highlighted the dynamic nature of national identity and the fragile coherence of nation-states, with hybrid teams playing before hybrid audiences with hybrid allegiances. Fletcher and Lusted (2017) propose that connection with and belonging to England and notions of 'Englishness' or

'Britishness' are context bound. As Burdsey (2007) articulates, sport embodies the fragmented nature of identity, which is indicated through the examination of the contrasting affiliations of young British Asians in football and cricket. This is significant because, as this article and previous literature demonstrates, whilst many British Asians articulate support for the national cricket teams from their respective countries of ancestry, there are certain contradictory trends that are evident, for example in relation to British Asians and English football fandom.

'Divided loyalties': British asians and football support.

Young British Asians are, in increasing numbers, demonstrating support for the England national football team (Burdsey 2007; Ratna 2014). Nevertheless, persisting British Asian support for their countries of ancestry in cricket has led to accusations that they might be caught 'between two cultures', and the belief that British Asians are not authentic England football fans because their loyalties are supposedly divided between England and their ancestral places of 'home' (Ratna 2014). However, there are many challenges to the idea that British Asians are in some way 'compromised' in their 'Britishness' by being loyal supporters of England at football and of national teams from their country of ancestry in other sports. This kind of reductive argument ignores the core complexity of British Asian identities, where 'celebrating India in cricket and England in football is just a hybrid aspect of who they are' (Ratna 2014, 300).

In contrast to the ardent displays of cricket fandom, perhaps unsurprisingly, there is very little evidence of any fully-fledged support or affiliation for the national football teams of the subcontinent (Burdsey 2007). The elite status and international successes of subcontinental national cricket teams, in contrast to the extremely weak official rankings of subcontinent football teams in FIFA's global 'league table' might go some way to explaining this (Burdsey 2007; Ratna 2014). Compared with cricket, football takes on an entirely different role within the construction of identities among young British Asians. Allegiance to football is related to their own permanent residence in England and, is an important part of mainstream British culture (Burdsey 2007). Nevertheless, in relation to football, certain contradictory trends regarding sporting allegiances do seem to be evident. For example, whilst cricket allegiance to teams in the subcontinent is often attributed to a rejection of exclusionary aspects of 'Englishness', young British Asians seem not to be expressing the same kind of rejection in football contexts.

Significantly, British Asians who choose to play football are often met with some of the same cultural constraints in relation to their participation in cricket. That many young British Asians in England closely follow the England national football team, and domestic English clubs is thus especially pertinent when considering that British Asians have faced significant barriers to entering English professional football as players (Kilvington 2016). British Asians following football in England have also been subject to racist abuse from some members of the White-British population (Burdsey and Randhawa 2012). As Burdsey (2007, 99) argues, the fact that increasing numbers of young British Asians now affirm their support for England in football does not change the fact that notions of 'Englishness' remain deeply problematic for them. Everyday experiences of racism, in and out of the football arena, continue to act as a reminder to British Asians that they are not uniformly accepted or welcomed and these experiences can, understandably, taint their sense of belonging to the nation (Ratna 2014). Thus, Burdsey (2007) suggests that we must remain cautious about the extent to which affiliation with the England football team signifies a palpable 'improvement' in racial equality, either in football or in the wider society.

Whilst there is a consensus that analysing the construction of national identities through sport can enable a wider sociological understanding of the nuances and complexities of contemporary British Asian identities, previous research in this area has focused almost exclusively on football and cricket. Furthermore, these issues of belonging and identity have, thus far, not been explored in the same way in relation to Britishness. In addition to discussions about football and cricket this article extends the analysis to explore national identity and sport affiliation through the lens of the London 2012 Olympic Games. Of particular interest is how the Games contributed to understandings and articulations of national identity, 'Britishness' and belonging.

Methods

Analysing how sport contributes to articulations of 'Englishness', 'Britishness', and feelings of belonging, relies on adopting research tools that can produce rich, in-depth data. This article is based on empirical data about national identity and sport that emerged from a wider project on the impact of the London 2012 Olympic Games for young British Asians in two English cities. The qualitative approach utilised foregrounds the oral testimonies of the participants, to explore the role sport plays in their lives and in their identity construction.

A total of twenty-eight semi-structured interviews were carried out with twelve female and sixteen male participants aged between sixteen and twenty-four. The interviews lasted between thirty and ninety minutes. A purposive sampling technique was adopted to recruit the participants, who were different in terms of their ethnicity, religious identity, class background and location. Twenty-five of the participants were born in England, two in India and one in Germany, and all had heritage connections to the Indian Subcontinent. All were active participants in sport or physical activity, ranging from recreational to county-level participation. The interviews were conducted in 2015 and focused on the impact of the London 2012 Olympic Games on the participants' levels of participation in sport and physical activity, sport consumption, national identity and sense of belonging. A thematic data analysis was conducted to code the interviews and condense the rich testimonies of the participants into core themes.

Complexities relating to the use of racial and ethnic categories within research, and the subsequent debate about the most appropriate way to describe those who have migrated to Britain from the Indian subcontinent, continue to persist (Bradbury 2011; Ratna 2014). The term 'British Asian' currently remains the most used terminology to describe British citizens who trace their ancestry back to the Indian subcontinent. Whilst 'British Asian' is a term that is conceptually understood by both British Asians themselves and the wider UK population, it nonetheless remains at risk of obscuring the fractured relationships that are apparent within the Indian subcontinent and the obvious heterogeneity of settlers who have migrated to Britain from different places and at different times.

I use the term 'British Asian', therefore, to refer to people who trace their ancestry back to the Indian subcontinent, but who, through birth or residence in Britain are afforded British citizenship. I apply the term 'South Asian' to describe the first generation of migrants in the period immediately after their migration to Britain, and in reference to South Asian heritage. Crucially, it is important to avoid homogenising British Asians and consequently, in the discussion, the self-defined ethnic identities of my participants will be used as a demographic marker. Pseudonyms have been used in this article to protect the identity of the participants.

Discussion

National identities and hybrid sporting affiliations

The context of sport is one of the most significant means through which notions of 'Englishness' and 'Britishness' are played out. Exploring national identity through a diasporic lens encourages us to acknowledge the 'multivocality of belongings' (Kalra, Kaur, and Hutnyk 2005, 29) that characterise being part of a British Asian diaspora. Although many British Asians are supporters of domestic English football clubs and the England national team, their professed 'love' of English football may be questioned if they also follow Pakistan or India in cricket: then they might be charged with being 'caught between two cultures' and displaying unacceptably divided loyalties (Fletcher 2012; Ratna 2014). However, hybrid national affiliations are not a reflection of British Asians' 'divided loyalties', nor should they result in accusations of being 'caught between cultures', arguments which are situated within essentialist conceptualisations of identity. Instead, hybrid affiliations centralise the need to appreciate the 'dynamic, fluctuating and fragmented nature of British Asian identities' that are underpinned by a wide range of diverse personal reasons and social factors (Burdsey 2006, 22).

Male participants Jas and Baasit, who in discussions concerning national identity both rejected an English identity in favour of identifying more comfortably with a wider British label, are passionate supporters of the England national football team. This example demonstrates that connections and attachments to England and Britain are flexible and context bound, supporting Burdsey's (2006) arguments that notions of 'Englishness' and 'Britishness' can possess different meanings in relation to concepts of citizenship and ethnicity, with reasons for identification often multiple, and contextually and temporally specific. As Fletcher and Lusted (2017, 18) explain:

> In some instances, minoritised ethnic communities may feel a strong association with English and/or British national identity and work hard to integrate and align themselves to such cultural markers, while on other occasions those same people may feel equally strongly excluded from such ideas and reject (and/or be rejected by) the idea of a national identity – or certainly one which calls itself "English".

Jas and Baasit's adoption of a British national identity is centred on feelings of a relative lack of belonging and the seemingly exclusive associations routinely made by others between 'Englishness' and Whiteness, something that their phenotypical Asian appearance calls into question. Yet their support for the England national football team indicates that the negotiation of identity can vary in different social fields. As Brah (1996, 193) proclaimed, identity is always plural and in process, and 'it is quite possible to feel at home in a place and, yet, the experience of social exclusions may inhibit public proclamations of the place as home'.

For others, demonstrating support for heritage teams is a way for British Asians to distance themselves from the specific elements of Englishness that they feel most uncomfortable about (Burdsey 2006). These constitute deeper reflections of issues around acceptance and belonging within British society. The following exchange with Zayn, for example, illustrates the latter in English football culture, and it may help to answer Fletcher's (2012, 619) persistent and important question: 'If British Asians are not supporting England, why not?

> **Zayn:** In this country, I don't feel like I'm *welcome* to play football. I understand why a lot of Asian fans don't support England. [If] you're not welcome to play football in your country why would you support your country's team? You live here, this is your identity, and you've socialised here but then you don't feel like you're a part of it. (British Pakistani male)

Some British Asians understand that their presence in England is not accepted or valued, and thus regard their place in the nation as 'outsiders within' (Ratna 2014). Zayn's experiences of exclusion within football taint his sense of belonging in England. Consequently, his presence as an 'outsider within' helps Zayn to justify his lack of support for English national teams. As Brah (1996) asserted, diasporic groups can feel at home in a place, even if social exclusions prohibit public declarations of that place as 'home'. There can be parallels drawn here between Zayn's experiences of exclusion within football circles and similar reported findings in relation to cricket (Fletcher 2012; Raman 2015; Valiotis 2009). Those who were excluded from mainstream cricket competition and subjected to hostility and racism as participants and spectators, consequently distanced themselves from supporting England, with the lack of acceptance deemed as justification for showing an affiliation to national teams from the subcontinent (Fletcher 2012; Raman 2015). These examples reinforce that national sporting affiliations can be defined by the social practices that shape the lived realities for young British Asians growing up in Britain.

Team GB, Britishness and belonging: national affiliations at the London 2012 Olympic Games

One of the key underlying issues regarding the rejection of an English identity related to feelings of a lack of belonging, based, in part, upon phenotypical appearance which excluded British Asians from ethnically exclusive White notions of 'Englishness'. The following extract from Jas illustrates the complexity of negotiating a manageable and functional British Asian identity, where generational differences are bound up with feelings of (dis)connection and belonging:

> **Jas:** If my family were together, everyone would be supporting India. My generation would be secretly supporting England but you wouldn't want to show it, especially with the older people. They would say "Are you actually Indian? Because you are there supporting the English and the English just call you a Paki!" If I would've told my grandad that I was buying an England shirt he would have said "What do you want to wear that for?" That's probably because [of] the way he was treated back when he first came over to England. (British Indian male)

One crucial part of the process of national identity formation is about understanding who is included and who is excluded, with ethnicity likely to play a defining role within this process (Fletcher and Lusted 2017). The consensus among my participants was that their acceptance as 'English' was predicated on meeting predetermined criteria based, in their case, largely on skin colour. Fletcher and Lusted (2017, 4) suggest that 'national cultures like the 'English' are not repositories of shared symbols to which the entire population accesses with equal ease.' Instead performances of 'Englishness' are heavily racialised. For those that did not meet such criteria, 'British' is considered a more fitting and 'open' identity, one which held prospects of representing both inclusion *and* difference.

During the London 2012 Olympic Games, knowledge of and support for the Indian and Pakistani Olympic teams was extremely limited within my sample of young British Asians. This may suggest that unless it is cricket, young British Asians are not really that interested in the sporting aspirations or the success of their countries of ancestry. Comments made by Jas about his support and interest in the Indian Olympic team summed up the general consensus of my interviewees. Were they interested in India at the Olympics?

> **Jas:** Not really, no, because I know the standard wouldn't be that high. So, I was only concerned with watching Great Britain. My family were following Britain as well; they weren't bothered about watching India. (British Indian male)

As in relation to football and cricket, my interviewees were only interested in watching India in sport if the latter offered prospects of success. Jas's response is of particular interest, especially because he reports that his family objected to him openly demonstrating support for England and were all big fans of the Indian national cricket team. Cricket, of course, helps maintain diasporic connectivity for those who trace their ancestry back to the Indian subcontinent. The elder generations of Jas's family rejects 'Englishness' based on their experiences of racism in England. It might seem a little surprising, then, that Jas's family did not take an interest in the fortunes of the Indian Olympic team. That Jas's family were following Team GB in 2012, perhaps indicates that even first and second generation British Asians - who have traditionally felt more closely affiliated with their countries of ancestry - feel increasingly able to identify, less problematically, with a more inclusive British identity in sporting contexts.

Zayn, who had expressed a resistance to showing support for England's national sports teams agreed that he felt much more comfortable adopting a wider and more inclusive British sporting identity for the 2012 Olympics. Thus, showing support for Team GB at London 2012 was not as problematic as showing support in sport for England:

> **Zayn:** Yes, I supported the GB team in the Olympics. I actually feel like it's more equal [than England]. Although it was still mostly people from White backgrounds, I liked the fact that there were people from different countries, and not just England. (British Pakistani male)

Zayn's positive response supports Fletcher's (2012, 624) argument that 'for many British Asians, the label 'English' is the very antithesis to their inclusion [and so] many... prefer to endorse the more liberal politics of "Britishness."' Similarly, Kumar (2010) acknowledges that British is a less essentialised identity that can be offered to groups of people that do not identify with an ethnicised or racialised Englishness. Here, Zayn seems to equate his own British Asian identity with those of the other constituent countries that make up Great Britain. Zayn's less problematic identification as 'British' is attributed to a sense of belonging to a wider collective who are not excluded by a British label in the same way that primarily White, ethnically exclusive, notions of 'Englishness' tend to exclude many people from alternative ethnic backgrounds.

Perhaps more compelling as a commentary about Zayn's complex identity politics through sport is a fascinating account of how British Muslims might align themselves with a figure like Mo Farah:

Zayn: Something that's quite common amongst the Muslim background is to support Muslims... they feel they're not a part of England, so they just support people with the same faith. I think that is why some people were interested in Mo Farah: Asian people can familiarise themselves with him because he's quite similar. He has suffered from racism and maybe they will relate to that and the fact that they don't really feel welcomed. That's why they might support him, as they've had a very similar up-bringing. Blood-wise, he's not English, he has come from somewhere else, but has been brought up here, just like most British Asians are. (British Pakistani male)

Zayn indicates what he called a 'blood-wise' notion of national identity and belonging. In this case, he rejects a sense of national identity and belonging relating to citizenship and birthplace, and implicitly suggests that British Asians might feel a stronger connection to their ancestral roots: a connection that's in their blood. For British-born Muslims, the conceptualisation of diaspora as a state of consciousness, as opposed to a sense of rootedness or belonging, facilitates a connection with others who share similar aspects of identity and experience. There is a perception here that British Asians who are Muslims would be able to identify with Farah because of their similar migratory experiences and their shared religious affiliations, even if they have different ethnic backgrounds. A shared religious identity and shared experiences of racism are the foundations for Zayn's connection with Farah.

Jas, who although supported England at football felt that an English cultural identity was more aligned with being 'White' English, also discussed the more inclusive messages circulating around sport, Great Britain and the Olympics. He articulated this in relation to his presence and feeling of acceptance at the London 2012 Games:

Jas: I was actually there [...] Even though I was Asian, I didn't feel as if I was any different from a White person. I felt like, yeah, I'm a part of this, I am finally being accepted. That is probably one of the only examples where I feel like I've been accepted in society, in terms of my colour. I felt proud to be British. (British Indian male)

These articulations are clearly related to a feeling of belonging in Britain that is not apparent when considering the potential of an English national identity. The international and cosmopolitan crowd present at the Games had an impact on Jas's sense of self and helped dissipate those feelings of alienation around England. Clearly, for both Jas and Zayn, a more inclusive British Olympic Team, including athletes from a range of different ethnic and faith backgrounds (although very limited British Asian representation), helped strengthen their feelings of belonging in Britain. The same incompatibility is not evident between being British, Asian, and demonstrating support for teams and athletes representing Team GB, as is experienced in relation to England.

Because 'Britishness' is not viewed by my participants as such an ethnically exclusive space, in the same way that they conflate 'Englishness' with Whiteness, then there is a stronger sense of belonging through sport, allied to positive experience of a more inclusive British identity. The feeling of acceptance discussed by Jas, *despite* his phenotypical British Asian appearance, allowed him to identify with his own - but also others' - understandings of 'Britishness'. In the case of London 2012, inhabiting a British sporting identity acts as a 'third space of hybrid identities', one where some British Asians can feel - and are comfortable demonstrating - a real sense of belonging, whilst also 'bridging the void between their national and ethnic identities without fear or constraint' (Fletcher and Lusted 2017, 15). Identifying as British Asian does not illicit the same exclusionary responses that are experienced when young British Asians demonstrate support for England's national teams.

Conclusion

Previous research has identified the hybridised nature of British Asian supporter preferences; many British Asians routinely demonstrate their support for the England football team, alongside their respective national subcontinent cricket teams (Burdsey 2007; Fletcher 2012; Ratna 2014). A sizeable group of my respondents also demonstrated hybrid supporter preferences through their 'multivocality of belongings' (Kalra, Kaur, and Hutnyk 2005), reflecting the permanency of settlement and wider connections to British culture, whilst at the same time retaining pride in their family heritage and cultural history. The notion of diaspora allows us to challenge the imposition of a single idea of belonging to the nation (Kalra, Kaur, and Hutnyk 2005). Exploring national identity formation through a diasporic lens enables us to appreciate the fragmented nature of British Asian identities, thus moving away from essentialist conceptualisations and associated accusations that differential supporter preferences must be evidence of 'divided loyalties'.

International sporting events – such as the Olympic Games – have been identified as providing important contexts for everyday articulations of the nation (Fox and Miller-Idris 2008). Whilst previous literature has explored the role of sport and national identity formation for the British Asian diaspora, these studies have focused almost exclusively on football and cricket and specifically *English* national identities. The structure of international competition in the Olympic Games – which uniquely 'dissolves' national differences in favour of a combined British identity – meant that London 2012 offered a sociologically significant lens via which to explore the nexus between 'Britishness', national identity, sport and belonging for young British Asians. It is on this wider and potentially more inclusive British national identity, explored through the lens of the London 2012 Olympic Games, that the original contribution of this article lies.

Significantly, for those who rejected an English national identity through sport, the Games presented an opportunity to connect with a more inclusive British version of sporting allegiance. My participants who had rejected 'Englishness', or at least certain exclusionary elements of an English national identity, were much more at ease at connecting to the Great Britain Olympic team. This alternative structure of international sporting competition engaged them in identity terms, and a seemingly more inclusive British moniker for national sporting identity offered them a way inside the national collective that had been previously lacking. My participants attributed this feeling of being included to a more compatible British Asian identity; one that allowed notions of acceptance via a global sporting event, regardless of phenotypical British Asian appearance. That 'Englishness' and 'Britishness' are often regarded as synonymous is problematic for many citizens of other UK home nations, a rationale for their weaker connection to a British identity (Vincent et al. 2018). Interestingly, this article has demonstrated the opposite for a small sample of British Asians, identifying a need for future research to move beyond narrow explorations of Englishness when exploring the nexus of sport, national identity and feelings of belonging for diasporic British Asian groups.

This article has utilised the concepts of diaspora and hybridity, with a view to showcasing the analytical utility of these concepts in studies of sport and national identity for diasporic groups. Diaspora disrupts homogenous ideas of nationality, and as is the case for British Asians, leads us to the possibility of a third space of hybrid identities (Bhabha 1996). However, these concepts are not without their limitations. As Kalra, Kaur, and Hutnyk (2005) have argued, the presence of diasporic groups has influenced conceptualisations of the nation much more than the institutional structures that make up the state. Furthermore, the concept of hybridity disguises 'deep-seated entrenched inequalities' whereby diversity has become a code-word 'that foregrounds the marketable aspects of neglected and run-down inner urban areas while maintaining a hegemonic base for capital' (Kalra, Kaur, and Hutnyk 2005, 89). The urban regeneration of five Olympic boroughs in East London that ultimately displaced lower income East-Londoners is perhaps a case in point.

Disclosure statement

No potential conflict of interest was reported by the authors.

References

Anthias, F. 2001. "New Hybridities, Old Concepts: The Limits of 'Culture." *Ethnic and Racial Studies* 24 (4): 619–641. doi:10.1080/01419870120049815.
Bhabha, H. 1996. "Culture's in-Between." In *Questions of Cultural Identity*, edited by S. Hall and P. du Gay, 53–60. London: Sage.
Black, J. 2016. "As British as Fish and Chips': British Newspaper Representations of Mo Farah during the 2012 London Olympic Games." *Media, Culture and Society* 38 (7): 979–996. doi:10.1177/0163443716635863.
Black, J., T. Fletcher, and R. J. Lake. 2020. "Success in Britain Comes with an Awful Lot of Small Print': Greg Rusedski and the Precarious Performance of National Identity." *Nations and Nationalism* 26 (4): 1104–1123. doi:10.1111/nana.12614.
Bradbury, S. 2011. "From Racial Exclusions to New Inclusions: Black and Minority Ethnic Participation in Football Clubs in the East Midlands of England." *International Review for the Sociology of Sport* 46 (1): 23–44. doi:10.1177/1012690210371562.
Brah, A. 1996. *Cartographies of Diaspora*. London: Routledge.
Burdsey, D. 2006. "If I Ever Play Football, Dad, Can I Play for England or India?': British Asians, Sport and Diasporic National Identities." *Sociology* 40 (1): 11–28. doi:10.1177/0038038506058435.
Burdsey, D. 2007. *British Asians and Football: Culture, Identity, Exclusion*. London: Routledge.
Burdsey, D. 2016. "One Guy Named Mo: Race, Nation and the London 2012 Olympic Games." *Sociology of Sport Journal* 33 (1): 14–25. doi:10.1123/ssj.2015-0009.
Burdsey, D., and K. Randhawa. 2012. "How Can Professional Football Clubs Create Welcome and Inclusive Stadia for British Asian Fans?" *Journal of Policy Research in Tourism, Leisure and Events* 4 (1): 105–111. doi:10.1080/19407963.2011.643060.
Carrington, B. 2015. "Assessing the Sociology of Sport: On Race and Diaspora." *International Review for the Sociology of Sport* 50 (4–5): 391–396. doi:10.1177/1012690214559857.
Devan, P. 2012. "Cricket and the Global Indian Identity." *Sport in Society* 15 (10): 1413–1425. doi:10.1080/17430437.2012.744210.
Ewen, N. 2012. "Team GB, or No Team GB, That is the Question: Olympic Football and the Post-War Crisis of Britishness." *Sport in History* 32 (2): 302–324. doi:10.1080/17460263.2012.681357.
Farrington, N., D. Kilvington, J. Price, and A. Saeed. 2012. *Race, Racism and Sports Journalism*. London: Routledge.

Fletcher, T. 2012. "Who Do 'They' Cheer for?" Cricket, Diaspora, Hybridity and Divided Loyalties Amongst British Asians." *International Review for the Sociology of Sport* 47 (5): 612–631. doi:10.1177/1012690211416556.

Fletcher, T. 2015. "Cricket, Migration and Diasporic Communities." *Identities* 22 (2): 141–153. doi: 10.1080/1070289X.2014.901222.

Fletcher, T., and J. Lusted. 2017. "Connecting 'Englishness', Black and Minoritised Ethnic Communities and Sport: A Conceptual Framework." In *Sport and English National Identity in a 'Disunited Kingdom*, edited by T. Gibbons and D. Malcolm, 95–110. Abingdon: Routledge.

Fletcher, T., and T. Walle. 2015. "Negotiating Their Right to Play: Asian-Specific Cricket Teams and Leagues in the UK and Norway." *Identities* 22 (2): 230–246. doi:10.1080/1070289X.2014.901913.

Fox, J. E., and C. Miller-Idris. 2008. "Everyday Nationhood." *Ethnicities* 8 (4): 536–563. doi:10.1177/1468796808088925.

Gibbons, T., and D. Malcolm. 2017. "Nationalism, the English Question and Sport." In *Sport and English National Identity in a 'Disunited Kingdom*, edited by T. Gibbons and D. Malcolm, 1–25. Abingdon: Routledge.

Hylton, K., and N. Morpeth. 2012. "London 2012: "Race" Matters and the East End." *International Journal of Sport Policy and Politics* 4 (3): 379–396. doi:10.1080/19406940.2012.656688.

Joseph, J. 2014. "Culture, Community, Consciousness: The Caribbean Sporting Diaspora." *International Review for the Sociology of Sport* 49 (6): 669–687. doi:10.1177/1012690212465735.

Kalra, V. S., R. Kaur, and J. Hutnyk. 2005. *Diaspora and Hybridity*. London: Sage.

Kilvington, D. 2016. *British Asians, Exclusion and the Football Industry*. London: Routledge.

Kumar, K. 2010. "Negotiating English Identity: Englishness, Britishness and the Future of the United Kingdom." *Nations and Nationalism* 16 (3): 469–487. doi:10.1111/j.1469-8129.2010.00442.x.

McSweeney, Mitchell, and Yuka Nakamura. 2020. "The "Diaspora" Diaspora in Sport? A Systematic Literature Review of Empirical Studies." *International Review for the Sociology of Sport* 55 (8): 1056–1073. doi:10.1177/1012690219869191.

Raman, P. 2015. "It's Because We're Indian, Innit?' Cricket and the South Asian Diaspora in Post-War Britain." *Identities* 22 (2): 215–229. doi:10.1080/1070289X.2014.887566.

Ratna, A. 2014. "Who Are Ya?' the National Identities and Belongings of British Asian Football Fans." *Patterns of Prejudice* 48 (3): 286–308. doi:10.1080/0031322X.2014.927603.

Smith, A. D. 2010. *Nationalism: Theory, Ideology, History*. 2nd ed. Cambridge: Polity Press.

Stanfill, M., and A. N. Valdivia. 2017. "(Dis)Location Nations in the World Cup: Football Fandom and the Global Geopolitics of Affect." *Social Identities* 23 (1): 104–119. doi:10.1080/13504630.2016.1157466.

Valiotis, C. 2009. "Runs in the Outfield: The Pakistani Diaspora and Cricket in England." *The International Journal of the History of Sport* 26 (12): 1791–1822. doi:10.1080/09523360903172408.

Vincent, J., J. S. Hill, A. Billings, J. Harris, and C. D. Massey. 2018. "We Are GREAT Britain": British Newspaper Narratives during the London 2012 Olympic Games." *International Review for the Sociology of Sport* 53 (8): 895–923. doi:10.1177/1012690217690345.

Whigham, S. 2015. "Internal Migration, Sport and the Scottish Diaspora in England." *Leisure Studies* 34 (4): 438–456. doi:10.1080/02614367.2014.923498.

Winter, A. 2013. "Race, Multiculturalism and the 'Progressive' Politics of London 2012: Passing the 'Boyle Test." *Sociological Research Online* 18 (2): 137–143. http://www.socresonline.org.uk/18/2/18.html. doi:10.5153/sro.3069.

Hegemony, domination and opposition: fluctuating Korean nationalist politics at the 2018 Winter Olympic Games in PyeongChang

Jung Woo Lee (iD)

ABSTRACT

This article is concerned with the contested nature of nationalism expressed through sport. The 2018 Winter Olympic Games in PyeongChang offers some useful episodes where I can investigate a different type of Korean nationalism represented through sport. At this Winter Olympics, I observed four distinctive discourses on Korean identity being displayed via the winter sporting competition: 1) unified Korean ethnic nationalism, 2) South Korean state patriotic nationalism, 3) postcolonial anti-imperialist nationalism, and 4) cosmopolitan Korean identity. The four variants of nationalism were vying for the dominant position in the hierarchy of South Korean politics, and the Winter Olympics presented a platform on which each nationalist group asserts the legitimacy of their sense of nationhood. Therefore, I conclude that the 2018 Winter Olympics in PyeongChang was not simply a physical contest between athletes but more importantly, was a field of the hegemonic struggle between adherents of different nationalistic views.

Introduction

Despite an increasing awareness of transnational solidarity, a nation continues to provide one of the strongest sources of collective identity in the world today (Bieber 2018; Wellings and Power 2016). Numerous scholars have examined the role that sport plays in the construction and dissemination of nationalism in different regions and contexts (Angelini et al. 2017; Bairner 2009; Maguire 2011; Scherer and Jackson 2010). Most studies tend to focus on the way in which sport reflects and reinforces a particular type of, frequently a dominant form of, nationalism. However, more recent literature on this topic also implies that sport can carry more than one form of nationalism within an established nation, and that different nationalist groups tend to exploit sport to claim the legitimacy of their sense of nationhood (Dolan and Connolly 2018; Ho and Bairner 2013; Thomas and Antony 2015). In such a case, instead of operating as a unifying force, sport can potentially divide the nation or, at least, it can reinforce an existing political fissure in the country.

This article concerns dominant, oppositional and emerging form of nationalism expressed through sport. The 2018 Winter Olympic Games in PyeongChang offers some useful episodes where a different type of Korean nationalisms being represented and contested in sporting arenas can be investigated. A few academics have examined the evolvement of Korean sporting nationalism over time (Cho 2009; Kim 2019; Park, Ok, and Merkel 2016). Yet, these studies paid little attention to the way in which sport mirrors the contentious relations between different nationalist groups. Thus, by looking at the circulation of multiple discourses of Korean nationalisms in conflict surrounding the winter sport mega-event, this article intends to extend the academic discussion on Korean sporting nationalism further. This would eventually make a useful contribution to the theoretical literature on sport and nationalism.

PyeongChang 2018 is arguably one of the most politicized Olympics mainly due to the demonstration of the unity between North and South Korea after the escalating military tensions (Rowe and Lee 2018). Yet, conservative groups in South Korea was not convinced by this symbolic union in the stadium, questioning the intent of communist Korea's rather sudden conciliatory gestures (McCurry 2018). At the same time, the Winter Olympics was a cultural theatre showing cosmopolitan Korean identity being emerged. In addition, anti-Japanism can also be noticed at this event because it took place when Japan and Korea were in a fierce diplomatic dispute (Panda 2018). The representation and circulation of these nationalistic sentiments at the Winter Olympics indicate the complexity of the articulation amongst sport, nationalism and national identity (Topič and Coakley 2010).

The aim of this study is to examine the power struggle between different nationalist politics in Korea during the 2018 Olympic Winter Games. Bairner (2015) stresses that the academic literature on sport and nationalism, instead of being heavily relied on media analysis, needs to present a theoretically informed discussion of nationalism. In this light, this paper will pay attention to some key incidents that reveal the tensions between different variants of Korean nationalism being displayed at the Winter Olympics and will discuss how the demonstration of these nationalist sentiments is related to the shifting power structure and to political ideologies in this country. Then, this study will attempt to conceptualize this fluctuating landscape of nationalist politics and its connection with sport in South Korea.

Nationalism as a field of a hegemonic struggle

While an academic debate on nationalism has been informed by a diverse range of theoretical underpinnings, it is difficult to deny that primordialism and modernism are conventionally the two major theories that significantly influence nationalism studies. Put simply, primordialism considers essential characteristics of particular ethnic groups and their cultural tradition as the origin of nationalism (Geertz 1973; Smith 1986) whereas modernism regards nationalism as a forged political ideology which began to emerge with the industrialization in the late eighteen centuries in Europe and their colonies (Anderson 1991; Gellner 1983). Arguably, Stalin (1913/1994, 20) offers one of the most succinct definitions of the essentialist view: 'a nation is a historically constituted, stable community of people, formed on the basis of a common language, territory, economic life, and psychological make-up manifest in a common culture.' A socio-biological and organic tie between people is the core component of this primordial nationalism (Özkirimli 2000). On the other hand, the modernist view of nationalism states that while a nation as a community may have a historical root, nationalism as a political movement was mainly constructed with the development of industrial capitalism which subsequently led to the formation of modern nation-states (Held 1995). In this nation building process, many cultural conventions were (re)invented and new artificial territorial boundaries are drawn in order to provide a sense of distinctive national characters (Anderson 1991; Hobsbawm 1983).

While the two major theoretical frameworks present a useful intellectual agenda in nationalism studies, the recent identity politics and culture war caused largely by globalization and immigration make a spectrum of nationalist movement more diverse and more complicated than the conceptualization that primordialism and modernism offer. To some extent, globalisation, by facilitating the free flow of financial assets and cultural products, weakens the function of the conventional sense of the nation as a sovereign and autonomous political unit although there is a group of people who still assert the need for defending national interest in response to this neoliberal globalisation (Buzan and Lawson 2015). Paradoxically, the weakening of exclusive sovereignty of the nation-state as a large political entity gives rise to a separatist movement, especially within established nations such as the Scottish and Catalan independent movement in the UK and Spain (Fukuyama 2018). At the same time, diminishing economic autonomy of the nation in the face of transnational capital and international labour forces frustrates a significant number of ordinary people, and their anger creates the condition in which right-wing nationalist populism flourishes (Collier 2018). In opposition to this surge of the conservative nationalist regime, some ethnic minority groups and cosmopolitan liberals also form a political alliance against such exclusive and essentialist nationalism (Castells 2015). In some cases, these liberals challenge the discourse of the official history by provoking post-colonialist sensitivity in order to demonstrate a more inclusive historical narrative that embraces cultural diversity within their nation (Malik 2020).

Such development leads to the situation that multiple discourses of the nation and nationalism can co-exist within the boundary of an established nation. Regarding a separatist movement, Seiler (1989, 191) notes earlier that 'nations seek its legitimacy through hegemony … or domination', and further argues that there exist tensions between central nationalism which is a dominant form of national discourse and peripheral nationalism which is related to an increasing awareness of regionalism that may resist the top-down centre nationalism. Today, such a struggle between central and peripheral nationalism has become more manifest in the context of globalisation where the hegemony of the official nationalism is increasingly challenged by both regional and transnational consciousness. While Seiler's concept of centre-peripheral nationalism mainly concerns geographical divisions within a nation, the hegemonic domination of national consciousness and its opposition can be extended to the tensions between left-wing and right-wing nationalism caused by the recent class and culture war in the West (Fukuyama 2018). Similarly, Anderson (1991) also distinguishes official and popular nationalism, former being nationalist ideology adopted by the ruling elites whether they are imperialists or an authoritarian regime, and the latter being vernacular national consciousness embraced by independent or democratic activists. Both Seiler (1989) and Anderson (1991) point out the dialectic nature of this power games between hegemonic and alternative nationalism, meaning that when popular or peripheral nationalism gains hegemony, this becomes a new official or central nationalist ideology which will subsequently be challenged by another antithetical nationalist movement. What their views imply is that the hierarchy of national identity politics is by no mean fixed but there is a constant struggle between different nationalist groups for the hegemonic position.

Sport is often exploited by both central and peripheral nationalist groups to assert their legitimacy. The articulation between sport and militarism in the West, most notably in the US and UK exemplifies the exploitation of sport by the right-wing nationalist group. In this respect, Kelly (2017, 279) identifies four different ways that sport is being utilized in the context of militarism: 'sport people paying respect to the military, injured military personnel becoming athletes, sports uniforms becoming militarized, [and] sponsors using sport to support the military'. Similarly, Butterworth (2012) observes the infiltration of war images and military individuals into the celebrational occasions in American professional sport. Such a sport and military connection tends to naturalize and neutralize the glorification of the armed forces and their duty abroad, and this cultural politics subsequently helps legitimate the way in which the conservative political groups construct their vision of national identity. At the same time, the use of sport by a counter-hegemonic nationalist group can also be seen. American anthem protest most notably by Colin Kaepernick and Megan Rapino can be considered as a ritual that imagines a different type of American identity (Schmidt et al. 2019). While a conservative group regard their activism unpatriotic (Park, Park, and Billings 2020) their human rights movement can equally be patriotic conduct to build fairer and more morally just America (Boykoff and Carrington 2020).

Nationalist politics in Korea and sport

The hegemonic struggle between the established and oppositional nationalist groups can also be found in Korea. It should be noted that the division of the Korean nation does not simply indicate the partition between North and South Korea. The nationalist politics within South Korea is also polarized. Therefore, it may be useful to explain, albeit briefly, three distinctive forms of nationalism in South Korea before I examine the contest of different types of Korean nationalist politics at the 2018 Winter Olympic Games in PyeongChang. These are postcolonial anti-imperialist nationalism, unified Korean ethnic nationalism, and South Korean state patriotic nationalism (Lee 2015). In addition to these three established national discourses, newly emerging cosmopolitan Korean identity will also be introduced in this section (Joo 2012).

First, the Korean Peninsula was occupied for 36 years (1910–1945) by Japan, and during this period of the occupation, Korean people had to endure repressive and exploitative colonial domination. The memory and legacy of colonialism embody one of the most noticeable features of Korean nationalism today, and sport is often exploited as a vehicle for displaying anti-Japanese sentiment in the postcolonial period (Tosa 2015). While this postcolonial nationalism widely spreads in the country, it is the liberal and left-wing political parties in Korea who mostly embrace and endorse this nationalist view in their policy (Choe 2019). As a result, when the liberal party is in power, this postcolonial sentiment is more easily observable in South Korea.

South Korean state patriotic nationalism is another important type of a nationalist sentiment in Korea. Anti-communism and the economic prosperity of the nation are some of the core components of this nationalist ideology, and the right-wing conservative parties adopt this view. This was the dominant form of nationalism from its liberation in 1945 to the early 2000s. As South Korea's anti-communist campaign and its economic development process during the Cold War required military support and financial assistance from the US and Japan, this state patriotic nationalism espouses a pro-American attitude and eschews an anti-Japanese feeling (Lee 2015). This was clearly official nationalism in Anderson's sense (1991) because the propagation of this nationalism had included the introduction of new patriotic rituals to Korean civic life since the foundation of the Korean Republic in 1948 (Shin 2006). In the same vein, since the 1960s, the conservative regime had systematically fostered its national sporting team in order to win more medals at international contests because such a sporting achievement would motivate its citizens to take part in the government-led industrialisation project (Park and Lim 2015). Additionally, the conservative party is adept at displaying the nation's economic development to the international community by hosting major global sport mega-event (Bridge 2008).

Unified Korean ethnic nationalism highlights an ethnic homogeneity of the nation and sets the unification between the North and South Korea as the main aim of this nationalism (Shin 2006). In fact, the myth of ethnic homogeneity is the concept shared by different nationalist groups. However, it is this Korean ethnic nationalism that actively utilizes this notion to justify the unification movement which this nationalism underpins. Since the partition of the nation and the subsequent Korean War in the 1950s, this nationalist group has campaigned for peace and reunification of the Korean Peninsula and has intended to maintain the momentum of dialogue and collaboration with North Korea (Lee 2015). One interesting fact is that while the rightest groups in the West generally embrace this primordialism, in South Korea, it is left-wing parties whose manifesto reflects this ethnocentric nationalism. During the Cold War, this nationalist view was severely repressed by the ruling right-wing regime and has only begun to emerge as a mainstream nationalist thought since the 2000s when the centre-left liberalist party was in power for the first time in its history (Campbell 2015). The very first joint march between the two Koreas at the Opening Ceremony of the 2000 Sydney Olympics under the Korean Unification Flag, a symbol of the reunification movement, exemplifies the demonstration of this nationalism through sport (Merkel 2008).

Additionally, a new cosmopolitan identity has recently begun to appear in the domain of South Korean culture. The adoption of a neoliberalist globalisation policy and the subsequent increase of migrated populations challenge the myth of ethnic homogeneity of the Korean nation, and this social change gives rise to multi-ethnic Korean national identity (Campbell 2015). It is too early to accept that this cosmopolitan culture as one of the major national characteristics, yet this new development surely deserves careful attention. Sport also mirrors this trend. After the 2002 FIFA World Cup when the South Korean football team advanced to the semi-finals, the manager of the team, Gus Hiddink, was awarded honorary citizenship of Korea, and he was praised as a national hero (Lee, Jackson, and Lee 2007). Additionally, when a half-Korean and half-black American NFL player, Hines Ward, visited Korea in 2006, his Korean-ness widely cerebrated by Korean media (Ahn 2014). Such cosmopolitanism may be temporal and transient emotion, merely reflecting a festive social climate forged by sporting achievements. However, this can equally be a sign of new multicultural Korean identity being emerged, albeit slowly.

The contest of nationalist politics at PyeongChang 2018

This section discusses a series of incidents that occurred during the Winter Olympics to demonstrate the power games amongst different nationalist groups in South Korea. It also shows an emerging cosmopolitan Korean identity being represented at this event

The surge of unified Korean ethnic nationalism

The worsening relations between the US and North Korea increased military tensions on the Korean peninsula and this became a major threat to PyeongChang until a few months before the Winter Olympics (Jin and Lough 2017). On New Year's Day 2018, however, North Korea suddenly declared that it would support the Winter Olympic Games to be held in the South, and it would also dispatch its delegation to the PyeongChang (Lee 2021). Then, the two Koreas reopened their direct communication channel after nearly two years of hiatus to discuss North Korea's participation in the upcoming Winter Olympics (Rowe 2019). This sudden shift created a political climate where unified Korean nationalism flourished during the Olympics.

The Opening Ceremony consisted of many symbols representing this unified Korean nationalism. The South Korean President Moon Jae-in sat next to Kim Yo-jong, the sister of the North Korean leader, at the grandstand in the Olympic stadium. Both Korean and international media paid attention to this amicable encounter between the two individuals (Rowe 2019). The Olympic Torch Relay was also arranged to signify the unity of the Korean nation. Two athletes from the unified Korean ice-hockey team were chosen to be joint torchbearers, each from North and South Korea respectively, for the last leg of the relay. The ignition of the Olympic Cauldron is the ritual that officially declares the opening of the sporting competition. Their collaboration at this ceremony symbolized this Olympics Games as a cooperative enterprise by the two Koreas, effectively reinforcing a unified Korean identity (Lee 2019). Moreover, under the Korean Unification Flag and under the banner reading 'Korea', the athletes from the two Korean states marched as one at the parade of nations. This was also highly emblematic moment to display a unified Korean nationalism to the world.

The unified female ice hockey team also embodies this ethnic Korean nationalism at the Olympics. This sporting union was particularly significant because it was the first time in the history that the two sides took part in the Olympics as a single entity. On 25 January, two weeks before the Olympics, twelve North Korean players with their coaching staff travelled to the Olympic training centre in South Korea. On their arrival, the ice-hockey team held a brief welcoming ceremony. A banner reading 'We are one' decorated the venue where this ritual took place. At this ceremony, the director of the training centre greeted the North Koreans, saying that 'although we only have a limited time to train together, let's make our best effort by being one heart and one mind (YTN 2018)'. A North Korean coach replied that 'I am very pleased to compete as a unified team at the Olympics. Let's put our heart and our strength together in order to obtain a good result (YTN 2018)'. This ceremony, which was relayed by the media, was also an occasion that celebrated unified Korean nationalism at the Olympics and reinforced this nationalist sentiment in the country.

With regard to the political groups' response to the North Korean team in PyeongChang, the centre-left and ruling Democratic Party of Korea (2018) claimed that 'our party welcomes the North Korean team's participation and the use of the name Korea [which describes unified Korea] and of the song *Ariang* [a traditional folk song which is popular on both sides] as an anthem of the unified Korean team.' On the day when the two Koreas agreed to march jointly at the opening ceremony and to field a unified ice hockey team, the leftist Justice Party (2018) announced that 'We wholeheartedly welcome this decision and wish that the Olympic Games will be staged without any accidents. We especially hope that this collaboration at the Olympics will lead to more regular exchanges between North and South Korea.' The Korean Confederation of Trade Union (2018) also published a press release which wrote that 'The PyeongChang Winter Olympics is a peace Olympics and furthermore it should be the Games leading to the reunification [of Korea]. ... It is really meaningful to welcome the North Korean guests, and to support our Olympic team waving the Korean Unification Flag together.' These commentaries from liberal and left-wing political groups all endorsed the union of the two Koreas at the Olympics, thereby fanning the feeling of unified Korean nationalism. With the Democratic Party in power for nearly six months before the Olympics, the reunification movement was being emerged as an official (or central) nationalism in South Korea. It appears that the ruling party with other left-wing political organizations used this Olympics as a tool for circulating this ethnic Korean nationalism to the country.

The rise of South Korean state patriotic nationalism

The right-wing political parties and conservative groups dismissed the emerging reunification movement simply as a leftist ideology and repudiated North Korea's peaceful gesture at the Olympics as communist's propaganda (Chung 2018). In order to understand the reason for this opposition more accurately, it is necessary to review briefly the domestic political environment at that time. In December 2016, the National Assembly voted to impeach a conservative South Korean president Park Guen-Hye because of the corruption scandals involving her. In March 2017, the constitutional court of South Korea upheld the impeachment and Park was removed from office. In the following snap election in May, the left-leaning Moon Jae-in was elected as a new president. This was the moment patriotic state nationalism began to lose its hegemony in the political landscape of South Korea. Yet, a number of right-wing parties and civic organizations refused to accept the impeachment and subsequent dismissal of Park, and fiercely protested against the court decision (Park and Chung 2017). The Winter Olympic Games was held midst this domestic political climate.

As the relations between North and South Korea is rapidly improving before the event, the two sides agreed to hold a cultural event at a tourist district in Mount Kumgang in North Korea prior to the Winter Olympics. They also scheduled a North and South Korea joint training session at the Masikryong ski resort which is also located in the North Korean territory (Kim 2018a). Conservative politicians and civic groups vehemently criticized these two events to be held in communist Korea, arguing that the music concert and joint training programme only served the interest of North Korea (Kim and Chung 2018). They claimed that it is clear evidence of the Winter Olympics being exploited by the communists to promote tourism in North Korea (Smith 2018). These responses from the right-wing groups clearly mirror their patriotic nationalist view which regards communist Korea as the main foe of the South Korean state (Lee 2015).

The rightist groups were also unhappy with the use of the Korean Unification Flag (KUF) and the folk song Arirang at the Olympics. It should be noted that the KUF is the flag often appeared in the left-wing student movement in South Korea against the authoritarian government in the 1980s (Knitter 2017). Therefore, the KUF to some extent signifies leftist political thoughts, of which unified ethnic Korean nationalism is an important part (Kim 2018). With the assertation that the KUF is alien to the South Korean state, conservative nationalists, including the three major opposition parties, voiced that the *Taegukgi* and the Patriotic Song, the national flag and anthem of South Korea, must be used at all times during the Olympics because it is essentially the sport mega-event to be staged in the South Korean town of PyeongChang (Kim 2018b).

On the opening day of the Winter Olympics, state patriotic nationalists organized a large demonstration outside the Olympic Stadium where the Opening Ceremony was to be held. Here, the protesters expressed their anger by satirizing this Olympic as Pyongyang [the North Korean capital] Games (Volodzko 2018). They also protested at the contamination of the Olympic Games by communist ideology. Interestingly, the demonstrators waved the US national flag alongside the *Taegukgi* (Baynes 2018). The display of these symbols reveals a unique aspect of conservative nationalism in South Korea. For this nationalist group, the nation's alliance with the US is considered an essential component of safeguarding the economy and security of South Korea (Lee 2015). This is an expression of nostalgic sentiment that the US military helped the South during the Korean War in the 1950s and provided economic aids to assist its industrial development after the civil war (Kang 2015). Subsequently, the patriotic state nationalism highlights the importance of the close tie between America and South Korea because this East Asian country is still technically at war with communist Korea.

These right-wing nationalists continued their anti-North Korean campaign until the end of the Olympics. Particularly, the Patriotic Party of Korea, a radical right-wing party led by the ardent supporters of the impeached president Park Guen-Hye, actively involved in anti-communist and anti-unified ethnic nationalist campaigns (Park and Shin 2018). At the close of the Winter Olympics, The United Future Party (2018), the main opposition party, stated that 'while this Olympic had a number of good memories, this event was seriously undermined by the North Korean intervention. President Moon Jae-in appears to be only interested in serving the guest from North Korea. We are fed up with such treacherous behaviour'. With left-leaning Moon as a new president, a unified ethnic nationalism was prevalent during the Olympics (Lee 2019). The protest and comments from the conservative parties clearly show their antipathy towards this circumstance, especially watching their hegemony in decline. In effect, flagging up South Korean state patriotic nationalism was their resistance to and culture war against the leftists.

The display of postcolonial nationalism

The demonstration of anti-Japanism is also observable during the Winter Olympics. The relations between South Korea and Japan often fluctuates. In 2018, the two sides were in a fierce dispute over the issue of the comfort women, the practice of sex slave by the Imperial Japanese Army during the Second World War. Many Asian women including Koreans were forced to be a sex worker to serve Japanese soldiers at the frontiers (Tanaka 2002). This matter has long been contentious, and this prevents the two nations from developing constructive partnerships (Tisdall 2015). In 2015, South Korea, which was led by a conservative president Park Guen Hye, settled a compensation deal with Japan which claimed to resolve this matter finally and irreversibly (Tisdall 2015). However, this pact deeply frustrated many South Korean citizens including the former comfort women because the compensation was insufficient, and the victims had also been seeking a formal apology from the Japanese government for their wrongdoing during the war (Kim 2015). In 2017 when the president Moon Jae-in was in power, his centre-left government requested the amendment of the 2015 deal (Jung 2017). Shinzo Abe's administration in Japan refused to accept this demand, claiming that the revision of the pact violates the diplomatic agreement between two sides. The dialogue then halted. Subsequently, Japan and Korea relations have been soured since the altercation.

On 8 February 2018, a day before the commencement of the Winter Olympics, a group of civic organizations in South Korea held a political rally in front of the Japanese Embassy in Seoul. The protestors displayed banners reading 'We won't welcome Shinzo Abe' and 'We are seeking apologies' (Nam 2018). They also pelted a large photograph of the Japanese Prime Minister with bags of ashes. This was not the first time that anti-Japan demonstrating took place prior to the Olympics. A few weeks earlier, a group of university students also organized a similar campaign against Mr Abe near the Japanese Embassy. Reflecting this diplomatic tension, Mr Abe was considering forgoing his attendance at the Opening Ceremony of the Winter Olympics (Kyoto 2017). However, two weeks before the Olympics, he confirmed that he would attend the Olympic ceremony. He further noted that he would seek a confirmation with Mr Moon the importance of the military alliance between Japan, the US and South Korea midst increasing North Korea's provocation in Northeast Asia (Osaki 2018). This message appeared to be disturbing the mood of inter-Korean reconciliation at the Olympics that has just been warmed up. This fanned the flame of postcolonial nationalism in Korea. A series of the protests taken place in front of the Japanese Embassy in Seoul reflected this nationalistic emotion.

Another incident that triggered this postcolonial nationalism at the Winter Olympic was the design of the Korean Unification Flag (KUF) to be used at the Olympics. In the East Sea/Sea of Japan, there are small islets, Dokdo, controlled and administrated by South Korea. This was a symbol of Korea's liberation because the nation reclaimed these islets from Japan when the imperial occupation ended (Mayali and Yoo 2018). Yet, Japan also claims that the islets are their territory called Takeshima. The original design of the KUF at PyeongChang contains a small dot representing Dokdo. Yet, Japan raised this issue to the IOC. Japan also voiced concern over the map, which include the islets, to be found on the official webpage of the PyeongChang Winter Olympics (Siripala 2018). The IOC asked Korean to remove the dot from the flag in order to avoid politicization of the Olympic Games, and the two Koreas heeded the IOC's recommendation as the host nation had no intention to provoke any further dispute with Japan (Yonhap 2018). Despite this tolerant response, Japan opened the Takeshima exhibition in Tokyo to claim its sovereignty over the islets. The South Korean government requested immediate closure of this display, but Japan rejected this demand (AFP 2018). This territorial row caused the rise of postcolonial nationalism in Korea during the Olympics. A group of protesters held a media conference before the Japanese Embassy in Seoul to condemn the Japanese claim on Dokdo. They also appealed to the Korean Sport Council to restore these islets on the unification flag. This quarrel over Dokdo and the design of the KUF at the Winter Olympics are clearly the legacies of Japanese colonialism over the Korean Peninsula.

The emergence of cosmopolitan identity

During the winter sport mega-event, cosmopolitan national identity can also be detected. Conventionally, the myth of ethnic homogeneity one of the essential elements of Korean nationalism (Shin 2006). The Opening and Closing Ceremonies of this Winter Olympics indeed contain a range of symbols that represent this organic nationalism (Lee 2019). Yet, South Korea is the country that actively embraces neoliberal globalisation, and the influx of foreign nationals from diverse cultural backgrounds have rapidly been transforming the composition of its population (Paik 2010). In this respect, the 2018 Winter Olympic was an occasion where an image of multi-ethnic Korean identity was gradually conjuring up. Again, with regard to the Opening Ceremony, the Rainbow Children Choir, whose members consisted of children from multicultural families settled in South Korea, sang the national anthem of the host country before the South Korean president formally declared the opening of the Olympic Games. Arguably, the performance of the national anthem was the most solemn moment in the ceremony which displays an official identity of the host nation (Lee and Maguire 2009). Clearly, the appearance of the multi-ethnic choir at this nationalistic ritual signifies cosmopolitanism that has slowly but surely been becoming one of the major characteristics of Korean identity.

Team South Korea at this Olympics, which consisted of 19 naturalized players, also implied multicultural Korea (Longman and Lee 2018). The Korean ice hockey teams, both male and female squads, present an interesting example in this respect. The unified Korean women's team not only consisted of players from North and South Korea. It also included four naturalized skaters from the US and Canada. Also, an American head coach, Sarah Murray, led the team at the Olympics. In that sense, the collaboration between North Korean, South Korean and naturalized Korean players graphically created an image of cosmopolitan Korea. As this women's ice hockey team received huge media attention mainly because of the inter-Korean connection, their multi-ethnic composition was also naturally publicized. Subsequently, the story of the four naturalized players also appears in the media (Park 2018). This media appearance in effect helped disseminate the notion of multiculturalism, defying the myth of ethnic homogeneity. The male hockey team attracted comparatively less attention from the media, but this team also consisted of seven foreign-born players (Harlan 2018). In fact, the men's hockey team was the first multi-ethnic Korean national team in the history of Korean sport. This trend symbolically shows cosmopolitanism being emerged gradually as one of the Korean identities.

The case of Chloe Kim offers another interesting episode. She is a Korean American snowboarder, and the athlete won Olympic gold in the women's halfpipe event in PyeongChang as a member of Team USA. When Chloe Kim became an Olympic champion, South Korean media highlighted her ethnic root and celebrated her victory as if she was one of fellow Koreans despite her being an American citizen (Jeon 2018, Park 2018). Notably, in her interview with NBC, an American broadcaster, the Olympic champion emphatically commented that she was proud to be a Korean American (Belvedere 2018). South Korean newspapers relayed an extract from this interview (Park 2018). Her comments may indicate transnational identity that can often be found in the diaspora community where both one's official nationality and their ethnic origin affect national identity politics of immigrants and their offspring (Darby 2010; Joo 2012). At the same time, the portrayal of this Korean American Olympian by Korean media may also be an indication that Korean society has begun to embrace a multitude of Korean-ness, challenging its conventional essentialist nationalism (Campbell 2015). It may be an exaggeration to argue that cosmopolitanism is now one of the core elements of Korean identity. Nevertheless, it seems certain that the migration of people from and to this East Asian nation has now been constructing a more flexible sense of Korean nationalism as the cases of naturalized Korean and Korean American athletes at the Winter Olympics show.

Discussion

Gellner (1983, 1) notes that 'nationalism is primarily a political principle, which holds that the political and the national unit should be congruent. ... Nationalist sentiment is the feeling of anger aroused by the violation of this principle, or the feeling of satisfaction aroused by its fulfilment'. In Korea, the memories of colonialism, of the civil war and of the partition significantly influence the formation of the modern Korean nationalism (Jager 2003). To some extent, Korea is the nation that Geller's political principle has not yet been realized because the nation is divided into two parts after the liberation against their will, and there is still a territorial dispute between Korea and Japan. Therefore, for Koreans, the memory of the unfortunate past is an ongoing lived experience that still affects their national consciousness.

At the 2018 Winter Olympic Games, I observed a number of different nationalist sentiments being aroused. Moreover, the demonstration of different types of nationalism also polarized South Korean society. This situation compels me to reconsider the nature of nationalism and the role that sport plays in evoking nationalistic emotion. Generally, nationalism including patriotism works as a unifying force as the nation provides the most powerful sense of collective identity (Smith 2001; Özkirimli 2000). Likewise, a few influential texts on Korean nationalism mainly perceive this political ideology or movement as a source of social integration (Jager 2003; Shin 2006). Yet, the current study shows that nationalism functions as both a force for unity and a source of division in contemporary South Korea. More interestingly, nationalist politics are divided according to the spectrum of political ideologies in this country. For instance, conservative politics underpins South Korean patriotic nationalism whereas progressive parties support a unified Korean ethnic nationalism. While both sides tend to share the sentiment of postcolonial anti-Japanese nationalism, it is the progressive politics that embraces and expresses this nationalism more actively. The right-wing politics tends to adopt a more pragmatic approach when it comes to the relations between Korea and Japan. Each nationalist sentiment and the way this feeling is represented work as a unifying force only within the same political community (i.e. a group of leftists or rightists). Nationalism turns into a source of disunity as the power games between different political communities in Korea intensify. Given Geller's principle is yet to be materialized in this nation, each political party and their supporters appear to envision a different image of the Korean nation.

In this respect, Seiler's notion of peripheral and central nationalism (Seiler 1989), and Anderson's official and popular nationalism (Anderson 1991) can be particularly noteworthy. They both admit a dialectic nature of nationalism which means that nationalist politics is by no means static but is dynamic. However, their main concerns are the existence of different national communities in a single territory, and the issue of their subjugation and subordination. The situation in Korea is less of the tensions between different national communities but more of between different political/ideological communities. Thus, in conceptualizing such characteristics of nationalist politics, instead of Seiler and Anderson's notion of the division between the major and minor ethnic groups and their conflict within the boundary of the nation, the hegemonic relations between a different type of nationalist politics in a single national community would better describe the nature of Korean national identity politics today. This means that the power balance between different nationalist groups is constantly shifting, and these groups assert their legitimacy through culture war. The key aim of this hegemonic struggle is not to establish a new nation or reinstate a lost nation but to change the characteristics of the existing nation.

There was an expectation that the 2018 Winter Olympics to be a patriotic game which would involve a range of national rituals to strengthen Korean nationalism domestically and to display its cultural identity to the world (Joo, Bae, and Kassens-Noor 2017; Merkel and Kim 2011). This appears to be partly correct. In fact, my observation reveals the Olympics an important site of this hegemonic struggle between different nationalist groups in this single nation-state. As political hegemony is gradually shifting towards left-leaning ethnic nationalists, the Winter Olympics turned into a cultural space where a unified Korean nationalism was being displayed and celebrated. This national discourse attached to the Winter Olympics actively permeates into the Korean public sphere, and subsequently makes the reunification of the Korean Peninsula a major agenda for the contemporary nationalist politics. Postcolonial anti-Japanese nationalism was also reminded through this Olympics, and this makes Korean citizens believe that Japan still poses a threat to the welfare of their home nation. Outside the Olympic stadium, right-wing patriotic nationalist groups displayed their anti-North Korean feelings in order to protect their political interest and to defend their declining hegemony. Additionally, cosmopolitan Korean identity was also demonstrated, and this emerging multiculturalism defies the myth of ethnically homogeneous Korea. Then, far from being a unifying force, the Winter Olympics offered a theatre where different nationalist groups show multiple images of the nation they envision.

Conclusion

This article examined a different type of Korean nationalism being displayed through the 2018 Winter Olympic Games in PyeongChang. Bairner (2001) states that sport is a cultural practice that triggers the most emotive sense of nationalism in peacetime. Topič and Coakley (2010) further note that the way in which sport represents national identity is complicated and diverse. Starting from these basic notions, this study attempted to conceptualise the complexity of nationalism being expressed through sport as a means of integration and as a cause of polarization. In terms of the theoretical underpinning of this study, I try to modify Seiler's (1989) and Anderson's (1991) duality of nationalism in the context of South Korean nationalist politics.

At PyeongChang 2018, 1) unified Korean ethnic nationalism, 2) South Korean state patriot nationalism, 3) postcolonial anti-imperialist nationalism and 4) cosmopolitan Korean identity are the four major forms of nationalist sentiment being aroused and represented through sport. Recently, the four variants of nationalism have been vying for a dominant position in the hierarchy of South Korean politics (Cho 2020; Lee 2015) and in the midst of intensifying national identity wars, the Winter Olympics presented a unique platform on which each nationalist group asserts the legitimacy of their sense of nationhood. Therefore, this investigation concludes that the 2018 Winter Olympic Games was not simply a sporting contest between athletes but more importantly was a field of the hegemonic struggle between adherents of different nationalistic views

Disclosure statement

No potential conflict of interest was reported by the author(s).

ORCID

Jung Woo Lee (iD) http://orcid.org/0000-0003-1850-1746

References

AFP. 2018. "South Korea Demands Japan Close Museum on Disputed Islands." *The Straits Times*, January 25. https://www.straitstimes.com/asia/east-asia/japan-opens-museum-on-disputed-islands.

Ahn, Ji-Hyun. 2014. "Rearticulating Black Mixed-Race in the Era of Globalization: Hines Ward and the Struggle for Koreanness in Contemporary South Korean Media." *Cultural Studies* 28 (3): 391–417. doi:10.1080/09502386.2013.840665.

Anderson, Benedict. 1991. *Imagined Communities: Reflections on the Origin and Spread of Nationalism*. Revised. London: Verso.

Angelini, James R., Paul J. Macarthur,Lauren Reichart Smith, and Andrew C. Billings. 2017. "Nationalism in the United States and Canadian Primetime Broadcast Coverage of the 2014 Winter Olympics." *International Review for the Sociology of Sport* 52 (7): 779–800. doi:10.1177/1012690215619205.

Bairner, Alan. 2001. *Sport, Nationalism, and Globalization: European and North American Pespectives*. Albany, NY: State University of New York Press.

Bairner, Alan. 2009. "National Sports and National Landscapes: In Defence of Primordialism." *National Identities* 11 (3): 223–239. doi:10.1080/14608940903081101.

Bairner, Alan. 2015. "Assessing the Sociology of Sport: On National Identity and Nationalism." *International Review for the Sociology of Sport* 50 (4–5): 375–379. doi:10.1177/1012690214538863.

Baynes, Charles. 2018. "Winter Olympics 2018: Protesters Clash with Police in Pyeongchang during Demonstration against North Korea." *The Independent*, February 9. https://www.independent.co.uk/sport/olympics/winter-olympics/winter-olympics-2018-pyeongchang-north-korea-protests-demonstration-police-violence-south-a8202596.html.

Belvedere, Metthew J. 2018. "Snowboarding Gold Medalist Chloe Kim: I Won't Work with Sponsors Whose Messages I Don't Agree with." *NBC*, February 13. https://www.cnbc.com/2018/02/13/snowboarding-gold-medalist-chloe-kim-needs-to-agree-with-sponsors-messages.html.

Bieber, Florian. 2018. "Is Nationalism on the Rise?: Assessing Global Trends." *Ethnopolitics* 17 (5): 519–540. doi:10.1080/17449057.2018.1532633.

Boykoff, Jules, and Ben Carrington. 2020. "Sporting Dissent: Colin Kaepernick, NFL Activism, and Media Framing Contests." *International Review for the Sociology of Sport* 55 (7): 829–849. doi:10.1177/1012690219861594.

Bridge, Brian. 2008. "The Seoul Olympics: Economic Miracle Meets the World." *The International Journal of the History of Sport* 25 (14): 1939–1952.

Butterworth, Michael L. 2012. "Militarism and Memorializing at the Pro Football Hall of Fame." *Communication and Critical/Cultural Studies* 9 (3): 241–258. doi:10.1080/14791420.2012.675438.

Buzan, Barry, and George Lawson. 2015. *The Global Transformation: History, Modernity and the Making of International Relations*. Cambridge: Cambridge University Press.

Campbell, Emma. 2015. "The End of Ethnic Nationalism?: Changing Cenception of National Identity and Belonging among Young Korean." *Nations and Nationalism* 21 (3): 483–502. doi:10.1111/nana.12120.

Castells, Manuel. 2015. *Networks of Outrage and Hope: Social Movements in the Internet Age.* Cambridge: Polity.

Cho, Younghan. 2009. "Unfolding Sporting Nationalism in South Korean Media Representations of the 1968, 1984 and 2000 Olympics." *Media, Culture & Society* 31 (3): 347–364.

Cho, Younghan. 2020. *Global Sports Fandom in South Korea: American Major League Baseball and Its Fans in the Online Community.* Singapore: Palgrave Macmillan.

Choe, Sang H. 2019. "Embattled at Home, South Korea's Leader Turns on Japan, Stoking Old Hostilities." *The New York Times*, August 30. https://www.nytimes.com/2019/08/30/world/asia/korea-japan-moon-jae-in.html.

Chung, Jane. 2018. "Anti-North Korea Protesters Burn Flags before Opening Ceremony." *The Reuters*, February 9. https://www.reuters.com/article/us-olympics-2018-northkorea-protest/anti-north-korea-protesters-burn-flags-before-opening-ceremony-idUSKBN1FT0WI.

Collier, Paul. 2018. *The Future of Capitalism.* London: Penguin.

Darby, Paul. 2010. "The Gaelic Athletic Association, Transnational Identities and Irish-America." *Sociology of Sport Journal* 27 (4): 351–370. doi:10.1123/ssj.27.4.351.

Democratic Party of Korea. 2018. "Afternoon Briefing." *Press Release*, January 21. Seoul.

Dolan, Paddy, and John Connolly. 2018. "Contested and Contingent National Identifications in Sport." In *Sport and National Identities: Globalization and Conflict*, edited by Paddy Dolan and John Connolly, 1–16. Abingdon: Routledge.

Fukuyama, Francis. 2018. *Identity: Contemporary Identity Politics and the Struggle for Recognition.* London: Profile Book.

Geertz, Clifford. 1973. *The Interpretation of Cultures.* London: Fontana.

Gellner, Ernest. 1983. *Nations and Nationalism.* Ithaca: Cornell University Press.

Harlan, Chico. 2018. "Can You Sing the Anthem? Okay, You Can Play Hockey for South Korea." *The Washington Post*, February 11. https://www.washingtonpost.com/sports/olympics/can-you-sing-the-anthem-okay-you-can-play-hockey-for-south-korea/2018/02/11/fe63fa36-0ef6-11e8-8b0d-891602206fb7_story.html.

Held, David. 1995. "The Development of the Modern State." In *Modernity: An Introduction to Modern Socities*, edited by Stuart Hall,David Held,Don Hubert, and Kenneth Thompson, 55–89. Cambridge: Polity.

Ho, Glos, and Alan Bairner. 2013. "One Country, Two Systems, Three Flags: Imagining Olympic Nationalism in Hong Kong and Macao." *International Review for the Sociology of Sport* 48 (3): 349–365. doi:10.1177/1012690212441160.

Hobsbawm, Eric. 1983. "Introduction: Inventing Tradition." In *The Invention of Tradition*, edited by Eric Hobsbawm and Terence Ranger, 1–14. Cambridge: Cambridge University Press.

Jager, Sheila M. 2003. *Narratives of Nation-Building in Korea: A Genealogy of Patriotism.* Abingdon: Routledge.

Jeon, Y.J. 2018. "Chloe Kim Sent an Inspiring Message to Girls in PyeongChang." *The Chosun Ilbo*, Feburary 13. https://news.chosun.com/site/data/html_dir/2018/02/13/2018021301311.html.

Jin, Hyunjoo, and Richard Lough. 2017. "France to Skip 2018 Winter Games If Security not Assured." *The Reuters*, September 21. https://www.reuters.com/article/us-olympics-2018/france-to-skip-2018-winter-games-if-security-not-assured-idUSKCN1BW2M5.

Joo, Miyung R. 2012. *Transnational Sport: Gender, Media, and Global Korea.* Durham: Duke University Press.

Joo, Yu M., Y. Bae, and Eva Kassens-Noor. 2017. *Mega-Events and Mega-Ambitions: South Korea's Rise and the Strategic Use of the Big Four Events.* London: Palgrave.

Jung, Min-kyung. 2017. "Moon Decries 2015 Korea-Japan 'Comfort Women' Deal as Flawed." *Korea Herald*, December 28. http://www.koreaherald.com/view.php?ud=20171228000905.

Justice Party. 2018. "Briefing." *Press Release*, January 18. Seoul.

Kang, Jung I. 2015. *Western-Centrism and Contemporary Korean Political Thought.* London: Lexington Books.

Kelly, John 2017. "Western Militarism and the Political Utility of Sport." In *Routledege Handbook of Sport and Politcs*, edited by Alan Bairner,John Kelly, and Jung Woo Lee, 277–291. Abingdon: Routledge.

Kim, Christine. 2018a. "South Korea Sends Athletes for Joint Training at North Korean Ski Resort." *The Reuters*, January 31. https://uk.reuters.com/article/uk-olympics-2018-southkorea-northkorea/south-korea-sends-athletes-for-joint-training-at-north-korean-ski-resort-idUKKBN-1FK02R.

Kim, Jinsook. 2019. "Why We Cheer for Viktor Ahn: Changing Characteristics of Sporting Nationalism and Citizenship in South Korea in the Era of Neoliberal Globalization." *Communication & Sport* 7 (4): 488–509. doi:10.1177/2167479518788842.

Kim, Kevin. 2015. "Japan and South Korea Agree WW2 'Comfort Women' Deal." *BBC*, December. https://www.bbc.co.uk/news/world-asia-35188135.

Kim, Max. 2018b. "The Korean Unification Flag Isn't as Unifying as It Seems." *The Atlantic*, February 9. https://www.theatlantic.com/international/archive/2018/02/korean-unification-flag-pyeongchang-olympics/552914/.

Kim, Richard, and S. Chung. 2018. "The PyeongChang Olympics: Peace Olympics or Pyongyang Olympics." *BBC News Korea*, January 19. https://www.bbc.com/korean/news-42741680.

Knitter, Jaclyn S. 2017. "The Evolution of South Korean Student Protests." *Peace Review* 29 (3): 383–391. doi:10.1080/10402659.2017.1344607.

Korean Confederation of Trade Union. 2018. "Our view on the opening ceremony of the PyeongChang Winter Olympics." *Press Release*, February 9. Seoul: KCTU.

Kyoto. 2017. "Abe Doubtful on Attending Pyeongchang Winter Games Given Seoul's Report on 'Comfort Women' Accord." *The Japan Times*, December 29. https://www.japantimes.co.jp/news/2017/12/29/national/politics-diplomacy/abe-might-skip-pyeongchang-games-opener-seouls-comfort-women-deal-reversal-source/#.XzfpADXTWUl.

Lee, Jung Woo. 2019. "Olympic Ceremony and Diplomacy: South Korean, North Korean and British Media Coverage of the 2018 Olympic Winter Games' Opening and Closing Ceremonies." *Communicaiton and Sport*. doi:10.1177/2167479519886544.

Lee, Jung Woo. 2015. "Examining Korean Nationalisms, Identities, and Politics through Sport." *Asia Pacific Journal of Sport and Social Science* 4 (3): 179–185. doi:10.1080/21640599.2016.1139533.

Lee, Jung Woo. 2021. "Sport Diplomacy at the 2018 Winter Olympics in PyeongChang: The Relations between North and South Korea." In *Routledge Handbook of Sport in Asia*, edited by Fan Hong and Lu Zhouxiang, 227–237. Abingdon: Routledge.

Lee, Jung Woo, and Joseph Maguire. 2009. "Global Festivals through a National Prism: The Global-National Nexus in South Korean Media Coverage of the 2004 Athens Olympic Games." *International Review for the Sociology of Sport* 44 (1): 5–24. doi:10.1177/1012690208101483.

Lee, Nammi, Steven Jackson, and Keunmo Lee. 2007. "South Korea's "Glocal" Hero: The Hiddink Syndrome and the Rearticulation of National Citizenship and Identity." *Sociology of Sport Journal* 24 (3): 283–301. doi:10.1123/ssj.24.3.283.

Longman, J., and Chang W. Lee. 2018. "South Korea got the Winter Games. Then It Needed more Olympians." *New York Times*, February 9. https://www.nytimes.com/2018/02/09/sports/olympics/south-korea-naturalized-citizens.html.

Maguire, Joseph. 2011. "Globalization, Sport and National Identities." *Sport in Society* 14 (7–8): 978–993. doi:10.1080/17430437.2011.603553.

Malik, Kenan. 2020. "Culture Wars Risk Blinding Us to just how Liberal We've become in the Past Decades." *The Observer*, June 21, 37.

Mayali, Laurent, and John C. Yoo. 2018. "Resolution of Territorial Disputes in East Asia: The Case of Dokdo." *Berkeley Journal of International Law* 36 (3): 504–550.

McCurry, Justin. 2018. "Frosty Reception for South Korea's Winter Olympics Detente with North." *The Guardian*, January 19. https://www.theguardian.com/world/2018/jan/19/frosty-reception-for-south-koreas-winter-olympics-detente-with-north.

Merkel, Udo. 2008. "The Politics of Sport Diplomacy and Reunification in Divided Korea: One Nation, Two Countries and Three Flags." *International Review for the Sociology of Sport* 43 (3): 289–311. doi:10.1177/1012690208098254.

Merkel, Udo, and Misuk Kim. 2011. "Third Time Lucky!? PyeongChang's Bid to Host the 2018 Winter Olympics-Politics, Policy and Practice." *The International Journal of the History of Sport* 28 (16): 2365–2383. doi:10.1080/09523367.2011.626691.

Nam, Youn H. 2018. "We Won't Welcome Abe." *MBN News*, February 8. https://www.mk.co.kr/news/society/view/2018/02/91546/.

Osaki, Tomohiro. 2018. "Abe Confirms Plan to Attend Winter Olympics Despite Tension with South Korea over 'Comfort Women' Pact." *The Japan Times*, January 24. https://www.japantimes.co.jp/news/2018/01/24/national/politics-diplomacy/abe-will-attend-pyeongchang-winter-olympics-opening-ceremony-source/.

Özkirimli, Umut. 2000. *Theories of Nationalism: A Critical Introduction*. London: Macmillan.

Paik, Young-gyung. 2010. "Not-Quite Korean" Children in "Almost Korean" Families: The Fear of Decreasing Population and State Multiculturalism in South Korea." In *New Millennium South Korea: Neoliberal Capitalism and Transnational Movements*, edited by Jesook Song, 130–141. London: Routledge.

Panda, Ankit. 2018. "Abe Will Go to PyeongChang, Despite Japan-South Korea Tensions." *The Diplomat*, January 25. https://thediplomat.com/2018/01/abe-will-go-to-pyeongchang-despite-japan-south-korea-tensions/.

Park, B., S. Park, and Andrew C. Billings. 2020. "Separating Perceptions of Kaepernick Separating Perceptions of Kaepernick from Perceptions of His Protest: An Analysis of Athlete Activism, Endorsed Brand, and Media Effects." *Communication & Sport* 8 (4–5): 629–650. doi:10.1177/2167479519894691.

Park, H. C. 2018. "A Bit Special National Team: The Stody of Four Naturalised Players in the Women's Hockey Team." *The Hankyoreh*, February 4. http://www.hani.co.kr/arti/sports/sports_general/830698.html.

Park, Jae Woo, and Seungyup Lim. 2015. "A Chronological Review of the Development of Elite Sport Policy in South Korea." *Asia Pacific Journal of Sport and Social Science* 4 (3): 198–201. doi:10.1080/21640599.2015.1127941.

Park, Kyoungho, Gwang Ok, and Udo Merkel. 2016. "Hosting International Events and Promoting South Korean Identity Discourses: Continuities and Discontinuities." *The International Journal of the History of Sport* 33 (18): 2307–2322. doi:10.1080/09523367.2017.1365708.

Park, S. H. 2018. "Chole Kim and the Issues around Olympic Athletes 'National Identity."The Hankyoreh, February 13. http://www.hani.co.kr/arti/international/international_general/832137.html.

Park, Yuna, and Hyonhee Shin. 2018. "Protesters Greet North Korean Olympic Delegation Touring Seoul." *The Reuters*, January 22. https://uk.reuters.com/article/olympics-2018-north-korea/protesters-greet-north-korean-olympic-delegation-touring-seoul-idUKL4N1PH2AL.

Park, Yuna, and Jane Chung. 2017. "Supporters of Ousted South Korea Leader Outraged over Jail for Samsung Chief." *The Reuters*, August 25. https://www.reuters.com/article/us-samsung-lee-protesters/supporters-of-ousted-south-korea-leader-outraged-over-jail-for-samsung-chief-idUSKCN1B50FL.

Rowe, David. 2019. "The Worlds that Are Watching: Media, Politics, Diplomacy, and the 2018 PyeongChang Winter Olympics." *Communication & Sport* 7 (1): 3–22. doi:10.1177/2167479518804483.

Rowe, David, and Jung Woo Lee. 2018. "2018 Winter Olympics Set to Begin against the Backdrop of Warm Words and Cold Politics." *The Conversation*, February 8. https://theconversation.com/2018-winter-olympics-set-to-begin-against-the-backdrop-of-warm-words-and-cold-politics-89967.

Scherer, Jay, and Steven J. Jackson. 2010. *Globalization, Sport and Corporate Nationalism the New Cultural Economy of the New Zealand All Blacks*. New York: Peter Lang.

Schmidt, Samuel H., Evan L. Frederick,Ann Pegoraro, and Tyler C. Spencer. 2019. "An Analysis of Colin Kaepernick, Megan Rapinoe, and the National Anthem Protests." *Communication & Sport* 7 (5): 653–677. doi:10.1177/2167479518793625.

Seiler, D.L. 1989. "Periperal Nationalism between Pluralism and Monism." *International Political Science Review* 10 (3): 191–207. doi:10.1177/019251218901000303.

Shin, G. W. 2006. *Ethnic Nationalism in Korea: Genealogy, Politics and Legacy*. Stanford: Stanford University Press.

Siripala, Thisanka. 2018. "Dokdo or Takeshima? Japan and South Korea Reopen Territorial Row Ahead of Olympic Games." *The Diplomat*, February 7. https://thediplomat.com/2018/02/dokdo-or-takeshima-japan-and-south-korea-reopen-territorial-row-ahead-of-olympic-games/.

Smith, Anthony D. 1986. *The Ethnic Origins of Nations*. Oxford: Blackwell.

Smith, Anthony D. 2001. *Nationalism*. Cambridge: Polity.

Smith, Nicola. 2018. "Kim Jong-un 'Handed Propaganda Victory' over North Korea's Luxury Ski Resort." *The Telegraph*, January 22. https://www.telegraph.co.uk/news/2018/01/22/critics-fear-handing-kim-jong-un-propaganda-victory-north-koreas/.

Stalin, Joseph. 1913/1994. "The Nation." In *Nationalism*, edited by John Hutchinson and Anthony D. Smith, 18–21. Oxford: Oxford University Press.

Tanaka, Yuki. 2002. *Japan's Comfort Women: The Military and Involuntary Prostitution during War and Occupation*. London: Routledge.

Thomas, Ryan J., and Mary Grace Antony. 2015. "Competing Constructions of British National Identity: British Newspaper Comment on the 2012 Olympics Opening Ceremony." *Media, Culture & Society* 37 (3): 493–503. doi:10.1177/0163443715574671.

Tisdall, Simon. 2015. "Korean Comfort Women Agreement Is a Triumph for Japan and the US." *The Guardian*, December 28. https://www.theguardian.com/world/2015/dec/28/korean-comfort-women-agreement-triumph-japan-united-states-second-world-war.

Topič, Mojca Doupona, and Jay Coakley. 2010. "Complicating the Relationship between Sport and National Identity: The Case of Post-Socialist Slovenia." *Sociology of Sport Journal* 27 (4): 371–389. doi:10.1123/ssj.27.4.371.

Tosa, Masaki. 2015. "Sport Nationalism in South Korea: An Ethnpgraphic Study." *Sage Open* October-December: 1–13.

United Future Party. 2018. "Comment." *Press Release*, February 26. Seoul.

Volodzko, David J. 2018. "'Pyongyang Olympics': How North Korea Stole the Winter Games." *This Week in Asia*, January 27. https://www.scmp.com/week-asia/politics/article/2130782/pyong-yang-olympics-how-north-korea-stole-winter-games.

Wellings, Ben, and Ben Power. 2016. "Euro-Myth: Nationalism, War and the Legitimacy of the European Union." *National Identities* 18 (2): 157–177. doi:10.1080/14608944.2015.1011110.

Yonhap. 2018. "Korea Not to Use Dokdo-Showing Flag during PyeongChang Olympics." *The Korea Herald*, February 6. http://www.koreaherald.com/view.php?ud=20180206000770.

YTN. 2018. "North Korean Advance Team, Ice Hockey Players Arrive in South Korea." *YTN news*, January 25. https://www.youtube.com/watch?v=k-c-GKPQVI8.

They are not 'Team New Zealand' or the 'New Zealand' Warriors! An exploration of pseudo-nationalism in New Zealand sporting franchises

Damion Sturm, Tom Kavanagh and Robert E. Rinehart

ABSTRACT

Often international sport can be viewed through a nationalistic lens, with sport allowing for nation-based team selections and competitions. Alternatively, we probe the notion of pseudo-nationalism in a New Zealand setting to examine two professional teams that, falsely, evoke familiar symbols and linkages to the nation. The first is 'Team New Zealand', which races in the global America's Cup yachting series but overtly manufactures nationalistic links between the corporate sport, syndicate and nation. The second is the 'New Zealand' Warriors which operates as a professional franchise in the Australian-based National Rugby League competition against 15 other Australian clubs. Despite their corporate structures, as well as circulation in non-nation-based sporting contests, both teams exhibit forms of pseudo-nationalism by conflating, obfuscating and masquerading as nationally-representative sports teams. Collectively, both teams proffer a contested vision of pseudo-nationalism by mimicking other national sport teams while projecting, evoking and imploring an allegiance to 'New Zealandness'.

Introduction

Sport is steeped in nation-based contests, nationalistic displays and potentially aligns specific teams to a sense of national identity, character and prosperity. More often than not, these associations are linked to nationally-selected teams that can claim to represent the nation in international sporting competitions against other nations. Thus, New Zealand have national representative teams that draw on national iconography and symbols such as the 'All Blacks' (rugby), 'Black Caps' (cricket), 'Silver Ferns' (netball), and 'Kiwis' (rugby league), offering a seemingly straight-forward linkage between the nation and sport.

We are interested in probing what we have termed 'pseudo-nationalism'—essentially when sports, syndicates and franchises masquerade as a national team and rely upon tapestries of national identity, affiliation and symbolism. 'Pseudo-nationalism' would logically be a sub-set of Silk, Andrews, and Cole (2005) notion of 'corporate nationalism' (see also

Scherer and Jackson 2010). While many of the factors they delineate with corporate nationalism still exist, there are distinctive characteristics which may mark out a 'pseudo' element within several contemporary sport forms. Specifically, our interest lies with two sports/teams that play on similar and familiar nationally representative tropes; drawing upon, conflating and arguably explicitly evoking elements of 'New Zealandness' through referential links to, and as, national teams, when in reality they are not. Interestingly, two of the more telling elements of these sporting teams are an emphasis on homogeneity of social class, targeting specific ethnic and/or economic factors; and a deliberate 'masking' of the relationships between corporate sponsors and the teams which propagates a heightened form of (misplaced) patriotic nationalism.

The first is 'Emirates Team New Zealand' (TNZ) which competes in the America's Cup. TNZ's assumed links between the nation and the syndicate are embellished and overstated for what is a global sailing event. The America's Cup is an elitist and corporate competition between various global yacht clubs, with crews drawn from an array of nationalities while relying upon public and private sources of funding. Nevertheless, TNZ have sought to galvanize nationalistic support, emphasise sporting underdog clichés, and foreground national 'loyalty' to their America's Cup campaigns. The second example is the 'New Zealand' Warriors (NZW)—an Auckland-based professional franchise that competes in the Australian National Rugby League competition. Despite only playing Australian-based teams in a club competition, the NZW conflate and confuse links between the team and the nation through a range of guises, including an obfuscation of pre-existing international teams and competitions. As a marginalised sport, the NZW also evoke, target and mobilize nationalistic-hued support among Māori and Pasifika supporters around aspiration, desire, community, family and working-class masculinities.

Imagined and invented nationalism

Nationalism is a complex and difficult phenomenon to define but, in simplistic terms, is an ideology that centres around concern for, and promotion of, the nation (Smith 2001). This takes form in the shape of a political economic structure, but also as a 'cultural formulation, a feeling of belonging, and a shared heritage' (Hardt and Negri 2000, 336). Nationalism is a discursive formation, a way of constituting the nation as a real and powerful dimension of social life that continues to be a significant influence in the structuring of individual lives and consciousness (Calhoun 2007; Silk, Andrews, and Cole 2005). Through these discourses, people construct meaning and identity, telling stories and memories that connect a nation's present with its past (Tuck 2003).

Nationalism categorises humans, informs upon these groups' notions that national identity is of basic importance, and stresses those who 'belong' and those who don't within a society (Tuck 2003). It claims and contests the legitimacy of governments, demands institutional reform, and may even become a device to advocate for ethnic cleansing (Calhoun 2007). Yet, while it often conjures negative associations with imagined social superiority, national identification is also about social solidarity, and dependence on others (Dolan and Connolly 2017). Nations, through shared historic experiences, 'values, myths, memories, traditions, institutions, customs, organisations and deep attachment to territory', generate a deep sense of belonging in a way that few historical communities can (Hargreaves 2002, 31). Subsequently, few movements have been as successful at mobilizing the masses to engage with the projects of the elites (Delanty and Kumar 2006).

To understand these ideas, we draw largely from Anderson's (1991) conceptualisation of nations as 'imagined communities', and Hobsbawm's (1983a, 1983b) notion of the 'invented tradition'. Anderson argues that for a nation to come into being, its members must share a sense of collective, despite the fact that the vast majority of the population will never meet one another. Rather, they must understand that they share certain interests, and act in accordance with these interests. Thus, the creation of the nation is an act of imagination. This is not to say that nations do not really exist, but that nations are produced through cultural practices which encourage members to formulate their identities within the nation. Anderson's concept helps us to understand this complexity by weaving together the tangible elements with the abstract (Bairner 2009). Everyday interactions that continue to reaffirm a common identity remind members of their relationship to one another and are crucial in the creation and maintenance of the nation (King 2006). Nationalism has thus been hugely influential in enabling people to imagine the world in terms of large-scale identities and composed of sovereign nation-states (Calhoun 2007).

Similarly, Hobsbawm's (1983a) 'invented tradition' refers to practices which seek to instill values and norms repetitively, which automatically imply continuity with the past. By this, Hobsbawm is not implying that all traditions are fictional, and makes clear the distinction between institutions that have adapted over time from fictive traditions that have distinct social and political functions. He was particularly concerned with the periods following the Industrial Revolution (how the state and dominant classes constructed narratives of tradition and past that legitimised their domination) and preceding World War I (how nation-states constructed narratives that engendered loyalty and social cohesion). Hobsbawm (1983b, 298) explicitly mentions sport in his writing, exclaiming that sport is 'one of the most significant of the new social practices of our period'. Sport not only enabled the middle and upper classes to draw class distinctions from the masses by implementing an emphasis on amateurism (and inventing the tradition that this was the original, pure version), but it provided a medium for national identification and factitious community. If we understand nationalism and sport as invented traditions, we then need to analyse their political roles in ensuring compliance and conformity of the masses through symbolic rituals (Dolan and Connolly 2017).

Sport and nationalism

Sport has proven to be a most effective means for generating a sense of belonging to a nation. Together with sport's capacity for reaffirmation and reinvention of groups' collective identity, sporting traditions thus create important 'anchors of meaning' for a nation's people (Smith 2004). Hobsbawm (1990) describes this importance:

> What has made sport so uniquely effective a medium for inculcating national feelings, at all events for males, is the ease with which even the least political or public individuals can identify with the nation as symbolized by young persons excelling at what practically every man wants, or at one time in his life has wanted, to be good at. The imagined community of millions seems more real as a team of eleven named people. The individual, even the one who only cheers, becomes a symbol of his nation himself. (143)

After war, sporting competition arguably provides the most tangible expression of imagined communities, and the nation temporarily becomes 'real' (Tuck 2003). The very nature of most sport, with its emphasis on physicality, competition and its appeal to the masses, provides the perfect platform for the expression of group identities, and international competition provides endless opportunities for the nation to become visible and prove itself against an 'other' (Billig 1995). International sports become 'patriot games'—flags are waved, national anthems are played and individual competitors become 'proxy warriors' that must embody these nations.

Orwell (1968) famously wrote on this topic, using a tour of Britain by the Moscow Dynamo football team to illustrate the negative impact sport has on national relations, and claiming that international sport is 'mimic warfare' or 'war minus the shooting':

> You do make things worse by sending forth a team of eleven men, labelled as national champions, to do battle against some rival team, and allowing it to be felt on all sides that whichever nation is defeated will 'lose face'. (63)

According to Orwell, the significant factor is not the players but the spectators who work themselves into furies, arguing that 'the whole thing is bound up with the rise of nationalism that is, with the lunatic modern habit of identifying oneself with large power units and seeing everything in terms of competitive prestige' (63). This competitiveness exhibits itself through celebrating often xenophobic ideas of who 'we' are in contrast to 'them' (Whannel 2008). Sport provides a platform for oppositional national identities to compete in the same space, which can exacerbate existing social divisions and incite conflict (Sugden and Bairner 1993). Sport offers something easily identifiable to cling to—a hero and a direct enemy in coloured shirts (Cronin 1999).

These notions have particular pertinence in New Zealand, where sport continues to be one of the dominant arenas for the reproduction and maintenance of national identity. Crawford (1985, 77) argues that the formation of national identity has 'been more sharply delineated in sport than in any other sphere of cultural activity', while Falcous and Newman (2016) clarify that select sports in particular have been appropriated as symbols of (male) national identity. For males, the 'Kiwi bloke' became the dominant representation of masculine national identity, promoting a pioneer/colonial identity through physical strength and stoicism. Specifically, the 'Kiwi bloke' celebrated the 'taming' of the land through settlement and rugby successes (while also aligning Māori 'comrades' in war and rugby with the 'Kiwi Bloke'), with the All Blacks historically one of New Zealand's most visible markers of nationhood (Phillips 1996; Sturm and Lealand, 2012). Concomitantly, the Kiwi woman was expected to embody a feminine 'ideal' of heterosexual, domestic displays coupled with the physical prowess to engage in hard labour in often rugged environments (Marfell 2019). The stereotypical linkages for women (and for many upper-class men) to nationalism were often seen as understated, humble, yet effective.

Sport, corporate nationalism and pseudo nationalism

By the early twentieth century, the power elites in many Western nations had capitalized on the widespread appeal of sport (Silk, Andrews, and Cole 2005). It quickly acquired a crucial role in the construction of a dominant national identity, and nation-states sought to use the high visibility of sport to promote themselves and enhance their prestige and influence internationally (Bairner 2017). Accordingly, those in control—and these range from national governments to local governments to private and public-private entities—of both national and international sport are fully cognisant of the material benefits of commercialization and governmental support, and form mutually beneficial partnerships with groups that serve their commercial and political interests (Hargreaves 2002).

Silk, Andrews, and Cole (2005, 7) corporate nationalism describes this commercialization of the nation through sport, whereby national culture is 'reduced to a branded expression of global capitalism's commandeering of collective identity and memory'. Sport is capitalized upon as a product which captures the attention of the nation, whilst delivering vast economic wealth to an opportunistic few. Scherer and Jackson (2010) explain in detail how this process has occurred with New Zealand's (men's) national rugby team, the All Blacks. Adidas continue to utilize themes of nationalism that draw upon Māori culture and a romanticized New Zealand history in their sponsorship of the All Blacks. However, rather than a straightforward acquisition of cultural capital, many of their initial advertising strategies were met with resistance by many rugby fans who saw through their promotional rhetoric and were disgruntled by the increasing commodification of the national team.

But what of sports teams that draw upon nationalism and the imaginary of a nation, yet are essentially corporate entities that do not represent the nation? Pseudo-nationalism, as a sub-set of corporate nationalism, extends beyond merely inventing a history or connection between a (national) audience and a (national) sporting organization. Pseudo-nationalism also contains facets of what Billig (1995) terms 'banal nationalism'. Banal nationalism relies on discourse, but at a level of 'prosaic, routine words, which take nations for granted' (Billig 1995, 93). The invention of a pseudo-nationalism based upon corporate, and banal nationalisms (including patriotism) is an attempt to fictionalize the linkages between privately-owned corporate sporting bodies and a national audience. Such an organization could be made up of individuals from anywhere (and arguably, could shift allegiance, marketing strategy and cultural imagining as global finances dictated), yet use nationalism as their preferred 'hook' for brand engagement.

Sporting teams with strong links to the 'nation' are able to leverage significant financial reward from tapping into the myths, the nostalgia and the imagery associated with national identities (Hobsbawm 1983a). The 'imagined community of millions' offers a ready-made fan base with a well-established national storyline to follow (Anderson 1991). A national team provides a sentimental sense of home and the idea of a cohesive collective. Pseudo-nationalism is effectively the acquisition of such concepts with no 'genuine' links. TNZ and the NZW are not representatives of the nation, and they are not part of (inter)national competitions—they are transnational organizations masquerading under the invention of nation, utilizing an imagined community for the acquisition of financial capital.

In 'pseudo' nationalism, corporate (or other privatized) entities consciously utilize and align these creations with shared cultural practices for their monetary and 'lifelong consumer' product. Much of the end game is obviously targeted for income production; but, just as Nike worked to enhance emotional desire and identification with their imagined lifestyle, these privatized corporates also strive for emotional attachment to TNZ and NZW.

More than those quite obvious markers of 'sport nationalism', when niche marketing is added, the targeting of both corporate nationalism and pseudo nationalism begins to become clearer. Middle class aspirations are linked with America's Cup through its explanatories of how the sport works, its obvious upper-class trappings and histories, and its disguised national linkages. The Warriors organization deliberately creates an imaginary where a Pasifika/Māori demographic become linked to desire. These provide spectators with perhaps the most-easily accessible medium to display their national identity (Bairner 2009). Subsequently, sport provides an important arena that has the ability to bind together people from around the world, but also to segment them into manageable niche markets (Maguire and Tuck 2005).

For TNZ and the NZW the allure is relatively simple. A significant, meaningful, loyal supporter base takes considerable time to establish, and this task is especially difficult when the sport is acutely elitist, and available to only a small proportion of the population or, historically, has been marginalized along class and racial lines. Rather than merely the imagined community of yachting or rugby league fans, by attaching their brand to the nation these organizations hope to engage a wider range of sport fans who strongly identify to the nation. Goldman and Papson (1996) suggest that,

> Evoking memory is a method of socially positioning viewers. Advertisers turn nostalgia into a talisman to ward off fear of constant upheaval. Since the inception of modern advertising, one dimension of advertising has been aimed at soothing distress about moral and ethical upheaval by speaking to, and about memories of the past. (117)

For these groups, speaking to myths of a settler/colonial past, of physical strength, of 'punching above their weight' and success on the sport field allows links to a common, unified collective. These themes can be dramatized for commercial effect, while those who do the storytelling benefit from these cultural economic practices (Scherer and Jackson 2010). Our attention now turns to yachting and rugby league as sites for pseudo-nationalism.

America's cup

America's Cup (AC), for New Zealand, is a good example of the changing and assimilative face of pseudo-nationalism reliant upon confusing corporate and banal nationalisms for it to be successful. By reinforcing the island nation's self-image of plying the seas, a nostalgic indigenous origination story of Māori 'discovery' in ocean-going waka (canoes), and an aspirational nationalism that benefits both a public 'sense of identity' (Coakley 2020, 411) and private entrepreneurship, New Zealand business interests arguably capitalize on a man-ufactured nationalism.

New Zealand, as a government and within its citizenry (heavily marketed by media) has had an interest in the AC since at least 1986, when 'KZ5, a NZ yacht skippered by Chris Dickson, won the first heat of the world 12 m championships' (Eagles 1986a, 1). But the history of the AC weaves into the imaginary for New Zealand as well. The 'America's Cup', then simply an unnamed challenge by the first Commodore of the New York Yacht Club (NYYC), John Cox Stevens, to British yachtsmen, began in 1851 when his *America* prevailed over fifteen yachts from Britain's Royal Yacht Squadron. Subsequently, the trophy/cup was named after the yacht *America*. The NYYC held the Cup against all challenges for 132 years until 1983, when Australia's (the yachts, though privately held, all are tied to nation-states) *Australia II* won over the NYYC's defender (Orams 2011).

How and why did this private, upper-class, very expensive hobby become conflated with nations and, somehow, patriotism itself? Over time, two things occurred: sport—even upper-classed sport—became more accessible to the masses and there was a growing awareness that yachtsmen (almost exclusively male) and yachting clubs required subsidization to remain afloat. Middle classes *aspired* to sail, to 'man' the crafts. In New Zealand, the nostalgic imaginaries for the *pakeha* Kiwi 'bloke', including the stereotypical images of an 'emphasis on success coupled with modesty, physical strength and courage, egalitarianism, and *understated patriotism* [emphasis added]' (Cosgrove and Bruce 2005, 344), have been exploited by TNZ and sport media alike.

Thus, the exclusivity of yacht clubs somewhat opened up, drawing sailors with less rigid views of membership, opportunity, and indeed, amateurism itself. As values toward the sport and access to funding changed, televisual broadcasting of AC exploded (Kerr 2016). More interest grew larger sponsors and multinational corporations became convinced that sport was good business. Arguably, the 'apolitical' nature of sport is a part of the banal components resulting in pseudo-nationalism.

At the start of a generated neoliberal worldwide economic shift, partnering sport with government via nationalistic calls proved to be quite effective for selling mega-events to publics. Thus, private entrepreneurs sought financial assistance from governments, encouraging public-private enterprises, through the canny vehicle of competition with other nations. Eagles (1986b, 4) suggests that the AC 'involves history and national prestige; has the thrill of danger and the spice of glamour; has rich prizes and great status for the winners. The clear winners, of course, are the (private) syndicates, who draw income, accolades, status and prestige from both public and private sources.

Research looking at the development of the various forms of nationalism surrounding the AC competition in Fremantle, Western Australia (e.g. Hartley 2016) and the Cup challenges in which New Zealand has participated (e.g. Barker, Page, and Meyer 2002a, 2002b; Evans 2004, 2007; Scherer and Jackson 2010; John and Jackson 2011; Barron 2020) demonstrates that tourism business interests sought more lucrative entrepreneurial, economic, and pseudo-nationalistic ties with AC. That they were successful is clear. For example, despite COVID-19 border restrictions for international tourists, the 2021 AC staged in Auckland had in attendance 'a 50,000-strong crowd ... [and] a huge spectator flotilla of up to 2000 vessels' (Todd 2021, para. 1) attended, with 'every other person [seeming] to have a Team New Zealand shirt on' (para. 18).

Interrelated are misplaced notions of national loyalty, particularly in the context of global corporate sport and the forms of pseudo-nationalism that may proliferate. For example, after 2000, when New Zealand sailors Russell Coutts and Brad Butterworth 'defected' from TNZ to sail with the Swiss syndicate Alinghi in 2003, a campaign attacking their loyalty was begun. Scherer and Jackson (2010, 17) note that the '*Blackheart*' campaign 'was a quintessential instance of banal nationalism (Billig 1995) that pitted loyal, ordinary New Zealanders against supposed traitors and public enemies'. Furthermore, Scherer and Jackson (2010, 17) explain that the backlash towards Coutts and Butterworth resulted from public resentment regarding 'increased flexibility of capital and citizenship in the context of globalization' when professional athletes chose to work in a more lucrative syndicate. National loyalty—even banal—has serious emotional linkages, but it demonstrates the pseudo nature of the tenuous linkage to nationalism: professional sportspersons, by virtue of their professional status, are often mercenaries without deep loyalty to their team, region, or even country. The question remains: are the syndicates within the AC cynically capitalizing on a pseudo-nationalism to increase audience affiliation?

Another facet of New Zealand's AC-manufactured nationalism was the marketing of patriotic and nationalistic fervour for the presumed winning yacht: 'Public enthusiasm for the event was aided by the expectation and eventual reality of the country successfully defending the Cup' (Barker, Page, and Meyer 2002b, 777). The plan was geared toward 'winning support and consent by naturalizing the relationship between corporate interests and citizens/consumers via nationalism' (John and Jackson 2011, 403). The rationale? It appears 'common-sensical', though tacit and largely undocumented, that 'intangible psychological benefits [are] reflected through the business community, visitors and residents, and widespread displays of national pride' (Barker, Page, and Meyer 2002a, 89). For businesses, customer loyalty (to their product or service, and to New Zealand) was strengthened and government monies assisted in the campaign.

A New Zealand-affiliated syndicate—nicknamed *TNZ*, representing the Royal New Zealand Yacht Squadron—has won the AC four times, in 1995, 2000, 2017, and 2021. In each of these triumphs over rivals, forms of pseudo- or corporate-type nationalism have aided in 'selling' the exclusive and elite sport of yacht racing. Though 'as a spectator sport it is an absolute bore' (Eagles 1986b, 4), the concept of collective, nationalistic support, buoyed up by an ideologically-imagined community (Anderson 1991; John and Jackson 2011) assisted in selling the sport to New Zealand. For example, in order to gain support for the privately-owned 'Black Magic' TNZ syndicate that would eventuate in 1995, some ideological preparation for public support was necessary. Thus, against a backdrop of rhetoric that 'we are building our national identity and finding our competitive advantage' (Mazany 1995, 3), was the expectation that '20 to 50 million dollars' (Schnackenberg, in Mazany 1995, ix) needed to be raised. One of the ways the government 'sells' the public and simultaneously generates public support for a sporting project is through a nationalistic and patriotic call.

The island nation that 'punches above its weight' is a theme that runs through much of New Zealand sporting rhetorics: media ply this slant for the Commonwealth Games, the Olympics, and for nearly every international sporting success story. It is so ubiquitous that slight reference to it resonates with the public. Note, for example, Sir Peter Blake's recollection of being a member of a nationalistically-laced TNZ in 1995, in preparation for the Cup defence in 2000: 'We genuinely felt we had 3.5 million people riding with us on *Black Magic* especially as the contest built to a climax' (Blake 2000, 13). This is another example of the banal nationalistic component of pseudo-nationalism.

However, this semi-emotional expression of gratitude from Blake comes after he has expressed thanks to the money:

> First, we are grateful for the generous support of our principal sponsors, Steinlager, Television New Zealand, Telecom New Zealand, the Lotteries Commission and Toyota New Zealand ... we salute the companies that are backing America's Cup 2000—Telecom New Zealand, Fuji Xerox, Air New Zealand and Ericsson. (Blake 2000, 13)

It is noteworthy that the private partnerships disguise some of the contributions of government, public entities that were state-owned at the time: Television New Zealand, the Lotteries Commission, Telecom (privatized in 1990), and Air New Zealand (since partially privatized). Private industry also became iconic sponsors of the syndicates, supplemented or replaced in more recent times by OMEGA, Toyota, Spark, and Sky City for TNZ, including the corporatization of naming rights via the rebranded 'Emirates TNZ'.

Finally, one of the markers of pseudo-nationalism is the composition of team members. In 2017, TNZ, in concert with Italian team Luna Rossa agreed that, for the 2021 AC, '20 per cent of sailors in competing teams must have passports or be citizens of that team's country, and the rest must meet residency requirements' (The Protocol 2017, para. 9). This change meant that sailors must be 'physically present in that country for a minimum of 380 days over a two year period' (para. 9). This manufactured attempt to reintegrate nationalism into global and corporate yachting syndicates further reinforces the elements of pseudo-nationalism at play.

The teams are 'pseudo nationalistic' because they don't represent, or even (realistically) potentially represent, the whole of their democratic nations. In 'corporate' nationalism, the exclusion of women, middle and lower economic classes, or brown people (in the case of AC), is leavened by a benign (corporate, banal, but mostly, pseudo based) neutrality: the pursuit of money. Fiduciary rewards, streamed through the public tax system, represent the corporate component of pseudo-nationalism. Kitsch-like markers describe 'banal' nationalism (banners, pennants, body painting, for example). While money and banality matter for banal and corporate nationalism, the non-democratic exclusion of classes of potential members, and then the cynical re-appropriation of them as patriotic supporters, marks out pseudo nationalism. Thus, collectively, tax dollars, private sponsorship, and public support based upon pseudo-nationalism have contributed to New Zealand's AC efforts.

'Bringing a nation together' through a mega sporting event may be aspirational on the part of business interests, governments who seek to align with successful syndicates, and tourism and hospitality concerns. In 1987, in support of New Zealand's effort, the song 'Sailing Away', a 'We-Are-the-World' type NZ anthem (to the tune of a nostalgic, recognizable, and emotive *Pokarekare ana*), held the number one slot for nine weeks (Sailing Away 1987). As well, in 1995,

> Red socks had become an emblem and fundraiser for the Kiwis' cup campaign, after Team New Zealand boss Peter Blake won an early race wearing a pair his wife had given him. A TV jingle urging fans to "get your lucky socks on" resulted in red socks flying from car aerials and flagpoles, and cladding Kiwi feet. (O'Neil 2015, para. 3)

These epiphanic markers form ideological archipelagoes, touchstones that resonate for generations of Kiwis who have been members of economic, entrepreneurial, and pseudo-nationalistic majority groups. A popular song and red socks are representative physical markers of the banal aspect of pseudo-nationalism (Billig 1995).

Whether hosting the AC is financially profitable or not, for an island nation-state like New Zealand, the social benefits have been sold to both government and the public, on the whole, as positive. However, in June of 2021, while the New Zealand Government offered a '$99 million bid to host the next America's Cup' (America's Cup 2021, para. 1), it was rejected. Further supporting the pseudo-nationalism aspect of TNZ's AC efforts, TNZ are now looking for other host countries, but TNZ CEO Grant Dalton stated, 'No matter where in the world we are, we will always be Team New Zealand' (ibid., para 8).

Celebrations of sporting victories, while fleeting, give the impression of a diverse group pulling together (Cosgrove and Bruce 2005)—and this can be powerful, as evidenced by the 'team of 5 million' statements following 2020s COVID-19. However, the audiences and citizens of the nation are being shepherded to support private, elite (and white male) sports and sportspeople without direct, informed insight.

The 'New Zealand' Warriors

The Vodafone or 'New Zealand' Warriors (NZW) are a professional rugby league franchise that competes in the Australian-based National Rugby League (NRL) competition. Such arrangements are not unique to New Zealand-based sport franchises, as currently the Wellington Phoenix, New Zealand Breakers and Auckland Tuatara (prior to COVID-19) compete in Australian national football (soccer), basketball and baseball leagues. However, what is intriguing and, indeed, problematic, is the use of the moniker 'New Zealand' for select sporting franchises that are professional and corporate entities physically located in Auckland, such as the Warriors, Breakers and TNZ, that are not necessarily representative of the nation or the nationally-affiliated namesake being deployed. We will unpack and analyze the contested and 'pseudo-national' elements to the NZW shortly. First, however, an overview of rugby league is required to contextualize and understand its operation.

Rugby league: marginalized nationalism

Given its lack of global impact, rugby league (RL) may perhaps be considered a 'pseudo-global' sport with a limited appeal to and concentration in parts of England, Australia, New Zealand, France and the Pacific Island nations. RL emerged via a split of the rugby codes, with the Northern Rugby Football Union formed in 1895 to professionalize the game in the North of England, seeking payment and compensation for the predominantly working-class players in the industrial age (Collins 2013). Arguably, RL's origins are steeped in divisions surrounding professionalism versus amateurism, north versus south, and class factions (Collins 2013), although Falcous (2017, 84) suggests that 'rugby league emerged as a symbol of an imagined northern Englishness' rather than as representative of the 'north' embracing RL. Currently, the UK Super League is in financial strife, with poor media deals and coverage, as well as static audiences (Wilson, Plumley, and Barrett 2015). Moreover, Falcous (2017) argues that narrow stereotypes centred around 'northern' working-class masculinities make problematic the forging or evoking of nationalistic sentiments around RL.

Australia has been the dominant RL force in terms of international results and the assumed status and success of the NRL (Phillips 1998), especially in New South Wales and Queensland. However, COVID-19 exposed the NRL's financial shortcomings, allegedly pushing the sport to the precipice (Tedeschi 2020) prior to games recommencing in May 2020. In New Zealand, RL remains ostensibly marginalized and mobilized around working-class masculinities as well as race, with the code governed by white/'Pakeha' males yet dominated by Māori and Pasifika players (Anderson 2020; Diversity of New Zealand Rugby League's Leaders Questioned 2020).

Critically, RL has been positioned in opposition to the dominant code of rugby union in New Zealand which, via historical successes, has been laced with mythic tapestries and a nostalgic aura of nation-building, nationalism and national unity (Scherer and Jackson 2010; Sturm and Lealand 2012). Alternatively, as noted earlier, an excessive projection of corporate nationalism (Silk, Andrews, and Cole 2005), that seeks to make Adidas synonymous with the national team, has seemingly reduced the All Blacks to a series of branded commodities (Scherer and Jackson 2010).

Nevertheless, despite the threat of various 'football codes', Falcous (2007, 426) asserts that 'amateur rugby was selectively elevated as the "national sport"'. Colonial elites actively promoted rugby union to help 'civilize' New Zealand settler society, while proclaiming the amateurism values, egalitarian attributes and classlessness of rugby (Phillips 1996). Hence, the success of the 'Pro-Blacks' (or later retitled 'All Golds') professional tours to Australia and England in 1907, which effectively created or consolidated RL in all three countries, as well as international competitions from 1908 (Falcous 2007), was largely marginalized. Rather, the colonial elite intentionally opposed the growth and significance of RL through attempts to prohibit or supress its playing and popularity. Specifically, players were excluded or expelled who did not remain loyal to rugby union, opposition to the game was disseminated politically and via the press, and numerous barriers were erected around access, facilities and funding, including banning RL from most schools (Falcous 2007).

RL still remains largely marginalized and maligned in New Zealand due to a lack of funding, no professional competition, and its operation as a grassroots sport with limited inter-school competitions, participatory rates or media coverage (Diversity of New Zealand Rugby League's Leaders Questioned 2020). The governance and diversity of RL has also been criticized, with both the New Zealand Rugby League (NZRL) and the Warriors critiqued for failing to have Māori, Pasifika or female representatives on their respective Boards (Anderson 2020; Diversity of New Zealand Rugby League's Leaders Questioned 2020). Ex-NZRL and Warriors coach and player, Tony Kemp, observed that,

> 60 percent of the participation rates for rugby league are in Auckland and "the reality of it is that the game is predominantly played by Māori north of Orewa and south of the Bombay Hills and it is Pasifika if you know anything about Auckland rugby league" (cited in Diversity of New Zealand Rugby League's Leaders Questioned 2020, para. 5)

Effectively, with RL dominated by Pasifika and Māori players, Kemp has been scathing of the NZRL for failing to adequately support these communities through equitable governance and representation, alleging that less than 3% of the purported $7 m the NZRL annually receives is distributed to grassroots RL.

'Warrior nation': projecting pseudo-nationalism

The Warriors first joined the NRL (then Winfield Cup) in 1995, operating as the Auckland Warriors which projected, as well as reflected, the city-based franchises already commonplace—such as the Brisbane Broncos, Canberra Raiders and later Melbourne Storm. The team was owned by Auckland RL and Auckland-based, with a jersey design that utilised Auckland RL's blue and white colours, combined with green for main sponsor DB Bitter. Additionally, the team actively recruited players from New Zealand, Australia and England (including an English coach), while also deploying Māori iconography and Pasifika-drummers at home matches. Ostensibly, the Warriors operated as a New Zealand-based professional franchise participating in an Australian sporting competition in its early years.

However, amid financial difficulties, the Warriors changed ownership twice, most notably with Eric Watson acquiring the Warriors in 2001. This acquisition would be significant for the fundamental re-presentation, re-positioning and re-branding of the franchise in relation to nationalism. Significantly, Vodafone was signed as naming rights sponsors, with the franchise officially operating as the Vodafone Warriors since 1999. Moreover, Watson would place an especial emphasis on its 'New Zealandness'. In effect, Watson rebranded the club as the 'New Zealand' Warriors (NZW) through his 17-year ownership (Long 2016), registering New Zealand Warriors Ltd as its business name, while encouraging the mass media and general public to adopt and use NZW as the shorthand trading name for the franchise. Clearly, elements of corporate nationalism underpin this process (Silk, Andrews, and Cole 2005), although corporate linkages to the nation are less pronounced than, for example, the overt branded relationship between Adidas and the All Blacks (Scherer and Jackson 2010). In contradistinction, as title sponsors, Vodafone is often not acknowledged due to an emphasis on the pseudo-nationalistic NZW namesake.

Collectively, across the past 20 years, the Warriors consciously projected, aligned and embedded links to nationalism within the franchise through a range of pseudo-nationalistic guises. Specifically, references to Auckland were removed and replaced with evocations of a 'New Zealand' team playing an Australian team every week (Long 2016) and further reinforced by the club recruiting mainly New Zealand players (St John 2020). The new black uniform explicitly constructed a pseudo-national dimension, with the black and white design between 2006 to 2011 largely imitating the colour scheme of most New Zealand national sports teams and operating as almost indistinguishable from the nationally representative NZRL team, the Kiwis, albeit with different sponsor logos and emblems. More broadly, 'New Zealandness' becomes embedded within, inscribed onto and permeates the NZW franchise during this time.

Pseudo-nationalism imagery and imaginary

NZW media coverage, promotions and advertisements also make tenuous links to nationalism. At its most blatant was the '*We Are New Zealand and We Are All Warriors*' 20-year anniversary campaign video (Vodafone Warriors 2015). The advertisement essentially plagiarised the concurrent 'Dream Big New Zealand' campaign run by the ANZ bank around their sponsorship of New Zealand Cricket (NZC) during the 2015 Cricket World Cup. Through its narrative and imagery, the ANZ advertisement provided an idyllic projection of cricket's assumed inclusiveness and place within the national fabric, with a nostalgic take on cricket interlaced with scenic New Zealand and voice-overs of 'everyday' cricket participants, administrators and prominent players (ANZ Bank 2015). The Warriors advertisement by-and-large replicates this, with similar imagery and participant voice-overs, albeit with a greater cross section of Māori and Pasifika fans than ANZ's arguably token display of 'brown' faces. Moreover, nationalistic sentiments are both explicit and highly contestable. The familiar tropes of the underdog and 'punching above our weight' are utilized, while notions of unity and 'New Zealandness' seemingly binds Warriors' fans together. As the narrative suggests: 'We are the few facing many. A tribe facing an army. A nation facing the world... We will stand strong. Because we are New Zealand. And we are all Warriors'. The advertisement then ends with the written statement—'We are your team' and then 'Vodafone Warriors'.

What is intriguing in this advertisement is the mobilization of pseudo-nationalism to elicit emotive appeals to both an imagined nation and an idealized Pasifika/Māori demographic. First, as a macro rendering of pseudo-nationalism, the 'Dream Big' campaign ran while NZC co-hosted a mega-event and played other cricketing nations on a weekly basis. Conversely, the NZW advertisement conflates their place in RL competitions, notably via the misnomer and hyperbolic claim to be 'a nation facing the world' despite this being an intra-Australian national sporting competition for Australian-based clubs/franchises. There is no 'world', nor any other nations involved in the NRL, aside from individual international players representing their respective NRL clubs. Furthermore, international teams and competitions for RL nations already exist, such as the Kiwis, that eligible NZW players need to gain selection for.

Additionally, a micro idealized version and aspirational vision of an imaginary Pasifika and/or Māori community inflects the pseudo-nationalistic links promulgated in NZW advertising. For example, the 2001 promotion 'Matter of Faith' (Vodafone Warriors 2014) provides a backdrop of multi-cultural Auckland foregrounded with a gospel-inspired and predominantly Pasifika and Māori congregation, dressed in black NZW jerseys, repeating the lines 'it's just a matter of faith', injected with an urban rap breakdown of 'the Warriors'. Collectively, the pseudo-national appeal to Pasifika and Māori communities is significant, if not problematic.

Anderson (2020) observes that 'over 45 percent of NRL players have Pacific Island heritage and over 70 percent of the New Zealand Warriors squad were of Māori or Pacific descent' (para. 16). Despite the prominence of these communities, Anderson (2020) notes that criticism around a lack of cultural values has been directed at the NZW for failing to understand Māori and Pacific cultures—both in terms of players and fans—as well as around forms of communication, name pronunciation, well-being, and general inclusion in decision-making processes.

Overall, as a marketing ploy, an idealized vision for Pasifika and Māori as a pseudo-national community of NZW fans is targeted. This is reinforced by the pronounced use of Pasifika cultural artefacts at games, such as Pasifika drummers, dancers and traditional dress, alongside Māori iconography, most notably by deploying a *tekoteko* (or carved human form) as the NZW logo. More broadly, familiar tropes that assume religious servitude and privilege a family and communal orientation are also emphasised, as the 'Matter of Faith' and 'We Are All Warriors' advertising reflected and reinforced. Additionally, with grassroots RL overwhelming comprised of Māori and Pasifika players, the NZW afford a potential pathway and aspirational end-goal to a professional RL career in New Zealand (Diversity of New Zealand Rugby League's Leaders Questioned 2020).

Problematically, this often also relies upon a narrowcasting of physicality and glorification of hypermasculinity. Hawkes (2018) observes that Pasifika players in the NRL are both glorified and demonised via the predominant emphasis on their physicality, operating as either heroes or dupes by being restricted to such hypermasculine displays. Stereotypically, physicality is equated with Pasifika sport stardom, while the need to serve families and communities add further layers of pressure and expectation to achieve RL success (Hawkes 2018; McDonald and Rodriguez 2014). In a similar vein, Māori male athletes have traditionally been encouraged, if not expected, to privilege their 'natural' physicality over other pursuits. As a result, this narrowcasting of physicality often evokes the 'Māori Warrior Gene' (Hokowhitu 2003), where troubling assumptions of a proclivity towards violence and aggression undergirds a dubious expectation for Māori to participate in stereotypically physical sports such as rugby and RL.

By using such language, imagery, symbolism, and stereotypes, alongside targeted aspirational and desire-laden motifs for Māori and Pasifika, the NZW are exploiting nationalistic links for commercial gains (i.e. corporate nationalism), while evoking and mobilizing a pseudo-nationalistic version of community as target market rather than communal partnership. Ultimately, this rendering of cultural capital may empower but also entrap such fans as a niche market 'buying' into these invented pseudo-national traditions and products of desire, particularly through the oversupply of NZW merchandise that trades in Māori and Pasifika iconography and signifiers.

Conclusion

While sport and nationalism are underpinned by elements that are always already 'imagined', 'invented' and contested, the emergence of forms of pseudo-nationalism, as a subset of corporate nationalism, further challenge and dismantle any assumed stable terrain. Corporate nationalism brands the nation through evocations, processes and practices that facilitate an often-explicit link between a national audience, a national sport and a particular transnational company or product. In turn, this can lead to the reappropriation of sports and nations by global corporations, as is evinced by Adidas' reworking of traditions, histories, and cultures to re-brand the All Blacks as a global commodity (Scherer and Jackson 2010). Pseudo-nationalism creates and constructs its own new myths around identity and belonging, positing signifiers that are not necessarily as affixed, endearing or enduring as longer held linkages between sports and nations conventionally conceived as 'representative' of a people, a place, an identity or a sporting tradition.

Specific to pseudo-nationalism is an overt fabrication, a deliberate manufacturing and an explicit overreach to ascribed imagined boundaries, invented traditions and assumed realities of what constitutes 'authentic' or legitimate forms of nationalism at play. The claimed links between sport, nation and corporation are tenuous, dubious to non-existent, with expressions of pseudo-nationalistic sentiment predominantly having commercial, global and mediated interests at heart. Fundamentally, pseudo-nationalism mimics, falsifies and masquerades, deploying processes that reassemble and rearticulate imagined and invented underpinnings of sporting nationalism while realigning franchises, syndicates, teams, and communities dubiously to a specific and identifiable nation-state. Pseudo-nationalism hints at both the fluidity and contestability of national identity through sport, as well as the potential to re-spin these sporting traditions as forms of cultural and financial capital that segment and target markets within the nation's imagined community. Hence, like corporate nationalism, pseudo-nationalism exposes a duplicitous and disingenuous manufacturing of corporate interests packaged as national interests, made all the more striking with pseudo-nationalism's appeal to aspiration and desire. Thus, as an exclusionary sport, the America's Cup can reappropriate middle-class aspirations of upward mobility to garner patriotic public support and funding to ostensibly finance a rich, white man's sport raced between global syndicates. Paradoxically, historically marginalized, the invention of a 'New Zealand' team moniker within Australian rugby league targets an idealized Pasifika/ Māori demographic with links to desire while obfuscating the stereotypes and exclusions permeating this imagined community.

Collectively, in New Zealand, pseudo-nationalism offers a short-hand and instant mechanism for generating interest, galvanizing support, and for forging forms of collective national identity. This may furnish sharing and celebrating franchise/syndicate successes as national successes and afford outpourings of communal unity, however temporary, perfunctory or manufactured they might be. Thus, rather than a simplistic dismissal of the falsehoods, implicit niche marketing and commercially-laden permutations in and around pseudo-nationalism, problematic though they are, the proliferation and percolation of pseudo-nationalism affords another rich layering to the imagined, invented and mythic components of sporting nationalism, community-building and New Zealand national identity.

Disclosure statement

No potential conflict of interest was reported by the authors.

References

America's Cup: Team NZ Rejects Government, Auckland Council Hosting Bid. 2021. *New Zealand Herald*. June 16. Accessed June 24, 2021. https://www.nzherald.co.nz/nz/americas-cup-team-nz-rejects-government-auckland-council-hosting-bid/6K4LEVFZI34OE6IZ5UX5MPVD3Q/#.

Anderson, Talei. 2020. Understanding Pasifika Culture Pivotal for Rugby League Success. *Radio New Zealand*. 12 August. Accessed September 5, 2020. https://www.rnz.co.nz/international/pacific-news/423314/understanding-pasifika-culture-pivotal-for-rugby-league-success.

Anderson, Benedict. 1991 [1983]. *Imagined Communities: Reflections on the Origin and Spread of Nationalism* (Rev. and extended ed.). London: Verso.

ANZ Bank. 2015. "Dream big New Zealand." *YouTube*. January 12. Accessed September 8, 2020. https://www.youtube.com/watch?v=f1jbCqi4ARs.

Bairner, Alan. 2009. "National Sports and National Landscapes: In Defence of Primordialism." *National Identities* 11 (3): 223–239. doi:10.1080/14608940903081101.

Bairner, Alan. 2017. "Sport and the Politics of National Identity in the Two Chinas." In *Sport and National Identities*, edited by Paddy Dolan and John Connolly, 226–242. London: Routledge.

Barker, Michael, Stephen Page, and Denny Meyer. 2002a. "Evaluating the Impact of the 2000 America's Cup on Auckland, New Zealand." *Event Management* 7 (2): 79–92. doi:10.3727/152599501108751498.

Barker, Michael, Stephen Page, and Denny Meyer. 2002b. "Modeling Tourism Crime: The 2000 America's Cup." *Annals of Tourism Research* 29 (3): 762–782. doi:10.1016/S0160-7383(01)00079-2.

Barron, Christopher. 2020. "Selling the 'City of Sails': Destination Branding through the 2021 America's Cup." Unpublished Master's Thesis, Auckland University of Technology (March). Accessed August 7, 2020. https://openrepository.aut.ac.nz/bitstream/handle/10292/13471/BarronC.pdf?sequence=3&isAllowed=y.

Billig, Michael. 1995. *Banal Nationalism*. Los Angeles: Sage.

Blake, Peter. 2000. *Message from Team New Zealand. The Road to America's Cup: 2000 New Zealand*. Auckland: Vision Publishing.

Calhoun, Craig. 2007. *Nations Matter: Culture, History and the Cosmopolitan Dream*. London: Routledge.

Coakley, Jay. 2020. *Sports in Society: Issues and Controversies*. 12th ed. New York: McGraw-Hill.

Collins, Tony. 2013. *Rugby's Great Split: Class, Culture and the Origins of Rugby League Football*. 2nd ed. London: Routledge.

Cosgrove, Amanda, and Toni Bruce. 2005. "'The Way New Zealanders Would like to See Themselves': Reading White Masculinity via Media Coverage of the Death of Sir Peter Blake." *Sociology of Sport Journal* 22 (3): 336–355. doi:10.1123/ssj.22.3.336.

Crawford, Scott. 1985. "The Game of 'Glory and Hard Knocks': A Study of the Interpenetration of Rugby and New Zealand Society." *The Journal of Popular Culture* 19 (2): 77–92. doi:10.1111/j.0022-3840.1985.00077.x.

Cronin, Mike. 1999. *Sport and Nationalism in Ireland: Gaelic Games, Soccer, and Irish Identity since 1884*. Dublin: Four Courts Press.

Delanty, Gerard, and Krishan Kumar, eds. 2006. *The SAGE Handbook of Nations and Nationalism*. London: Sage.

Diversity of New Zealand Rugby League's Leaders Questioned. 2020. *Radio New Zealand*. August 31. Accessed September 5, 2020. https://www.rnz.co.nz/news/sport/424865/diversity-of-new-zealand-rugby-league-s-leaders-questioned.

Dolan, Paddy, and John Connolly, eds. 2017. *Sport and National Identities: Globalization and Conflict*. London: Routledge.

Eagles, Jim. 1986a. "On February 2, 1986." *National Business Review America's Cup Outlook: New Zealand's Challenge for the America's Cup*, 1. Wellington: Fourth Estate Newspapers.

Eagles, Jim. 1986b. "Battling for the Plunder." *National Business Review America's Cup Outlook: New Zealand's Challenge for the America's Cup*, 4–5. Wellington: Fourth Estate Newspapers.

Evans, Bryn. 2004. "Commercialising National Identity: A Critical Examination of New Zealand's America's Cup Campaigns of 1987, 1992 and 1995." Unpublished Master's Thesis, Auckland University of Technology. Accessed July 31, 2020. https://openrepository.aut.ac.nz/handle/10292/209.

Evans, Bryn. 2007. "KZ7, the Mass Media, and the Ascent of Entrepreneurial Nationalism 1984–1987." *Communication Journal of New Zealand* 8 (1): 7–22.

Falcous, Mark, and Joshua Newman. 2016. "Sporting Mythscapes, Neoliberal Histories, and Post-Colonial Amnesia in Aotearoa/New Zealand." *International Review for the Sociology of Sport* 51 (1): 61–77. doi:10.1177/1012690213508942.

Falcous, Mark. 2007. "Rugby League in the National Imaginary of New Zealand Aotearoa." *Sport in History* 27 (3): 423–446. doi:10.1080/17460260701591684.

Falcous, Mark. 2017. "Rugby League and the Negotiation of Englishness." In *Sport and English National Identity in a 'Disunited Kingdom'*, edited by Tom Gibbons and Dominic Malcolm, 79–92. London: Routledge.

Goldman, Robert, and Stephen Papson. 1996. *Sign Wars: The Cluttered Landscape of Advertising*. New York: Guilford.

Hardt, Michael, and Antonio Negri. 2000. *Empire*. Cambridge, MA: Harvard University Press.

Hargreaves, John. 2002. "Globalisation Theory, Global Sport, and Nations and Nationalism." In *Power Games: A Critical Sociology of Sport*, edited by John Sugden and Alan Tomlinson, 25–43. London: Routledge.

Hartley, J. 2016. "A Political Theory of Progressive Individualism? Western Australia and the America's Cup, 30 Years on." *Thesis Eleven* 135 (1): 14–33. doi:10.1177/0725513616657883

Hawkes, Gina. 2018. "Indigenous Masculinity in Sport: The Power and Pitfalls of Rugby League for Australia's Pacific Island Diaspora." *Leisure Studies* 37 (3): 318–330. doi:10.1080/02614367.2018.1435711.

Hobsbawm, Eric. 1983a. "Introduction: Inventing Traditions." In *The Invention of Tradition*, edited by Eric Hobsbawm and Terence Ranger, 1–14. Cambridge: Cambridge University Press.

Hobsbawm, Eric. 1983b. "Mass Producing Traditions: Europe, 1870–1914." In *The Invention of Tradition*, edited by Eric Hobsbawm and Terence Ranger, 263–307. Cambridge: Cambridge University Press.

Hobsbawm, Eric. 1990. *Nations and Nationalism since 1780: Programme, Myth, Reality*. Cambridge: Cambridge University Press.

Hokowhitu, Brendan. 2003. "Physical Beings: Stereotypes, Sport and the Physical Education of New Zealand Māori." *Sport in Society* 6 (2–3): 192–218. doi:10.1080/14610980312331271599.

John, Alistair, and Steve Jackson. 2011. "Call Me Loyal: Globalization, Corporate Nationalism and the America's Cup." *International Review for the Sociology of Sport* 46 (4): 399–417. doi:10.1177/1012690210384658.

Kerr, Roslyn. 2016. *Sport and Technology: An Actor-Network Theory Perspective*. Manchester: Manchester University Press.

King, Anthony. 2006. "Nationalism and Sport." In *The SAGE Handbook of Nations and Nationalism*, edited by Gerard Delanty and Krishan Kumar, 249–259. London: Sage.

Long, David. 2016. "Eric Watson Wants to Put 'New Zealand' Back into the Warriors Name."*Stuff*. April 23. Accessed September 8, 2020. https://www.stuff.co.nz/sport/league/79241058/eric-watson-wants-to-put-new-zealand-back-into-the-warriors-name.

Maguire, Joe, and Jason Tuck. 2005. "National Identity, Rugby Union and Notions of Ireland and the 'Irish.'" *Irish Journal of Sociology* 14 (1): 86–109. doi:10.1177/079160350501400106.

Mazany, Pete. 1995. *TeamThink: Team New Zealand: The "Black Magic" of Management behind the 1995 America's Cup Success*. Auckland: VisionPlus Developments.

Marfell, Amy. 2019. "'We Wear Dresses, We Look Pretty': The Feminization and Heterosexualization of Netball Spaces and Bodies." *International Review for the Sociology of Sport* 54 (5): 577–602. doi:10.1177/1012690217726539.

McDonald, Brent, and Lena Rodriguez. 2014. "'It's Our Meal Ticket': Pacific Bodies, Labour and Mobility in Australia." *Asia Pacific Journal of Sport and Social Science* 3 (3): 236–249. doi:10.1080/21640599.2014.972537.

O'Neil, Andrea. 2015. "Red Socks Became Part of the National Uniform." *Stuff*. March 30. Accessed 11 August 2020. https://www.stuff.co.nz/dominion-post/capital-life/67545131/red-socks-became-part-of-national-uniform.

Orams, Mark. 2011. "America's Cup." In *Encyclopedia of Sports Management and Marketing*, edited by Linda E. Swayne and Mark Dodds, 62. Thousand Oaks, CA: Sage.

Orwell, George. 1968. *The Collected Essays, Journalism and Letters of George Orwell*. London: Secker and Warburg.

Phillips, Jock. 1996. *A Man's Country? The Image of the Pakeha Male—A History*. Auckland: Penguin.

Phillips, Murray. 1998. "From Suburban Football to International Spectacle: The Commodification of Rugby League in Australia, 1907–1995." *Australian Historical Studies* 29 (110): 27–48. doi:10.1080/10314619808596059.

Sailing Away. 1987. *NZ On Screen Iwi Whitiāhua*. Accessed August 11, 2020. https://www.nzon-screen.com/title/sailing-away-1986.

Scherer, Jay, and Steve Jackson. 2010. *Globalization, Sport and Corporate Nationalism: The New Cultural Economy of the New Zealand All Blacks*. Oxford: Peter Lang.

Silk, Michael, David Andrews, and Cheryl Cole, eds. 2005. *Sport and Corporate Nationalisms*. Oxford: Berg.

Smith, Adrian. 2004. "Black against Gold: New Zealand—Australia Sporting Rivalry in the Modern Era." In *Sport and National Identity in the Post-War World*, edited by Dilwyn Porter and Adrian Smith, 168–193. London: Routledge.

Smith, Anthony. 2001. *Nationalism: Theory, Ideology, History*. Malden, MA: Polity.

St John, Mark. 2020. "'They Need Australians': Kent Blasts Warriors' National Focus in Club Competition." *Fox Sports Australia*. June 22. Accessed September 14, 2020. https://www.fox-sports.com.au/nrl/nrl-premiership/nrl-2020-paul-kent-vs-warriors-new-zealand-vs-australia-stephen-kearney/news-story/7ce7b8713d12d20574883c1a8e0f13ac.

Sturm, D., and, G. Lealand. 2012. "Evoking 'new Zealandness': representations of Nationalism during the (New Zealand) 2011 Rugby World Cup. " MEDIANZ: Media Studies *Journal of Aotearoa New Zealand* 13 (2): 46–65. doi:10.11157/medianz-vol13iss2id15.

Sugden, John, and Alan Bairner. 1993. *Sport, Sectarianism, and Society in a Divided Ireland*. Leicester: Leicester University Press.

Tedeschi, Nick. 2020. "Squandered Money and a Lack of Planning puts NRL on Precipice." *The Guardian*. March 24. Accessed September 1, 2020. https://www.theguardian.com/sport/2020/mar/24/squandered-money-and-a-lack-of-planning-puts-nrl-on-precipice.

The Protocol for the 36th America's Cup. 2017. *America's Cup*. September 17. Accessed March 17, 2021. https://www.americascup.com/en/official/the-protocol.

Todd, Katie. 2021. "America's Cup Crowds a Winner for Auckland Hospitality, Events, Businesses." *RNZ*. March 15. Accessed March 25, 2021. https://www.rnz.co.nz/news/national/438435/america-s-cup-crowds-a-winner-for-auckland-hospitality-events-businesses.

Tuck, Jason. 2003. "Making Sense of Emerald Commotion: Rugby Union, National Identity and Ireland." *Identities* 10 (4): 495–515. doi:10.1080/714947402.

Vodafone Warriors. 2014. "Matter of Faith." *YouTube*. August 6. Accessed April 23, 2021. https://www.youtube.com/watch?v=nq5MyLuAnhA.

Vodafone Warriors. 2015. "We are New Zealand and We Are All Warriors." *Vodafone Warriors*. February 18. Accessed September 8, 2020. https://www.facebook.com/vodafonewarriors/videos/927046214006439/.

Whannel, Garry. 2008. *Culture, Politics and Sport: Blowing the Whistle, Revisited*. London: Routledge.

Wilson, Rob, Daniel Plumley, and David Barrett. 2015. "Staring into the Abyss? The State of UK Rugby's Super League." *Managing Sport and Leisure* 20 (6): 293–310. doi:10.1080/23750472.2016.1141367.

Nation as a product of resistance: introducing post-foundational discourse analysis in research on ultras' nationalism

Mateusz Grodecki (ID)

ABSTRACT
The aim of the paper is to introduce the post-foundational discourse analysis (PDA) in nation studies, in particular, in research on football supporters' (ultras) national(istic) discourse. The value of the PDA for nation studies lies in its analytical tools, which allow to give visibility to different national(istic) discourses creating meanings of nation and thus to explore how these meanings are created, how they become institutionalized and reproduced in social practices and how they are challenged. The PDA's specific value for research on ultras' nationalism lies in its conceptualisation and analytical tools for the study of social change. Considering the findings from different European countries showing that ultras' nationalism is shaped by their resistance against current mainstream political nationalisms and ideologies expressed by rival ultras groups, the PDA can be a useful tool for empirical studies of the processes that have had an impact on its development.

Introduction

The aim of this article is to introduce and adopt the post-foundational discourse analysis (PDA) in nation studies. PDA defines discourse as a range of practices of articulation which create and regulate the social meaning of an object (Martilla 2015). Drawing on both structuralist (Saussure 1916) and post-structuralist conceptions of discourse (Derrida 2001), it adopts the view that practices of articulation creating discourses originate based on contingency logic, i.e. on rules established by already existing practices of articulation. The relative stability of discourse is achieved owing to the mechanism of sedimentation, which consists in the concealment of the origins of a discourse on the one hand, and the materialization of practices of articulation on the other. The former translates into the perception that the meaning created by discourse 'has always been there'. The latter is apparent in the emergence of institutions and subject roles which regulate practices of articulation 'by making them accept and stick to discourse-specific conceptions of the world' (Martilla 2015: 12). This builds the relative stability of discourse and thus establishes the meaning of a specific object within a particular period of time. The practices of articulation that create and reproduce current meanings are defined as hegemonic. The change of meaning occurs when counter-hegemonic articulations undermine and redefine it and thus attendant ideas become sedimented in the institutional context (Martilla 2015).

In the PDA approach, nationalism will be understood as a national(istic) discourse, i.e. a set of practices of articulation creating the meaning of nation. Thus, this study is situated within discursive approach to nation-building process (e.g. Billig 1995; Sutherland 2005; Łuczewski 2012) which fits constructivist dimension of nation research in broader perspective. Contrary to traditional approaches, i.e. primordialism, modernism and ethno-symbolism (see Smith 2008) which study top-down strategies of nation building and aim to define what nation is, this approach focuses more on questions of who, how and where reproduces the meaning of nation (Hearn and Antonsich 2018: 602). This conceptualization fits constructivist dimension of nation studies as it allows to analytically distinguish national(istic) discourses on the basis of reconstruction of practices of articulation giving meaning to nation and explore their material dimension visible in institutions which regulate the coherency of articulations and reproduce given meanings. The value of PDA for research on nation-building process thus lies in its analytical tools, which allow to give visibility to different national(istic) discourses, to explore how the current meanings of nation are (re)created, how they become sedimented in practices and institutions, and who and how challenges them.

This paper argues that PDA can be a particularly valuable methodological approach in research on ultras' nationalism for three reasons. Firstly, existing studies on the issue (e.g. Testa and Armstrong 2010; Maniou 2019; Djordjević and Pekić 2018; Grodecki 2020b) clearly indicate that ultras groups create distinctive forms of nationalism. They use football stands as a space where they intentionally present their views on the nation using different means, like choreographies, flags, banners, chants, etc. Secondly, the same studies show that ultras' nationalism is shaped by their resistance against current mainstream political and national ideologies, and forms on the basis of contrariety to other ideologically distinctive ultras groups (e.g. Spaaij and Viñas 2005; Doidge 2013). In other words, ultras' nationalism is a result of counter-hegemonic acts against articulations of mainstream nationalisms on the one hand, and rivalry between ultras groups on the other. In this perspective, the PDA's conceptualisation of social change provides useful tools to analyse processes that have been shaping elements of ultras' nationalism. Thirdly, there is a considerable gap in sports fandom research regarding potential theoretical and methodological approaches that could be applied in empirical studies exploring supporters' nationalism. Existing studies have often employed only general terms like nationalism, xenophobia, extreme right-wing, etc. as explanatory categories for individual cases. Thus, further research on ultras' nationalism needs proposals for theoretical and methodological approaches which could foster more nuanced explanatory models in empirical projects.

The article is divided into four sections. The first section introduces the main postulates and premises of the post-foundational discourse analysis. The second one situates PDA within the current conceptions of nation-building process and discusses its implementation in nation research. The third section illustrates how the PDA's theoretical codes and analytical tools (synchronic and diachronic analyses) can be applied in research exploring nationalism among ultras groups. It uses examples from Polish ultras' national(istic) discourse, concerning such constructs as traditional Polish family, anti-communism, national heroes and anti-refugee campaign. The paper concludes with final remarks and part discussing the limitations of the proposal.

The post-foundational discourse analysis

This article draws on Tomas Martilla's (2015) proposal of a research programme for the post-foundational discourse analysis. PDA conceptualizes discourse as a range of coherent practices of articulation which create and regulate the meaning of an object. Discourse is 'a structural arrangement of discursive elements that originates from practices of articulation, and which, in its turn, constrains social subjects' potential practices of articulation' (Martilla 2015: 22). Practices of articulation are specified as every social practice that establishes relations between elements and thus creates theirs identity (Laclau and Mouffe 1985). In this view, discourse does not refer only to narrowly defined content, but most importantly to a range of social processes creating and reproducing meaning. This conceptualisation of discourse means that the main aim of PDA is to analyse the process of (re)production of meaning.

PDA draws on both structuralist (Saussure 1916) and post-structuralist conceptions of discourse (Derrida 2001). Following Saussure's 'relational epistemology of meaning' revised by Derrida, it claims that social practices are not regulated by any objective rules but are a contingent result of already existing practices. In consequence, 'social rules persist only as long as they are maintained by consecutive social practices' (Martilla 2015: 5). This translates into the assumption that discourses are established on the basis of contingency rules – they are a contingent outcome of already existing practices of articulation. 'The conceived self-evidentiality of a discourse results from the process of discursive "sedimentation"' (Martilla 2015: 10). Sedimentation is vital for the relative stability of a discourse due to the fact that only enduring discourses can create meaning. Sedimentation is evinced in the concealment of discourse origins and the materialization of practices of articulation. The former is achieved when the social meaning that it creates is perceived as something taken for granted, something that 'has always been there'. The latter refers to the perpetuation of social meanings in the structure. Discourses give rise to institutions and subject roles which regulate the existing practices of articulation and make them coherent with the existing meanings (Martilla 2015: 10-11). PDA defines subject roles as positions with a potential to influence and regulate discourse. Institutions, in turn, are understood as every structuralized form which regulates practices of articulation by supporting existing practices and meanings, punishing deviations and establishing rules of access to subject roles. In other words, institutions deliver resources for maintaining the stability of discourse. However, the effectiveness of institutions 'depends on the presence of corresponding institutional populace, which accommodates itself to the functional needs of institutions and adapts social practices that support institutional operations' (Martilla 2015: 39; see also Torfing 1999).

Considering the fact that discourses are processual and fluid in nature, they achieve relative stability of created meaning only in a certain period of time. The social change (i.e. a change of meaning within discourse) is conceptualized in PDA on the basis of ontology of conflict theory. The practices of articulation which establish and reproduce current meanings are considered hegemonic, while the practices which aim to undermine, redefine or bend the existing meanings are defined as counter-hegemonic. A change of meaning occurs when new ideas stemming from counter-hegemonic articulations become sedimented in the institutional context (Martilla 2015). Counter-hegemonic acts may also undermine the 'obviousness' and the 'primeval' character of hegemonic meanings and, consequently, contribute to the destabilization of hegemonic discourse.

The usefulness of PDA mostly lies in its potential to deconstruct processes (discourses) which shape the social meaning of an object. Its main aim is 'to lend empirical visibility to all parts of discourses constituting and structuring social life' (Martilla 2015: 49). In PDA, discourses are not viewed as entities existing in the objective sense, but are co-constructed by the researcher. This means that they are abstract analytical models, distinguished in order to examine processes which have been shaping the meaning of an examined object. They are recognized based on (1) coherency of practices of articulation (Glynos and Howarth 2007), visible in nodal points (Laclau and Mouffe 1985; Torfing 1999), (2) distinction from other discourses (Laclau and Mouffe 1985) (Martilla 2015).

Following Glynos and Howarth (2007), Martilla points out that coherency of practices of articulation becomes apparent in 'patterns of discursive articulation', which can be captured in discursive 'relations' and 'identities'. Relations are built by practices of articulation upon linked elements that are present in discourse and thus create identities. Both categories are considered in PDA as 'theoretical codes' suitable to build middle-range explanations (Martilla 2015: 20-21). There are four types of discursive relations in PDA: contrariety, representation, equivalence and difference (Martilla 2015: 24-28). The relation of contrariety is crucial for the very existence of a discourse as it defines what belongs to it (what is 'in') and what is excluded ('out'). Some more specific relations can be distinguished within this type: antagonism (where two elements of a discourse are in mutual opposition), dissociation (distinction between marked and unmarked elements which establish discursive boundaries) and incommensurability (where two or more elements are evaluated differently in regard to a more general element of reference). The relation of representation, in turn, symbolizes shared elements of a given discourse. It constitutes so called 'nodal points' around which discourses are organized (Norval 2000: 328) and which create the common identity of discursive elements. The relations of equivalence and difference are strongly linked. Elements could be defined as different only when 'they are also mutually equivalent – partly with regard to the nodal points, which represent their common identity, and partly with regard to their distinction from other discourses' (Martilla 2015: 27).

The analytical category of discursive identities aims to capture the syntagmatic coherency of practices of articulation. Drawing on second order-hermeneutics, PDA points out that analysis of identity meanings should be placed in relation to the context in which they occur. Considering that the distinctiveness of discourses is defined based on the logic of difference from other discourses, this category is divided into negatively and positively marked identities (with reference to the vision of a given discourse). Martilla introduces three main analytical categories of discursive identities: values, subjectivity and activity. The first of them is divided into 'ethical ideals', expressed by nodal points as a certain ideal state, and 'antagonists' – actors and processes threatening the ideal state. 'Subjectivity' defines and assigns roles to particular actors. These roles are divided into 'protagonists', who defend values, 'opponents', who hinder the attainment of values (the ideal state), 'helpers', who support protagonists or opponents, 'destinators', who are considered initiators of actions and ideas, and 'receivers', on behalf of whom activities are carried out. The category 'activity' is subdivided into 'actions' undertaken by entities (actors or institutions), 'interactions' that connect these entities with their actions, 'objects' used for activities or on which activities are oriented, 'resources' that enable entities to pursue their actions, and 'strategies' defining the course of action to achieve specific goals (Martilla 2015: 30–33).

PDA also provides analytical tools for the study of current discourses (synchronic analysis) and for their historical reconstruction (diachronic analysis). The first step of synchronic analysis aims to identify practices of articulation creating a particular discourse and thus the meaning of an analysed object. The second step proceeds to the reconstruction of the content of the practices in focus. Using theoretical codes described above (i.e. discursive relations and discursive identities), this stage examines the coherency of practices of articulation, identifies nodal points of the discourse and determines its boundaries. Further on, synchronic analysis focuses on the reconstruction of the material dimension of the discourse: the aim is to identify its subject roles and institutions regulating practices of articulation. The final results of synchronic analysis are findings showing processes which create and reproduce the meaning of an analysed object (Martilla 2015: 44-45)

The principal aim of diachronic analysis, in turn, is to reconstruct historical processes which have shaped the discourse under investigation. As the conceptualisation of social change is crucial here, it is worth reminding that PDA draws on the ontology of social conflict and defines a shift in meaning as a result of influence of counter-hegemonic acts on hegemonic discourse. Diachronic analysis begins with identification of the hegemonic discourse and counter-hegemonic practices of articulation in a given time period. Next, it focuses on content analysis which aims to reconstruct the contested discourse (i.e. discursive relations, identities, nodal points). This makes it possible to gather data on changes in meaning that have occurred in a particular period under the influence of counter-hegemonic acts. In the final stage, diachronic analysis concentrates on changes in the material dimension of the contested discourse. In particular, it needs to focus on the roles and institutions that have supported its stability and the extent to which they have been changed (Martilla 2015: 46).

Applying PDA in nation studies

The PDA's conceptualisation of (re)production of meaning through discourse makes it a useful analytical tool in nation-building research situated within constructivist approach. It allows to analytically distinguish national(istic) discourses on the basis of (1) reconstruction of practices of articulation giving meaning to nation and (2) their material dimension visible in institutions which regulate the coherency of articulations and reproduce given meanings. The value of PDA for nation studies lies particularly in addressing the latter dimension using the concept of discursive sedimentation (i.e. the materialization of a discourse and the concealment of its genesis). Additionally, PDA provides a useful conceptualisation of social change which makes it possible to capture not only how the meanings of nation have been changed but also what influenced the process. As such, then, PDA is particularly valuable for the study of nation-building process: its analytical tools allow to give visibility to different national discourses, to explore how the current meanings of nation are created, how they become sedimented in practices and institutions, and who and how challenges them.

The role of discourse has been underlined in many theoretical proposals aiming to conceptualize the process of (re)production of nation (e.g. Verdery 1995; Billig 1995; Calhoun 1997; Sutherland 2005; Łuczewski 2012). These studies have followed constructivist logic defining nation as a product of national(istic) discourse, viewed as a set of widely defined practices of articulation which associate different social constructs (like values, territory, history, religion, stereotypes) with concepts and symbols related to nation. Most importantly, national(istic) discourse binds the vision of nation with a given population, creating 'imagined community' (Anderson 1983), and thus builds the sense of belonging to a particular nation. Consequently, such practices contribute to the naturalization of nation and create a sense that the world is 'naturally' divided into different nations (Smith 1988). In general, national(istic) discourse is the space where nation and its meaning are created and reproduced (e.g. Billig 1995; Łuczewski 2012).

PDA also conceptualizes nation as a product of discourse where discourse refers to the content of articulations, and most importantly to processes which shape and reproduce the meaning of nation. The presupposition of the contingent genesis of nation (Brubaker 1996), which is constructed by practices of articulation, results in its processual and fluid nature. National(istic) discourse nationalizes various social constructs (elements) by linking them with nation and national symbols. Since PDA treats discourses as analytical models, national(istic) discourses do not exist in objective terms. They can be analytically distinguished on the basis of the empirical criteria mentioned above: (1) consistency of practices of articulation, (2) clear distinction from other discourses.

National(istic) discourses are clearly visible in practices of articulation referring to the nodal point 'nation' (Przyłęcki 2013). This establishes the general boundaries of national(istic) discourses separating them from other (non-nationalistic) discourses: in order to create a discursive national identity, given elements have to be linked with nation (or national symbols). The question is how to analytically distinguish one national(istic) discourse from another. According to the premises of PDA, this should be done by investigating 'patterns of discursive articulation', which are visible through application of discursive 'relations' and 'identities' as theoretical codes. These analytical tools allow to examine the coherence of articulated content and therefore assign practices of articulation to a particular national(istic) discourse. In this step, it is crucial to explore 'contrariety' relations between specific national(istic) discourses, as they clearly establish the mutual boundaries between different meanings of nation (and thus, between discourses). However, this strategy refers only to the content dimension of discourse analysis. Martilla (2015: 23) argues that 'analytical focus must be extended beyond the analysis of discursive structures, and also involve analysis of the reciprocal relations between discourse and discursive materiality'. In other words, the analytical distinction of a particular national(istic) discourse also needs to consider its material dimension as the consistency of articulations is regulated by institutions and subject roles. Applying this conceptualisation in research on nation-building process requires developing a model of relations between institutions creating national discourses.

It is argued here that the 'regulative dimension' of discourse emphasized by PDA constitutes the key value of this approach for research on nation-building process as the institutional anchor of nation is one of the central aspects highlighted in studies considering the role of discourse in shaping the meaning of nation (e.g. Billig 1995; Brubaker 1996, Kilias 2004, Łuczewski 2012). However, the study of institutional materialization also needs to take into account the distribution of power, i.e. the extent of impact and influence of a given institution. The main institution regulating the meaning of a given nation is obviously nation-state. It was established by nationalist movements which defined a specific nation (created a national(istic) discourse) and formalized (institutionalised) this idea in the form of nation-state (e.g. Gellner 1997; Hobsbawm 2012). The nation-state has established and controls a wide range of institutions reproducing 'its' national(istic) discourse: education (Jaskułowski, Majewski, and Surmiak 2018), national symbols (Dumitrica 2019), national holidays (Fox 2013), national sports teams (Houlihan 1997) or state policies in general (Brubaker 1996).

Although nation-state can be considered as the biggest actor (re)producing the national(istic) discourse through its institutions, this does not mean that this discourse (the meaning of nation) is not contested by other actors who attempt to modify it. Contrary to traditional approaches to nationalism (e.g. Gellner 1997; Hobsbawm 2012; Kilias 2004; Smith 2008) – which tend to presuppose the top-down nature of the nation-building process, stressing that nation is invented by 'national elites' and consumed and reproduced in this form by the rest of society – contemporary studies emphasize the agency of 'ordinary' people (e.g. Skey 2010; Łuczewski 2012; Fox and Van Ginderachter 2018; Dumitrica 2019), who (re)create nation in their everyday practices. This also translates into the possibility of forming new visions of nation and therefore into the emergence of other national(istic) discourses.

Therefore the general model of studying mutual relations between national(istic) discourses should consider at least two dimensions: the relation between a given national(istic) discourse and the nation-state nationali(istic) discourse, and mutual relations between a given national(istic) discourse and other (non-state) national(istic) discourses. These relations can be analysed using the PDA's conceptualisation of change of social meaning (to reiterate: the current meaning is created by hegemonic articulations, while counter-hegemonic ones try to change/expand it). The first dimension, the relation between a given national(istic) discourse and the nation-state national(istic) discourse, could be conceptualized by defining the latter as a 'major nationalism', which the former, a 'minor' nationalism, struggles to undermine (Sutherland 2005). In other words, minor national(istic) discourses are created on the basis of counter-hegemonic articulations against a major national(istic) discourse. These counter-hegemonic articulations create different discursive identities and, in result, different meanings of nation to some extent (e.g. different historical figures defined as national heroes, different range of territorial resentments, characteristics of members of the nation, etc.). A distinctive national(istic) discourse emerges when this newly established meaning and contrariety between a minor and a major national(istic) discourse become materialized, i.e. when a minor discourse gives rise to subject roles and institutions reproducing these articulations. In this sense, the PDA analysis could be used to study both nation-state nationalism (i.e. one regulated by state institutions) and minor nationalisms, which can be associated with various political doctrines/parties, national minorities or other groups articulating their visions of nation (like national movements, football supporters – ultras etc.) and their mutual relations. The second dimension follows the same pattern, but concerns mutual relations between 'minor' national(istic) discourses. Counter-hegemonic articulations creating different discursive identities (and, in result, different meanings of nation) can also refer to other minor nationalisms: they can influence one another both in terms of creating common identities and by establishing mutual contrariety.

In result, PDA allows to analytically identify different national(istic) discourses and the dynamics of their mutual relations creating the meaning of nation. The identification of national(istic) discourse is based on its reference to the nodal point 'nation' (or national symbols). Distinction from other national(istic) discourses is established by mutual contrariety and by different institutions and subject roles which are created by a given discourse. It needs to be emphasized, however, that the 'natural' range of (nationalistic) discourse is not limited to particular institutions or populations (Martilla 2015: 52). Nevertheless, as analytical constructs they can be conceptualized as 'products' of a given community as their effectiveness stems from 'corresponding institutional populace' which adapts to their rules (see the previous section).

Applying PDA in the study of ultras' national(istic) discourse

This proposal argues that PDA is a methodological approach which can be valuable in nation studies in general, and in research on ultras' nationalism in particular. The ultras culture is strongly coupled with performative manifestations of their identity and views. Ultras groups 'create the cultural performance by bringing elements of everyday life into the stadium. The stadium atmosphere magnifies these elements and puts them on display for the immediate public as well as the larger media audience' (Guschwan 2007: 252). In other words, stadiums can be considered contemporary *agoras* (Testa and Armstrong 2010) where ultras groups voice their views by means of different forms, including spectacular choreographies, banners, flags and chants. The performative sphere also extends beyond stadiums: their murals and graffiti are visible in public space (Gibril 2018). These performances are also used to articulate ultras' views on nation.

Ultras' national(istic) discourse can be analytically distinguished on the basis of PDA's empirical criteria introduced in previous sections of the paper: (1) consistency of practices of articulation, (2) content and institutional distinction from other discourses. Firstly, as any other national(istic) discourse, ultras' nationalism can be observed in the articulations referring to the nodal point 'nation' (directly or by means of national symbols). Secondly, the distinctiveness of ultras' nationalism can be visible in the relations of contrariety to other national(istic) discourses. Existing studies clearly show that it is shaped by their resistance against current mainstream political and national ideologies (e.g. Guschwan 2007; Testa and Armstrong 2010; Djordjević and Pekić 2018; Maniou 2019; Grodecki 2020a), and by contrariety to rival ultras groups (defined mostly by the right-wing vs left-wing dichotomy) (see Spaaij and Viñas 2005; Doidge 2013).

Practices of articulation creating the national(istic) discourse of ultras can display a various extent of cohesion. On the one hand, different groups of ultras within one nation can articulate different forms of nationalism. This is the case for instance in Italy (see Testa and Armstrong 2010; Doidge 2013), Germany (Daniel and Kassimeris 2013) or Spain (Spaaij and Viñas 2005). On the other hand, the national(istic) discourse of ultras may be common to all or a vast majority of such groups in a given country. This is the case in Poland (Kossakowski, Przemysław and Woźniak 2020), Russia (Gloriozova 2018) or Serbia (Djordjević and Pekić 2018). The extent of coherence of ultras' national(istic) discourse can be empirically visible in mutual rivalry. In countries where ultras groups differ in terms of their nationalism, the articulations of their vision of nation emphasizing contrariety to rival visions will be present during direct confrontations between their teams (see Testa, Armstrong 2010; Doidge 2013). In turn, in countries where ultras share national(istic) discourse, its expressions will be limited to the games played around 'special occasions' like national holidays or moments of perceived threat to national interests (Grodecki 2020a). In the latter case, direct confrontations will be dominated by performances focussed on intergroup rivalry.

PDA allows to give visibility to discourse creating the meaning of nation in ultras community, to show how it is reproduced and to reveal its genesis. To this end, the national(istic) discourse of ultras can be analysed using both synchronic and diachronic analysis. The main aim of synchronic analysis would be to deconstruct current ultras' discourse giving meaning to nation and mechanisms of its reproduction. Diachronic analysis, in turn, would aim to reconstruct its genesis by analysing the hegemonic and counter-hegemonic dynamics of social change. To go beyond an abstract description, the individual stages of both types of analysis will be illustrated with examples from the national(istic) discourse of ultras groups in Poland.

Synchronic analysis should begin with identification of practices of articulation creating the national(istic) discourse of ultras. As mentioned above, they can be found mainly in the performative sphere of ultras activities. Owing to their intended public display, they can be viewed as 'representations' of ultras' nationalism. In the next step, identification of practices of articulation allows to reconstruct the content of national(istic) discourse. The content analysis should start with investigating articulations linking different social objects (elements) with the nodal point 'nation' (directly or by means of national symbols). Then, following the PDA's theoretical codes of discursive relations and identities, it is possible to reconstruct 'the extent of paradigmatic and syntagmatic coherence of articulations' (Martilla 2015: 45). This should also reveal content-related boundaries separating ultras' national(istic) discourse from other national(istic) discourses. Discursive elements will create 'positive' (what and who belongs to the nation) or 'negative' identities (defining contradictions to and antagonists of the nation).

For instance, Polish ultras connect the 'traditional' heterosexual family with the cornerstone of the Polish nation. It is opposed to modern forms of family 'imposed' by 'rotten' liberal Western Europe and leftist and liberal political parties in Poland. This relation can thus be described as a combination of logics of equivalence and contrariety: the traditional 'Polish' family is contrasted with its threatening foreign (European) modern equivalent. This contrariety also creates a line between ultras' nationalism and liberal nationalism. The other typical construct that Polish ultras connect with nation is anti-communism. This connection can be illustrated by displays commemorating introduction of Martial Law in Poland by communist authorities, like banner of Lech Poznań ultras that reads, 'Poles always against communism 13.12.81' (Pol. *Polacy zawsze przeciwko komunie*) or by Ślask Wrocław ultras' choreography that originally showed an eagle in the crown (Poland's national coat of arm) and then the crossed-out hammer and sickle. Those kind of displays create the antagonist type of contrariety relation between the Polish nation and communism, thus connecting true Polishness with anti-communistic attitudes. National(istic) discourse of Polish ultras is apparent also in commemorations of historical figures identified by ultras as national heroes. Mostly soldiers or former state leaders who were fighting against different occupants of Poland are defined as national heroes. They are pictured by ultras as figures to follow due to their sturdy resistance against enemies of the nation-state or because of their loyalty to compatriots. The banner of Zagłębie Lubin ultras, 'Cursed by communists, sturdy for us – Zagłębie shall not forget' (Pol. *Wyklęci przez komunistów, w naszych oczach niezłomni - Zagłębie nie zapomni*) commemorates the Cursed Soldiers – one of the major figures honoured by the Polish ultras. It serves as a very telling illustration. Such performances establish the positive discursive identity by defining these figures as 'protagonists' of the 'ethical idea' (Polish nation-state) who undertake laudable 'strategies' for its sake. Such displays not only connect historical figures with nation but also define enemies of the nation (in this example, communists) and, most importantly, they nationalize specific behaviours creating the virtues of true Poles.

The last step of synchronic analysis of ultras' national(istic) discourse should concentrate on its material dimension which regulates the range of practices of articulation. Following the case of Polish ultras, there are a few dimensions which could be examined in order to cover this issue. Firstly, such an analysis should explore the structure of this environment. It is strongly hierarchical, which means that every new idea on display (choreography, banner, flag) has to be approved by the leaders (see Grodecki 2019). Therefore, this structure should be examined in terms of specific subject roles responsible both for introducing the ideas of displays and for their approval. These subject roles then need to be explored as regards the decision-making process concerning the national content. This should reveal the fundamental boundaries of discourse (e.g. the main filter for introducing displays related to nation, the basic limits: what cannot ever be shown, etc.). Secondly, the materialization of national(istic) discourse is visible in processes of intergroup social control, which has a strong impact on the uniformity of articulations in the environment of Polish supporters. Ultras' rivalry is based on emphasizing mutual distinctions, demonstrated in displays during games played between teams they support. One perfect illustration of this process is the case of Ruch Chorzów ultras, who used to manifest their Silesian identity (using the German language and Silesian symbols). Their individuality was attacked many times by other Polish ultras groups, including Lechia Gdańsk ultras, who presented a choreography with a banner reading 'This is Silesia, This is Poland'.

However, the greatest potential for applying PDA in research on ultras' nationalism can be seen it its conceptualisation of social change. It is worth reminding that, as established in literature, ultras internalize national(istic) discourses present in public sphere at some historical point and, following their attitude of resistance, transform them into discourses distinctive for their environment. Thus, ultras' national(istic) discourse can be considered a contingent outcome of some historical processes (combining the emergence of supporters' subculture with wider social sentiments) and a result of counter-hegemonic acts against external articulations of other nationalisms. Applying diachronic analysis should allow to grasp these dynamics and reveal processes of change in detail, thus contributing to the understanding of their mechanics.

Diachronic analysis of ultras' national(istic) discourse needs first to determine the time period of research (which will be most often dictated by the combined factors of the purpose of the study and the availability of data). Then, on the basis of existing knowledge on the discourse, it should map the moments of social change within it. This opens a possibility to identify hegemonic and counter-hegemonic practices of articulation in the examined period of time. Following the case of Polish ultras, their anti-refugee campaign will be used as an illustration of this type of analysis. In 2015 they presented stadium displays (mostly banners and chants, but also a few themed choreographies) containing anti-refugees slogans. These displays voiced resistance against the migration policy of the EU and the Polish government aiming to relocate Syrian refugees to Poland. This was the first time when articulations against an ethnic and cultural group appeared in Polish stadiums on the nation-wide scale in an organized way.

The second step of diachronic analysis focuses on the content of both hegemonic and counter-hegemonic articulations. To continue with the example, Polish ultras' performances were based on the slogan 'Stop the Islamisation of Poland' and expressed critical attitude towards the EU and government (e.g. 'Instead of following Orban's example, you're on your knees before Angela'). Their displays created 'contrariety' relations between the Polish nation and Syrian refugees. The 'ethical idea', which for ultras in this case was ethnoculturally defined Polish nation and ethnically oriented nation-state, was under threat. The refugees were defined as 'antagonists' and 'receivers' (actors threatening the ideal state in the name of which activities are carried out), and politicians – as 'antagonists' and 'destinators' (the initiators threatening the ideal state) who introduce asylum policy as a 'strategy' to achieve political goals. The counter-hegemonic practices appeared in ultras' national(istic) discourse in response to narratives present in the 'major' discourse, pointing out the necessity (both moral and political) to support the culturally and ethnically different minority. They also came in response to some ultras groups from other European countries who displayed the opposite slogan: 'Refugees welcome'.

The final stage of diachronic analysis examines the relation between new articulations and discourse in terms of their materialization potential. It aims to study the extent to which subject roles and institutions have been influenced (changed or replaced) by counter-hegemonic articulations. The 'anti-refugee' campaign in the stadiums expanded the national(istic) discourse of Polish ultras by establishing the relation of contrariety between the Polish nation and Islamic culture. As ultras groups are based on informal structures, their influence on ultras' national(istic) discourse (change in norms) can be captured directly only by conducting interviews with supporters. However, it is also possible to examine this dimension indirectly by analysing the material products of ultras. Thus, the materialization of contrariety relation between the Polish nation and Islamic culture in ultras' national(istic) discourse was visible in anti-Islamic symbols (crossed-out *hilal*, crossed-out mosque), disseminated on scarves (e.g. a Śląsk Wrocław scarf with the mentioned symbols and the slogan 'Poland for Poles'), stickers (e.g. a sticker produced by Lechia Gdańsk supporters with the slogan 'There is no excuse it hurts, Lechia fans from Malbork fuck Islam', Pol. *Nie ma, że boli, malborska Lechia Islam pierdoli*) or in graffiti (e.g. a Wisła Kraków graffiti with the crossed-out mosque and ISIS caption with the slogan 'Every Arab needs to remember, Poland is sacred to us', Pol. *Każdy Arab niech pamięta, dla nas Polska to rzecz święta*).

The diachronic analysis of ultras' national(istic) discourse should consider, however, two important issues. Firstly, regarding the 'relational epistemology' it needs to be remembered that relations between elements appearing in discourse are linked on the basis of already existing social rules. As a result, counter-hegemonic (new) articulations follow them as well. This was clearly apparent in the case of the anti-refugee campaign. The domination of rules which can be generally characterized as ethnic nationalism (Breton 1988) in ultras' national(istic) discourse could only establish the 'contrariety' relation with pro-refugee elements. But these rules only create certain 'boundaries' or 'guidelines'. The way they are followed fits contingency logic. Secondly, thus, new discursive relations and identities can be a contingent outcome of existing rules of articulation. This can be illustrated by another example from the national(istic) discourse of Polish ultras: the development of performative commemorations of national holidays. They were developed on the basis of imitation of first demonstrations of local collective memory (i.e. some local historical events), in which ultras groups linked their local memory with national symbols. By doing this, they followed the pattern (rules) established during the communist period whereby nation was a symbol of community wider than the family, but different than the state. Thus, nation was used as a symbol marking such communities, especially in the moments of resistance against the communist state. However, in the process of imitation some other ultras groups mimicked only demonstrations of national identity and began to express it by celebrating national holidays or commemorating events from national history. As a result, the national(istic) discourse of ultras came to be extended by including both types of manifestations (Grodecki 2020b).

Final remarks

This paper has aimed to introduce the post-foundational discourse analysis (PDA) in nation studies, and argued that it can be a particularly valuable methodological approach in the study of ultras' nationalism. Having discussed arguments for the usefulness of PDA in both fields above, in the final section the article focuses on limitations of this methodological programme.

The principal aim of applying PDA in nation studies is to reveal the process of (re)production of the meaning of nation by giving (analytical) visibility to the (national) discourse and by analysing its material dimension which regulates the existing practices of articulation. PDA, however, does not make it possible to study what social constructs produced by discourse actually mean for the actors, to show their interpretations of the meaning nor to examine their overall motivations (Martilla 2015: 50). In other words, the analysis using PDA is concerned with how the discourse (re)produces the meaning of nation, and not on what nation actually is. This stems from the epistemological consequences of drawing on second-order hermeneutics, which, in general, is focussed on social structures that exist beyond the actors' consciousness. Thus, firstly, the sedimentation of discourse (i.e. its materialization and concealment of its origins) results in the fact that 'the social meaningfulness of an object is separated from social subjects' self-conscious conceptions of this object'. and secondly, there is no possibility to 'achieve an access to sedimented meanings that rationalize different social practices' (Martilla 2015: 54). Still, its analytical aims are consistent with the constructivist approach to nation which is concerned with how nation is reproduced rather than what nation is.

Finally, the model of adopting PDA in nation studies introduced here was strongly inspired by the current knowledge on the dynamics shaping ultras' nationalism. Thus, the usefulness of the presented mechanics beyond the study of ultras' national(istic) discourse could be overstated. Nevertheless, ultras groups have been proven to create distinctive meanings of nation. Therefore, analysing the process of how these meanings are produced in this environment can bring new insights into our understanding of the process of (re)production of nation in general. Attempts to introduce new methodological and theoretical approaches in research on ultras' nationalism are required even more due to the lack of consistent theoretical models in this field so far. The understanding of this phenomenon can be developed only by adapting different theoretical perspectives to empirical research.

Disclosure statement

Author has nothing to disclose.

Funding

This work was supported by the National Science Centre, Poland (grant number 2018/31/B/HS6/00148).

ORCID

Mateusz Grodecki (iD) https://orcid.org/0000-0003-3156-2850

References

Anderson, Benedict. 1983. *Imagined Communities: Reflections on the Origin and Spread of Nationalism.* London: Verso.

Billig, Michael. 1995. *Banal Nationalism.* London: Sage.

Breton, Raymond. 1988. "From Ethnic to Civic Nationalism: English Canada and Quebec." *Ethnic and Racial Studies* 11 (1): 85–102. doi:10.1080/01419870.1988.9993590.

Brubaker, Rogers. 1996. *Nationalism Reframed: Nationhood and the National Question in the New Europe.* Cambridge: Cambridge University Press.

Calhoun, Craig. 1997. *Nationalism.* Buckingham: Open University Press.

Daniel, Petra, and Christos Kassimeris. 2013. "The Politics and Culture of FC St. Pauli: From Leftism, through anti-Establishment, to Commercialization." *Soccer & Society* 14 (2): 167–182. doi:10.1080/14660970.2013.776466.

Derrida, Jacques. 2001. *Writing and Difference.* London: Routledge.

Djordjević, Ivan, and Relja Pekić. 2018. "Is There Space for the Left? Football Fans and Political Positioning in Serbia." *Soccer & Society* 19 (3): 355–372. doi:10.1080/14660970.2017.1333678.

Doidge, Mark. 2013. "The Birthplace of Italian Communism: political Identity and Action Amongst Livorno Fans." *Soccer & Society* 14 (2): 246–261. doi:10.1080/14660970.2013.776471.

Dumitrica, Delia. 2019. "The Ideological Work of the Daily Visual Representations of Nations." *Nations and Nationalism* 25 (3): 910–934. doi:10.1111/nana.12520.

Fox, Jon, and E. 2013. "National Holiday Commemorations: The View from below." In *The Cultural Politics of Nationalism and Nation-Building*, edited by Rachel Tsang and Eric Taylor Woods. Abingdon: Routledge.

Fox, Jon E., and Maarten Van Ginderachter. 2018. "Introduction: Everyday Nationalism's Evidence Problem." *Nations and Nationalism* 24 (3): 546–552. doi:10.1111/nana.12418.

Gellner, Ernest. 1997. *Nationalism.* New York: University Press.

Gibril, Suzan. 2018. "Shifting Spaces of Contention. An Analysis of the Ultras' Mobilization in Revolutionary Egypt." *European Journal of Turkish Studies* 26: 1–31.

Gloriozova, Ekaterina. 2018. "Russia." In *The Palgrave International Handbook of Football and Politics*, edited by Jean-Michael, De Waele, Suzan, Gibril, Ekaterina, Gloriozova, and Ramón, Spaaij. New York: Springer.

Glynos, Jason, and David Howarth. 2007. *Logics of Critical Explanation in Social and Political Theory.* London: Routledge.

Grodecki, Mateusz. 2019. "Building Social Capital: Polish Football Supporters through the Lens of James Coleman's Conception." *International Review for the Sociology of Sport* 54 (4): 459–478. doi:10.1177/1012690217728728.

Grodecki, Mateusz. 2020a. "Occasional Nationalists: The National Ideology of Ultras." Nationalities Papers doi:10.1017/nps.2020.25.

Grodecki, Matuesz. 2020b. "Contingent nationalism: The genesis of ultras' nationalist discourse." *International Review for the Sociology of Sport.* doi:10.1177/1012690220968116.

Guschwan, Matthew. 2007. "Riot in the Curve: Soccer Fans in Twenty-First Century Italy." *Soccer & Society* 8 (2-3): 250–266. doi:10.1080/14660970701224467.

Hearn, Jonathan, and Marco Antonsich. 2018. "Theoretical and Methodological Considerations for the Study of Banal and Everyday Nationalism." *Nations and Nationalism* 24 (3): 594–605. doi:10.1111/nana.12419.

Hobsbawm, Eric J. 2012. *Nations and Nationalism since 1780: Programme, Myth, Reality.* Cambridge: Cambridge University Press.

Houlihan, Barrie. 1997. "Sport, National Identity and Public Policy." *Nations and Nationalism* 3 (1): 113–137. doi:10.1111/j.1354-5078.1997.00113.x.

Jaskułowski, Krzysztof, Piotr Majewski, and Adrianna Surmiak. 2018. "Teaching the Nation: history and Nationalism in Polish School History Education." *British Journal of Sociology of Education* 39 (1): 77–91. doi:10.1080/01425692.2017.1304205.

Kilias, Jarosław. 2004. *Wspólnota Abstrakcyjna: Zarys Socjologii Narodu.* Warszawa: Wydawnictwo IFiS PAN.

Kossakowski, Radosław, Przemysław Nosal, and Wojciech Woźniak. 2020. *Politics, Ideology and Football Fandom: The Transformation of Modern Poland*. London: Routledge.

Laclau, Ernesto, and Chantal Mouffe. 1985. *Hegemony and Socialist Strategy*. London: Verso.

Łuczewski, Michał. 2012. *Odwieczny Naród. Polak i Katolik w Żmiącej*. Toruń: Wydawnictwo Naukowe Uniwersytetu Mikołaja Kopernika.

Maniou, Theodora. 2019. "Political Conflicts in the Cypriot Football Fields: A Qualitative Approach through the Press." *Soccer & Society* 20 (1): 123–138. doi:10.1080/14660970.2016.1267630.

Martilla, Tomas. 2015. "Post-Foundational Discourse Analysis: A Suggestion for a Research Program." *Forum Qualitative Sozialforschung/Forum: Qualitative Social Research* 16 (3).

Norval, Aletta J. 2000. "The Things we Do with Words: contemporary Approaches to the Analysis of Ideology." *British Journal of Political Science* 30 (2): 313–346. doi:10.1017/S0007123400000144.

Przyłęcki, Paweł. 2013. "Założenia Teorii Dyskursu Ernesta Laclaua i Chantal Mouffe." *Przegląd Socjologiczny* 62 (4): 9–24.

Saussure, Ferdinand de. 1916. *Course in General Linguistics*. London: Fontana/Collins.

Skey, Michael. 2010. "A Sense of Where You Belong in the World: National Belonging, Ontological Security and the Status of the Ethnic Majority in England." *Nations and Nationalism* 16 (4): 715–733. doi:10.1111/j.1469-8129.2009.00428.x.

Smith, Anthony. 1988. "The Myth of the 'Modern Nation' and the Myths of Nations." *Ethnic and Racial Studies* 11 (1): 1–26. doi:10.1080/01419870.1988.9993586.

Smith, Anthony. 2008. *Cultural Foundations of Nations: Hierarchy, Covenant and Republic*. Oxford: Blackwell.

Spaaij, Ramón, and Carles Viñas. 2005. "Passion, Politics and Violence: A Socio-Historical Analysis of Spanish Ultras." *Soccer & Society* 6 (1): 79–96.

Sutherland, Claire. 2005. "Nation-Building through Discourse Theory." *Nations and Nationalism* 11 (2): 185–202. doi:10.1111/j.1354-5078.2005.00199.x.

Testa, Alberto, and Gary Armstrong 2010. *Football, Fascism and Fandom: The Ultras of Italian Football*. London: A&C Black.

Torfing, Jacob. 1999. *New Theories of Discourse: Laclau, Mouffe and Žižek*. Oxford: Blackwell.

Verdery, Katherine. 1995. *National Ideology under Socialism: Identity and Cultural Politics in Ceaușescu's Romania*. Berkeley: University of California Press.

Guerrilla patriotism and mnemonic wars: cursed soldiers as role models for football fans in Poland

Przemysław Nosal ⓘ, Radosław Kossakowski ⓘ and Wojciech Woźniak ⓘ

ABSTRACT
Most national symbols – the flag, the coat of arms, the anthem, the pantheon of historical figures – belong to the common symbolic space. However, there are also those which divide the society: controversial figures or historical events which are difficult to assess and vulnerable to contradictory interpretations. In Poland, one case in point are the Cursed Soldiers. This paper discusses a specific mode of patriotism of football fans influenced by the figures of Cursed Soldiers. The first part provides a theoretical frame for further arguments. The second draws the relation between Polish football fans and nationalism. The third introduces the figure of Cursed Soldiers: their history, political context and social perceptions. The fourth part analyses fans' *guerrilla patriotism*. It revolves around performative content produced within football fandom, mainly by ultras groups. The article concludes with a discussion of specifics and universals of the proposed model of *guerrilla patriotism*.

Introduction

The relation between sport, nation and patriotism is an important topic in social studies (see Bairner 2001; Houlihan 1997; Smith and Porter 2004; Ward 2009). Sports rivalry is frequently built around national identity: nation is an essential category for sport federations, teams and tournaments; sport stars function as national heroes; national sports teams represent the unity of the nation and the media coverage of their performance provides a specific image of the whole nation (Blain, Boyle, and O'Donnell 1993). Likewise, teams or players (e.g. Bradley 2002; Gibbson 2011), sport successes (see Hilvoorde van, Elling, and Stokvis 2010; Kavetsos and Szymanski 2010), events (e.g. Tour de France), stadiums (frequently referred to as "national arenas") or outfits (e.g. yellow football jerseys of Brazil) may become elements of the patriotic universe and an important part of country-branding. There is a wider agreement that they are inherent elements of national identity (e.g. Marks 1998). Besides, sport arenas provide space for patriotic manifestations (Morgan 1997; Dixon 2000), where fans use flags, emblems, national colours or anthems. They also demonstrate their attachment to national history by displaying banners featuring historical figures and events. Supporters also present special choreographies to commemorate important anniversaries or to insult rival teams. All these activities make fans visible actors of performative patriotism. In effect, they are both participants and creators of official national narratives (see Jarvie and Walker 1994; Cronin 1999; Tuck 2003). However, there are certain symbols which divide the society: controversial figures, historical events which are difficult to assess, symbolic songs or slogans confusing for the public opinion also appear in the stadiums. This leads to discussion about the current shape of patriotism.

In Poland, such figures are Cursed Soldiers – members anti-communist Polish resistance movements formed in the later stages of World War II. Over the past decade they have become an important element of the patriotic narrative in Polish terraces. They serve as an example of anti-establishment, victimised, ready-to-fight pro-national attitude – *guerrilla patriotism*.

The aims of this paper are as follows: (a) to draw a picture of complex interrelations between nation, patriotism and football fans; (b) to provide a thorough description of Cursed Soldiers – their social, historical and political dimension; (c) to introduce and discuss the concept of *guerrilla patriotism* – a mode of patriotism unique to Polish fans.

Nation, nationalism, and sport

Studies describing the relation between sport and nationalism focus on several issues. First of all, the category of "nation" is considered as the foundation on which modern sport is built (Allison 2004; Tomlinson and Young 2005; Leeds and Leeds 2009). Andrews and Cole argue that the "'nation' remains a virulent force in everyday lived [sport] experience" despite the current "global moment'" (Andrews and Cole 2002, 123). Nation and nationality provide tools to control the institutional order. The world of sport is organised around national federations, leagues and training systems, around "domestic" and "international" rivalries, around sport mega events which gather teams from all the nations. Despite the processes that seem to weaken the role of nation in sport, like globalisation or migrations (see Giulianotti and Robertson 2009; cf. Topic and Coakley 2010; Ariely 2012), the national perspective still remains fundamental (Seippel 2017).

As observed, the idea of nation is essentialised by sport (Bairner 2009). The basic assumption is that every nation has only one official representation in a particular discipline (e.g. one men's national football team). The official team legitimises the state in the public opinion, which is why unrecognised countries strive to compete in official international tournaments (MacLean and Field 2014; Deeley 2019). International sports rivalry makes use of a limited numbers of national/state symbols which frame the concept of nation as such: coats of arms, anthems and flags. The system of sport gives no space for discussion on the idea of nation: there is no place for representations of autonomous ethnic minorities, trans-national areas or quasi-independent territories (cf. Hargreaves 2000). It offers a clear vision: one coherent nation with its official symbols. By extension, this vision strengthens the sense of the imagined community (Anderson 1991). Supporting the same national team or national representative helps people to perceive themselves as members of one nation. Apart from sharing a common language, media, government or currency, people also share a common national team (cf. Lechner 2007; Gleaves and Llewellyn 2014).

So, on the one hand, then, sport is an arena of pop-patriotism. Hobsbawm writes (1990, 143):

What has made sport so uniquely effective a medium for inculcating national feelings, at all events for males, is the ease with which even the least political or public individuals can identify with the nation as symbolized by young persons excelling at what practically every man wants, or at one time in his life has wanted, to be good at. The imagined community of millions seems more real as a team of eleven named people.

Owing to its cultural characteristics, sport has an important performative value. Players and fans embody the idea of nation in the stadiums, in the streets and in the media. They "play the nation" together. Edensor presents the concept of "performing the nation", which is especially relevant to the role of elite athletes who represent their nations. He argues that "probably the most currently powerful form of national performance is that found in sport" (Edensor 2002, 78). He claims that the concept of performance "enables us to look at the ways in which identities are enacted and reproduced, informing and (re)constructing a sense of collectivity" (Edensor 2002, 69). However, the role of supporters is particularly important and all of the above observations are relevant in the case of team sports rather than individual sporting competitions. They make use of symbols, chants and slogans (see Giulianotti 1995). Consequently, this mode of displaying nationality becomes eye-catching and spectacular. Sports events, along with some public holiday festivals or military parades, provide a unique space for celebrating nationality: they offer intense emotions and the experience of togetherness.

On the other hand, owing to the same cultural features, sport is also a domain of nationalism, chauvinism or right-wing ideology. The relation between narrowly defined nationalism and sport, including football, has been deeply explored (e.g. Mills 2009; Brentin 2016). Sport provides space and tools for expressing hostility towards others. There is a long list of issues which occasion nationalist performances: proclaiming the superiority of one nation over another; international historical animosities; ethnic, religious or racial conflicts; tension between nations within one country; the sense of external threat; or specific internal political atmosphere. All of them can release the nationalist potential of sport. The catalogue of supporters' nationalist behaviours includes a wide range of activities: stadium chants, slogans and banners, and out-of-stadium marches and demonstrations as well as street violence. Of course, there is a fine line between pop-patriotism and nationalism: the former is focused on praising one's own nation, the latter – on diminishing another. However, they are both mingled in fans' activities (see Brentin 2014). It is also worth noting that supporters' violent nationalism can appear in collaboration with political authorities as "official nationalism" (Arnold 2018), or, conversely, emerge in opposition against the current political power (see Krugliak and Krugliak 2017). It can be used as a political tool (Molnar and Whigham 2021), or function as a grass-root force out of control (cf. Kossakowski, Nosal, and Woźniak 2020, 209–211).

Billig emphasises the role of sport in banal nationalism – everyday representations of the nation which build a shared sense of national belonging among people (Billig 1995). He notes that this kind of nationalism is "simultaneously obvious and obscure" (14): it refers to all those familiar, unnoticed, taken-for-granted forms of nationalism embedded in the routines of social life that serve as constant reminders of nationhood. Sport reports, which are distinguished by country or stress the results of "ours", teach people how to perceive social life in terms of nations – home country and others (see Poulton 2004; Vidacs 2011). Besides, it is an effective instrument of banal nationalism owing to constant repetition of national symbols and almost subliminal nature (see Bowes and Bairner 2019). Billig writes about "indication": "Daily, the nation is indicated, or 'flagged', in the lives of its citizenry. Nationalism, far from being an intermittent mood in established nations, is the endemic condition" (Billig 1995, 6) while Edensor argues that "sport is increasingly situated in the mediatised matrix of national life, is institutionalised in schools, widely represented in a host of cultural forms and is an everyday practice for millions of national subjects. These every day and spectacular contexts provide one of the most popular ways in which national identity is grounded" (Edensor 2002, 71, 78).

In conclusion, sport is undoubtedly an area where the nation is reproduced. Modern sport promotes the vision of one coherent nation and one coherent patriotism. However, as it offers only the basic or essential concept of the nation, the forms of expressing patriotism in sport mostly rely on obvious symbols, colours, figures and slogans. The media usually do not focus on the supporters who go beyond this official discourse by using unpopular national symbols or praising controversial historical figures. The available studies rarely, if at all, record athletes' or fans' criticism of the official concept of their nations. Nevertheless, there are examples of supporters' search for their distinct language of patriotism, manifested in stadium banners, chants, and choreographies. Although their patriotic narrative sometimes complements and sometimes contests the official discourse, it always contributes to discussion on the idea of patriotism. One case in point with several threads to be analysed is the example of Polish fans and Cursed Soldiers.

Polish football fans and nationalism

Political ideologies played a crucial role in the history of Polish football from its early days, mainly in relation to class cleavages and inter-ethnic divisions within multi-ethnic composition of the society (Kossakowski, Nosal, and Woźniak 2020, 69-83). In the years 1945–1989 Poland was under communist rule. During this period, sport served as a tool of official propaganda in the clash with the Western world. On the other hand, national team supporters treated matches with the Soviet Union as an opportunity to manifest their political hostility towards the "Big Brother" (Kossakowski, Nosal, and Woźniak 2020, 84-88 and 186-188).

The nationalist potential of football came to the fore again after the fall of the system in 1989, when many fans of Polish clubs supported extreme right-wing ideology. In the first years of democracy it was quite usual to see them turn to the skinhead subculture and display symbols like the Celtic cross or even the swastika. This ideological pattern had an enormous impact on the next stage of the development of fandom culture. Although such extreme symbols gradually vanished from the stadiums (due to the civilising process of the fan world as such, but also as a result of growing pressure from authorities of different kind), right-wing ideology is a strong characteristic of Polish fans. As discussed in our other studies (see Kossakowski, Nosal, and Woźniak 2020; 2019), fans of Polish football clubs are characterised by cohesive, non-democratic structures, the rule of violence, support to conservative and traditional values, reluctance towards otherness (refugees, LGBT people, left-wing ideology, etc.) and nationalist attitude.

In recent years, however, club fans have gradually withdrawn from supporting the national team (mostly due to a conflict with football authorities). Recently, Polish team matches are extremely popular and mostly sell out, which means that it is possible to fill the stadium with middle-class clients. The "pricing-out" of lower-class fans has also changed the "ideological" atmosphere in the stadiums: nationalist and hostile attitudes of club fans have been supplanted by "others-friendly" pop-patriotism. The "new" national team fan pays attention to the aesthetic value of the game and buys fan merchandise (hats, scarves, etc.) in national colours. While pop-patriotism (or banal nationalism) dominates in national team matches, strong right-wing tendencies prevail among fans of Polish clubs. The latter make selective use of symbols and content referring to the Polish history in their performative activity. One of the most important themes is "Cursed Soldiers" – fans' role models and heroes.

Polish politics of memory and cursed soldiers: an unlikely alliance of mnemonic warriors among football fans and the political elite

"Cursed Soldiers" is the umbrella term covering a large spectrum of heterogeneous underground movements which continued the guerrilla war against the Soviet Army operating on the Polish territory and against the institutions of the emerging Polish communist state in the aftermath of World War II. During the most active period (until 1947), their total manpower is estimated at around 80,000, but active units were far less numerous later. Despite large-scale operations of the Polish and Soviet military forces, the last remaining soldier survived underground until 1963 (Wnuk 2007; Gut 2016).

Growing significance and massive resonance of narratives about Cursed Soldiers may be effectively analysed applying a new conceptualisation of the politics of memory and commemoration, introducing the terms "mnemonic actors" and "memory regimes" as offered by Bernhard and Kubik (2014). This actor-centred approach underlines the role of various individual (teachers, parents, historians, artists, intellectuals) and collective (institutional) actors who contribute to the creation of historical memory.

Memory regime is understood as a set of cultural and institutional practices designed to commemorate some past events or processes (Bernhard and Kubik 2014, 14–15). Although this approach was developed for large scale analysis of memory regimes (national politics of memory), it may also prove useful in analysing case studies like the one presented here. Mnemonic actors are those who influence the shape of historical memory by various (conscious or unconscious) activities or by negligence. "Mnemonic warriors" are those mnemonic actors who pay special attention to this area of politics, drawing a sharp line between themselves (the depositories of the "true" vision of the past) and other actors who cultivate "wrong" or "false" versions of history. For them, memory is the field of constant struggle in which all means may be used to win (Bernhard and Kubik 2014, 9–14).

The mnemonic regime prevalent in Poland since the beginning of the transition period resembles what Bernhard and Kubik (2014, 18) call a "fractured memory regime", one that draws a line between us: "the guardians of the 'true' version of the past, and 'them' – the prevaricators or opportunists who do not know or care about the 'proper' shape of collective memory". It was designed by centre-right and right-wing governments and implemented by numerous educational and cultural institutions. The key actor behind the politics of memory is the Institute of National Remembrance (*Instytut Pamięci*

Narodowej, hereafter IPN), established in 1999. One of the most generously funded state institutions, it combines historical research and public prosecution powers (in cases of war crimes or crimes against the Polish nation). In recent years, however, its work has focused on the design and implementation of politics of memory on both national and local level.

Bernhard and Kubik (2014, 17) stress that memory regimes are fluid. In Poland, the more radical version of politics of memory moved up on the political agenda when more radical right-wing parties were in power as a part of the ideological foundations of the so called "Fourth Republic", a new iteration of the Polish state present in their narrative. For many years, the main trope of the politics of memory was the Warsaw Uprising, portrayed as a heroic, ill-fated operation of World War II. The gross strategic miscalculation of Polish Home Army's military command led to about 20,000 members of resistance forces being killed or missing in action; at least 150,000 civilians murdered by German forces. The entire population of Warsaw was expelled and the city was systematically destroyed with explosives: about 85–90 per cent of the buildings were turned into rubble (Davies 2003; Borodziej 2006; Ciechanowski 2009). However, the myth of the Warsaw Uprising, or the story of the Polish Underground State (officially: The Government Delegation for Poland) and the Home Army (the largest underground resistance army in occupied Europe), could not be adapted in the nationalist narratives pursued by radical right-wing organisations and political activists throughout the period of transformation – the Underground State was pluralist and its political manifestos had openly socialist undertones (Karski 2014).

Therefore, there was a space and the need for yet another mythological narrative in the nationalist imaginary. According to Wnuk (2016) the term "cursed soldiers" was introduced to the vocabulary of history and politics in Poland in the 1990s by intellectuals (journalists and activists) associated with radical right. These mnemonic warriors – who, as Bernhard and Kubik (2014) shows, often use history for instrumental and utilitarian reasons – succeeded in introducing this new trope both to the official memory policy and into the imaginary of right-wing-oriented football fans.

"Cursed soldiers" is an ideological construct born out of the assumption, widely spread among right wing politicians and activists, that equalises the German occupation of Poland between 1939 and 1945, with the period of post-war Soviet dominance disregarding the disproportion in human losses between the two and the scale of atrocities committed by the Nazis.

During the communist period (1945-1989) they were ignored by the official historiography, and their come back to the fore of the debates and historical were closely connected to the resurgence of nationalist undertones in memory policy.

Although in the 1990s in Poland we have witnessed the resurgence of the radical right, also at the football terraces, it was not until the twenty first century when the nationalist narratives infiltrated the official discourse and political agenda. The previous period was much more pluralist when it comes to the mnemonic work with postcommunist party being the major political force. Since the demise of so called "postcommunist cleveage" in the 2005 (Kossakowski, Nosal, and Woźniak 2020, 50-68), Polish mainstream politics is dominated by two right-wing political parties (Civic Platform and Law and Justice) with the leadership of the later one paying far more attention to the transformation of the mnemonic regime in Poland deploying its mnemonic warriors to the variety of institutions, particularly those responsible for education. The IPN currently plays the key role in official commemoration of Cursed Soldiers, including numerous exhibitions, publications and pop-cultural production relating to their stories, such as feature films or comic books (see e.g. IPN 2020) at the same time downplaying well-documented cases of their participation in anti-Jewish and anti-Ukrainian pogroms (Kułak 2001; Brzoza 2004; Rokicki 2015).

The cult of Cursed Soldiers has been adopted and consecrated by the ruling political elite. The official Cursed Soldiers' Day was declared in 2011 from the initiative of the late president Lech Kaczyński of Law and Justice by the then president Bronisław Komorowski of Civic Platform. Since the double electoral victory of the Law and Justice party in 2015 they have become the key figures of the national pantheon, and the state has generously sponsored numerous activities devoted to their commemoration (Woźniak 2017).

The Cursed Soldiers phenomenon has resulted from the synergy between the grass-roots activities of mnemonic warriors and their official state-affiliated counterparts. They became a recurring motif in ultras' choreographies all over the country. Fans willingly engaged in various commemorations, took care of their graves, organised meetings with surviving members of the troops or wore franchised clothing with old military insignia or symbols assigned to Cursed Soldiers. First popular among football fans (ultras and hooligans), these "patriotic brands" (e.g. Semper Patria or Red is Bad) were mainstreamed and are currently available for instance in shops of state museums (see Kossakowski, Szlendak, and Antonowicz 2018; Kossakowski, Nosal, and Woźniak 2019).

Application of Bernhard and Kubik's conceptualization of mnemonic regime *in statu nascendi* works well with constructionist approaches by Anderson (1991) and Hobsbawm (1990). The apparent need of the new "imagined community" which would satisfy the ideological expectations of part of the society (for instance football fans) was – since Cursed Soldiers were officially adopted by the state and its mnemonic actors –fulfilled by the invention of new tradition: the mythology of "Cursed soldiers". It may be assumed that the enthusiastic response among the fandom towards the new heroes became a testing ground for mnemonic warriors of the current memory regime before proceeding with a large scale ideological campaign focused on them (Kossakowski, Nosal, and Woźniak 2019, 8).

The features of Polish memory regime mentioned above and the activities of Polish mnemonic warriors may also be viewed as an example of what Pascale (2019) has recently called the "weaponisation" of language. She frames this process as a discursive *modus operandi* of many radical right movements. In Poland, it may be viewed as a result of mainstreaming of radical right discourse by the ruling Law and Justice party in an attempt to push back more radical and extreme political rivals. Violent language used against the hostile fan group characterises football fandom anywhere, though the discursive "weaponry" is mainly aimed at the arch-rivals of the preferred football club. In Poland however, this overlaps with the broader political context. For instance, since 2015 declaratively anti-establishment Polish football fandom went shoulder to shoulder with Law and Justice in the campaigns against the refugees (refusal to accept the refugees by Polish government was supported in numerous choreographies in some stadiums).

	OFFICIAL PATRIOTISM	GUERRILLA PATRIOTISM
Patriotic symbols	*mainstream*	*specific*
Self-location in social landscape	*being in community*	*being marginalised*
Self-perception in social landscape	*neutral*	*being scapegoated for being disobedient or provocative*
Main enemy	*none or external*	*internal (besieged fortress syndrome)*
Relations with the establishment	*supported by the establishment*	*anti-establishment*
Mode of activities	*using strategy*	*using tactics*
Political character	*non-political common universe (but also used by politicians)*	*beyond current politics (but also used by politicians)*
Mode of patriotism	*holistic*	*fragmented*
Attitudes towards the ideology of official patriotism	*incorporation*	*selection*
Effects on the ideology of official patriotism	*reproduction*	*critical redefinition*

The concept of *guerrilla patriotism*

The aim of this paper is to introduce the concept of *guerrilla patriotism* - specific pattern of football fans' nationalist attitudes. Its idea is based on the opposition between *guerrilla* and official patriotism in the terraces. Although it is inspired by the analysis of the case of Cursed Soldiers, the proposed categories aspire to be universal and the proposed model is a framework for further empirical consideration. The main features of official and guerrilla patriotism are summarized in the table.

The proposed types of patriotism are theoretical constructs aimed at facilitation of the sociological analyses of the relation between official patriotism and *guerrilla* patriotism. In real life the lines dividing those types are blurred, and expressions of football supporters' patriotism fall along a two-dimensional continuum rather than into a clear-cut type. Nevertheless, the presented typology can be helpful in the mapping of patriotic engagement of football fans.

Specific symbols. The important feature of guerrilla patriotism is a selective choice of patriotic symbols. Fans do not make use of the most obvious tools: well-known signs, common heroes or patriotic gadgets. Instead, they tend to look for distinctive ones. Their attention is focused on a less recognisable symbolic universe. Moreover, the figures they praise are often controversial and divide public opinion. The language and symbolism used in this kind of communication is often expressive, solemn and bombastic; sometimes the message is weaponised and aimed directly at the groups perceived as antagonistic.

The feeling of being marginalised. Guerrilla patriots view themselves as figures who are marginalised and stigmatised for their beliefs and their actions, mainly for various forms of disobedience against the dominant elitist politics. They do not tend to see themselves as being in the same community as the "official", patriots (or see themselves on its margins). Their sense of honour, bravery and loyalty to the group is coupled with the conviction that they are lone fighters for the old, "real" patriotic values who never surrender or make a compromise with authorities.

The sense of being scapegoated. The side effect of being marginalised is the besieged fortress syndrome. Guerrilla patriots feel that they are under attack from the media and politicians. This strengthens the sense of internal cohesion of the group and the conviction that they should keep on fighting.

Internal enemy. Guerrilla patriots see their main enemies within the society they live in: the government, other political authorities, media, successors of the former regime; ethnic or religious minorities may also be included on the list. On the other hand, external threats are not really considered important (with some exceptions, like Germans, Russians or Muslims in the Polish case).

Anti-establishment attitudes. The establishment is seen as the enemy. Political and, to some extent, cultural and economic elites are accused of pursuing only their own interests. They are also blamed for promoting wrong values instead of "real" patriotism.

Tactics. Recalling Michel de Certeau's distinction between strategies and tactics (1984), guerrilla patriots rely on the latter. They do not have their own forum or efficient media channels to proclaim their ideas. In effect, they use public space (stadiums, streets, sport events) and performative tools (banners, chants, choreographies, pyrotechnics, marches). Furthermore, their message almost exclusively reflects on the glorious past of heroic struggle against the enemy, or voices harsh criticism of the current political situation and the ruling elites (economic, political, media). There is no positive agenda about the desired shape of the national or political community: fans do not offer any coherent vision of nation or nation state.

Being beyond current politics. Consequently, guerrilla patriots do not perceive themselves as political actors, in the sense that they neither pursue nor promote any coherent agenda that is possible to achieve. Rather, they support or oppose particular issues. They are not strongly tied to any institutions or political parties, and the views they hold are "worldviews" or even "no-specific-idea views" rather than strictly "political views". When they undertake political activities, they are not inspired by politicians. Of course, politicians set the agenda to which fans react, but their worlds are separate universes even if they share similar worldviews.

Fragmented picture. Fans focus on specific aspects of patriotism. They do not approach it coherently and holistically. Instead, guerrilla patriots see the pro-national orientation as an eclectic assemblage of various elements that appeal to the patriotic or nationalist attitudes dominant in the group.

Selective patriotism. As a result, guerrilla patriotism is a patchwork which combines features of official patriotism and marginalised aspects. Some mainstream themes are accepted and some are rejected. The guerrilla-patriotism-as-a-whole is often heterogenous and self-contradictory.

Critical redefinition of official patriotism. The proliferation of guerrilla attitudes can also transform official patriotism. Some elements of guerrilla patriotism enter the mainstream and reconfigure the existing order. One example of this process is the case of Cursed Soldiers: they are currently a major topic of memory policy. The ruling party recognised them as particularly attractive in terms of memory policy aimed at younger generations (see Kończal 2019).

The concept of *guerrilla patriotism* is a theoretical proposition, grounded in empirically observed phenomena. The empirical examples of this type of attitudes from Polish terraces will be presented in the next part of paper.

The performance of *guerrilla patriotism*

The legend of the "cursed soldiers" as heroic and honourable troops which never surrendered to the communist oppressors became particularly attractive for football fans who glorify them in the choreographies and on murals who may be described not only as mnemonic actors but also as mnemonic warriors. Although they use a range of means of expression (banners, chants or giant crowd flags covering most of the ultras terrace), the scale of their performances is naturally limited – the show is a short form, mostly with a strongly stressed theme and a brief slogan. The whole process of presentation rarely takes longer than a few minutes. Ultras' performances aim to draw attention of broader audience and to familiarise them with the moral and cultural values of the group. This explains why they often rely on controversial images and divisive slogans: they raise discussion, even if it means criticism and condemnation. For example, Legia Warsaw ultras unfurled a giant crowd flag commemorating the Warsaw Uprising, featuring the image of a German soldier holding a gun to a child's head, accompanied with the caption (in English) reading: "During the Warsaw Uprising Germans killed 160,000 people. Thousands of them were children". In contemporary digital times, such a strong message instantly received wide coverage in the international media.

Considering the Cursed Soldiers theme, the form of these aesthetic shows is similar. Basically, they include a strong, persuasive slogan and a well-prepared image. As we present below, performances devoted to Cursed Soldiers are based on few components that, put together, create a properly – in ideological terms – designed and desired image (the "dark side" of some Cursed Soldiers formations is thus tactically omitted). This image not only plays a role in a particular memory regime but also constitutes a role model for fans as a group. In fact, as clearly visible in a comment from a Polish fan, only positive and inspiring attributes of Cursed Soldiers have been incorporated (Jantych 2016 after Kossakowski, Nosal, and Woźniak 2020, 170–171):

> [They] are perceived as ideal role models, romantic and tough-minded fighters for a lost cause who were fighting in the name of honour, principles and their oath of allegiance. In addition, they fought against communists and – according to fans – Polish elites who try to destroy fandom descend from the communist circles. Therefore, fans feel they are not only successors, but also continuators of the Cursed Soldiers' struggle

Another fan puts emphasis on the lack of attractive ideological proposals (Kossakowski, Nosal, and Woźniak 2020, 171):

> As I see it, that was a moment of a kind of ideological chaos; (…) I'd say, no distinct ideology that fans would find appealing. And such an ideology has to fulfil some criteria; the first thing is that it has to be distinct, it has to appeal to steadfast people, people who go against the current of the surrounding reality. (…) And I think that such values like steadfastness, refusal to make compromises, make it possible for fans to identify with Cursed Soldiers.

It also needs to be stressed that this choice of role models stems from the military structure of fandom. Considering that fan groups are characterised by hierarchical, punitive and coercive management, coupled with physical endurance and hegemonic masculinity (Kossakowski, Antonowicz, and Jakubowska 2020), it is hard to imagine that historical figures of a different kind could serve as role models.

Moral steadfastness and prowess in fight

Of the culture of ultras is based on such qualities as extremism (also in political terms), physical violence and non-democratic, hierarchical style of operating (Kossakowski

Szlendak, and Antonowicz 2018).: Simultaneously, 'The men's world of Polish ultras promotes (...) an idealistic image in which steadfast fighters obeying the principles of honour struggle in the name of noble values, defend the local/national territory and bring up young, "unspoilt" generations' (Kossakowski 2021). As a result, many slogans and images referring to Cursed Soldiers invoke such features as prowess, courage, fearlessness and steadfastness. For example, Legia Warsaw fans painted an image of a soldier holding a rifle kneeling on one knee in front of a cross with a soldier's helmet on top and a white-and-red ribbon bound around it (typical for soldiers' graves in Poland). The image is accompanied with the words: "I won't fear the enemy even if I am to die in battle" (*Wroga się nie ulęknę choćbym miał zginąć w walce*). Likewise, fans of Korona Kielce displayed a large banner with the words (and the symbol of the wolf, typically added to the Cursed Soldiers imaginary): "Without fear, they did not give up" (*Nie bojąc się niczego, nie dali za wygraną*). For fans, Cursed Soldiers represent noble values which perfectly fit the "weaponisation of language": like soldiers, fans are prepared "to die in battle" – the former for homeland, the latter for their club. The imaginary dimension of these slogans is important for building the fighting spirit and for the ideological glue binding the groups. At the symbolic and identity levels, fans are convinced about peculiar transmission, as can be seen in a slogan displayed by Śląsk Wrocław fans: "Your prowess lives in us" (*W nas trwa waleczność twoja*).

Being against the system

Fans tend to glorify and identify with Cursed Soldiers owing to their perceived anti-establishment attitude, discrimination and oppression by authorities. These are characteristics that fans assign also to themselves (fans as deviants and "public enemy", see Kossakowski 2017). In their iconography and performances, Cursed Soldiers are often associated with the symbol of the wolf. For example, Legia ultras presented a huge show featuring the image of the wolf in the centre of the Polish national flag; the accompanying caption read: "In the shadows of the night, in the darkness of the trees, called by the homeland" (*Wśród cieniów nocy, w mroku drzew, wezwani na ojczyzny zew*; a line from a Cursed Soldiers' song). It captures the "hidden" and "underground" nature of their mission – they need to operate at night (they risk being caught during the day) and to live in abandoned places (woods) beyond control of the forces of establishment (communist authorities). As it is today, fans' tactics and modes of operation also involve abandoned places; for example, arranged fights between hooligan groups are organised in the woods to avoid the police.

The symbol of the wolf – which has many meanings in various mythologies; it may be identified as "out-of-place" animal, master of the hunt, a symbol of the wild (see Figari and Skogen 2011) – has also appeared in other performances devoted to Cursed Soldiers. Legia fans displayed a banner with the word "Cursed" (*Wyklęci*), Polish national colours and the symbol of the wolf. Fans of Jagiellonia Białystok, in turn, presented a large card stunt featuring the symbols of the wolf; the caption read: "The evening darkness bade them farewell as they went into battle" (*Żegnał ich wieczorny mrok, gdy ruszali w bój*). Again, Cursed Soldiers live and operate in darkness.

Marginalised heroes need to be remembered

For many years, Cursed Soldiers were excluded from official narratives. Therefore some performances pointed out education as the key to restoring their memory. This was emphasised by a banner displayed by Śląsk Wrocław fans that stated: "Listen children, are you taught at school who Cursed Soldiers were?" (*Słuchajcie dzieci - czy uczą Was w szkole, kim byli żołnierze wyklęci?*). Likewise, Widzew Łódź supporters painted graffiti saying: "The most important lesson of patriotism is a history lesson" (*Najważniejsza lekcja patriotyzmu to lekcja historii*), with three figures of Cursed Soldiers, three wolves and a hooded figure reading a book (most likely representing the fan; such a figure is often used by fans to promote the "deviant" image of themselves).

Fans of Górnik Zabrze, in turn, presented a banner with the slogan: "Cursed Soldiers. The real heroes live in our memory" (*Żołnierze wyklęci. Prawdziwi bohaterowie żyją w naszej pamięci*). This sentence can be interpreted in terms of stressing the authenticity and "pureness" of those who are glorified, in contrast to "bad" heroes of mainstream ideologies (mainly: people promoting liberal and progressive values). These categories refer to a broader discussion on moral and cultural patterns that should dominate in public space. In terms of fans' memory regime, there is only space for one "real" type of authority figure. Therefore, one of the most popular chants during patriotic events in Polish stadiums (Independence Day or Cursed Soldiers' Day) is "Honour and glory to the heroes" (*Cześć i chwała bohaterom!*).

Cracovia ultras prepared an impressive choreography referring to Cursed Soldiers in the context of the Independence of Poland. The choreography was accompanied by the following inscription: "An independent Poland was the most important issue for you. Cursed Soldiers, Cracovia will never forget!" (*Dla Was Niepodległa Polska była najważniejszą sprawą. Żołnierze Wyklęci, Cracovia nie zapomni!*) (Kossakowski 2021). The memory of Cursed Soldiers will last in the future owing to the importance of guerrilla actions and attitudes. This idea was invoked by Lechia Gdańsk ultras, who displayed a choreography presenting wolves at a soldier's grave, accompanied by the following caption: "When everyone was on their knees, you had the strength to stand. The memory of your deeds will last forever" (*Gdy wszyscy już klęczeli, mieliście siłę stać. Pamięć Waszych czynów na wieki będzie trwać*). And again, this performance puts emphasis on the element that seems to be crucial for fans – steadfastness (perseverance when others give up).

As above examples demonstrate, fans cultivate politics of memory using highly visible aesthetic forms. Their performances can be treated in terms of a mnemonic regime, as most choreographies present one topic in a consistent way. Their politics of memory is devoid of ambivalence or consideration of nuances: it never includes questions or threads that could raise doubts about the nature of their historical heroes. This mechanism of excluding all shades of grey casts doubt on the reliability and historical credibility of fan performances. However, reinforcing it reinforces fan identity and community.

Conclusion

To sum up, guerrilla patriotism can be defined as fans' mode of patriotism, characterised by anti-establishment, apolitical, victimised and ready-to-fight pro-national attitudes. However, this conclusion leads to further research questions: about the internal dynamics of particular cases of guerrilla patriotism, and about issues which have potential to generate it. A general overview of the situation in the terraces in Europe indicates that some other fan cultures also include examples of chants or choreographies commemorating various insurgents, guerrilla movements, paramilitary troops or even terrorist organisations. This may be exemplified by the UPA (Ukrainian Insurgent Army) in Ukraine, the Ustaša organisation in Croatia, Arkan's Tigers (Serbian Volunteer Guard) in Serbia, the ETA in the Basque Country and the IRA in Scotland (among some Celtic Glasgow fans), or Che Guevara in some European countries (among 1. FC Sankt Pauli or Livorno supporters).

A thorough analysis of these cases would require examining the relation between the activity of mnemonic warriors and the official discourses of respective memory regimes in each national context. Some other questions should be put forward as well: Is looking for controversial symbols and figures a form of fans' distinction? Do fans use such symbols to stress their "deviant" character? How important is it to incorporate extremist content in fans' identity work? Is praising local characters an act of resistance against the globalised and commercialised football? Or perhaps is it that the militant and strongly cohesive structure of fan groups can only be bound by extraordinary ideological glue? Most fan groups emerge owing to resistant and antagonist attitudes to various actions. Democratic and progressive values may be ineffective to fuel such attitudes. When it is necessary to be ready for "war", only steadfast figures, like Cursed Solders, are useful role models.

Disclosure statement

No potential conflict of interest was provided by the author(s).

ORCID

Przemysław Nosal (iD) http://orcid.org/0000-0002-4794-1479
Radosław Kossakowski (iD) http://orcid.org/0000-0002-4150-9730
Wojciech Woźniak (iD) http://orcid.org/0000-0002-9720-6595

References

Allison, L. 2000. "Sport and Nationalism." In *Handbook of Sports Studies*, edited by J. Coakley and E. Dunning, 344–355. London: Sage.

Allison, L. ed. 2004. *The Global Politics of Sport. The Role of Global Institutions in Sport.* London: Routledge.

Anderson, B. 1991. *Imagined Communities: Reflections on the Origin and Spread of Nationalism.* New York: Verso.

Andrews, D., and C. Cole. 2002. "The Nation Reconsidered." *Journal of Sport and Social Issues* 26 (2): 123–124. doi:10.1177/0193723502262001.

Ariely, G. 2012. "Globalisation and the Decline of National Identity?" *Nations and Nationalism* 18 (3): 461–482. doi:10.1111/j.1469-8129.2011.00532.x.

Arnold, R. 2018. "Sport and Official Nationalism in Modern Russia." *Problems of Post-Communism* 65 (2): 129–141. doi:10.1080/10758216.2018.1425093.

Bairner, A. 2001. *Sport, Nationalism, and Globalization: European and North American Perspectives.* Albany: State University of New York Press.

Bairner, A. 2009. "National Sports and National Landscapes: In Defence of Primordialism." *National Identities* 11 (3): 223–239. doi:10.1080/14608940903081101.

SPORT AND NATIONALISM

Bernhard, M., and J. Kubik. 2014. "A Theory of the Politics of Memory." In *Twenty Years after Communism* edited by M. Bernhard and J. Kubik, 7–34. New York: Oxford University Press.

Billig, M. 1995. *Banal Nationalism*. London: SAGE.

Blain, N., Boyle, R., and O'Donnell. H. 1993. *Sport and National Identity in the European Media*. Leicester, London, New York: Leicester University Press

Borodziej, W. 2006. *The Warsaw Uprising of 1944*. Madison: University of Wisconsin Press.

Bowes, A., and A. Bairner. 2019. "Three Lions on Her Shirt: Hot and Banal Nationalism for England's Sportswomen." *Journal of Sport and Social Issues* 43 (6): 531–550. doi:10.1177/0193723519850878.

Bradley, J. 2002. "The Patriot Game: Football's Famous 'Tartan Army." *International Review for the Sociology of Sport* 37 (2): 177–197. doi:10.1177/1012690202037002004.

Brentin, D. 2014. "Now You See Who is a Friend and Who an Enemy.' Sport as an Ethnopolitical Identity Tool in Postsocialist Croatia." *Sudosteuropa. Journal of Politics and Society* 62 (2): 187–207.

Brentin, D. 2016. "Ready for the Homeland? Ritual, Remembrance, and Political Extremism in Croatian Football." *Nationalities Papers* 44 (6): 860–876. doi:10.1080/00905992.2015.1136996.

Certeau de, M. 1984. *The Practice of Everyday Life*. Berkeley: University of California Press.

Ciechanowski, J. 2009. *Powstanie Warszawskie: zarys Podłoża Politycznego i Dyplomatycznego [Warsaw Uprising: political and Diplomatic Background]*. Warszawa: Bellona.

Cronin, M. 1999. *Sport and Nationalism in Ireland: Gaelic Games, Soccer and Irish Identity since 1884*. Dublin: Four Courts Press.

Davies, N. 2003. *Rising '44: The Battle for Warsaw*. New York: Macmillan.

Deeley, C. 2019. *Forgotten Nations: The Incredible Stories of Football in the Shadows*. Sussex: Pitch Publishing.

Dixon, N. 2000. "A Justification of Moderate Patriotism in Sport." In *Values in Sport: Elitism, Nationalism, Gender Equality, and the Scientific Manufacturing of Winners*, edited by T. Tannsjo and C. Tamburrini, 74–86. New York: E & FN Spon.

Doidge, M., R. Kossakowski, and S. Mintert. 2020. *Ultras. The Passion and Performance of Contemporary Football Fandom*. Manchester: Manchester University Press.

Edensor, T. 2002. *National Identity, Popular Culture and Everyday Life*. Oxford: Berg.

Figari, H., and K. Skogen. 2011. "Social Representations of the Wolf." *Acta Sociologica* 54 (4): 317–332. doi:10.1177/0001699311422090.

Gibbson, T. 2011. "English National Identity and the National Football Team: The View of Contemporary English Fans." *Soccer and Society* 12 (6): 865–879. doi:10.1080/14660970.2011.609685.

Giulianotti, R. 1995. "Football and the Politics of Carnival. An Ethnographic Study of Scottish Fans in Sweden." *International Review for the Sociology of Sport* 30 (2): 191–220. doi:10.1177/101269029503000205.

Giulianotti, R., and R. Robertson. 2009. *Globalization and Football*. London: Sage

Gleaves, J., and M. Llewellyn. 2014. "Ethics, Nationalism, and the Imagined Community: The Case against Inter-National Sport." *Journal of the Philosophy of Sport* 41 (1): 1–19. doi:10.1080/00948705.2013.785427.

Gut, W. 2016. *Józef Franczak ps. "Lalek". Ostatni Partyzant Poakowskiego Podziemia*. Toruń: Wydawnictwo Adam Marszałek.

Hargreaves, J. 2000. *Freedom for Catalonia? Catalan Nationalism, Spanish Identity and the Barcelona Olympic Games*. Cambridge: Cambridge University Press.

Hilvoorde van, I., A. Elling, and R. Stokvis. 2010. "How to Influence National Pride? The Olympic Medal Index as a Unifying Narrative." *International Review for the Sociology of Sport* 45 (1): 87–102. doi:10.1177/1012690209356989.

Hobsbawm, E. 1990. *Nations and Nationalism since 1780: programme, Myth, Reality*. Cambridge: Cambridge University Press.

Houlihan, B. 1997. "Sport, National Identity and Public Policy." *Nations and Nationalism* 3 (1): 113–137. doi:10.1111/j.1354-5078.1997.00113.x.

IPN 2020. *Accursed soldiers. Pro-independence underground 1944-1963*. Warszawa: Institute of National Remembrance. https://ipn.gov.pl/download/1/383928/A3ENzolnierzewykleciwy stawaelementarna.pdf

Jantych. 2016. *Kibice w polityce. Lata 2004-2016 [Fans in politics. years 2004-2016]*. Warszawa: PZI Softena.

Jarvie, G. and Walker G, eds. 1994. *Scottish Sport in the Making of the Nation: Ninety-Minute Patriots ?* Leicester: Leicester University Press.

Karski, J. 2014. *Story of a Secret State*. Washington: Georgetown University Press.

Kavetsos, G., and S. Szymanski. 2010. "National Well-Being and International Sports Events." *Journal of Economic Psychology* 31 (2): 158–171. doi:10.1016/j.joep.2009.11.005.

Kończal, K. 2019. "The Invention of the 'Cursed Soldiers' and Its Opponents: Post-War Partisan Struggle in Contemporary Poland." *East European Politics and Societies and Cultures* 20 (10): 1–29. doi:10.1177/0888325419865332.

Kossakowski, R. 2017. *Od Chuliganów Do Aktywistów. Polscy Kibice i Zmiana Społeczna*. Kraków: Universitas.

Kossakowski, R. 2021. *Hooligans, Ultras, Activists. Polish Football Fandom in Sociological Perspective*. London: Palgrave Macmillan.

Kossakowski, R., D. Antonowicz, and H. Jakubowska. 2020. "The Reproduction of Hegemonic Masculinity in Football Fandom. An Analysis of the Performance of Polish Ultras." In *The Palgrave Handbook of Masculinity and Sport*, edited by R. Magrath, J. Cleland, and E. Anderson, 517–536. London: Palgrave Macmillan.

Kossakowski, R., P. Nosal, and W. Woźniak. 2019. "A squad with no left wingers: The roots and structure of right-wing and nationalist attitudes among Polish football fans." *Problems of Post-Communism* 67 (4): 511–524. doi:10.1080/10758216.2019.1673177.

Kossakowski, R., P. Nosal, and W. Woźniak. 2020. *Politics, Ideology and Football Fandom. The Transformation of Modern Poland*. London: Routledge.

Kossakowski, R., T. Szlendak, and D. Antonowicz. 2018. "Polish Ultras in the Post-Socialist Transformation." *Sport in Society* 21 (6): 854–869. doi:10.1080/17430437.2017.1300387.

Krugliak, M., and O. Krugliak. 2017. "The Unlikely Alliance of Ukrainian Football Ultras." In *Football Fans, Rivalry and Cooperation*, edited by C. Brandt, F. Hertel, and S. Huddleston, 170–184. London: Routledge.

Kułak, J. 2001. "Pacyfikacja Wsi Białoruskich w Styczniu 1946 [Pacification of Belarussian Villages in January 1946]." *Biuletyn Instytutu Pamięci Narodowej*. 8: 49–54.

Lechner, F. 2007. "Imagined Communities in the Global Game: soccer and the Development of Dutch National Identity." *Global Networks* 7 (2): 215–229. doi:10.1111/j.1471-0374.2007.00166.x.

Leeds, M., and E. Leeds. 2009. "International Soccer Success and National Institutions." *Journal of Sports Economics* 10 (4): 369–390. doi:10.1177/1527002508329864.

MacLean, Malcolm, and Russell Field. 2014. "Performing Nations, Disrupting States: sporting Identities in Nations without States." *National Identities* 16 (4): 283–289. doi:10.1080/14608944. 2014.930427.

Marks, J. 1998. "The French National Team and National Identity: cette France D'un Bleu Métis." *Sport in Society* 1 (2): 41–57. doi:10.1080/14610989808721815.

Mills, R. 2009. "It All Ended in an Unsporting Way. Serbian Football and the Disintegration of Yugoslavia, 1989–2006" *The International Journal of the History of Sport* 26 (9): 1187–1217. doi:10.1080/09523360902941829.

Molnar, G., and S. Whigham. 2021. "Radical Right Populist Politics in Hungary: Reinventing the Magyars through Sport." *International Review for the Sociology of Sport* 56 (1): 133–148. 1–16. doi:10.1177/1012690219891656.

Morgan, W. 1997. "Sports and the Making of National Identities: A Moral View." *Journal of the Philosophy of Sport* 24 (1): 1–20. doi:10.1080/00948705.1997.9714536.

Pascale, C.-M. 2019. "The Weaponization of Language: Discourses of Rising Right-Wing Authoritarianism." *Current Sociology* 67 (6): 898–917. doi:10.1177/0011392119869963.

Poulton, E. 2004. "Mediated Patriot Games: The Construction and Representation of National Identities in the British Television Production of Euro '96." *International Review for the Sociology of Sport* 39 (4): 437–455. doi:10.1177/1012690204049072.

Rokicki, P. 2015. *Glinciszki i Dubinki. "Zbrodnie Wojenne na Wileńszczyźnie w Połowie 1944 Roku i Ich Konsekwencje we Współczesnych Relacjach Polsko-Litewskich."* ["Glinciszki and Dubinki. War

Crimes in Vilnius Region in Mid- 1944 and Their Consequences for Contemporary Relations between Poland and Lithuania]." Warszawa: Instytut Pamięci Narodowej.

Seippel, O. 2017. "Sports and Nationalism in a Globalized World." *International Journal of Sociology* 47 (1): 43–61. doi:10.1080/00207659.2017.1264835.

Smith, A., and D. Porter, eds. 2004. *Sport and National Identity in the Post-War World.* London: Routledge.

Tomlinson, A., and C. Young. 2005. "*National Identity and Global Sports Events: Culture.*" *Politics, and Spectacle in the Olympics and the Football World Cup.* Albany: State University of New York Press.

Topic, M., and J. Coakley. 2010. "Complicating the Relationship between Sport and National Identity: The Case of Post-Socialist Slovenia." *Sociology of Sport Journal* 27 (4): 371–389. doi:10.1123/ssj.27.4.371.

Tuck, J. 2003. "Making Sense of Emerald Commotion: Rugby Union, National Identity and Ireland." *Identities* 10 (4): 495–515. doi:10.1080/714947402.

Vidacs, B. 2011. "Banal Nationalism, Football, and Discourse Community in Africa." *Studies in Ethnicity and Nationalism* 11 (1): 25–41. doi:10.1111/j.1754-9469.2011.01105.x.

Ward, T. 2009. "Sport and National Identity." *Soccer & Society* 10 (5): 518–531. doi:10.1080/14660970902955455.

Wnuk, R. 2007. *Atlas Polskiego Podziemia Niepodległościowego 1944-1956 [Handbook of Polish Underground].* Warszawa: IPN.

Wnuk, R. 2016. "Wokół mitu żołnierzy wyklętych." [On the Myth of Cursed Soldiers.] *Przegląd polityczny.* http://przegladpolityczny.pl/wokol-mitu-zolnierzy-wykletych-rafal-wnuk/

Woźniak, W. 2017. "Bieganie Jako Deklaracja Ideowa, Biegi Masowe Jako Element Polityki Pamięci." [Running as an Ideological Declaration, Mass Running Events as an Element of Memory Politics."] In *Polska Moda na Bieganie – Zapiski Socjologiczne* [Polish Running Trends – Sociological Inquiries], edited by J. R. Stempień, 21–40. Łódź: Wydawnictwo Uniwersytetu Medycznego.

Index

Note: *Italic* page numbers refer to figures.

Abe, S. 172
Adam, T. 28
Adenauer, K. 35
AFC *see* Asian Football Confederation (AFC)
Agergaard, S. 7
Agnew, J. 92
All Blacks 181
Allen, J. 152
Alli, D. 92
ambivalence 43
American fascism 103–115
America's Cup (AC) 182, 186–189
'America's Own V Campaign' 112
Anderson, Benedict 6, 8, 14, 26, 27, 44, 45, 49, 51, 75, 80, 82, 94, 111, 112, 134, 166, 168, 193, 218; deep horizontal comradeship 41; imagined community 2, 4, 5, 40, 105; invented tradition 183; nationalism 26, 29, 40; print capitalism 106
Andrews, D. 2, 3, 181, 185
antagonisms 119, 121, 122, 125
anti-communism 8, 167
Anti-extradition Bill movement (2019) 43, 44
anti-Japanism 165, 171
Arendt, H. 125
Argentina 29
Arsenal FC 99
Asamoah, G. 97
Asian Football Confederation (AFC) 42, 43
Asianness 150
athletes 32; Muslim women 141; naturalization of 5, 41; Saarland 33

Bairner, A. 2, 4, 19, 42, 91, 134, 165, 175
Balogun, O. 106
Bambi Award 87
banal Europeanism 5, 58, 66; conceptionalisation 67; Europeanisation of football and 59–66
banal nationalism 2, 5, 55–67, 185, 214
Bayar, M. 12
Bellamy, C. 152

Ben-Amos, A. 106
Bentley, N. 124, 126
Bernard Shaw, G. 107
Bernhard, M. 216–218
Bhabha, H. 7, 151
Billig, M. 2, 5, 55, 57, 61, 66, 75, 82, 185, 214, 215
Birmingham 20
The Birth of a Nation 109
Black Caps 181
Black Country 19–21
Black, J. 6
Blake, P. 188
'blood and soil' nationalism 19
Bonde, H. 30
Bora, T. 58
The Border Cradle 16
Border landscape 15, 17–18
Border towns 15–16
Bosman case 62–63
Bouchers, G. 127
boundary-making processes 133–136
Bourdieu, P. 57, 95
Bowmont Valley 18
Brah, A. 157
"Braw Lads or Lasses" 16
Brexit 20, 59, 79, 80
British Asians 149, 150; cricket 154–155; diaspora 150; football support and 155–156; hybridity 151; *vs.* national sporting identity 151
British multiculturalism 152–153
Britishness 150–156, 158–161
British Olympic Committee 79
broadcasting rights, central marketing of 63–65
Bundesliga 26
Burdsey, D. 153, 155, 156
Butterworth, B. 187
Butterworth, M. L. 167

Calver, G. W. 112
van Campenhout, G. 5, 6

INDEX

capitalism 40, 76
Carrington, B. 150, 151
Cartwright, Anthony: Black Country 19–21; *Heartland* 12; *Iron Towns* 12; primordialism 21
Certeau de, M. 220
Champions League (CL) 60
Chan, A. H. N. 49
Chile 33
China 42–44, 47
China League One 44
Chinese Football Association (CFA) 43, 44, 47
Chineseness 5, 41, 45, 47, 48, 51
Chinese Super League (CSL) 44
Chinn, C. 19
Chiu, A. 4, 5
Choi, Y. 42
citizenship 47; British Asians 149; formal 95, 96; moral 95, 96; political regulations of 136
civic order 15
The Civilizing Process 73
The Clansman 109
Cogdell, C. 111
Cole, C. 2, 3, 8, 181, 185
Common Riding festivals 15
Commonwealth Games 188
Connor, W. 4, 13, 20
Coolidge, C. 110
corporate-cultural nation 3
corporate nationalism 8, 181, 184–186
Corwen, L. 20
cosmopolitan identity 172–174
cosmopolitanism 168
Coughlan, R. M. 12
counter-hegemonic 200
Coutts, R. 187
COVID-19 pandemic 79
Cram, L. 56, 58
Crenshaw, K. 136
cricket 151, 154–155
Cronin, M. 3
cultural reintegration 33
cultural supremacy 151
Cursed Soldiers 212–224

Danishness 142
Darnell, S. C. 143
Daume, W. 32
Dean, J. 125, 126, 128
deep horizontal comradeship 41
Delanty, G. 73
Denmark 133, 138; Muslim women in 138; national and local politicians in 138; sports facilities 140; women-only swimming 138
deservedness 98
desire 118
diachronic analysis 202, 207, 208

diaspora 150; as conceptual tools 150–151; cricket 154–155; divided loyalties 155–156; national identity 150
Dieke, I. 152
Die Zeit 28
divided loyalties 7, 155–156
Dixon, T. 109, 110
domination 93
drag-effect 6, 72–83; contemporary English national identity and sport 78–81; nationalism 74–78
Drumond, M. 109
dual nationality 92

Eagles, J. 187
EC *see* European Commission (EC)
ECA *see* European Club Association (ECA)
ECJ *see* European Court of Justice (ECJ)
Edensor, T. 3
Edinburgh 18
Eichmann, A. 125
Elias, Norbert 2, 5, 6, 93; drag-effect 72–83; sociological perspective of 72–74
Eller, J. D. 12
Elshtain, J. B. 106
embodied nationalism 6, 105–107
England 4, 14, 22, 42, 122, 150
Englishness 150–156
English Premier League 49, 63, 64
enhabitation 55–67
enjoyment 118, 119
Ennis, J. 153
Ernst, R. 108
ethnicity 13, 21, 97, 136
ethnic 'other' women, in sport 136–138
ethno-nationalism 134
ethno-symbolism 199
ethnosymbolist 3
EURO 2020 79
Europa League (EL) 60
Europe 2, 19, 55, 56; competitions 61; enhabitation of 61; ethno-nationalism 134; fascism 104; identity and 57–59; physical culture 104; political integration project in 58
European Club Association (ECA) 65
European Commission (EC) 60, 64
European Court of Justice (ECJ) 60, 62, 64
Europeanisation, of football 55–67
Europeanism 56, 63
European Union (EU) 56, 58
evoking memory 186

Falcous, M. 184, 190
fantasy 119, 120, 124–125, 127–129
Farah, M. 153, 160
fascism 103–115
FC Saarbrücken 31

INDEX

FC Schalke 04 99
Federal Republic of Germany 28
Fédération Internationale de Football Association (FIFA) 43, 56, 92
Feldman, A. 106
figurational sociology 5, 6
Finlayson, A. 121, 122
Fletcher, T. 150, 151, 154, 157–159
football 4, 19, 137, 151, 199; banal Europeanism 5; banal nationalism in 58; British Asians 155; broadcasting rights of 63–65; centralisation of 5; contextualizing 42–44; Europeanisation of 55–67; Germany 25; Hong Kong 5, 44, 46; international 5, 26, 86–99; Poland 8, 9; Saarland 30; unified Chineseness in 44; United Kingdom 20
Football Association (FA) 79
Football Association of Wales (FAW) 79
Football Kingdom of the Far East 42
Forbes, A. 7
formal citizenship 95, 96
Fourth Republic 217
Fox, J. E. 58, 152
fractured memory regime 216
France 34, 92
François-Poncet, A. 34
Frankenberg 18
French Football Association 31
functional democratisation 78

Geertz, C. 4, 12, 13, 75
Gellner, E. 6, 74, 105, 106, 174
German Democratic Republic 28
German Football Association 32–33
German Football Federation 36
German Poles 97
German Turk 97
Germany 4, 86, 104, 156; Allied powers 28; cultural memory 28; English Premier League 64; model minorities 87; physical training 104; western border of 28
Gibbons, T. 5, 151
Giggs, R. 152
Glasgow 18
Gleaves, J. 31
globalisation 73, 152, 166
Glynos, J. 201
Goldman, R. 186
Grandval, G. 32
Gray, J. N. 17, 18
Griffith, D. W. 109
Grodecki, M. 8
Guen-Hye, P. 170
guerrilla patriotism 9, 212–224; anti-establishment attitudes 220; beyond current politics 220; feeling of being marginalised 219; fragmented picture 220; internal enemy 220; marginalised

heroes 223; moral steadfastness and prowess 221–222; official patriotism 220; performance of 220–223; selective patriotism 220; sense of being scapegoated 219; specific symbols 219; tactics 220
Guibernau, M. 82

habitus: emotional 80; national 73; social 73
Hage, G. 95
Haig, N. 16
Hargreaves, J. 137
Hatherley, O. 124, 125
Hawick 16
Hawkes, G. 193
Heartland 12, 21
Heffernan, C. 6
hegemonic struggle 165–167
Hiddink, G. 168
historical emergence 119
Hitler, A. 104, 112
Hobsbawm, E. 3, 8, 26, 36, 41, 75, 91, 105, 120, 183, 214, 218
Hong Kong: as diverse, international city 47–49; football 5; '519 incident' in 46; internationalness 48; naturalized footballers 40–51; 'One Country, Two Systems' 46; paradoxes 49–51; repetitive contents, stadium 45–47; self-determination 43; (sub)national identity in 42–44
Hong Kong Football Association (HKFA) 43–45, 49
Hong Kong Kickass 45, 46
Hong Kongness 5, 41, 45, 47–51
van Houtum, H. 5, 6
Howarth, D. 201
Hudson-Odoi, C. 92
Hüger, D. 32
Hunt, T. 6
Hurley, A. 4, 5
Hutnyk, J. 150, 162
hybrid identities 7
hybridity 150–151
hybrid sporting affiliations 157–158
Hylton, K. 153

identification process 121–127
identity negotiation 43
ideology 7, 120; communist 171; national 82; political 11, 138
Ignatieff, M. 19
imagined community 2, 4, 5, 26–29, 40, 41–42, 91, 105, 106, 203, 218
immigration 138, 166
519 incident 46
Independent Saarland Football Association 26
India 156
industrial capitalism 166

INDEX

Industrial Revolution 183
Instagram 87
interdependency 73
International Olympic Committee (IOC) 43, 80
invented traditions 120, 183
IOC *see* International Olympic Committee (IOC)
Ireland 3, 14
Irish Football Association (IFA) 79
Iron Towns 12, 19, 20
irrationality 26, 27
Israel 106
Italy 6, 104, 107–111

Jackson, S. 185, 187
Jansen, J. 95
Japan 165, 171; compensation deal 171; Korean
   Peninsula 167; military alliance 172
Jews 124
Joseph, J. 153

Kaepernick, C. 167
Kalra, V. S. 150, 162
Kaur, R. 150, 162
Kavanagh, T. 8
Kedourie, E. 74
'Keep Calm and Carry On' 124
Kelly, R. T. 22
Kemp, T. 191
Kim, C. 173
Kingsbury, P. 122, 127–129
Kiwis 181
Klose, M. 97
Kohn, H. 47
Korea: civic life 168; ethnic nationalism 168–170;
   nationalist politics in 167–168
Korean Confederation of Trade Union 170
Korean Unification Flag (KUF) 170, 171
Kossakowski, R. 8, 9
Kubik, J. 216–218
Kuhn, T. 58
Kumar, K. 159
Kupfer, C. 108

Lacan, J. 123–125
Laidlaw, R. 14, 16
Lawrence, S. 19, 20
legal nationality 95
Lenneis, V. 7
'Lion Rock Spirit' 50
Littlejohn, J. 18
Little, K. 152
Lleweyn, M. 31
London 2012 Olympic Games 7, 149, 152–153,
   156, 158–161
Lui, T. L. 43
Lundeen, E. 112
Lusted, J. 151, 154, 157, 159

Macdonald, C. 104
Macfadden, Bernarr 6, 103–115; Italy 107–111;
   Portugal 107–111; 'sports and athletic revival'
   108; 'unbounding energy' and 'dynamism' 108;
   wartime nationalism and 111–113
Maguire, J. 2, 79
Malcolm, D. 151
marginalized nationalism 190–191
Martilla, T. 200, 201
Marxist 74
materialism 127
Matless, D. 22
May, A. 4
McLaren, B. 14, 16, 17
McSweeny, M. 154
Melrose Rugby Football Club 17
memory regimes 216
Mennell, S. 81, 82
Merton, R. 13
methodological nationalism 92
migrants, in international football 86–99
Miller-Idris, C. 152
Millington, R. 143
The Miracle at Bern 34
The Mirror 81
Mitchell, W. J. T. 22
mnemonic actors 216
mnemonic warriors 216
mnemonic wars 212–224
modernism 199
Mohanty, C. 134
monopoly mechanism 76
Moon Jae-in 169, 172
moral citizenship 95, 96
Morgan, T. 108
Morneau, J. 107
Morpeth, N. 153
multiculturalism 152–153
multiple identities 150
multivocality of belongings 150, 157, 161
Murtha, R. 6
Muslim women 7; athletes 141, 142; burka and
   niqab 141; in Denmark 138–140; ethnic 'other'
   136; leisure time physical activity 138–140;
   political and public discourses 137; social
   media 141; in sport 137
Muslim women and sport 137
Mussolini, B. 6, 103–115

Nadim, N. 141–143
Nakamura, Y. 154
nation 2, 4, 12, 26, 40, 74, 112, 175, 213–215;
   hegemony 8; homeland and 154; imagined
   community 194; legitimacy 40; sport 2,
   121–127
national habitus 73
national heritage 121

INDEX

national identity 1, 2, 7, 27, 120, 134, 136, 181; 'blood-wise' notion of 160; Britishness 151–156; contemporary English 78–81; contested concepts of 151–156; diaspora 150; Englishness 151–156; in Hong Kong 42–44; hybrid sporting affiliations and 157–158; nationhood and 41; New Zealand 184; *vs.* sport 72–83
nationalism 1–4, 11, 12, 26, 73, 82, 105, 133, 152, 164, 213–215; banal 2, 5, 55–67; 'blood and soil' 19; corporate 8, 181; drag-effect in 74–78; embodied 6, 105–107; everyday 3; fascism and 105; football and 27; hegemonic struggle 165–167; identifying philosophy 27; imagined and invented 182–183; irrationality 26, 27; Korean ethnic 8; marginalized 190–191; Marxist interpretation of 74; methodological 92; New Zealand 183–184; Polish football fans and 215–216; postcolonial 171–172; post-modernist approaches 151; primordial 165; South Korean state patriotic 8; ultras' 198–209; wartime 111–113; Yuval-Davis, Nira, studies of 138–141
nationalist politics: in Korea 167–168; PyeongChang (2018) 168–174; in sport 167–168
national myths 121
national 'others' 141–143
national patriotism 105
national popular 119
national reconciliation 120
National Rugby League (NRL) 190
national sports 2, 3
national Thing 119, 122–124, 127–129
nationhood 40–51, 164
naturalization 41–42
Nazi Germany 124
negotiation 151
neoliberal globalisation 166
Netherlands 92, 97
Neuberger, H. 26, 35
Neville, G. K. 15
Newman, J. 184
New York Yacht Club (NYYC) 186
New Zealand 8, 16, 18; America's Cup 186–189; corporate nationalism 184–186; imagined and invented nationalism 182–183; 'New Zealand' Warriors 190; pseudo-nationalism 181–195; rugby league 190–191; sport and nationalism 183–184
New Zealand Cricket (NZC) 192
New Zealand Rugby League (NZRL) 191
'New Zealand' Warriors (NZW) 182, 186, 190–192
Nigeria 106
non-emotional identity 82
North America 2, 19

Northern Ireland 57
North Korea 8, 165, 168
North Wales 18
Norway 154
Nosal, P. 8, 9

Obert, J. C. 15
Odonkor, D. 97
Olympic legacy 153
O'Mahony, P. 73
'One Country, Two Systems' 46
Orwell, G. 80, 184
Owomoyela, P. 97
Özil, M. 6, 63, 86–99, *88–91*

Pakistan 157
Palmer, C. 137
pan-European league system 60–62
pan-European quasi-league system 55
Papson, S. 186
parallel society 139
Parran, T. 113
Parva, W. 77
Pascale, C.-M. 218
passionate intensity 27
patriotic brands 218
patriotism: America 6; guerrilla 9, 212–224; 80 minute 15; 90 minute 15; official 220; selective 220
PDA *see* post-foundational discourse analysis (PDA)
Pearl Harbor 112
Pentre people 18
perennialist 3
personal pronoun model 2
Phillips, D. R. 49
physical activity 7, 138–141
Physical Culture 6, 103, 106–111, 114
physical fitness 107, 108, 111
physical training 104
Podolski, L. 97
Poland 205, 206; Cursed Soldiers 216–219; football fans 215–216; German occupation of 217; Home Army 217; politics of memory 216–219
Poli, R. 42
politics of belonging 135
pop-patriotism 216
Portugal 63, 104, 107–111
postcolonial anti-imperialist nationalism 8
postcolonial feminism 135
postcolonial nationalism 171–172
post-foundational discourse analysis (PDA) 198–209; contrariety 201; counter-hegemonic 200; diachronic analysis 202; difference 201; equivalence 201; in nation studies 202–205; representation 201; sedimentation 200;

social change 199, 200; ultras' national(istic) discourse 205–208; usefulness of 201
Poulton, E. 79
power of fascination 27
primordialism 4, 12–13, 21, 165, 199
primordialist 3
primordial nationalism 165
print capitalism 106
professionalism 16
progressive primordialism 21
projected fantasy 153
pseudo-nationalism 8, 181; corporate nationalism and 184–186; imagery and imaginary 192–194; sport and 184–186; 'Warrior nation' 191–192
PyeongChang Winter Olympics (2018) 7, 8

Quran 86

race 21
Raman, P. 154
Ranger, T. 3
Rapino, M. 167
Ratna, A. 137
Real Madrid CF 99
Renwick, J. 14, 16, 17
Rice, D. 92
Rinehart, R. 8
Rooney, W. 129
Roosevelt, F. D. 107, 110
Roosevelt, T. 110
rugby, in Borders 16–17
rugby league (RL) 190–191
rugby union 15
Rutherford, J. 14, 16

Saarland 5, 25–29; Peace Treaty (1920) 30; soccer and 29–33; sport history 28; World Cup (1954) 28
Salazar, António de Oliveira 104, 109
Scherer, J. 185, 187
Schiller, N. G. 92
Schön, H. 25, 26
Schumacher, K. 33, 34
Scotland 13, 14, 18, 22; borders of 14–18; independence 15, 79; rugby union 15
Scotson, L. 77, 87, 93
Scottish Football Association (SFA) 79
Scottishness 18
Scott, W. 15
sedimentation 200
Seiberth, K. 97
Seiler, D. L. 166, 174
self-identity 120
sense of natural affinity 12
Senyuva, O. 58
Sharpe, M. 127
Shaulis, D. 113

Shils, E. 12
Silk, M. 2, 3, 8, 181, 185
Silver Ferns 181
Skey, M. 94
Slide, A. 109
Smith, A. 74, 75
Smith, A. D. 3, 105, 120
soccer 26–33, 104
social change 199, 200
Social Democratic Party 139
social habitus 73
society of individuals 77
sociological autobiography 13
Solomon, Ty. 121, 128
Sorek, T. 107
South Korea 8, 165, 168; multicultural families 173; patriotic nationalism 170–171
sovereignty 151
Spaaij, R. 97
Spain 63
sport 1–4, 14–18, 104, 151, 167, 213–215; academic study of 2; contemporary English national identity and 78–81; for diasporic groups 153–156; ethnic 'other' women in 136–138; fantasy 124–125; globalization of 127; imagined community 2; irrationality 26, 27; Muslim women's experiences of 7; nationalism and 74–76; nationalist politics in 167–168; national Thing 122–124, 127–129; nation and 121–127; New Zealand 183–184; other/other 125–126; Real 126–127; recognition 122; research 41–42; unity through 33–36; West Germany 28; Yuval-Davis, Nira, studies of 138–141
Stalin, J. 165
Stanfill, M. 154
Stanley, L. 13
stereotypes 79
Stevens, J. C. 186
Stewart, P. J. 19
'Stop the Islamisation of Poland' 207
Strathearn, A. 19
Sturm, D. 8
Summer Olympic Games (1984) 16
symbolization 126

Taiwan 42, 44
Takeshima 172
Tarkowski, J. 92
taxation 76
Taylor, N. 152
Team GB 152, 153, 158–161
Team New Zealand (TNZ) 182, 186, 188
Tebbit, N. 149–151
Telfer, J. 14, 16–18
Thacker, D. 109
Thatcher, M. 21

INDEX

Thiel, A. 97
third-wave feminism 134
Toffoletti, K. 137
Townsend, G. 14, 16, 17
traditionalism 75
transactionalist theory 58
transnational club coordination 65–66
transnational critique 29
transnational feminist 134–136
transnational solidarity 164
Tumblety, J. 104
Turkey 86, 96
Twitter 87
two cultures 98–99

Ukraine 224
ultras' nationalism 198–209
Umbrella Movement (2014) 43
unified Chineseness 44
unified Korean ethnic nationalism 169–170
Union of European Football Association (UEFA) 56, 60, 65
United Kingdom (UK) 4, 15, 79, 149, 150; Asian-specific cricket teams 154; football 20; neoliberal politics in 22
United States 105, 108, 113; athleticism 108; Canada and 173; fascist movements in 104; Japan 167; nationalism 105; North Korea and 169; South Korea and 172; sterilization 111

Valdivia, A. N. 154
Vincent, J. J. S. 152
violence 76

Walle, T. 154
Warner, M. J. 112
wartime nationalism 111–113
Watson, E. 191

Weber, R. 5
Weir, D. 14, 18
Weiss, M. 106
Welsh, I. 19, 22
Werder Bremen 99
West Germany 4, 5, 25, 34; cultural identity 28; sport 28; World Cup (1954) 28
Whigham, S. 130, 153
Wiggam, A. E. 110, 111
Wimmer, A. 92
Winter Olympic Games in PyeongChang (2018) 164–176; cosmopolitan identity 172–174; nationalist politics 168–174; postcolonial nationalism 171–172; South Korean state patriotic nationalism 170–171; unified Korean ethnic nationalism 169–170; 'Warrior nation' 191–192
Wnuk, R. 217
women-only swimming 139
Wood, K. 126
Woo Lee, J. 7
Woolridge, J. 13
World War I 29, 30, 183
World War II 9, 30, 33, 213, 216, 217
Woźniak, W. 8, 9

xenophobia 79

Yo-jong, K. 169
Yung, S. C. 49
Yuval-Davis, Nira 7, 134, 135; Danish Muslim women's leisure time physical activity 138–140; nationalism 138–141; politics of belonging 136; sport 138–141

Zimmerman, H. 34
Žižek, S. 6, 7, 118, 119, 121, 122, 124, 126–128, 130
Zweiniger-Bargielowska, I. 104

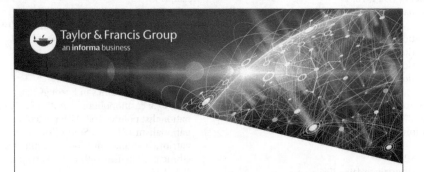